D1737204

STRESS AND ANXIETY

THE SERIES IN CLINICAL AND COMMUNITY PSYCHOLOGY

CONSULTING EDITORS
Charles D. Spielberger and Irwin G. Sarason

IN PREPARATION

STRESS AND ANXIETY

Volume 12

Editors
Charles D. Spielberger
University of South Florida

Irwin G. Sarason
University of Washington

Guest Editor of this Volume
Jan Strelau
University of Warsaw

SCHOOL OF
CALIFORNIA PROFESSIONAL
PSYCHOLOGY
LOS ANGELES

⬤HEMISPHERE PUBLISHING CORPORATION
A member of the Taylor & Francis Group

New York   Washington   Philadelphia   London

STRESS AND ANXIETY: Volume 12

1 2 3 4 5 6 7 8 9 0   B R B R   8 9 8 7 6 5 4 3 2 1 0 9

This book was set in Times Roman by Hemisphere Publishing Corporation. The editors were Susan E. Zinninger and Todd Baldwin; the production supervisor was Peggy M. Rote. Cover design by Sharon M. DePass.
Braun-Brumfield, Inc. was printer and binder.

Library of Congress Cataloging-in-Publication Data

Advanced Study Institute on Stress and Anxiety in Modern Life,
Murnau, Ger., 1973.

Stress and anxiety: [proceedings] /edited by Charles D. Spielberger,
Irwin G. Sarason. Washington: Hemisphere Publ. Corp.
  v. :ill.: 24 cm. (v. 1–2: The series in clinical psychology
  v. 3–5: The series in clinical and community psychology)

  Includes bibliographies and indexes.
  1. Stress (Psychology)—Congresses.   2. Anxiety—Congresses.
I. Sarason, Irwin G., ed.   II. Spielberger, Charles Donald, date, ed.
III. North Atlantic Treaty Organization. Division of Scientific Affairs.
IV. Title. [DNLM: 1. Anxiety.   2. Stress, Psychological. WM 172 S755a]

BF575.S75A38   1973   616.8' 522   74-28292
                                       MARC

ISBN 0-89116-890-7
ISSN 0146-0846
ISSN 0364-1112

Contents

II
SITUATIONAL DETERMINANTS
OF STRESS AND ANXIETY

IV
COPING WITH STRESS AND ANXIETY

V
STRESS, EMOTIONS, AND HEALTH

Contributors

M. J. *APTER*, University College, Cardiff, Wales, UK

J. R. *AVERILL*, University of Massachusetts, Amherst, MA, USA

W. *BATTMANN*, Freie Universität Berlin, Federal Republic of Germany

G. *BAGDY*, National Institute for Nervous & Mental Disease, Hungary

M. *BEN-RAFAEL*, Tel Aviv University, Israel

J. *BRZEZINSKI*, Adam Mickiewcz University, Poland

P. B. *DEFARES*, University of Wageningen, the Netherlands

K. L. P. *DE SOOMER*, University of Wageningen, the Netherlands

S. E. *DOTZENROTH*, Ministry of Correctional Services, Canada

H. F. *DRIES*, State University of Ghent, Belgium

H. J. *EYSENCK*, University of London, UK

P. R. J. *FALGER*, Faculty of Medicine, University of Limburg, Maastricht, the Netherlands

N. *GIRAULT*, Université René Descartes, Paris, France

M. *GIRODO*, University of Ottawa, Canada

J. *GEIER*, Eötvös Loránd University, Budapest, Hungary

J. W. *HINTON*, University of Glasglow, Scotland

M. *JERUSALEM*, Freie Universität Berlin, Federal Republic of Germany

E. *KARCZYKOWSKA*, University of Warsaw, Poland

T. *KLONOWICZ*, University of Warsaw, Poland

M. *KOFTA*, University of Warsaw, Poland

Z. *KULCSÁR*, Eötvös Loránd University, Budapest, Hungary

L. *KUTOR*, Kandó Kálman College, Hungary

C. *LEVY-LEBOYER*, Université René Descartes, Paris, France

J. *MATYSIAK*, University of Warsaw, Poland

P. *McREYNOLDS*, Universty of Nevada, Reno, NV, USA

G. *MOSER*, Université René Descartes, Paris, France

U. *NEUMANN*, Freie Universität Berlin, Federal Republic of Germany

K. *OWCZAREK*, University of Warsaw, Poland

J. *SCHELLENBERG*, Humboldt Universität Berlin-OST, German Democratic Republic

L. R. B. *SCHOMAKER*, University of Nijmegen, the Netherlands

W. *SCHÖNPFLUG*, Freie Universität Berlin, Federal Republic of Germany

R. *SCHWARZER*, Freie Universität Berlin, Federal Republic of Germany

G. SEDEK, University of Warsaw, Poland

A. P. SMITH, University of Sussex, UK

T. SOSNOWSKI, University of Warsaw, Poland

S. J. STEIN, Thistletown Regional Centre, Canada

J. STRELAU, University of Warsaw, Poland

S. SVEBAK, University of Bergen, Norway

M. TYSZKOWA, Adam Mickiewcz University, Poland

A. J. J. M. VINGERHOETS, Free University of Amsterdam, the Netherlands

S. WATRAS-GANS, University of Warsaw, Poland

Preface

Volume 12 of this continuing series on Stress and Anxiety is based on papers that were initially presented at an international conference held in Rynia, Poland, in September 1983. Sponsored by the Polish Academy of Science and the Faculty of Psychology at the University of Warsaw, the conference attracted participants from 15 countries. Professor Jan Strelau of the University of Warsaw was primarily responsible for organizing the Conference, and he has served as Guest Editor for this volume.

The volume is organized into four main parts. The chapters in Part I examine critical theoretical issues in contemporary stress research. Although there is as yet no generally accepted theory of stress and anxiety, as McReynolds notes in Chapter 1, cognitive mediators and coping mechanisms have received increasing attention from theorists in this field. In chapter 2, Averill discusses recent trends in stress research within psychology and medicine, and Apter and Svebak examine stress phenomena from the perspective of Reversal Theory in Chapter 3. In the final chapter of this section, Girodo and Dotzenroth review theoretical issues and empirical findings pertaining to self-esteem and perceived coping adequacy as determinants of social anxiety.

Part II provides a cross-cultural perspective on stress research. Reports of research findings from six countries examine the interaction of environmental stress and personality factors as determinants of stress reactions. The individual chapters investigate stress reactions as a function of a variety of individual difference variables and environmental factors, ranging from learned helplessness and Type-A behavior to stressful noise and examination situations.

The physiological changes that occur during stress reactions and in anticipation of stressful events are examined in Part III. Research findings on the effects of stressful stimulation on electrodermal responses, cardiovascular reactions and brain self-stimulation are reported in the individual chapters. Planning, information processing, and other cognitive strategies for coping with stress and the prevention of stress reactions are considered in the three chapters that encompass Part IV.

Recent empirical findings from the burgeoning research literature in behavioral medicine and health psychology are reported in the final section of this volume. Increasingly, over the past decade, stressful life events, lifestyle factors, and individual differences in personality, emotional reactions to stress, and psychological defenses for controlling unacceptable emotions have been identified as significant contributors to the etiology of heart disease and cancer.

In organizing the conference on which this volume is based and in the preparation of the manuscript for publication, the editors would like to express their gratitude to a number of colleagues who have worked with us. For their dedicated efforts in planning and coordinating the conference activities, and for creating a climate in which there was optimal opportunity for intellectual exchange, we are indebted to the faculty and graduate students of the Department of Psychology of Individual Differences at the University of Warsaw. We would also like to express our appreciation to Tatiana Klonowicz and Tytus Sosnowski of the University of Warsaw, and to Susan Krasner and Richard Rickman of the University of South Florida, for their invaluable contributions in reviewing the manuscripts. Finally, we would like to thank Virginia Berch for her expert assistance in preparing the manuscript for publication.

Charles D. Spielberger
Irwin G. Sarason
Jan Strelau

I

STRESS AND EMOTION:
THEORETICAL AND
ASSESSMENT ISSUES

1

Toward a General Theory of Anxiety

Paul McReynolds
University of Nevada

At the present time there is no generally accepted overall theory of anxiety. Rather, there are a number of restricted conceptions that concentrate upon limited aspects of the human anxiety experience. For example, existential theorists are concerned with a particular kind of angst, namely, that assumed to arise from an individual's perception of problems inherent in the nature of things, such as the gap between the desire for immortality and the realization that one is mortal. Psychoanalytic thinkers focus on internal problems that an individual struggles with as he or she attempts to cope with the world; often these struggles are described in battle-like metaphors, such as conflicts between two motives, or between the ego and the superego. Behavioral theorists call our attention to specific anxieties, such as phobic fears, that appear to be traceable to particular traumatic experiences. Still other limited scope conceptions of anxiety could easily be listed.

It is obvious that an adequate general theory of anxiety would be highly desirable. This is true not only in the interests of scientific elegance—it is hard to believe that there is not some meaningful symmetry underneath the apparent different kinds, or foci, of anxiety—but also because such a comprehensive theory would almost certainly suggest improvements in clinical practice.

Several years ago, in an attempt to further our understanding of anxiety, I put forth (McReynolds, 1976) a broad model integrating what appear to be the two major classes of anxiety—those arising from internal mental processes and those set off by specific environmental stimuli. Though this model was well received, it remains somewhat programmatic, and requires considerable theoretical elaboration and additional support in order to be fully viable.

In this paper I will summarize the anxiety theory that I have proposed—we may refer to it as the assimilation theory of anxiety—and will carry the theoretical analysis somewhat further than heretofore. In particular, I wish to examine the implications for the model of certain recent theory and data in the field of conditioning. Finally, I will indicate some of the research directions that have been stimulated by the model.

GENERAL THEORY

In order to outline my theory of anxiety as succinctly as possible, it will be helpful to begin with a brief statement of the core conception of cognitive processing on which it is based. This underlying paradigm is derived largely from the pioneering theoretical work of Bartlett, Lewin, Piaget, Bruner, and others. It conceives that the individual tends to order his ongoing experiences into an overall organized system. This system, as encoded in the brain, represents in its entirety the individual's conception of reality; it is the bank of data in terms of which the person sorts, collates and makes sense of new inputs. Similar in a general way to what Herbart meant by the "apperceptive mass," this system is nowadays often referred to as the individual's overall "cognitive structure." If we think of it as made up of innumerable interrelated units functioning as different categories, then we may perhaps more properly designate it as the "category system" (McReynolds, 1971).

New input data may or may not find an immediate fit in the person's category system. There is presumably some kind of rapid search-and-match process, and when a sufficiently congruent match between input and certain internal representations is obtained, those categories, with modifications, tend to be what the individual perceives. The category system of course undergoes relatively continuous development and change as it is modified through the individual's ongoing experiences. The impetus for the continuous restructuring can be attributed to the incapacity of the category system's match-mismatch process to readily resolve inputs that do not "fit." We may use the term *assimilation* to refer to the process whereby input data are matched readily and congruently with units of the existing category system. A number of terms, including restructuring, reorganization, and accommodation, have been employed to refer to the changes effected in the category system to permit assimilation to occur.

This, very briefly, is the core input processing conception that underlies the writer's theory of anxiety. It is, to be sure, not a universally accepted model, and working out the details of the schematization described clearly poses tremendous problems. But it would seem that something of the nature just described is essential in order to explain the manifold functions that the human data processing system obviously does accomplish.

Primary Anxiety

In order to construct a theory of anxiety based on the cognitive processing paradigm previously summarized, several additional assumptions have to be made. We assume first that when there is an input for which there is no readily available match in the category system, that is, when there is a mismatch, the immediate response of the person is what has been variously termed startle, the investigatory reflex, or the orienting reaction. This reaction includes a limited degree of tension, or arousal, which motivates the person to attend to the stimulus, which in turn tends to result, when possible, in such reorganization of the category system as will remove the incongruency between input and the internal representations. We may presume that a similar reaction occurs when it is a thought process, rather than an external stimulus, that does not fit.

This general pattern—the sudden increment in tension and arousal following a perception that is incongruent with the category representations to which it tends to be assigned—is, I believe, the basic process underlying anxiety, though of course it typically produces only a minute amount of affect. To see how more intense affects of the level that we would label anxiety are produced, we must bring in some further assumptions and additional theoretical apparatus.

First, I assume that the more involved conceptual inputs—that is, contents such as one's perceptions of oneself, including personal values, attitudes, and beliefs, of other persons, including the individual's perceptions of *their* values, attitudes, and feelings, and all manner of covert contents that enter one's awareness—are also processed according to the general paradigm that I sketched above. Indeed, there seems little reason to doubt that this is the case, even though, on a dimension of content complexity, the gap between the types of disparities typically involved in instances studied under the rubric of orientation reaction's (e.g., a woman hearing a loud noise that she hadn't expected) and those involving life-event experiences with personal meaning (e.g., a man being rejected by a woman he loves) is obviously very wide.

The assumption that anxiety is generated when there is an incongruent relationship between a personally meaningful experience and the relevant aspects of the individual's existent category system takes us into the domain studied by personality and social psychologists under such terms as incongruency, cognitive dissonance, cognitive imbalance, and cognitive inconsistency. There is, of course, an extensive literature in this area, and there is solid evidence (reviewed in McReynolds, 1976) to support the prediction that disparities of this kind—I will employ the generic term *discrepancy* to cover them all—do result in measurable degrees of tension or arousal, or, I assume, anxiety.

However, the deduction of a principle to the effect that experience of cognitive discrepancies of a personally meaningful sort lead to feelings of anxiety is hardly sufficient in itself to explain the intense affective states that we ordinarily have in mind when we use the word *anxiety*. This is true, first, because the anxiety resulting from the perception of such discrepancies appears to be quite transitory; and second, because the magnitude of anxiety generated by such discrepancies, at least so far as laboratory studies are concerned, is relatively mild. Of course, it must be noted that laboratory-contrived instances of anxiety are, as a matter of necessity, quite mild compared to real-life cognitive inconsistencies.

In any event, I have proposed as the major conceptual device for the explication of anxiety the assumption that the effects of experienced mental discrepancies tend to be accumulative. In order to elaborate this proposition I must discuss the concept of assimilation somewhat further. In a metaphorical sense we can think of assimilation as the process whereby input data—percepts, thoughts, and feelings—are entered congruously into the overall category system, and become part of that system. The greater the number of percepts assimilated into a given sub-part of the system, the more stable that sub-part is conceived to be. Input data which because of significant discrepancies do not have adequate fit to be assimilated are considered to remain unassimilated—until and unless the category system is so reorganized as to permit assimilation to occur.

Whereas simple perceptual incongruences—such as hearing an unexpected sound or viewing an ambiguous figure—are generally readily resolved, this is frequently not the case for personally meaningful material. Thus, for example, experienced data involving discrepancies between two strong motives (e.g., the desire to be independent and the desire to be dependent), between one's value system and one's actual behavior (guilt), or involving other dynamic internal constellations, may be impossible to assimilate. Further, because of the stability of the various categories involved, it may sometimes be extremely difficult to bring about the necessary cognitive reorganizations to make assimilation possible. Hence, it is not implausible to assume that in some instances there may be a very significant accumulation of unassimilated material.

Now, the theory posits that the level of anxiety in an individual (trait anxiety) is a monotonic function of the magnitude of unassimilated data in the person's cognitive processing system. The accumulation of such unassimilated material can be thought of as a kind of "cognitive backlog" of unworked-through experiences, attitudes and feelings.

Let me elaborate the points just made. I am positing that in the structure of the human mental apparatus, in the way it is laid down genetically, there is an arrangement whereby experiences that are unassimilable into the prevailing category system tend to be placed in a kind of holding bin—I am of course speaking figuratively—until they become assimilable by virtue of appropriate modifications in the category system; and further, that the felt affect associated with such a backlog is anxiety, which serves the function of motivating the individual to engage in such mental or behavioral processes as will bring about assimilation of the pent-up material.

We may term this kind of anxiety *cognitive anxiety*. It can also be referred to as *primary anxiety,* since its development is conceived to be inherent in the human design. It should be noted that this class of anxiety is content free; it is not tied theoretically to any particular human experiences, such as anticipation of loss, fear of separation, or concerns with selfness.

There appear to be three ways in which increments in cognitive anxiety can occur: (1) by the gradual buildup of the cognitive backlog; (2) by a rapid input of data which are in principle assimilable, but which enter awareness too rapidly to be readily processed (input overload); and (3) by the sudden deassimilation of a mass of previously assimilated material.

The discussion so far has centered on the explication of what are generally conceived by clinicians as internally determined anxieties. These focus on personal problems that arise in the course of living, such as concerns about interpersonal relations, feelings of guilt, worries about achievement, and the search for meaning in life; in other words, the kinds of problems that psychodynamically and cognitively oriented therapists see every day. In the early stages of the development of the present theory, which was designed with anxieties of this kind primarily in mind, I believed that it could adequately encompass all instances of anxiety. Later, (McReynolds, 1976), I concluded that this was not the case, and that it is necessary also to take systematic account of anxieties attributable to the conditioning process.

Secondary Anxiety

At the clinical level, as well as in everyday experience, there is strong evidence for the existence of anxiety that is basically associative, or conditioned. Theoretically, such an interpretation is the most expeditious way of explaining many strong fears, including those of phobic intensity. From the theoretical perspective the crucial question, however, is this: What is it that the originally neutral stimuli, which gain the capacity to set off or catalyze anxiety, are conditioned to? That is, What is the unconditioned stimulus (US) for which the conditioned stimulus (CS) is substituted? This is a question that exponents of the conditioning interpretation of anxiety have not adequately faced. They have been content, for the most part, simply to conceive that an individual experiences some kind of fear, and that this fear is conditioned so that it is later elicited by conditioned stimuli. On basic nature of the *original* fear—what its sources are, and the circumstances that give rise to it—behavior theorists have been essentially silent.

In the present theory, it is posited that conditioned anxiety arises from the adventitious pairing of neutral cues with states of primary (cognitive) anxiety, as previously defined. This proposal offers a straightforward, systematic method of bringing cognitive and conditioned anxiety into the same model in an integrated way. In this context conditioned anxiety can be thought of as "secondary," since it is based on prior instances of anxiety; this designation, however, does not imply that conditioned anxiety is any less real or less important than cognitive anxiety. The assumption that cognitive anxiety or some characteristic of it can be conditioned makes the present model quite different from the orthodox anxiety conditioning conceptualization, which has traditionally conceived of conditioning as applying only to specific fears. The present approach implies that not only may focal fears be the results of conditioning, but also that this may be the case, under certain circumstances, for some of the more generalized, nonspecific feelings of anxiety.

To reiterate, the anxiety model proposed has the following major features. In terms of origins, there are two types of anxiety, which do not (as far as we know) differ phenomenally. One type, designated as primary, is cognitive in nature and is posited to be a function of the backlog of unassimilated perceptual (experiential) data; the other type, designated as secondary, is conditioned in nature and is conceived to result from pairings of neutral stimuli with instances of intense primary anxiety. These two types are not incompatible, and it may be presumed that in real life they may frequently occur together. Though other theorists (Buss, 1962; Hamilton, 1959; Morris & Liebert, 1970; Mowrer, 1939) have also posited twofold conceptions of anxiety, all these differ in significant ways from the present model.

IMPLICATIONS OF MODERN CONDITIONING THEORY

Though there are a number of theoretical issues growing out of the present anxiety model that merit further discussion, I will limit myself in this paper to two of these. Both are related to a crucial feature of the model, namely, the assumption that one kind of anxiety is derived from specific cues conditioned to the other type. I will first examine the process of conditioning as such, and will then consider the problem of specific phobias, generally conceived to be instances of conditioned anxiety.

A particularly difficult problem in conditioning theory is what we may refer to as the selectivity of conditioning. It is manifestly obvious that not every neutral stimulus present during instances of conspicuous primary anxiety become conditioned to it. Indeed, it seems obvious, on the basis of general observation, that most potential conditioned anxiety stimuli do not become carriers of anxiety. What are the factors that determine which few of the available cues actually become conditioned? A difficult question in the laboratory, one can imagine how much more puzzling it is in the real-life complexities of the clinic.

Some relevant preliminary suggestions have been made by various authors. Wolpe and Rachman, in 1960, posited that "Any 'neutral' stimulus . . . that happens to make an *impact* on an individual at about the time that a fear reaction is evoked, acquires the ability to evoke fear subsequently . . ." (p. 145; italics added). Later Rachman and Costello (1961) proposed that neutral stimuli which are particularly relevant are more likely to be conditioned, and that connections are more likely to be formed when the fear is intense. I myself have suggested (McReynolds, 1976, p. 69) in a speculative way and with respect to assimilation theory that conditioning is particularly likely to occur in response to a sudden increment in the level of unassimilated material, as contrasted with a high but stable level.

It is important to note that the fundamental understanding of classical conditioning has undergone drastic change in recent years. While no one doubts the reality of conditioning in an empirical sense, the view of a simple CS-US pairing due to contiguity is now not deemed adequate. Thus, Bolles (1979) concludes that "We can no longer take for granted that conditioning produces an automatic connection of some response to the CS" (p. 155), and Bower and Hilgard (1981), after summarizing relevant studies, refer to "the utter inappropriateness of the simplistic doctrine that temporal contiguity of a CS and US is all that is necessary and sufficient to obtain strong conditioning" (p. 279).

Although complete consensus on the basic nature of conditioning among authorities in this area has yet to be achieved, there are several important theoretical developments that have gained wide acceptance and are particularly pertinent to the present anxiety model. Generally speaking, the trend is toward a more informational interpretation of the conditioning process. As Bower and Hilgard (1981) put it, "evidence is accumulating that, in order to become conditioned, the CS must impart reliable information about the occurrence of the US; it must be a useful predictor of the time, place, and quality of the US" (p. 277). And to quote Bolles again, with respect to the common laboratory procedure for studying fear conditioning in animals, "It appears . . . that fear becomes conditioned to a CS not when it is paired with shock but . . . when the CS predicts shock" (p. 156). In terms of the present anxiety model this suggests that stimuli that are conditioned carriers of anxiety are those that have a history of having predicted the occurrence of primary anxiety. It will be noted that the notions of information and prediction are cognitive rather than contiguity concepts. Since the present interpretation of primary anxiety is also cognitive, this fact suggests the possibility of a more basic integration of the two types of anxiety than I have yet developed.

Modern developments in conditioning theory, especially the work of Rescorla and Wagner (1972; Wagner and Rescorla, 1972; Rescorla, 1978), Kamin (1969), and others, also have important implications for understanding the selectivity of conditioning. Kamin discovered the "blocking" effect, namely, the fact that if stimulus A is first conditioned to a given US, then this tends to block the conditioning of stimulus B to the same US when B is part of the compound stimulus AB. Kamin attributes the degree of conditioning to the surprise value, or unexpectedness of the US. In the present context, this suggests that incongruent inputs, that is, those which are not readily assimilable and hence lead to primary anxiety, are most likely to be conditioned. The Rescorla-Wagner conditioning model, currently the most widely accepted overall systematization, assigns the amount of conditioning to a given cue that occurs on each trial to the amount of conditioning that has already taken place, the intensity of the US, and the relative degree of associative strength of other cues present in the stimulus array.

Various temporal values are of course also involved in determining whether conditioning takes place, though these are perhaps not as crucial in a predictive approach as in a contiguity approach. The Garcia effect (Garcia & Koelling, 1966) indicates that under certain circumstances the CS and the US may be far separated in time with conditioning still occurring. Another important factor is individual differences. Thus, work by Eysenck (1976) indicates that introverts are more subject to conditioning than are extraverts.

In summary, current conditioning theory emphasizes a predictive (cognitive), rather than a strict contiguity, approach. The present conceptualization of anxiety, with its cognitive basis, appears to be highly congruent with the newer view of conditioning. Within recent years considerable progress has been made at a basic theoretical level in delineating the factors involved in the selectivity of conditioning.

PHOBIAS

We turn next to the topic of phobias. For the last several decades, the most generally accepted explanation for phobias has been the conditioning paradigm, and this interpretation would seem to be very congenial to the present overall theory of anxiety. In recent years, however, the conditioning explanation of phobic anxieties has come under strong attack, most notably from behaviorists themselves, including some investigators who previously were strong supporters of the conditioning theory of phobias. Thus Rachman (1977, 1978) has stated that "the conditioning theory of fear acquisition is neither comprehensive nor adequate" (1977, p. 383). And Emmelkamp (1982) recently concluded that "There is little evidence that classical conditioning is involved in the development of clinical phobias. While there is some evidence that it might play a part in the development of specific phobias in agoraphobia it plays only a minor part" (p. 39).

These conclusions obviously raise important questions. As far as the present anxiety theory is concerned the presumption has been that conditioning is indeed centrally involved in the origin of phobias. Though cognitive factors are also important, especially in agoraphobia, I will center my remarks here on the role of conditioning in the onset of phobias. The question is, How plausible is a conditioning interpretation of this disorder?

First, we observe that Rachman does not reject the conditioning explanation of fear acquisition; he merely concludes that it is inadequate, and proposed two cognitive processes (vicarious behavior and direct instruction) to supplement it. Second, both Rachman and Emmelkamp appear to base their arguments on the older, pure contiguity conception of conditioning. In this connection we may note that a provocative interpretation of phobias, in terms of the newer conditioning model, and which appears to bypass some of the criticisms of Rachman and others, has recently been offered by Reiss (1980).

The strongest support for a conditioning explanation of phobias comes from two facts. First, phobic anxiety is set off by very specific stimulus situations (except for agoraphobia, which is probably not a phobia in the usual sense; cf. Hallam, 1978) and does not exist independently of this situation (or of its anticipation): this fact clearly suggests that the catalytic stimuli are playing the role of a CS. Second, phobic anxiety is typically most expeditiously relieved by techniques that can be ordered to the concept of extinction—desensitization, flooding, participant modeling, and in vivo exposure—and is less successfully treated by cognitive restructuring approaches.

One major criticism of the conditioning theory of phobias is easily countered. It is sometimes inferred from the fact that phobic patients are frequently unable to recall any traumatic event leading to their affliction (a person with a fear of dogs may not recall any frightening experience with a dog) that no conditioning was involved. However, there are several other equally good explanations. Perhaps a traumatic experience with a dog did occur, but was repressed. Or possibly such an event never took place, but was imagined; imaginings, as well as perceptions of real events, can be conditioned.

Actually, it does not seem absolutely essential that the original conditioning involve the object of the fear at all—in other words, a person could develop a dog phobia without ever having had a bad experience with a dog, even in fantasy. All that would be necessary is that the individual comes to believe the CS (dogs) to be *predictive* of anxiety. This belief would normally come about by awareness of the dog → high anxiety sequence, though the actual causes of the anxiety could be anything. It would not be essential, in this kind of analysis, that the person's belief as to the predictiveness of a given cue be correct, so long as he or she firmly believes it. From this perspective we can define a phobic object as one which an individual perceives to be unfailingly predictive of high anxiety. It can immediately be seen that a number of factors other than contiguity may be involved in the establishment of a conditioned fear reaction. One of these, no doubt, would be social facilitation, in the sense of suggesting to the individual possible anxiety predictors (i.e., possible phobic objects).

Cognitive factors can be expected to interact with conditioning in the development of phobias. For example, in the illustration just given, the subject, in order to rationalize (assimilate) the anxiety aroused by dogs, might come to see them as dangerous, even if this were not part of the original conditioning.

In another objection to the conditioning interpretation of phobias it is sometimes noted that people only rarely develop phobic-level fears of such everyday objects as cars, guns and electric outlets, even though these may frequently cause or be associated with stressful episodes. It is true that on a simplistic contiguity formulation such objects might be expected to be feared more frequently than they are. According to the more modern view, however, the key factor is the degree to which a prospective CS is uniquely predictive of the US. In this context, a stimulus such as an electric outlet would not normally be predictive of anxiety, since though it might frequently have been paired with the existence of anxious episodes it would also frequently have been paired with their absence.

The problem of phobias is exceedingly complex, and I do not suggest that the present anxiety theory, in its current level of development, offers a solution. I believe, however, that a conditioning approach to the acquisition of fears, as subsumed by the present overall theory, is still viable, and further that the present conceptualization, with its twin moorings in cognitive and conditioning factors, offers a basis for further progress in the study of phobic disorders.

RESEARCH DIRECTIONS

I will now discuss some of the research directions that have been generated by the assimilation theory of anxiety. As illustrations of the kind of research that the theory leads to, I will focus on two projects that are currently under way (for a review of earlier studies see McReynolds, 1976).

Mental Discrepancies

An important component of the theory is the assumption that input data involving significant internal discrepancies are difficult or impossible to assimilate. Though this assumption can be strongly defended, it must be granted that it has a certain programmatic quality that calls for a more formal and rigorous analysis of the nature of mental discrepancies. A project now under way, in which my associates are Robert Jenkins, Ingrid Moore, William Crabbe, and Patricia White, is directed to this problem.

Specifically, the aim of this research program is to develop and apply a system for conceptualizing, identifying and classifying instances of mental discrepancies as these occur in real life. Our procedure has been to collect and examine a large number of instances of actual mental discrepancies in different individuals. These instances have been obtained from several sources: an earlier study, based on therapy transcripts, by Peer (1975); data on patients obtained from various therapists; and questionnaire data solicited from students.

It now seems evident that all mental discrepancies can be phrased as disjunctive statements, specifically, as "but statements," that is, of the form x but y, where x and y are discrepant in some formal manner. Examples would be "I know I should love my father but I detest him," and "I want to get married but I also want to be single."

It is immediately clear from the examination of a collection of real-life mental discrepancies that these fall into various groups, that they differ in formal ways and can be classified in terms of these differences. Our goal has been to discover what might be thought of as the basic grammar of mental discrepancies, and to develop a coding system for describing such discrepancies. In this endeavor we have identified a number of elements, that is, systematic aspects in terms of which the two sides of a discrepancy can differ in meaningful ways. Earlier work on mental discrepancies emphasized to an almost exclusive degree the inconsistencies among cognitions, from which it might be inferred that cognitions are the only kind of element in terms of which an individual may experience discrepancies in mental processing. Our work, however, demonstrates clearly that this is not the case. Indeed, it has been evident for some time, to others as well as ourselves, that mental inconsistencies may involve affective as well as cognitive experiences.

Further, it has long been obvious, from the work of psychodynamic therapists, that individuals frequently manifest strong discrepancies (conflicts) among their various desires.

The coding system that we have devised includes a large number of elements, including actions, affects, attitudes, beliefs, desires, intentions, morals, values, and understandings. In any given instance two of the elements are in a discrepant relationship. For example, in the phrase "I should love my father but I detest him," the discrepancy is between a moral imperative and an affect. In the statement "I want to get married but I also want to stay single," the discrepancy is between two desires. In a study of college students with a preliminary version of the coding system, White (1982) found desires, affects, beliefs, and reality judgments to be the most frequent elements in self-reported mental discrepancies, and conflicts between desires and affects to be the most frequent type of discrepancy.

Perhaps development of the mental discrepancy coding system will open the way for a variety of studies on individual differences in cognitive structure, and will lead to a better understanding of the nature of cognitive anxiety.

Differentiation of Cognitive and Conditioned Anxieties

A central theme of the present conceptualization is the postulation of two types of anxiety, cognitive and conditioned. This distinction, if valid, has important clinical as well as theoretical implications. This follows from the fact that different methods are involved in the reduction of anxiety of the two types. For cognitive anxiety, which is theoretically due to a buildup of unassimilated material, anxiety can be decreased by methods that reduce the magnitude of unassimilation, that is, by methods that bring about assimilation. The primary process of this kind is cognitive restructuring, using alterations in the category system that resolve and remove the discrepancies that are preventing assimilation. For conditioned anxiety, the core method of anxiety reduction is through extinction of the strength of the CS. Translated into implications for therapeutic procedures, this analysis indicates that some version of self-examination and insight therapy is indicated for cognitive anxiety, and one of the behavioral techniques, such as desensitization or flooding, for conditioned anxiety.

These therapeutic implications, as well as the research requirements, point up the need for a technique to determine, in any given instance of anxiety, whether that anxiety is chiefly cognitive or conditioned (I say "chiefly" because it is presumed that in most clinical instances, some of each type would necessarily be involved). For these reasons two of my colleagues, James Eyman and Patricia White, and I have undertaken the construction of an inventory, to be filled out by the subject with respect to a given episode of anxiety, which would indicate whether and to what degree that particular anxiety is cognitive or conditioned. Test development work on this inventory has not yet been completed, and therefore the comments to follow are in the nature of a progress report, as was the case with respect to the mental discrepancy research.

In constructing the inventory, which we refer to as the Personal Anxiety Report (PAR), we first derived on rational grounds a listing of specific criteria that appear to be characteristic of the two types of anxiety, as these are experienced by the anxious person. Among the criteria developed were the following. For cognitive anxiety: problem typically takes the form of *x* but also *y* (inconsistency); person can't get away from problem—it goes with him; and person ruminates about problem and tries to solve it. For conditioned anxiety: problem typically takes the form of A then B (temporal sequence); anxiety is tied to particular places and situations; person tries to avoid situations setting off anxiety.

On the basis of these and other rational criteria a large number of items were devised; these were eventually reduced to a 25-item test, including 15 cognitive items and 10 conditioned items. The general format of test administration is that the subject first writes a brief description of a particular anxiety experience, and then answers the 25 questions about it, each framed in 4-point Likert scales. An example of a cognitive item is, "Wherever I go the anxiety is with me," and of a conditioned item, "Even though I know better, I get anxious whenever I get in a certain situation."

Reliability estimates (alpha coefficients) on the two scales, obtained from several different samples, range from the high .70s to the high .80s. Obtained interrelations between the two scales have been uniformly low. Two preliminary studies provide some evidence of test validity. In one study judges selected, from subject's descriptions, 55 relatively pure cognitive anxiety experiences and 32 relatively pure instances of conditioned anxiety; these two groups were significantly discriminated by the test. In the second study students who identified themselves as having test-taking anxiety were compared on the PAR with students whose primary concern was vocational choice. It was reasoned that, in the main, the former anxiety was primarily conditioned, and the latter chiefly cognitive. The findings were in accord with this prediction.

Work on the PAR is continuing, and it is anticipated that the research form of the test will be available in the near future. The inventory appears to have considerable potential value, not only for basic research on the nature of anxiety, but also for certain clinical applications.

CONCLUSIONS

The purposes of this paper were to outline the essential points of the writer's assimilation theory of anxiety, to examine certain theoretical issues related to the theory, and to indicate the kinds of research generated by the theory.

The assimilation theory is based on a cognitive processing model. It assumes that unassimilable inputs tend to accumulate, and that primary (cognitive) anxiety is a function of the magnitude of unassimilated experiential material. Secondary (conditioned) anxiety is conceived to arise from the association of neutral cues with states of high primary anxiety.

The implications of modern conditioning theory, with its emphasis on predictive value of conditioned stimuli, were examined and found to be congruent with the anxiety model. The conventional theoretical view that conditioning is involved in the etiology of phobias was considered, and judged to be plausible.

Finally, two examples of research stimulated by the anxiety theory were presented. The first concerned the development of a system for identifying and categorizing instances of inconsistencies (discrepancies) in mental input, which, it is held, tend to be unassimilable. The second concerned the development of an inventory designed to discriminate between instances of cognitive and conditioned anxiety.

REFERENCES

Bolles, R. C. (1979). *Learning theory* (2nd ed.). New York: Holt, Rinehart & Winston.

Bower, G. H., & Hilgard, E. R. (1981). *Theories of learning* (5th ed.). Englewood Cliffs, NJ: Prentice-Hall.

Buss, A. H. (1962). Two anxiety factors in psychiatric patients. *Journal of Abnormal and Social Psychology, 65,* 426–427.

Emmelkamp, P. M. G. (1982). *Phobic and obsessive-compulsive disorders.* New York: Plenum.

Ensenck, H. J. (1976). The learning theory model of neurosis—A new approach. *Behaviour Research and Therapy, 14,* 251–267.

Garcia, J. & Koelling, R. (1966). Relation of cue to consequence in avoidance learning. *Psychonomic Science, 4,* 123–124.

Hallam, R. S. (1978). Agoraphobia: A critical review of the concept. *British Journal of Psychiatry, 133,* 314–319.

Hamilton, M. (1959). The assessment of anxiety states by rating. *British Journal of Medical Psychology, 32,* 50–59.

Kamin, L. J. (1969). Predictability, surprise, attention, and conditioning. In B. A. Campbell & R. M. Church (Eds.), *Punishment and aversive behavior* (pp. 279–296). New York: Appleton-Century-Crofts.

McReynolds, P. (1971). The three faces of cognitive motivation. In H. I. Day, D. E. Berlyne, & D. E. Hunt (Eds.), *Intrinsic motivation: A new direction in education* (pp. 33–45), Minneapolis: Winston.

McReynolds, P. (1976). Assimilation and anxiety. In M. Zuckerman & C. D. Spielberger (Eds.), *Emotions and anxiety: New concepts, methods, and applications* (pp. 35–86). Hillsdale, NJ: Erlbaum.

Morris, L. W. & Liebert, R. M. (1970). Relationship of cognitive and emotional components of test anxiety to physiological arousal and academic performance. *Journal of Consulting and Clinical Psychology, 35,* 332–337.

Mowrer, O. H. (1939). A stimulus-response analysis of anxiety and its role as a reinforcing agent. *Psychological Review, 46,* 553–565.

Peer, A. E. (1975). *A naturalistic study of the assimilation process in psychotherapy.* Unpublished doctoral dissertation, University of Nevada-Reno, Reno, Nevada.

Rachman, S. (1977). The conditioning theory of fear-acquisition: A critical examination. *Behaviour Research and Therapy, 15,* 375–387.

Rachman, S. (1978). *Fear and courage.* San Francisco: W. H. Freeman.

Rachman, S. & Costello, C. (1961). The aetiology and treatment of children's phobias. *American Journal of Psychiatry, 118,* 97–105.

Reiss, S. (1980). Pavlovian conditioning and human fear: An expectancy model. *Behavior Therapy, 11,* 380–396.

Rescorla, R. A. (1978). Some implications of a cognitive perspective on Pavlovian conditioning. In S. H. Hulse, H. Fowler, & W. Honig (Eds.), *Cognitive processes in animal behavior* (pp. 15–50). Hillsdale, NJ: Erlbaum.

Rescorla, R. A., & Wagner, A. R. (1972). A theory of Pavlovian conditioning: Variations in the effectiveness of reinforcement and nonreinforcement. In A. Black & W. F. Prokasy (Eds.), *Classical conditioning: II. Current research and theory.* New York: Appleton-Century-Crofts.

Wagner, A. R., & Rescorla, R. A. (1972). Inhibition in Pavlovian conditioning: Application of a theory. In R. A. Boakes & M. S. Halliday (Eds.), *Inhibition and learning* (pp. 301–336). New York: Academic Press.

White, P. (1982). *A study of cognitive anxiety and mental conflicts.* Unpublished doctoral dissertation, University of Nevada-Reno, Reno, Nevada.

Wolpe, J., & Rachman, S. (1960). Psychoanalytic evidence: A critique based on Freud's case of Little Hans. *Journal of Nervous and Mental Disease, 131,* 135–145.

2

Stress as Fact and Artifact: An Inquiry into the Social Origins and Functions of Some Stress Reactions

James R. Averill
University of Massachusetts

Perhaps I should say at the outset exactly what I mean by stress as fact and artifact. That, however, is what the chapter is all about; by the end of the chapter, I hope my meaning will be clear. Still, a few words of clarification are needed by way of introduction. A stress-like reaction might be regarded as artifactual for either of two reasons. First, the response may only approximate or simulate stress—in the way, say, that hysterical blindness simulates actual blindness. Second, the stress may be genuine enough, but it may occur in response to an innocuous situation, as when a claustrophobic becomes alarmed at the prospect of riding in an elevator.

Needless to say, both of the above senses of stress-as-artifact are quite ambiguous in the absence of a clear-cut definition of stress-as-fact. With respect to the first sense, for example, the concept of stress may be so broadly defined that it is almost impossible to say when a response is an instance of "true" stress and when it is only "stress-like." And with regard to the second sense, how do we know when a particular situation represents a realistic threat? The claustrophobic's fear of elevators may be unrealistic by almost any standard, but most threats that concern people cannot be classified as either clearly hazardous or clearly innocuous.

It is not my intention in this chapter to propose a set of criteria for identifying "true" stress or "realistic" threats. Many such proposals have been made, but none has been widely accepted. Another proposal is not needed. It is sufficient for my purposes if we can agree that some proportion—undoubtedly the major proportion—of the incidence of stress is grounded in fact. My concern is with the incidence of stress that is artifactual. Specifically, the purpose of the chapter is

I would like to thank Drs. Seymour Epstein and Patricia Wisocki for their helpful comments on an earlier version of this manuscript, and Debbie Hardy for her assistance in compiling relevant statistics.

15

twofold: first, I will review evidence suggesting that the incidence of artifactual stress—though perhaps small in proportion to the total amount of stress experienced in the modern world—is not insignificant and is perhaps increasing; and, second, I will examine some broad cultural trends (neoromanticism) as well as some more narrow professional interests (on the part of psychologists and other health-care professionals) that might contribute to an increase in stress-as-artifact.

For reasons that will become clearer later in this chapter (if they are not obvious from what already has been said), data do not exist that would allow a definitive statement with regard to the incidence of stress as either fact or artifact. However, there is an indirect source of data that we can draw upon; a source, moreover, that is of considerable interest in its own right. I am referring to the ever increasing amount of research being devoted to stress (as reflected in publication statistics), and to the application of this research in the burgeoning field of stress-management. The endeavors of researchers and health-care professionals can serve as a rough barometer of the presumed importance of stress within a society.

RECENT TRENDS IN STRESS RESEARCH

In 1983, *Psychological Abstracts* contained 615 references under the heading of *stress* and its various subcategories (environmental stress, occupational stress, physiological stress, psychological stress, social stress, and stress reactions).* Another 180 references were cited under the closely related heading, *coping*. The topic of stress has not always enjoyed such popularity. Stress was not indexed in the *Psychological Abstracts* until 1944, in which year four articles appeared. Subsequently, the number of references to stress has increased exponentially, both in absolute numbers and as a percentage of the total number of abstracts. When plotted on a logarithmic scale, the trend is almost linear. Even if emotional reactions were included under the rubric of stress, it would not affect the present argument substantially. Elsewhere (Averill, 1979, 1980a, 1980b, 1982), I have argued that such standard emotions as grief and anger can best be conceptualized as socially constituted syndromes. In a sense, this chapter extends a similar line of reasoning to some subset of stress reactions.

What accounts for the dramatic increase in interest in stress during the last 40 years? One possibility is that *stress* simply represents a relabeling of phenomena that, in earlier years, were discussed under different headings. But that cannot be the entire story, or even a very large part of it. Prior to 1944, topics that might now be included under the heading of stress were typically listed under such headings as *emotion* and *conflict*. An examination of entries in the *Psychological Abstracts* does not suggest that these categories have diminished in importance with the increased interest in stress. Quite the contrary: research on emotion, in particular, has enjoyed a resurgence lately.

Another possibility is that major scientific advances have been made in recent years, so that a breakthrough in our understanding of stress is imminent. But that

---

*The *Psychological Abstracts* contains nonevaluative summaries of the world literature (journals, articles, books, dissertations, etc.) in psychology and related disciplines. During 1983, articles were abstracted from 958 journals.

also seems unlikely. A sampling of the thousands of articles on stress that have been published during the past few years does not reveal a coherent field of inquiry; and although marked advances have been made in restricted areas, one does not get a sense of steady scientific progress. This point deserves brief elaboration.

The Institute of Medicine (a branch of the United States National Academy of Sciences) recently commissioned a review of research on the relationship between stress and human health. This is an issue about which I will have more to say later in the chapter. For the moment, I only want to comment on an observation made by David Hamburg in a forward to the report. According to Hamburg (1982) "hardly a week passes without a new course, book, article, or movie on ways of dealing with stress in industry, education, government, or marriage—as well as in medical settings. Yet, there has been a discrepancy between the high level of public interest and the low priority of scientific commitment to this subject" (p. ix).

Hamburg is certainly correct about the high level of public interest in stress. However, the statistics presented in Fig. 1 do not suggest a lack of commitment on the part of the scientific community. It is always tempting to attribute a lack of progress to a lack of commitment. I hope to demonstrate that the problem lies deeper than that.

A third possible reason for the trends depicted in Fig. 1 is that the concept of stress serves as a mantle for a broad range of scientific activities, including the organization of conferences and the publication of scholarly volumes. This is true, and I do not want to gainsay the value of such endeavors. But invariably, conferences on stress, anthologies of stress research, and the like bring forth the complaint that the endeavor lacks coherence. This complaint is often accompanied by the hope that, with additional research, the way will be opened toward a unified theory of stress. I may be unduly pessimistic, but I strongly suspect that a unified theory of stress eludes us, not because of a paucity of research, but because stress does not represent a unified field of inquiry.

Still a fourth possibility for the current interest in stress is that the occasions for stress have increased during the last 40 years. In order to evaluate this possibility, it is helpful to distinguish between microstressors and macrostressors (Schönpflug, 1983). Microstressors are the minor hassles and inconveniences that plague our daily lives that an objective observer might consider relatively innocuous. Macrostressors are the major catastrophies or changes in life-style that almost any person would regard as stressful.

Changes in the incidence of microstressors are very difficult to document. Schönpflug (1983) describes an unpublished study by Brunke, Sange, and Treziak (1978) which involved a content analysis of newspaper reports, as well as interviews with senior citizens (ranging in age between 75 and 92 years). The time period studied was from 1900 to the mid-1970s with the war years excluded, and the locale was restricted to a suburb of Berlin. Newspaper reports on stressful situations have increased since 1900; on the other hand, senior citizens tended to endorse such statements as, "Life is much easier now." But even if they perceived life as more difficult in earlier years, many senior citizens also believed that "We were more content than people nowadays."

As Schönpflug notes, data such as these are little more than anecdotal. Newspaper accounts tend to be biased by what people find interesting at any particular time; and this may have only a tenuous relationship to the underlying incidence of the phenomenon being reported. Also, the reminiscences of older persons may be influenced by nostalgia and faulty memory for minor incidences long past, as well as by a distorted image of present conditions (e.g., due to their own poor health and limited coping resources).

Human beings are remarkably capable of adapting to situations of potential stress; conversely, when things are going well, many people will nevertheless find grounds for discontent, while others will seek new challenges. For these reasons alone, it seems unreasonable to expect gross changes in microstressors from one period to another. Such is not the case with respect to macrostressors. In general, people are healthier and safer today, and they live longer than at any time in history. Since this is an important point that has implications for later discussion, let me digress briefly.

Figure 2 presents estimates of life expectancy for various historical epochs. Examination of skeletal remains indicates that in prehistoric times the average life expectancy of humans was between 20–25 years. Persons who were fortunate enough to reach their 20th birthday could expect to live approximately another 20

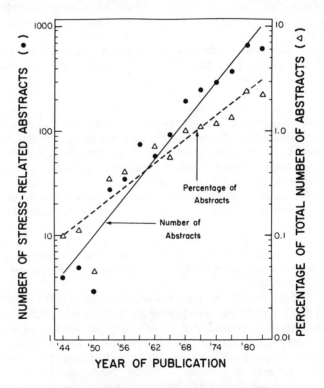

Figure 1 Number and percentage of stress-related abstracts published in the *Psychological Abstracts* at three year intervals from 1944 to 1983. The solid line is the regression line for the log number of abstracts on year of publication ($r = .96$). The regression of the log percentage of abstracts on year of publication is represented by the broken line ($r = .92$).

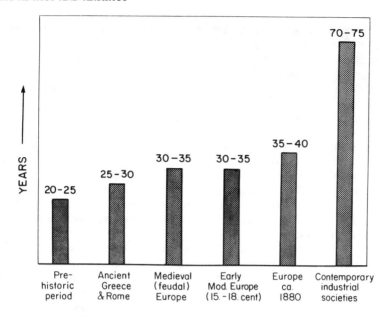

Figure 2 Average life expectancy during various historical epochs (based on data compiled by Acsadi & Nemeskeri, 1970; and Dublin, Lotka, & Spiegelman, 1949).

years. Thus, roughly three quarters of the people were dead by the age of 40. A modest increase in life expectancy (25–30 years) may have occurred in ancient Greece and Rome and again during the middle ages (30–35 years). These increases, however, were not very dramatic, being only about 10 years, and even this figure may be an overestimate. The available data (tomb epitaphs, death records, as well as skeletal remains) are biased toward older persons and persons of higher social status. Until the 19th century, it is probably safe to say that the average life expectancy was between 20 and 30 years.

The above figures also do not take into account major shifts in mortality rates due to pestilence, famine, and warfare. During the Black Death of the 14th Century, Europe lost perhaps 40% of its population. This was, of course, exceptional. But more regional epidemics of other diseases (e.g., smallpox, cholera, diphtheria, influenza) were not uncommon, and the death toll was often great. Famines have also taken a heavy toll. For example, the population of Denmark fell by more than 20% between 1650 and 1660; and Finland may have lost over a quarter of its population a few decades later (1696–1697). Many of the deaths were not due to outright starvation, but to infectious diseases that afflicted the malnourished population. A similar statement could be made about the many wars that have swept over Europe. Fewer deaths were caused by the wounds of conflict than by the disruption of harvests and the spread of disease. According to Wrigley (1969), years of heavy mortality occurred roughly once every generation in most parts of Europe until relatively recent times (19th century). If anything, the situation has been even worse in other parts of the world. Between 108 B.C. and 1911 A.D., an estimated 1800 famines occurred in China—almost one per year. Most of these were confined to a few provinces. Yet, during any person's lifetime, several famines might have been experienced (Peterson, 1961).

There is no need to elaborate further. The point I want to make is simply that the average life expectancies depicted in Fig. 2, grim though they may be, do not adequately reflect the vagaries and uncertainties of life during most of human history.

It was not until 100 years ago (ca. 1880) that a dramatic rise in life expectancy began to occur, first in a few countries of Europe, and then in the rest of the world. But progress has been very uneven. In many undeveloped countries today, life expectancy is not much greater than during the earlier epochs depicted in Fig. 2.

Of course, there are other sources of stress than those that involve a direct threat to one's life. Rapid social change, economic fluctuations, rising expectations, and the like can produce conditions of alienation and anomie. Still, it is difficult to find extended periods of time in history that were less stressful on these grounds than the present.

I do not wish to deny or downplay the ample grounds for stress in the contemporary world; I only wish to assert that these grounds are insufficient to account for the current, almost faddish interest in stress. To explain the latter, we must examine not only the objective risks and dangers that individuals face (stress as fact), but also the manner in which stress is adventitiously related to broader social concerns and interests (stress as artifact). In the remainder of this chapter, I will argue that the broader social conditions accounting for the recent increase in interest in stress are of the two types: first, a general cultural milieu (neoromanticism) that elevates stress to a status of ennobling condition; and, second, a rapid growth in health-care professionals whose esteem and livelihood depend on the identification and alleviation of stress.

But before proceeding further, a caveat is in order. Whenever one focuses on social determinants of behavior, the analysis is necessarily tied to conditions existing in a particular society at a particular time. The present analysis pertains primarily to conditions currently existing in the United States. The extent to which comparable considerations apply to other societies is not an issue that I am prepared to address. However, as is amply illustrated by the *International Conference on Stress and Anxiety*, on which this volume is based, an interest in stress is not limited to any one country; nor, I presume, are some of the broader cultural and scientific trends that have helped foster that interest. But that is for others to judge. To the extent that my analysis is culture-specific, this chapter may be viewed as a study in ethnopsychology.

NEOROMANTICISM
AND THE ENNOBLEMENT OF STRESS

On the most general level, the current interest in stress is linked, I believe, to a revival of romanticism. The term *Romanticism* is usually used to refer to the literary, artistic, and social movement that became dominant during the early decades of the 19th century. I am using the term "neoromanticism" to distinguish current trends from those of the last century. In a broader sense, however, romanticism is not limited to a few periods of history. It is a recurrent set of attitudes and orientations that has waxed and waned throughout Western history. The secondary literature on 19th century Romanticism alone is vast. A brief introduction and annotated bibliography is provided by Furst (1976). Romanticism is not a unitary philosophy or *Weltanschauung,* and hence it is difficult to describe concisely. For our purposes, that is not necessary. It suffices to note two common features of most romantic movements. One feature is an emphasis on what (for want of a better term) might be called "naturalness," and hence on the distorting effects of all that is nonnatural, especially established social institutions and technology. A second feature of Romanticism is an elevation of feeling to a higher status than reason or rational inquiry; one manifestation of this elevation—about which I will have much to say later—is a belief in the ennobling effects of suffering.

A few quotations from both 19th century and contemporary sources will help illustrate the romantic outlook. The emphasis on feeling, and on the goodness and wisdom to be found in nature, was epitomized by Wordsworth in his poem, *The Tables Turned,* written at the turn of the 19th century (1798, to be exact):

> *Books! 't is a dull and endless strife:*
> *Come hear the woodland linnet,*
> *How sweet his music! on my life,*
> *There's more wisdom in it.*

> *Enough of Science and of Art;*
> *Close up those barren leaves;*
> *Come forth, and bring you a heart*
> *That watches and receives.*

Mary Shelley gave even more dramatic expression to the potential dangers of technology in her Gothic tale of Dr. Frankenstein. Alluding to this story, the historian, Roszak (1974), has posed the following questions about the role of science in the modern world:

> Asked to nominate a worthy successor to Victor Frankenstein's macabre brainchild, what should we choose from our contemporary inventory of terrors? The cyborg? The genetically synthesized android? The behavioral brain washer? The despot computer? Modern science provides us with a surfeit of monsters, does it not? (Roszak, 1974, p. 17)

Where there are terrors, there must, of course, be victims who are terrorized. An ennoblement of the victim is also a common feature of romanticism. Sontag (1978) has described how suffering from tuberculosis was elevated by 19th century romantics to the status of high fashion.

> Many of the literary and erotic attitudes known as "romantic agony" derive from tuberculosis and its transformations through metaphor. Agony became romantic in a stylized account of the disease's preliminary symptoms (for example, debility is transformed into languor) and the actual agony was simply suppressed. Wan, hallow-chested young women and pallid, rachitic young men vied with each other as candidates for this mostly (at the time) incurable, disabling, really awful disease. (Sontag, 1978, pp. 28–29)

Persons suffering from a terrible affliction deserve our sympathy, and to the extent that they bear their burden with courage and dignity, also our admiration. It is not surprising, then, that people may sometimes create terrors to legitimize their own (presumed) victimization. Romanticism simply magnifies this all-too-human frailty. Commenting on contemporary society, Sennet (1980) has noted how many people seek moral legitimacy in the role of the victim:

> Most of all, the ennobling of victims means that in ordinary middle-class life we are forced constantly to go in search of some injury, some affliction, in order to justify even the contemplation of questions of justice, right and entitlement in our lives . . . The need to legitimate one'e beliefs in terms of an injury or suffering to which one has been subjected attaches people more and more to the injuries themselves. (Sennett, 1980, p. 150)

Needless to say, injury need not actually occur. The mere threat of injury —in other words, psychological *stress*— may be regarded as ennobling. However, not just any injury, or threat of injury, will ennoble the victim. The injury must be viewed as imposed from without and as undeserved. But these considerations raise further questions. How do we determine when an injury has been imposed from without? Who, for example, is responsible when a person who smokes two packs of cigarettes a day develops lung cancer? And even if we agree that a certain injury is imposed from without, under what conditions is it regarded as undeserved or morally wrong? In most modern societies, being struck by lightning is a morally neutral event, no matter how tragic. Among the Lele people of Zaire, being struck by lightning is attributed to specific types of immorality, in which the victim is generally seen as innocent and blame is attributed to some village elder or other powerful leader (Douglas & Wildavsky, 1982).

The attitudes of the Lele toward lightning are particularly interesting since these people take a more objective and morally neutral view of the many tropical diseases that pose a constant threat to their existence. As Douglas and Wildavsky (1982) note:

> Each social arrangement elevates some risks to a high peak and depresses others below sight. This cultural bias is integral to social organization. Risk taking and risk aversion, shared confidence and shared fears are part of the dialogue on how best to organize social relations. (p. 8)

It is not difficult to pinpoint in contemporary American society certain risks that have become elevated "as part of the dialogue on how best to organize social relations." The fear of atomic energy is one example.

> Why do people have almost phobic reactions, when scientific analysis says there is no real risk? The probability of dying from cancer of the lung is very high if you smoke, but people aren't afraid of smoking. The probability of a nuclear reaction accident is practically negligible, but there is all sorts of mass hysteria associated with it. (Yalow, 1982)

Yalow, who received the 1977 Nobel prize for her work in nuclear medicine, believes that the "almost phobic fear of radiation" would be an interesting problem for psychologists to investigate. But she also suspects "that social scientists have promoted these fears, by not knowing enough about radiation." She may be correct that social scientists have helped promote such fears, but not simply out of ignorance. For many Americans, atomic radiation has much the same symbolic significance as lightning has for the Lele. The issue is more social than technical.

It is interesting to speculate why some risks become emphasized while the significance of other dangers are ignored. But that is not my present concern. What is peculiar about contemporary society is that many risks have become the focus of concern simultaneously. To an extent, this may reflect a breakdown in social consensus, with different groups championing their own favored lists of dangers. But it is also due, I would suggest, to a general cultural milieu in which technological society is itself viewed as a source of danger, and in which suffering (stress) is elevated to the level of a status symbol.

Neoromanticism in Psychology

As an empirical science, psychology is supposedly immune from the value judgments and ideological concerns that are essential ingredients of larger social debates. Objectivity is indeed a worthy goal, one that should be striven after in any discipline that calls itself a science. But few psychologists today are so naive as to believe that psychology can remain insulated from movements in the society at large.

Neoromanticism in psychology is perhaps best reflected in what Maslow has termed the "third force." In one of his many expositions on the topic, Maslow (1970) recounts Drucker's (1939) thesis that western Europe, since the beginning of Christianity, has been dominated by four successive concepts of how individual happiness and welfare should be sought. The first of these concepts is that of the spiritual man (Middle Ages); the second, the intellectual man (Renaissance); the third, economic man (capitalism and Marxism); and the fourth, heroic man (the fascist counterpart of the economic man of capitalism and Marxism). Each of these concepts or myths has failed, according to Maslow, but a new and more adequate one is taking shape, namely, "the concept of the psychologically healthy man, or the eupsychic man, who is also in effect the 'natural' man. I expect that this concept will affect our era as profoundly as have the ones mentioned by Drucker" (Maslow, 1970, p. 269).

I believe Maslow was correct in his prediction about the emphasis to be placed on psychological health in contemporary society, but not necessarily with the results that he foresaw. In any case, Maslow's (1970) concept of the psychologically healthy person encompasses the two themes of Romanticism that we have been discussing. First, the healthy person is the "natural" person: "Psychopathology results from the denial or the frustration or the twisting of man's essential nature" (p. 269). The second theme is the elevation of feeling to a status at least equal to that of reason in the determination of truth and value: "After all, the limit to which the 'pure' scientist approaches is not an Einstein or a Newton but rather the Nazi 'scientist' of the concentration-camp experiments or the 'mad' scientist of Hollywood" (p. 3).

Maslow's "third force" was defined as much by its opposition to behaviorism and psychoanalysis as it was by any particular conception of human nature. As such, it drew inspiration from diverse sources, not all of which are compatible with one another in important respects. One of these sources is existentialism. In general, existentialist writers take a much more pessimistic view of human nature than do Maslow and many other humanistic psychologists. For most existentialists, life is basically absurd, and the touchstone of human feeling is angst not ecstasy. Persons who are serene in their "contemplative cognitions of the highest goods" (Maslow's phrase) are probably suffering from false consciousness or inauthenticity. The hero of the existentialist novel is not the self-actualized person envisioned by Maslow; rather, he/she is more akin to Sisyphus, who was condemned to roll a boulder to the top of a mountain, only to have it fall back again of its own weight. In Camus' (1955) interpretation of this ancient myth, Sisyphus is a tragic figure only because he is conscious of the absurdity of his task. Camus implies that the fate of Sisyphus is the fate of all of us, although few have the insight or courage to recognize the fact.

Rollo May (1981), a leading spokesman for existential psychology, expresses a similar theme: "Authentic despair is that emotion which forces one to come to terms with one's own destiny. It is the great enemy of pretense, the foe of playing ostrich. It is a demand to face the reality of one's life. . . . Despair is the smelting furnace which melts out the impurities in the ore" (p. 235).

Stressful experiences do frequently have beneficial as well as harmful effects. As described by Tyszkowa (1983), only by meeting and overcoming difficulties do we acquire the capacities to cope successfully with the major and minor hardships that inevitably confront us. With their overemphasis on the negative effects of frustration, humanists tend to overlook this basic truth; by contrast, the existentialists tend to go to the opposite extreme, almost making suffering an end in itself, a badge of one's humanity. Yet, both points of view have one thing in common: Each in its own way paints a picture of the individual sufferer as a tragic but noble victim.

Neoromanticism has not only influenced the attitudes of many psychologists toward stress, but also the means by which stress might be identified or diagnosed. A brief historical digression may help clarify this issue.

The 19th century Romantics popularized a theory of aesthetics in which a work of art was considered to be the embodiment of the thoughts and feelings of the artist. Correspondingly, to understand a work of art, one must try to think what the artist was thinking, and to feel what the artist was feeling. Aesthetic appreciation is thus an act or re-creation, one that mirrors the artist's original act of creation.

Baumann (1978) has traced the extension of this conception of understanding from its origins in Romanticism to its application in contemporary social science.

> *Social phenomena, since they are ultimately acts of men and women, demand to be understood in a different way than by mere explaining. Understanding them must contain an element missing from the explaining of natural phenomena: the retrieval of purpose, of intention, of the unique configuration of thoughts and feelings which preceded a social phenomenon and found its only manifestation, imperfect and incomplete, in the observable consequences of actions. (p. 12)*

In other words, an understanding of social phenomena falls more within the realm of art than of science as traditionally conceived. Diagnostic procedures that involve "pinning numbers on people" are particularly to be avoided as "dehumanizing." This attitude toward assessment, combined with the neoromantic emphasis on suffering, can easily lead to the detection of stress in almost any situation.[†]

THE PROFESSIONALIZATION OF STRESS

Broad cultural factors, such as neoromanticism, may provide a climate that is conducive to stress as artifact. However, in order to account for current trends, more specific factors must also be taken into account. In the present section, therefore, I will examine certain professional developments that would, given an appropriate cultural climate, help make stress a focus of concern. Specifically, I will argue that the present emphasis on stress is, in part, a function of the resources available for the alleviation of stress. Since there are no empirical data that bear directly on this issue, I will develop an argument by analogy. First, I will examine the various factors that influence the incidence of surgery; a topic that has been much investigated. I will then show how some of the same considerations apply *mutatis mutandis* to the identification and treatment of stress. In adopting this strategy, I am not simply acting like the drunk who has lost his keys down the street, but who searches for them under the lamppost because that is where the light is. On the contrary, my argument is actually a conservative one. There are many more constraints on the practice of surgery than on the management of stress (e.g., in terms of diagnostic criteria, outcome evaluation, and the reticence of most people to undergo surgery). Hence, to the extent that the same or similar considerations apply to rates of surgery, on the one hand, and to the identification and management of stress, on the other, the latter should be even more subject to variations than the former.

Factors Influencing Rates of Surgery

In the United States, the rate of surgery per capita is twice as high as in England and Wales (Bunker, 1970). This is true for a wide range of operations, including inguinal herniorrhaphy, cholecystectomy, tonsillectomy, hemorrhoidectomy, hysterectomy, and partial and radical mastectomies. When considering such variations in rates of surgery (more instances of which will be cited below), four interrelated factors must be taken into account: (1) the incidence of the disease in the population; (2) attitudes of the patient toward the disease and its treatment; (3) resources available; and (4) the professional interests of the physician. Let us consider briefly how these four factors influence rates of surgery. We will then consider the analogous situation with respect to stress.

[†]For a detailed analysis of some of the unfavorable effects that neoromanticism (or at least its more "irrationalistic" aspects) has had on the training of recent psychologists, see Strupp (1976).

Incidence of the Disease in the Population

Ideally, the rate of surgical intervention should be directly related to the incidence of the condition being treated. Unfortunately, the actual incidence of most diseases is difficult to determine. Diagnosis is often uncertain, even after a thorough workup; hence, much depends on the judgment and acumen of the diagnosing physician, about which I will have more to say shortly. But even if diagnostic procedures were completely accurate, the notion of what constitutes a disease is often ambiguous and subject to dispute. This point deserves brief elaboration, for it is central to much of the discussion that follows.

In the medical literature, it is becoming increasingly common to distinguish between disease and illness (e.g., Fabrega, 1979). A disease is a pathological condition resulting in an impairment of the organism as a biological system. Plants, animals, and humans can all have diseases. By contrast, illness is primarily a human phenomenon. An illness is comprised not only of the symptoms of a disease, if there be an underlying biopathology, but also of psychological reactions and socially conditioned responses to the disease.

There is often a close association between a particular disease and an illness. However, a disease can occur without a corresponding illness, provided the disease is not too debilitating and is accepted as normal by the society. Conversely, there may be illness with no corresponding disease. A hysterical conversion reaction is a familiar example.

The distinction between disease and illness is easy enough to draw in the abstract. In practice, however, the distinction is necessarily blurry. Once a diagnostic category is accepted within a culture, the corresponding illness is also created. The extent to which the illness is linked to a particular disease may vary in an unknown fashion from one condition to another.

Attitudes of the Patient Toward the Disease/Illness

Some persons have an almost phobic reaction to "the knife," avoiding surgery at all cost; other persons have a neurotic eagerness for surgery, demanding repeated operations for vague and uncertain conditions (Titchener & Levine, 1960). But these are only the extremes of the distribution. Within the normal range, marked individual differences exist in the utilization of surgical procedures. One indication of this can be seen in the response of individuals to a second opinion regarding the necessity of surgery. Since 1972, the Cornell-New York Hospital has been conducting such a second-opinion program. In this program, patients are assigned to groups in which second opinions on the need for surgery are either mandatory or voluntary. For simplicity, we will consider only the "mandatory" group, which now totals more than 273,000 patients (Finkel, McCarthy, & Ruchlin, 1982). Unless these patients seek a second opinion (free of charge), they face the possible loss of insurance coverage for the expense of the operation. The second opinion need not be followed, only obtained. Of the 273,000 patients who have participated in this program, 18% were not confirmed as needing surgery. Almost 40% of these patients (i.e., those who received a negative—disconfirming—second opinion) elected to have the surgery anyway. At the other extreme, 12% of the patients who were confirmed for surgery failed to have the operation performed within one year following the confirmation.

There is no simple explanation as to why some people elect to undergo surgery that may not be needed, while others refuse surgery that is clearly indicated (e.g., by a second opinion). Most research and speculation on this issue has emphasized individual psychodynamics (e.g., anxiety, defense mechanisms, unconscious wishes, body image, and the like). In keeping with the general focus of this chapter on social rather than individual dynamics, I will limit the present discussion to an illustration of how subtle and pervasive cultural influences can be.

Zborowski (1969) studied four groups of male patients at a Veterans Administration Hospital in New York City. The groups consisted of Old (Yankee) Americans, and Americans of Irish, Italian, and Jewish descent. Most of the individuals in the latter groups were born in America of immigrant parents. The primary focus of the study was on the experience of pain, but attitudes toward medical procedures, including surgery, were explored as well.

Irish and Old Americans tended to downplay the significance of pain more than did their Italian and Jewish compatriots. Members of the former groups also were more likely to delay contacting a physician when in pain; on the other hand, once placed on a medical regimen, they expressed more confidence in the procedures. Zborowski describes the attitudes of the Old Americans in the following way:

> *A large number of Old American patients show a tendency to reduce every organic distur-*
> *bance to a mechanical cause, thus making it identifiable, controllable, and reparable . . . The*
> *mechanistic explanation of pain and illness makes it easier for the patient to accept various*
> *aspects of the medical treatment, including the most frightening one: the [surgical] operation.*
> *(pp. 84–85)*

The Irish Americans tended to view the body in more holistic than mechanistic terms, and they were more ambivalent than the Old Americans about the prospects of surgery. The orientation of the Jewish Americans was different still. These patients were more likely than the other groups to focus of the long-range implications of their symptoms and to participate actively in determining a course of treatment. The Italian Americans were similar in many respects to the Jewish Americans, but they were more oriented toward the present rather than the future, and they were especially reluctant to undergo surgery.

The results of Zborowski's study are based on rather small samples of subjects that are not necessarily representative of the ethnic groups involved. Nevertheless, some of the findings, such as those respecting differences in reaction to painful stimuli, have been replicated in a controlled laboratory setting (Sternback & Tursky, 1965). Be that as it may, the main significance of Zborowski's study for the present discussion lies not in the specific differences observed; its significance is, rather, that *any* differences were observed. The groups studied, it should be emphasized, are much more similar than different in general cultural background and orientation. That subtle and not easily definable subcultural differences still had discernable effects is the most remarkable finding of all.

Resources Available

Rates of surgery tend to vary in proportion to the number of surgeons in an area. As noted earlier, the rate of surgery is twice as high in the United States as in England and Wales; and there are also twice as many surgeons per capita in the

United States (Bunker, 1970). Surgery, as well as other forms of medical care, require hospital beds. Both in England (Klarman, 1969) and in the United States (Anderson & Andersen, 1972), hospitalization tends to vary in proportion to the supply of beds. In a careful statistical analysis of such variation in different counties of New York State, Harris (1975) has presented a strong case, that, beyond a certain point, an increase in hospital beds increases the demand for usage beyond that required for sound medical care.

I am not suggesting that the rate of surgery (or hospitalization) bears any simple or direct relationship to the number of surgeons (or hospital beds), although these are certainly important factors. In addition to sheer numbers, one must take into account the way medical practice is organized and financed. Bunker (1970) attributed the difference in rates of surgery between the United States and England/ Wales as much to these latter factors as to differences in manpower. Group practice with consultation among specialists is more characteristic of the British system. Also, in Britain most physicians are salaried, whereas in the United States reimbursement is usually on a fee-for-service basis. The importance of these factors is also evident within the United States. Persons with fee-for-service insurance plans, such as Blue Cross/Blue Shield, undergo surgery at twice the rate as do persons with pre-paid or capitation plans, such as the Kaiser Foundation or the Federal Employees Health Benefits Program (Perrott, 1966). (It is also common for pre-paid plans to involve group as opposed to individual practice, and to have a larger patient-to-physician ratio. Hence, there is a confounding between number of physicians, type of organization, and mode of reimbursement.)

Professional Interests of the Physician

In addition to the resource variables discussed above (i.e., the number of surgeons, financial remuneration, group vs. individual practice), perhaps the major factors influencing the rate of surgery are the skills and attitudes of the individual physicians. In many instances, indications for surgery are vague and imprecise, and a wide latitude of surgical practices may be consistent with good health care, at least as reflected in mortality statistics. (If one considers the costs of medical care, both financial and personal—e.g., during convalescence—then the latitude is narrowed considerably.)

Tonsillectomy provides a good illustration, although similar conclusions could be drawn from more serious forms of surgery (e.g., appendectomy, hysterectomy, cholecystectomy). Fifty years ago (1934), the American Child Health Association conducted a study (cited by Gittlesohn & Wennberg, 1977) on a sample of 1,000 New York school children 11 years of age. By that age, 60% of the children already had had their tonsils removed. The remaining 40% were examined by school physicians, who selected 45% for tonsillectomy. Those not selected were reexamined by still another group of physicians, and 46% of these were recommended for tonsillectomy.

Tonsillectomies are no longer performed so routinely, but in some respects the situation has not changed greatly. Gittelsohn and Wennberg (1977) compared the rates of tonsillectomy in 13 areas of the state of Vermont. For the entire state, the chances of having one's tonsils out by the age of 20 is approximately 1 in 5 (22%), but the range varies from 9% to 60% depending upon the area in which one lives. Only 5 physicians accounted for over one-quarter of the operations, averaging about 135 tonsillectomies per year apiece. More than 80% of the operations were performed by a mere two dozen physicians.

Most tonsillectomies are performed by the primary physician, that is, they are not referred to other specialists. When more complicated forms of surgery are considered, the rate of surgery often varies as a function of the training of the physician. During the 1950's, for example, two modes of therapy were common for thyrotoxicosis, thyroidectomy or treatment with radioiodine. The conditional probability of one or the other treatment was largely dependent on whether the physician was a surgeon or an internist (Gittelsohn & Wennberg, 1977). Another example of the same phenomenon is reported by Finkel, McCarthy, and Miller (1982). These investigators reviewed the second opinions for surgery in a podiatry program. Initial recommendations for surgery were confirmed 94.3% of the time when the consultant was a podiatrist, but only 49.5% of the time when the consultant was a orthopedist.

Like other specialists, surgeons tend to do what they have been trained to do, and what they are rewarded for doing, both financially and in terms of professional prestige.

Extensions to the Domain of Stress

Now let us consider how each of the four factors that have been shown to influence rates of surgery might also influence the identification and management of stress.

The Incidence of Stress

We have seen how rates of surgery may vary, in part, because of vagueness in the criteria for identifying the underlying condition (e.g., inflammation of the appendix); and we noted how the situation is further complicated by the need to distinguish between a disease state (the underlying pathology) and an illness (the way the pathology, real or presumed, is institutionalized within the society). The incidence of an illness is obviously much more free to vary as a function of the other factors that we have been considering (attitudes of the patients, available resources, professional interests of the health-care provider) than is the incidence of a disease.

Is stress more like an illness or a disease? This is a difficult question to answer, since there is no agreed-upon definition of stress. If we interpret stress along the lines advocated by Selye (1982)—that is, as a definite syndrome of physiological changes initiated by any actual or perceived trauma to the organism—then stress has many of the characteristics of a disease. However, not all researchers agree with Selye's conception of stress, even on the animal level (Mason, 1975). With respect to psychological stress on the human level, it is safe to say that, in practice if not in theory, the concept of stress is much more similar to the concept of illness than it is to the concept of disease. That is, psychological stress is constituted by the person's appraisal of the situation, mediated, in part, by cultural values and expectancies.

Because stress can be manifested in so many and varied ways, accurate assessment is extremely difficult. This problem is made even more difficult by the neoromantic emphasis on empathy as opposed to rational diagnosis (as discussed earlier in the section on Neoromanticism). Under these conditions, one can speak of the "true" incidence of stress in only the most general terms. The criteria for identifying stress and the means of assessing it are simply too vague to allow precise determinations.

Attitudes Toward Stress

But the problem is not simply one of diagnosis on the part of health-care professionals. Since psychological stress is constituted, in part, by a person's appraisal of the situation and by his or her coping resources, the incidence of stress is obviously sensitive to the beliefs and attitudes that people have toward the risks inherent in everyday life and toward their own capacity to deal with those risks. I have already discussed the general cultural climate (neoromanticism) that would facilitate a favorable attitude toward and even expectancy of stress among the general population. There is no need to repeat that discussion here. Of course, not everyone is a romantic. Few persons, however, can escape being influenced by the images of stress that bombard us daily on television and in the press. It is difficult to think of any situation that has not been depicted as a source of stress, at least for some people some of the time. Stress has become legitimized. For many people, it is now more acceptable to admit to being stressed than it is to deny it.

Resources Available

Of all the factors that might account for the recent increase in interest in stress, the availability of resources to deal with stress is perhaps the most important. Many groups have an interest in stress and its management, but I will limit the present discussion to Ph.D.-level psychologists.

In the United States, the growth of psychology as a discipline has been phenomenal. The American Psychological Association was founded in 1892. By 1900, it had 127 members; and by 1920, 393 members. In 1950, there were 7,273 members of the American Psychological Association; by 1982, this number had increased more than 650%, to 54,282. (In the same time period, the population of the country had increased only about 50%, to 232 million.) The rapid growth of the Association reflects the expansion of psychology as a profession in the United States. It does not, however, provide an adequate index of the absolute number of psychologists. It is estimated that only about half of the psychologists who are eligible actually belong to the American Psychological Association. For a history of professional psychology in the United States, see Napoli (1981). Each year, more than 3,000 new psychologists are being added to the discipline (Syverson, 1982).

What do all these psychologists do? The traditional place of employment for psychologists has been academia. However, the academic job market has become saturated. As late as 1970, 61% of the recipients of doctoral degrees in psychology still found employment in a university, medical school, or college. By 1980, that number was down to 33% (Syverson, 1982). Full-time employment in universities, where most basic research is conducted, is especially tight, accounting for only 18% of the jobs for new Ph.D.'s in 1980. (This last figure varies considerably according to subfield, from a high of about 40% for the experimental and developmental psychologists, to a low of about 9% for clinical psychologists—Stapp & Fulcher, 1982).

Based on a recent survey (VandenBos & Stapp, 1983), an estimated 34,000 to 36,000 psychologists are involved in the delivery of health services (most on a part-time basis). These psychologists see an estimated 2,400,000 clients or patients per year, each client averaging 14 visits. These are impressive numbers. They do not, however, address the question of need. In an address to the American Psychological Association (reported by Turkington, 1983), Blau has argued that the United Stated could absorb an additional 17,000 to 20,000 psychologists in independent practice alone. In evaluating these figures, the size of the total population of the United States (over 230 million people) must be kept in mind. Comparisons with other nations should be made on a per capita basis. Because of differences in the way psychology is defined, and psychologists are counted, precise cross-national comparisons are difficult. Nevertheless, it appears that Israel and the Scandinavian countries, and perhaps others as well (e.g., the Netherlands, Belgium, and Switzerland), may have more psychologists per capita than does the United States (Rosenzweg, 1984).

A more complete analysis of the resources available for stress management would also have to take into account professions other than psychology. The most obvious of these is psychiatry. In the United States, psychiatry is not one of the more popular medical specialties, and the number of psychiatrists has not increased as rapidly in recent years as the number of psychologists. Nevertheless, there are currently about 26,000 members of the American Psychiatric Association—a good number. Social workers represent a third discipline that is heavily involved in stress management. In fact, social workers provide more direct patient care than either psychiatrists or psychologists. The National Association of Social Workers was formed in 1955 with a membership of 22,027; by 1976, it had grown to 70,046 members (Turner, 1977). Perhaps the most significant recent development is the "discovery" of stress by lawyers. Stress is increasingly being cited as a mitigating circumstance in criminal cases; and in civil liability cases, stress is also being treated as a type of "personal injury" for which compensation may be sought.

There is little doubt that the expansion of psychological services in recent decades has been in response top a real need, and that some segments of the American population (e.g., the elderly, some minority groups, and people living in rural as opposed to urban areas) still remain undeserved. Nevertheless, it would be naive to assume that the increase in psychological services is *just* a response to need. One last set of statistics may serve to illustrate this point. Each year, over 100,000 students receive Bachelor's degrees in psychology from colleges and universities in the United States, and about 9,000 receive Master's degrees. Thus, the 3,000 or so new Ph.D.'s each year reflects a considerable narrowing of the pipeline at the top. There is a great deal of interest on the part of students to obtain advanced degrees and to pursue careers in psychology. Much of the current demand for psychologists represents pressures from within the discipline itself, and is not simply a response to societal needs.

To summarize briefly, over the past several decades there has been a steady rise in the number of psychologists, and at the same time a steady increase in the proportion of psychologists entering applied settings. Roughly one-half of all psychologists are involved in the delivery of health services, at least on a part-time basis, health services being defined "as assessment and intervention procedures used for understanding, predicting, or alleviating emotional, psychological, and behavioral disability and discomfort" (VandenBos & Stapp, 1983, p. 1331). Health services thus defined encompass much of what we mean by stress. It is important to note, however, that interest in stress is not limited to clinical or medical settings. Stress management in nonclinical settings has also burgeoned, occupying many social, educational, industrial and organizational psychologists, as well as clinical psychologists.

In discussing the relationship between available resources and rates of surgery, I noted that the number of surgeons is not the only variable of importance. Equally, if not more important, are the way services are organized and financed. To recapitulate briefly, the conditions most conducive to high rates of surgery are independent practice on a fee-for-service basis, with the same physician both diagnosing the disorder and providing treatment. It is difficult to compare the delivery of psychological services with surgery on these dimensions. Psychologists work in many diverse settings; and specialization (and hence consultation and referral) within psychology differs in important respects from specialization within medicine. Nevertheless, at least in the delivery of health services, the psychologist is increasingly coming to resemble the general practitioner in medicine. Most psychologists are "generalists" in that they do not limit their practice to clients with only one type of disorder. (Anxiety, depression, and problems in interpersonal relationships are the most common complaints that bring clients for treatment.) Also, the same psychologist typically does both diagnosis and treatment; in the absence of organic pathology, referral to other specialists is the exception rather than the rule. Finally, third-party payment (e.g., through an insurance company or government agency) on a fee-for-service basis is becoming increasingly common. In other words, trends in the way psychological services are being organized and financed may also be conducive to an increase in stress-as-artifact, if our experiences in medicine are any guide.

Professional Interests

In his Presidential Address to the American Psychological Association, George Miller (1969) expressed the belief that our responsibilities as psychologists "is less to assume the role of experts" and more "to give it [psychology] away to the people who really need it—and that includes everyone" (p. 107). Miller was somewhat pessimistic about the willingness of the public and established institutions to adopt alternative ways of thinking and behaving based on psychological research. In certain respects, his pessimism was misplaced. In areas where psychological findings are congruent with broader cultural trends, the public has proved to be an eager consumer of psychological findings. As if to recognize this possibility, Miller also warned against the evils of superficiality. Unfortunately, warnings are more easily offered than heeded.

What exactly is psychology to give away? Psychology is not renown as a storehouse of esoteric knowledge. Of course, factual knowledge is not the only thing that can be given away. Skills and services are also valuable. But psychologists are no more able to give their services away than are carpenters, engineers, plumbers, or architects; and with the production of psychologists far in excess of the demands of the traditional market place (i.e., teaching and research), young psychologists have been well advised to find or create new markets for their services. For a large number of psychologists (not just clinicians), stress management is one such market.

I am not suggesting that the professional interests of psychologists are simply pecuniary, or that pecuniary interests are necessarily bad where they do exist. By the time a student receives a Ph.D. in psychology, a great deal of time and effort may have been devoted to the acquisition of skills that can be applied to the management of stress. And for most young psychologists, there is a sincere desire to apply their skills to the alleviation of human suffering. But for whatever reasons, psychologists—like surgeons and specialists in any other field—will tend to do what they have been trained to do, even if the need for their services is somewhat artifactual.

STRESS AND DISEASE

Before concluding this analysis, one further issue needs to be addressed. It might be objected that the recent upsurge of interest in stress is due, not to the kinds of factors I have been discussing, but to the demonstrated link between stress and disease. As many of the more immediate causes of disease (particularly acute, infectious diseases) have been brought under control, health care has moved into a new and vastly more complex stage. Our concern must now be with more distal and subtle causes. Why, for example, does one person contract a disease and another not, when both are exposed to the same pathogen?

The above line of reasoning is reflected particularly in the movement toward "holistic medicine." As the name implies, holistic medicine attempts to treat the individual as a whole, restoring and maintaining a harmonious relationship between mind and body, and between the individual and the environment. Within this context, stress—which signifies disharmony—is given a prominent place as one of the causes of disease.

I will discuss in a moment some of the ways in which stress may be related to disease. First, however, it is worth noting that the popularity of holistic medicine is not simply the inevitable result of traditional medicine's past successes and present shortcomings. Holistic medicine is also very congenial to the kind of neoromantic outlook discussed earlier in this chapter. In speaking of 19th century Romanticism, McGann (1983) notes "a repeated concern to achieve various types of harmonies, systems, and reconciliations, and to establish these unified configurations in conceptual terms. . . . This obsession with restoring what was perceived—mythologically in every sense—as a lost sense of total order was a function of an age marked by extreme cultural upheavel throughout Europe" (p. 40).

In other words, the current interest in stress cannot be attributed in any simple way to advances in holistic medicine. Rather, the appeal of both holistic medicine and stress is firmly rooted in the same cultural soil. This is not to say that there are no direct and demonstrable links between stress and disease. But those links are extremely complex and not nearly as unambiguous as many popular accounts would lead one to believe. Let us examine the issue a little more closely.

Stress may be linked to disease in at least five ways.

1. Acute stress, as in sudden fright, may have short-term but sometimes fatal consequences, for example, by inducing cardiac arrhythmias.

2. Chronic stress may be accompanied by autonomic and endocrine changes that lead directly to tissue damage in vulnerable organs, as in the case of ulcers.

3. Some of the physiological changes accompanying stress (particularly, but not only, secretion of adrenocortical steroids) may have a secondary effect of inhibiting the immune system, thus increasing susceptibility to a wide range of diseases, from the common cold to cancer.

4. Stress may also lead to coping behaviors (e.g., drug abuse, improper diet, recklessness) that increase the risk of contracting a disease or sustaining injury.

5. Stress may influence the way a person responds to a discrete already contracted (e.g., symptom recognition, the utilization of health services), thus altering the course of the disease.

Because stress is such a global concept, and because stress reactions (physiological and behavioral) can interact with disease processes in so many different ways, it is easy to exaggerate or misinterpret the link between stress and disease. There are, in fact, both logical (based on evolutionary considerations) and empirical reasons for interpreting with caution the etiological significance of stress. In order to keep the present discussion simple, I will limit consideration to only one of the above ways that stress may be linked to disease, namely, through inhibition of the immune system.

As is well known, one of the most common manifestations of stress is increased adrenocortical activity, including secretion of cortisol (in humans) and related hormones. Cortisol has anti-inflammatory properties; this can be important in preventing over-reaction to infection or injury, such as might lead to rheumatoid arthritis when the inflammation is in the joints. However, cortisol also impairs functioning of the immune system, thus increasing susceptibility to disease. Other, nonadrenal hormones may also inhibit the immune system (see, for example, Keller, Weiss, Schleifer, Miller, & Stein, 1983). The nature of these other hormones is not understood, but presumably the argument outlined below would apply to them as well as to cortisol. The basic question that must be addressed is the following: To what extent does stress-induced suppression of the immune system increase susceptibility to disease?

Because of advances in modern medicine, we tend to forget what a deadly scourge disease has been throughout most of human history, and how maladaptive even a minor increase in susceptibility can be. At the outset of this chapter, I described how, until about 100 years ago, the average life expectancy of most human beings was between 20 and 30 years. This rather grim statistic is relevant to the present discussion in two respects. First, historically, the threat of death was constant—if not one's own death, then that of a friend or loved one. For most people, life was as Hobbes described it: "solitary, poor, nasty, brutish, and short"—in a word, stressful. Second, it is relevant to note that the most common cause of death was disease. Even during periods of famine and warfare, more people typically died of disease than of starvation or wounds received in combat. The Russo-Japanese War of 1904–1905 was probably the first major war in which more soldiers died as a direct consequence of their wounds than died as a result of disease (Cartwright & Biddiss, 1972).

At a time when many potentially fatal diseases were endemic—that is, for most of human history—it would have been highly maladaptive if the inevitable stresses of everyday life were to result in significant impairment of the immune system, thus increasing susceptibility to disease. Stated somewhat differently, if people became more prone to disease whenever they experienced stress, they would be placed in double jeopardy: first, from whatever danger the original stressor might involve; and, second, from an increased susceptibility to disease. From an evolutionary point of view, one would expect strong selective pressures *against* such a state of affairs. An exception to this conclusion would be if the physiological changes during stress were of sufficient survival value (e.g., enabling the individual to overcome the direct risks posed by the stressor) to offset any longer-term risks that resulted from impairment of the immune system. The present argument assumes that most stressors are not *in themselves* life-threatening or seriously debilitating; that is, the direct risk that they pose is less—not greater—than the risk posed by disease.

In the final analysis, of course, it is not logical or evolutionary arguments that will settle the issue, but rather, empirical data. What does experimental research tell us about the relationship between stress, immune functioning, and disease? There is obviously not space here to review the relevant findings in any detail. Fortunately, that is not necessary. For one thing, excellent reviews are readily available (e.g., Jemott & Locke, 1984; Monjan, 1981; Rogers, Dubey, & Reich, 1979; Riley, 1981). For another thing, even a detailed review would not allow many specific conclusions. There is, however, one broad generalization that can be drawn from this body of research, namely: For some individuals (or animals) some kinds of stressors may inhibit aspects of immune functioning, thus reducing resistance to some kinds of disease; but for other individuals, other stressors, and other diseases, no effects—or even the opposite effects (i.e., increased resistance to disease)—have been observed. The factors responsible for such conflicting findings have yet to be sorted out and placed in meaningful order.

Actually, the above generalization should come as no surprise considering the evolutionary argument outlined earlier, as well as the great variety of ways that stress has been operationalized for research purposes, the complexity of the physiological regulatory systems related to immune functioning, the different demands placed on the body by different diseases, and possible changes in the relationship between stress, immunity, and disease as a function of time or chronicity.

Let us return now to the issue raised at the outset of this section: Can the recent upsurge of interest in stress be accounted for by the presumed link between stress and disease, as opposed to the other kinds of factors I have been discussing (i.e., neoromanticism and professional interests)? To a certain extent the answer to this question is yes. But that obviously cannot be the entire answer.

CONCLUSIONS

Iatrogenic diseases are maladies that result from medical treatment. For example, the procedures used to treat one disease may result in tissue damage, thus causing the patient to suffer another disease. One way of interpreting the argument I have been making in this chapter is that a certain unknown proportion of the incidence of stress is the social-psychological equivalent of iatrogenic. Professional concerns, coupled with a general cultural climate of neoromanticism, may lead—and I would maintain, have led—not only to an increased interest in stress on the part of the public and scientific community alike, but also have artifactually increased the incidence of stress, and stress-like reactions.

And having raised the issue, what do I recommend? That is the most difficult question of all, and one for which I have no satisfactory, or satisfying, answer. Certainly, nothing I have said should be construed as an argument for less research on topics generally subsumed under the rubric of stress. That would be like arguing for less medical research simply because some procedures have untoward side-effects. Nothing could be more short-sighted.

Nor would I maintain that the concept of stress is without heuristic value simply because it is vague. Vagueness is often a sign of intellectual ferment and innovation; and a premature demand for precision can have a stifling influence, cutting off fruitful avenues of investigation. However, it is always legitimate to ask: When is a demand for precision premature?

In reviewing the history of the concept of stress in medicine, Hinkle (1973) maintained that the concept served a useful function during the 1930's and 1940's, when it helped to focus attention on the multiple causes of disease. Hinkle went on to argue, however, that the multitude of specific mechanisms that mediate the reactions of the organism to its physical and social environment can be better understood without invoking a special variable called *stress*. I know of no findings during the past decade that would contradict Hinkle's argument. The concept of stress has become so inclusive as to be virtually meaningless from a scientific standpoint; the result may be to impede rather than to facilitate understanding.

This being the case, it might seem reasonable to recommend that the concept of stress be greatly restricted in scope, or else eliminated entirely as a scientific construct. I am not so naive to believe, however, that such a recommendation would be adopted. The concept of stress is obviously too useful in too many different (albeit not necessarily scientific) ways for it to be lightly abandoned.

What, then, can be done? Mainly this: As we pursue our individual research interests, let us step back once in a while and take a broad look at our collective endeavors, not for the sake of integrating or summarizing the "state of the art," but in an attempt to see where we are coming from and where we are going. Science does not proceed in a vacuum. What we do is influenced by the attitudes and interests of society at large; and, in turn, the results of our research filters back into society, often with effects that are not foreseen. Simply being aware of a problem—attempting to foresee the unforeseen—is sometimes the most important step one can take toward a solution.

REFERENCES

Acsadi, Gy., & Nemeskeri, J. (1970). *History of human life span and mortality* (K. Balas, Trans.). Budapest: Akademiai Kiado.

Anderson, O. W., & Andersen, R. M. (1972). Patterns of use of health services. In E. Freeman (Ed.), *Handbook of medical sociology* (pp. 386–406). Englewood Cliffs, NJ: Prentice Hall.

Averill, J. R. (1979). The functions of brief. In C. Izard (Ed.), *Emotions in personality and psychopathology.* New York: Plenum.

Averill, J. R. (1980a). A constructivist view of emotion. In R. Plutchik & H. Kellerman (Eds.), *Theories of emotion*. New York: Academic Press.

Averill, J. R. (1980b). On the paucity of positive emotions. In K. R. Blankstein, P. Pliner, & J. Polivy (Eds.), *Assessment and modification of emotional behavior*. New York: Plenum Press.

Averill, J. R. (1982). *Anger and aggression: An essay on emotion*. New York: Springer-Verlag.

Bauman, Z. (1978). *Hermeneutics and social science*. New York: Columbia University Press.

Brunke, Ch., Sange, P., & Treziak, M. (1978). *Belasctringsfaktoren eines Grosstadtlebins*. Unpublished thesis, Institut für Psychologie, Free University of Berlin, FRG.

Bunker, J. P. (1970). Surgical manpower: A comparison of operations and surgeons in the United States and in England and Wales. *New England Journal of Medicine, 282*, 135–144.

Camus, A. (1955). *The myth of Sisyphus* (J. O'Brien, Trans.). New York: Knopf.

Cartwright, F. F., & Briddiss, M. D. (1972). *Disease and history*. New York: Thomas Y. Crowell.

Douglas, M., & Wildavsky, A. (1982). *Risk and culture*. Berkeley: University of California Press.

Drucker, P. F. (1939). *The end of economic man*. New York: John Wiley.

Dublin, L. I., Lotka, A. J., & Spiegelman, M. (1949). *Length of life: A study of the life table* (rev. ed.). New York: Ronald Press.

Fabrega, H. (1979). The ethnography of illness. *Social Science and Medicine, 13A*, 565–576.

Finkel, M. L., McCarthy, E. G., & Miller, D. (1982). Podiatric surgery: The need for a second opinion. *Medical Care, 20*, 862–870.

Finkel, M. L., McCarthy, E. G., & Ruchlin, H. S. (1982). The current status of surgical second opinion programs. *Surgical Clinics of North America, 62*, 705–719.

Furst, L. R. (1976). *Romanticism* (2nd ed.). London: Methuen.

Gittelsohn, A. M., & Wennberg, J. E. (1977). On the incidence of tonsillectomy and other common surgical procedures. In J. P. Bunker, B. A. Barnes, & F. Mosteller (Eds.), *Costs, risks, and benefits of surgery* (pp. 91–106). New York: Oxford University Press.

Hamburg, D. A. (1982). Forward: An outlook on stress research and health. In G. R. Elliott & C. Eisdorfer (Eds.), *Stress and human health*. New York: Springer.

Harris, D. M. (1975). An elaboration of the relationship between general hospital bed supply and general hospital utilization. *Journal of Health and Social Behavior, 16*, 163–172.

Hinkle, L. E. (1973). The concept of "stress" in the biological and social sciences. *Sciences, Medicine and Man, 1*, 31–48.

Jemmott, III, J. N., & Locke, S. E. (1984). Psychosocial factors, immunologic mediation, and human susceptibility to infectious disease: How much do we know? *Psychological Bulletin, 95*, 78–108.

Keller, S. E., Weiss, J. M., Schleifer, S. J., Miller, N. E., & Stein, M. (1983). Stress-induced suppression of immunity in adrenalectomized rats. *Science, 221*, 1301–1304.

Klarman, H. E. (1969). Approaches to moderating the increase in medical care costs. *Medical Care, 7*, 175–190.

Maslow, A. H. (1970). *Motivation and personality* (2nd ed.). New York: Harper & Row.

Mason, J. W. (1975). A historical view of the stress field. Parts 1 and 2. *Journal of Human Stress, 1*, 6–12, 22–36.

May, R. (1981). *Freedom and destiny*. New York: Norton.

McGann, J. J. (1983). *The romantic ideology*. Chicago: University of Chicago Press.

Miller, G. (1969). Psychology as a means of promoting human welfare. *American Psychologist, 24*, 1063–1075.

Monjan, A. A. (1981). Stress and immunologic competence: Studies in animals. In R. Ader (Ed.), *Psychoneuroimmunology*. New York: Academic Press.

Napoli, D. S. (1981). *Architects of adjustment: The history of the psychological profession in the United States*. Port Washington, NY: Kennikat Press.

Perrott, G. S. (1966). Utilization of hospital services. *American Journal of Public Health, 56*, 57–64.

Petersen, W. (1961). *Population*. New York: Macmillan.

Riley, V. (1981). Psychoneuroendocrine influences on immunocompetence and neoplasia. *Science, 212*, 1100–1109.

Rogers, M. P., Dubey, D., & Reich, P. (1979). The influence of the psyche and the brain on immunity and disease susceptibility: A critical review. *Psychosomatic Medicine, 41*, 147–164.

Rosenzweig, M. R. (1984). U.S. psychology and world psychology. *American Psychologist, 39*, 877–884.

Roszak, T. (1974). The monster and the titan: Science, knowledge, and diagnosis. *Daedalus, 103*, 17–32.

Schönpflug, W. (1983). Coping efficiency and situational demands. In G. R. J. Hockey (Ed.)., *Stress and fatigue in human performance*. New York: Wiley.

Selye, H. (1982). *The stress of life* (rev. ed.). New York: McGraw-Hill.

Sennett, R. (1980). *Authority.* New York: Knopf.

Sontag, S. (1978). *Illness as metaphor.* New York: Vintage Books.

Stapp, J., & Fulcher, R. (1982). The employment of 1979 and 1980 doctorate recipients in psychology. *American Psychologist, 37,* 1159–1185.

Sternbach, R. A., & Tursky, B. (1965). Ethnic differences among housewives in psychophysical and skin potential responses to electric shock. *Psychophysiology, 1,* 241–246.

Strupp, H. H. (1976). Clinical psychology, irrationalism, and the erosion of excellence. *American Psychologist, 31,* 561–571.

Syverson, P. D. (1982). Two decades of doctorates in psychology: A comparison with national trends. *American Psychologist, 37,* 1203–1212.

Titchener, J. L., & Levine, M. (1960). *Surgery as a human experience.* New York: Oxford University Press.

Turkington, C. (1983, October). Independent practice: Wooden desks. *APA Monitor,* p. 21.

Turner, J. B. (Ed.). (1977). *Encyclopedia of social work,* Vol. 2. (17th ed.). Washington, DC: National Association of Social Workers.

Tyszkowa, M. (1983, September). *A situational-cognitive conception of psychological hardiness.* Paper presented at the International Conference on Stress and Anxiety, Warsaw.

VandenBos, G. R., & Stapp, J. (1983). Service providers in psychology: Results of 1982 APA human resources survey. *American Psychologist, 38,* 1330–1352.

Wrigley, E. A. (1969). *Population and history.* New York: McGraw-Hill.

Yalow, R. S. (1982, December). Psychology tomorrow: The Nobel view. *Psychology Today,* p. 26.

Zborowski, M. (1969). *People in pain.* San Francisco: Jossey-Bass.

3

Stress from the Reversal Theory Perspective

Michael J. Apter
University College, Cardiff, Wales

Sven Svebak
University of Bergen, Bergen, Norway

The concept of stress is one of the most confused in the whole of psychology. Many different definitions have been given (e.g. see Hinkle, 1973), many of them only marginally related or even inconsistent with each other. Part of the reason for this may be that stress is too broad a concept, and one which contains within it a number of varieties which may even be opposite to each other in some way. (In this respect, the situation may be not unlike that associated with the concept of depression, as discussed in Apter, 1982). The aim of the present paper is to try to unravel these different types of stress and set them in a meaningful framework: the framework of reversal theory.

Holroyd and Lazarus (1982) pointed out that contemporary research on psychological stress emerged from studies of life-threatening events such as military combat (Grinker & Spiegel, 1945), imprisonment in the concentration camp (Bettelheim, 1943), bereavement (Lindemann, 1944), and traumatic injury (Hamburg, Hamburg & deGoza, 1953). The prevailing assumption was made that exposure to extreme situations provokes such extreme responses as psychotic behavior, severe and chronic anxiety and bodily disease like bleeding ulcers (Paster, 1948; Swank, 1949). The formulation of general principles was made to account for the association of such extreme responses to extreme situations, and these principles have been subsumed under the concept of stress. It is a prevailing feature of the research on psychological stress, however, that a strong relation between stressful life events (Holmes & Masuda, 1974; Gunderson & Rahe, 1974) and the stress experience has failed to be found (see, in particular, Rabkin & Struening, 1976). Dohrenwend and Dohrenwend (1979) argued that methodological refinement would help towards the emergence of the predicted relationship between stressful life events and the stress experience. We do not dispute the importance of methodological refinement within this field. On the other hand, a method is limited by the power of the conceptions which guide the investigator. The approach taken in the present article is in harmony with that of Brenner, Roskies and Lazarus (1980) who argued that stress cannot be understood merely in terms of the stressful event. Most individuals suffer if they are placed in extreme circumstances, such as a concentration camp (Eitinger & Strom, 1973), but a few individuals emerge apparently safe and sound even from such extreme situations (Antonovsky, Maoz, Dowty, & Wijesenbeck, 1971). One source of the robust nature of some individuals would appear to be their biological makeup which seems to enhance their powers of resistance in stressful situations. The nature of the *experience* of stressful situations may also act as a moderator of responses, and the focus of the present analysis is upon the structure and dynamics of the experience of stressful situations.

In accordance with the whole approach of reversal theory (Apter, 1982), the way in which stress will be analyzed is essentially phenomenological, although the different types of stress and degrees of stress will be expected to have physiological and behavioral concomitants. At the same time, and also in consonance with reversal theory, the dynamics of stress situations will be conceived of cybernetically.

TENSION–STRESS AND EFFORT–STRESS

At the outset, we believe that it is necessary to distinguish between two fundamentally different types of stress which we refer to as "tension-stress" and "effort-stress." They can be defined as follows: (1) Tension-stress is that which is felt when there is a discrepancy between the preferred and actual level of some salient motivational variable, and (2) Effort-stress is that which is felt when one expends effort to reduce tension-stress. It should be noted that the definitions are phenomenological, and are in terms of the individual's mental state rather than in terms of environmental or other conditions. Note also that the second type of stress is a possible consequence of the first. An analogy would be to the way in which the body may be disturbed first by an infection, and then second by the body's own defense against the infection.

The distinction can be put more precisely in cybernetic terms: (1) Tension-stress is the recognition of a discrepancy from a preferred level of some variable (i.e. the detection of an "error"); and (2) Effort-stress is the concomitant of negative feedback action which is taken to overcome this discrepancy (i.e. reduce the "error"). This action, of course, may or may not be successful.

So tension-stress is the experience of a disturbance, and effort-stress is the experience of an attempt to adapt to the disturbance. In counseling terms, tension-stress may be the experience of a crisis situation, and effort-stress the attempt to cope with this situation. Of course, *coping* is ambiguous as a term in the counseling literature, sometimes implying that the coping is successful, sometimes that an attempt is being made whether successful or not (see e.g. Murgatroyd, 1981); clearly we are using the word in the second sense here.

The term *tension* has been used in a number of different ways in the medical, psychiatric, and psychological literature. One example is the use of the term as a synonym for anxiety within the currently active research on alcohol use and abuse (see e.g. Cappell, 1975). This use of the term seems to imply that drinking can

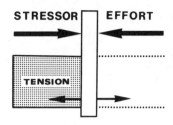

Figure 1 The relationship between tension-stress and effort-stress: the relationship between the power of the stressor and the effort defines the position of the bar and hence the intensity of tension-stress.

only occur with the aim of overcoming unpleasant high arousal and never as a response to unpleasant low states of arousal. Our use of the term comes closer to that of Wilson (1982) who elaborated on the tension-reduction theory of alcohol use and adopted the term *tension* to describe negative emotional states like feelings not only of anxiety, but also of depression and boredom. It should be emphasized, however, that we are using the term in a special way here, following its use in reversal theory (Apter, 1982), where it is defined as a feeling which accompanies, and is proportional to, the degree of mismatch at a given time between the actual and preferred level of a salient variable. However, this reversal theory use is consistent with its use in everyday speech where it depicts a feeling of unease, a sense that "things are not what they should be" and that "one needs to do something."

The term *effort* can also be used in different ways (see e.g. Svebak, 1982a). The way in which we are using it here does not mean being highly energized, since one can produce high effort in our sense even with little energy. Indeed, one needs more effort in such a case, to make up for the lack of energy. What we intend is the kind of experience which is described in every day language as "pushing oneself," as "exerting willpower," "not giving way," or as "working at it." It is about striving and determination.

The relationship between tension-stress and effort-stress can be depicted in the way shown in Fig. 1. This figure shows that some stress-situation or stressor causes a discrepancy which is experienced as some degree of tension, and that this tension is opposed by effort, which is felt as effort-stress. In this figure the intensity of the experienced tension is represented by the area of the rectangle to the left of the vertical bar, and one is to imagine that this vertical bar moves to the left or the right depending on whether, and to what extent, the stressor is more powerful than the effort, or vice versa. (In this figure and in Figs. 3 and 4 the strength of stressor and of effort is represented by the size of the arrows which depict them).

The dynamics of the situation over time can be represented graphically as shown in Fig. 2, where effort on the first occasion prevents tension being felt and on the second occasion counteracts tension which is already being experienced.

It should be clear that both tension and effort, as defined here, differ from arousal (i.e. felt arousal). Effort may be a response to some level of arousal, but is not the arousal itself. Effort may not even be a function of arousal: Thus much anxiety may call forth little effort in some people and much in others (or in the same people at different times). Moreover, tension may be directly proportional to the felt level of arousal, or inversely proportional to it, depending on the ongoing meta-motivational state (i.e. the telic or paratelic state) outlined in reversal theory as will be explained below. For these reasons, then, the reversal theory concept of tension cannot be equated with arousal as such.

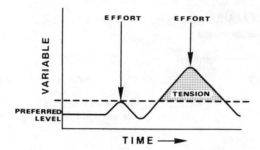

Figure 2 The dynamics of effort-stress and tension-
stress over time.

Tension and effort, as defined here, also differ from the concept of *activation*. Whether activation is defined physiologically (Pribram & McGuiness, 1975), or phenomenologically (Bohlin & Kjellberg, 1975) in terms of how energetic one feels, this is still different from effort, just as arousal is. Certainly, effort requires activation; but to some extent effort and activation are inverse, since the less the activation the greater the effort required to achieve a given goal. The same applies, inversely, to fatigue. It should be clear that tension, in the way defined, is also not the same as activation.

Clearly, overt activity cannot be equated with effort in any simple way, since some forms of high overt activity require little effort (e.g. children running around aimlessly in a playground), while other forms of low overt activity may require much effort (e.g. playing chess). Effort may be experienced in a variety of different ways apart from energetic overt behavior. Thus it may require much effort to concentrate or to reappraise a situation. Similarly, tension cannot be equated with activity; high tension may relate to little activity and vice versa.

EFFORT, STRESS, AND PERFORMANCE

A more elaborate presentation of the concept of effort as used here provides the opportunity to distinguish between different types of effort. Thus, effort may be required for either or both of two purposes: action and concentration. Action, for example, solving a problem, working hard physically, or running away, may involve either physical effort, or psychological effort in the sense of "hard thinking," or both. Effort may also be required for concentration on the task in hand. (In an earlier paper by Apter and Murgatroyd, 1980, concentration and effort were equated in this respect). For the purpose of concentration, effort can work in two opposite ways at different times. In the first case, effort is required to keep attention *on* some situation (e.g. to solve a problem), despite such factors as its intrinsic unpleasantness or certain distractions. In the second case, effort is needed to keep attention *away* from an unpleasant situation (e.g. one which the individual can do little about), despite its unpleasant demands on attention or the individual's tendency to persevere; this may be achieved through the suitable control of attention or through repression.

Type of effort notwithstanding, the amount of effort required for successful performance would appear to be a function of many different factors which can be subsumed into four categories:

1. *Task factors,* like intellectual difficulty and interest, associations with pleasant or unpleasant ideas or sensations, amount of energy required, and duration of time required;
2. *Physiological factors,* like activation (the less the energy, the more the effort required to maintain a given level of performance), fatigue and sleepiness;
3. *Psychological factors,* such as the felt importance and significance of a goal, the existence of conflicting goals, self-confidence in attaining the goal, the amount of energy felt to be available, and distractibility; and
4. *Contextual factors,* including distractions, frustrating forces (e.g. faulty equipment), the appropriateness of the social and environmental setting, and comfort.

These items bring out some of the complexities involved when effort-stress operates to reduce tension-stress. Clearly, there is much interrelation between the various factors. For example, fatigue will relate to many of these factors (e.g. activation, self-confidence); frustrating forces may be seen as part of the task difficulty, as may distractions; time needed may be a function of task difficulty; distractibility may relate to existence of conflicting goals or intellectual interest; self-confidence may be a function of such factors as fatigue, sleepiness, and task difficulty. It is characteristic of the present perspective on stress, however, that effortful striving of any kind represents one type of stress (effort-stress) whatever the actual circumstances and the quality of the performance.

RELATION TO TELIC AND PARATELIC STATES

As defined, both tension-stress and effort-stress can be experienced in both the telic and paratelic meta-motivational states. These states have been extensively described by Apter (1982). For the present purpose it is essential to note that arousal avoidance is a characteristic feature of the telic state. In this state the experience of low arousal is pleasant relaxation whereas high arousal is experienced as anxiety, which is intrinsically unpleasant. The inverse relation of hedonic tone and felt level of arousal is a characteristic feature of the paratelic state, since high arousal is sought after in this state, and the feeling of high arousal is experienced as pleasant excitement. In contrast, low arousal is felt as unpleasant boredom in the paratelic state; the lower the arousal the more intense the feeling of boredom. Since each state has its own optimal level, it will be appreciated that reversal theory breaks with optimal arousal theory in which there is only one optimal, that is, preferred, level of arousal.

Additional defining features of the two states involve the distinction between serious-mindedness and playfulness, and between planning orientation and impulsivity, as characteristics of the telic and paratelic states respectively (see Apter, 1982). It is argued in reversal theory that individuals reverse backwards and forwards between the two states with some frequency (due to satiation, contingent

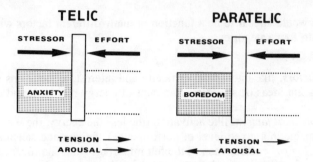

Figure 3 The telic and paratelic state-specific relations between
tension-stress and effort-stress: telic anxiety-tension is
high with high felt arousal whereas paratelic boredom-
tension is high with low felt arousal.

effects and frustration). It is also argued in this theory that some individuals have
an innate tendency to be dominated most of the time by one or other of the two
states whereas others are more likely to spend more nearly equal periods of time in
each. (A psychometric measure of degree of dominance in one direction or the
other is the Telic Dominance Scale by Murgatroyd et al., 1978).

Tension-Stress

Figure 1 represents tension-stress in both the telic and paratelic states, except
that in one case decreasing tension represents increasing arousal up to a high
preferred arousal level (the paratelic state) and in the other case down to a low
preferred arousal level (the telic state). So if the horizontal dimension of this
diagram (Fig. 1) represents arousal, then this is inverted from one state to the
other. Tension-stress is therefore always experienced as unpleasant in both states,
but for opposite reasons (i.e. under opposite circumstances in relation to arousal).
These state-specific relations between tension and felt arousal have been illustrated
in Fig. 3.

Effort-Stress

Figure 1 also represents effort-stress in both states. Here the situation is different from that in relation to tension stress: although effort-stress in the telic state is
always felt as unpleasant to some degree or another, effort-stress in the paratelic
state will be felt as more or less pleasant (whereas, as we have seen, tension-stress
is experienced as unpleasant in both types of state). There is therefore an asymme-
try in the relation between stress and hedonic tone in the effort and tension cases.

Telic effort-stress perhaps comes closest to what most people mean by the word
stress in everyday life: It is what is felt when one expends effort in performing an
activity which one does not wish to perform for its own sake. In other words, it is
felt in those situations in which one is experiencing effort in pursuit of some goal
over and beyond the activity itself, that is, when one is serious-minded.

This is to be distinguished from paratelic effort-stress, which would be effort expended in relation to a task which is intrinsically enjoyable. In this case the effort is felt not as stressful but as a kind of joyful striving, which is undertaken with keenness and enthusiasm. The situation in which this striving occurs is seen to involve challenge rather than threat or duty. Psychologically, therefore, the experience is not really stressful at all, and the word *stress* in this case should perhaps be put in inverted commas to remind us of this.

Telic effort-stress is also to be distinguished from telic low effort, which would be the experience of easy coping, that is, the pursuit of an essential goal which does not require much effort to be attained. (Note that easiness here is also phenomenological and cannot necessarily be defined operationally as, e.g. task difficulty, or in relation to internal factors like activation at the time in question.)

Paratelic low effort is probably not unpleasant, but simply not particularly pleasant. In this respect we would remember that in the paratelic state there are a number of sources of pleasure including intensity of sensation and high felt arousal, so it is possible to enjoy experience in the paratelic state even without striving in an effortful way (Apter, 1982).

THE RELATION OF TENSION–STRESS TO EFFORT–STRESS

The general relationship between tension-stress and effort-stress has already been shown in Figs. 1 and 2. There are three possible outcomes of the relationship between tension-stress and effort-stress in both the telic and paratelic states, and these are represented in Fig. 4. Let us look at these first of all in relation to the telic state.

Telic State

In the telic state, high arousal is felt as anxiety (see Fig. 3). Effort may be part of the response to such anxiety and an attempt to overcome it. (It should be quite clear that anxiety and effort are not the same thing.)

The first possible outcome of the relationship between tension-stress and effort-stress experienced in the telic state is illustrated in level 1 of Fig. 4. Here the individual is able, through effort, to reduce the anxiety, for example by removing the threat, or by achieving some goal which is felt to be essential. The extreme form of the outcome here is high effort and no anxiety, that is, high effort-stress and no tension-stress.

The second possible outcome in the telic state (level 2 of Fig. 4) is that in which the individual gives up trying to overcome the anxiety (e.g. through achieving a goal) and instead experiences intense anxiety in perhaps an acute form such as a panic attack. The extreme form of the outcome here is no effort and high anxiety, that is, no effort-stress and high tension-stress.

A third possible outcome in the telic state (level 3 of Fig. 4) is the case in which the individual may experience the worst of all possible worlds, by attempting to overcome the anxiety by means of high effort, but being unable to do so. The

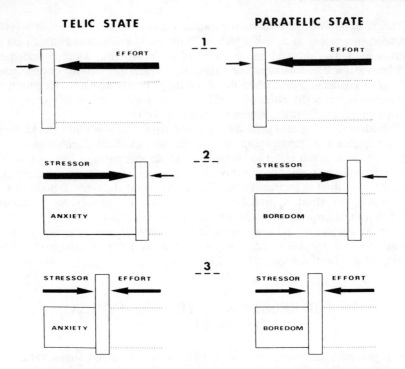

Figure 4 The three outcomes of the tension-stress and effort-stress relationship in telic
and paratelic states; the relative power of the stressor and the effort-stress is
indicated by the size of the arrows, and the intensity of the tension-stress by
the size of the hatched area to the left of the bar.

extreme form of the outcome in this case is high effort and high anxiety, that is,
high effort-stress and high tension-stress.

Effort-stress can therefore occur with and without tension-stress; it can produce
success or failure in overcoming tension. Conversely, tension-stress can occur with
and without effort-stress since the individual may continue to strive or give up. All
this emphasizes again that anxiety and stress (in the effort sense) are not the same.
In particular, it should be emphasized again that people who are subject to stressors do not necessarily experience anxiety, since they may overcome their various
problems, as they arise, through effort. And people who are anxious are not
necessarily stressed in the effort sense.

Paratelic State

As for the telic state, there are three possible types of outcome from the interaction between a stressor (which in the paratelic case is more likely to be a situation
which fails to give rise to high felt arousal rather than a specific stressor) and
effort (see Fig. 4). The only difference now is that high tension is felt in this case
as boredom rather than anxiety. (Note how the direction of the arousal dimension
is the inverse of that which obtains in the telic state, as was illustrated in Fig. 3.)

The amount of effort which an individual feels he or she is typically willing to expend in the pursuit of goals must presumably be regarded as a personality characteristic in itself. It is possible that this propensity to be effortful is related to the type A/B distinction. It is therefore of interest that this distinction has been found to be orthogonal to Telic Dominance (Svebak and Apter, 1984), which is what might be expected from the present analysis.

STRESS AND SYMPTOMATOLOGY

The outcomes labeled 1 and 2 in Fig. 4 may be expected in an extreme form to produce different types of pathology, and to do so differently in the telic and paratelic states. The outcome labeled 3 in Fig. 4 may be expected to involve a mixture of the pathologies associated with the outcomes labeled 1 and 2. Let us look tentatively at what these types of pathology might be expected to be.

High Effort-Stress and No Tension-Stress

In the telic state, if effort-stress is prolonged, then it is likely to give rise to the classic stress symptoms of chronic muscle tension problems (e.g. backache, tension migraine; see e.g. Malmo, 1975; Svebak, 1982b, 1983a), and risk of coronary heart disease (e.g. Svebak, 1983b). Behaviorally, high telic effort-stress may take the form of obsessional ritual (see Fontana, 1981), and a prolonged state of high effort-stress with no tension-stress may result in neurasthenia.

In the paratelic state, the effort-stress is likely in extreme cases to be expressed through excitement-seeking behavior which produces interpersonal problems, such as crime and hooliganism, and through high risk behavior, which may be detrimental (e.g. physically or financially) to the individual himself or others, including especially his or her family.

No Effort-Stress and High Tension-Stress

Tension-stress in the *telic* state appears to give rise to the classic neurotic symptoms of chronic anxiety, phobias, and the like. In the case of chronic tension-stress, various psychosomatic symptoms may result (e.g. tics and bedwetting in children, peptic ulcers and ulcerative colitis in adults, etc.). In this way, chronic tension-stress with little effort-stress may incorporate the "implicit set" factor in the theory of psychosomatic disease proposed by Sternback (1966) this being a factor which incorporates a variety of prolonged unpleasant emotional states. When tension-stress is high due to a transitory cessation of effort-stress, this may cause acute tense anxiety which triggers hyperventilation with the secondary psychosomatic effects of alkalosis described by Lum (1981).

Tension-stress in the *paratelic* state may take the form of a general listlessness; or low effort strategies may be used in the attempt to overcome the boredom, such as drug-taking where bodily effects may act to cause increased levels of felt arousal (and therefore reduced tension in this state).

It can be seen that *telic effort-stress* comes closest to what is known as *stress* in the medical and physiological literature. On the other hand, *telic tension-stress* comes closest to the way in which the term *stress* is used in certain parts of the counseling and psychotherapy literature. The present analysis shows not only how these two stress concepts are related, but also shows that there are other types of experience and behavior which can also be labeled as forms of stress. The reversal theory perspective on tension-stress and effort-stress, as outlined here, may help to avoid some of the confusion which occurs when the term *stress* is applied in a blanket manner to explain symptomatology.

IMPLICATIONS FOR THERAPY

It is the purpose of this section to point out briefly the main implications of the stress concept developed here in relation to therapeutic intervention or to stress-management training. First of all, certain interventions may be counterproductive, for example, those which aim to increase the effort which the individual expends on his or her problems, when these problems are of the effort-stress type. Conversely, a cultivated low arousal program would be counterproductive in the case of boredom (paratelic tension-stress).

A second implication of the reversal theory perspective upon stress management relates to the case where it is possible to solve the presenting problems, but at the expense of causing another problem. The present analysis shows how such "symptom substitution" may be brought about. For example, one may lower an individual's effort, in order to reduce the risk of heart attack, but at the expense of increased feelings of anxiety and perhaps other psychosomatic symptoms due to tension-stress (e.g. ulcers; see above). Such trade-offs may, of course, be considered to be worthwhile. Thus, anxiety and related neurotic symptoms may be considered preferable to the chance of a heart attack or to the incapacitating effects of chronic low back pain.

Instead of bringing about a change from high effort-stress to high tension-stress or vice versa (i.e. between the outcomes labeled 1 and 2 in Fig. 4), it may be preferable (e.g. to avoid symptom substitution) to try and induce switches between the telic and paratelic states instead. In this way, high effort, or high felt arousals, both of which are unpleasant in the telic state and may lead to symptoms, can be enjoyed if the paratelic state is induced, and be symptom free (unless they lead to dangerous behavior). Alternatively, the problem of dangerous and anti-social behavior in the paratelic state may possibly be solved by inducing the telic state. (For a related discussion of reversal theory and the treatment of stress-related disorders through the induction of reversals, see Svebak and Stoyva, 1980).

RELATIONS TO CURRENT
PERSPECTIVES ON STRESS

It is widely accepted today that stress is involved in the etiology of physical as well as psychological disorders (e.g. Krantz, Glass, Contrada, & Miller, 1981). Typically, the disorders said to be due to stress include anxiety, schizophrenia, depression, peptic ulcers, hypertension, coronary heart disease, immune system suppression, organ damage and general anhedonia (see, e.g. Amkraut & Solomon, 1977; Hamilton, 1979; Ross & Glomset, 1976; Selye, 1956, 1982; Weiner, 1977; Wise, 1982).

Despite the fact that stress is a popular diagnosis and a term frequently used as an explanatory concept in relation to illness, many issues pertaining to its causes, effects and measurements still remain unsolved. Recently, psychologists such as Baum, Singer and Baum (1981) have attempted to integrate biological and behavioral approaches to provide a framework for multilevel assessment of stress. The development of self-report measures (e.g. Holmes & Masuda, 1974; Rahe, 1969; Johnson & Sarason, 1979; Baum, Gatchel, Fleming & Lake, 1981; Lazarus & Lannier, 1978), performance measures (e.g. Evans, 1978; Zajonc, 1965; Frankenhaeuser & Jarpe, 1963; Cohen, 1980), psychophysiological measures (e.g. Cohen, Evans, Krantz, & Stokols, 1980; Lazarus, Speisman, Mordkoff, & Davidson, 1962; Malmo & Shagass, 1949; see also Svebak, Storfjell, & Dalen, 1982), and biochemical measures (e.g. Selye, 1956; Mason, 1975; Frankenhaeuser, 1975) are necessary contributions towards advances within the study of stress. However, unlike such writers as Baum, Grunberg and Singer (1982), it is implicit in our own argument that the simultaneous assessment of psychological, behavioral, physiological and endocrine factors is not sufficient; rather, we believe that advancement in the conceptualization of stress is also essential at this stage.

The reversal theory perspective on stress, presented earlier, offers a coherent way of understanding the paradoxical relation between arousal and hedonic tone (e.g. Hebb, 1955; see also Svebak, 1982b). Furthermore, the distinction between tension-stress and effort-stress may help to clarify the distinctive features of so-called bad stress and good stress (e.g. Frankenhaeuser, 1980; Ursin & Murison, 1983) and the relation between successful coping and stress (e.g. Levine, 1983; see also Carlson, 1982). It also explains why stress in some cases produces psychosomatic symptoms and in other cases symptoms of mental illness, as found for example by Cooper and Melhuish (1980) who identified two such patterns of response to stress in their study of senior British executives. Similarly, it gives one kind of explanation for the inverse relationship which has been found between lung cancer and neuroticism (see reviews by Eysenck, 1980, and in this volume).

In general, reversal theory would seem to have the potential of integrating a number of recent approaches to stress. Thus the distinction made by Holroyd and Lazarus (1982) between (1) appraisal of what is at stake and (2) appraisal of coping appears to be related to our distinction between tension-stress and effort-stress. This distinction is also in concert with the observation reported by Folkman and Lazarus (1980), that stressful encounters in real life are met by a dynamic constellation of both emotion-focused and problem-focused coping activities. Further, it appears that Janis (1982a, 1982b) has offered an excellent analysis of the role of decision-making in telic effort-stress while Mandler (1972, 1982) could be said to have elaborated on the relation between physiological arousal, concentration and planned performance in telic effort-stress.

In conclusion we think that the reversal theory perspective offered here (1) provides a systematic conceptual framework within which different approaches to stress can be compared and related to each other; (2) helps in its own terms to clarify the relation of stress to psychopathology, psychosomatic disorders and the so called stress symptoms; and (3) has important practical implications for stress management.

DISCUSSION

In this chapter the phenomenological/cybernetic approach of reversal theory was applied to the conceptualization of stress in order to distinguish between different types of stress within an integrative theoretical framework.

First, a distinction was made between tension-stress and effort-stress. Tension-stress was defined as the experience of a discrepancy between the preferred and actual level of some salient motivational variable and effort-stress as the experience of effort expended to reduce tension-stress. Differences were pointed out between the concepts of tension and effort on the one hand and arousal, activation, and activity on the other.

The concept of tension-stress was then applied to the distinction between telic and paratelic states as outlined in reversal theory: In the paratelic (arousal-seeking) state tension-stress is experienced as boredom whereas in the telic (arousal-avoiding) state, tension-stress is experienced as anxiety. Tension-stress is therefore experienced as unpleasant in both states, but for opposite reasons. In contrast, effort-stress is experienced as pleasant in the paratelic state and unpleasant in the telic state. Joyful striving is inherent in the former while feelings of threat and duty characterize the latter.

The constellations of (1) high effort-stress and no tension-stress, (2) no effort-stress and high tension-stress, and (3) high effort-stress and high tension-stress were explored in relation to the distinction between the telic and paratelic states. Finally, the resulting framework was used to account systematically for the different possible outcomes of stress including neurotic symptoms, addictions, and other behavioral problems and psychosomatic disorders of one type or another.

REFERENCES

Amkraut, A. & Solomon, G. F. (1977). From the symbolic stimulus to the pathophysiologic response: Immune mechanisms. In S. J. Lipowski, D. R. Lipsitt & P. C. Whybrow (Eds.), *Psychosomatic medicine: Current trends and clinical applications.* New York: Oxford University Press.

Antonovsky, A., Maoz, B., Dowty, N. & Wijesenbeck, H. (1971). Twenty-five years later. *Social Psychiatry, 6,* 186–193.

Apter, M. J. (1982). *The experience of motivation: The theory of psychological reversals.* London: Academic Press.

Apter, M. J. & Murgatroyd, S. (1980). Concentration: A central concept for educational technologists. *Programmed Learning and Educational Technology, 17,* 48–52.

Baum, A., Gatchel, R. J., Fleming, R. & Lake, C. R. (1981). *Chronic and acute stress associated with the Three Mile Island accident and decontamination: Preliminary findings of a longitudinal study.* Washington, D.C.: U.S. Nuclear Regulatory Commission.

Baum, A., Grunberg, N. E. & Singer, J. E. (1982). The use of psychological and neuro-endocrinological measurements in the study of stress. *Health Psychology, 1,* 217–236.

Baum, A., Singer, J. E. & Baum, C. S. (1981). Stress and the environment. *Journal of Social Issues, 37,* 4–35.

Bettelheim, B. (1943). *The informed heart: Autonomy in a mass age.* New York: Free Press.

Bohlin, G. & Kjellberg, A. (1975). Self-reported arousal: Factorial complexity as a function of the subjects' arousal level. *Scandinavian Journal of Psychology, 16*, 203-208.

Brenner, P., Roskies, E. & Lazarus, R. S. (1980). Stress and coping under extreme conditions. In J. E. Dimsdale (Ed.), *Survivors, victims and perpetrators: Essays on the Nazi Holocaust*. Washington, DC: Hemisphere.

Cappell, H. (1975). An evaluation of tension models of alcohol consumption. In R. J. Gibbins, Y. Israel, H. Kalant, R. E. Popham, W. Smidt & R. G. Smart (Eds.), *Research advances in alcohol and drug problems* (Vol. 2). New York: Wiley.

Carlson, J. G. (1982). Some concepts of perceived control and their relationship to bodily self-control. *Biofeedback and Self-Regulation, 7*, 341-375.

Cohen, S. (1980). Aftereffects of stress on human performance and social behavior: A review of research and theory. *Psychological Bulletin, 87*, 578-604.

Cohen, S., Evans, G. W., Krantz, D. S. & Stokols, D. (1980). Physiological, motivational and cognitive effects of aircraft noise on children: Moving from the laboratory to the field. *American Psychologist, 35*, 231-243.

Cooper, C. L. & Melhuish, A. (1980). Occupational stress and managers. *Journal of Occupational Medicine, 22* (9), 588-592.

Dohrenwend, B. P. & Dohrenwend, B. S. (1979). The conceptualization and measurement of stressful life events: An overview of the issues. In R. A. Depue (Ed.), *The psychobiology of the depressive disorders: Implications for the effects of stress*. New York: Academic Press.

Etinger, L. H. & Strom, A. (1973). *Mortality and morbidity after excessive stress*. New York: Humanities.

Eysenck, H. J. (1980). *The causes and effects of smoking*. London: Maurice Temple Smith.

Evans, G. W. (1978). Human spatial behavior. In A. Baum & Y. Epstein (Eds.)., *Human response to crowding*. Hillsdale, N. J.: Erlbaum.

Fontana, D. (1981). Obsessionality and reversal theory. *British Journal of Clinical Psychology, 20*, 299-300.

Folkman, S. & Lazarus, R. S. (1980). An analysis of coping in a middle-aged community sample. *Journal of Health and Social Behavior, 21*, 219-239.

Frankenhaeuser, M. (1975). Sympathetic-adrenomedullary activity, behavior and the psychosocial environment. In P. H. Venables & M. J. Christie (Eds.), *Research in psychophysiology*. New York: Wiley.

Frankenhaeuser, M. (1980). Psychobiological aspects of life stress. In S. Levine and H. Ursin (Eds.), *Coping and health*. New York: Plenum.

Frankenhaeuser, J. & Jarpe, G. (1963). Psychophysiological changes during infusions of adrenaline in various doses. *Psychopharmacologia, 4*, 424-432.

Grinker, R. R. & Spiegel, J. P. (1945). *Men under stress*. New York: McGraw-Hill.

Gunderson, E. K. E. & Rahe, R. H. (1974). *Life stress and illness*. Springfield: Thomas.

Hamburg, D. A., Hamburg, B. & deGoza, S. (1953). Adaptive problems and mechanisms in severely burned patients. *Psychiatry, 16*, 1-20.

Hamilton, V. (1979). Information processing aspects of neurotic anxiety and the schizophrenias. In V. Hamilton & D. M. Warburton (Eds.), *Human stress and cognition: An information processing approach*. Chichester: Wiley.

Hebb, D. O. (1955). Drives and the C. N. S. (Conceptual Nervous System). *Psychological Review, 62*, 243-254.

Hinkle, L. E. (1973). The concept of "stress" in the biological and social sciences. *Science, Medicine and Man, 1*, 31-48.

Holmes, T. H. & Masuda, M. (1974). Life change and illness susceptibility. In B. S. Dohrenwend & B. P. Dohrenwend (Eds.), *Stressful life events: Their nature and effects*. New York: Wiley.

Holroyd, K. A. & Lazarus, R. S. (1982). Stress, coping and somatic adaptation. In L. Goldberger & S. Breznitz (Eds.), *Handbook of stress: Theoretical and clinical aspects*. New York: Free Press/Macmillan.

Janis, I. L. (1982a). Decision making under stress. In L. Goldberger & S. Breznitz (Eds.), *Handbook of stress: Theoretical and clinical aspects*. New York: Free Press/Macmillan.

Janis, I. L. (1982b). *Stress, attitudes and decisions: Selected papers*. New York: Praeger.

Johnson, J. H. & Sarason, I. G. (1979). Recent developments in research on life stress. In V. Hamilton & D. M. Warburton (Eds.), *Human stress and cognition: An information processing approach*. Chichester: Wiley.

Krantz, D. S., Glass, D. C., Contrada, R. & Miller, N. E. (1981). *Behavior and health*. National Science Foundation's second five-year outlook on science and technology, 1981.

Lazarus, R. S. & Launier, R. (1978). Stress-related transactions between person and environment. In L. A. Pervin & M. Lewis (Eds.), *Internal and external determinants of behavior*. New York: Plenum.

Lazarus, R., Spiesman, J., Mordkoff, A. & Davidson, L. (1962). A laboratory study of psychological stress produced by a motion picture film. *Psychological Monographs, 76*, (Whole No. 553).

Levine, S. (1983). Coping: An overview. In H. Ursin & R. Murison (Eds.), *Biological and psychological basis of psychosomatic disease: Advances in the biosciences* (Vol. 42). Oxford: Pergamon.

Lindemann, E. (1944). Symptomatology and management of acute grief. *American Journal of Psychiatry, 101*, 141–148.

Lum, L. C. (1981). Hyperventilation and anxiety state. *Journal of the Royal Society of Medicine, 74*, 1–4.

Mandler, G. (1972). Comments. In C. D. Spielberger (Ed.), *Anxiety: Current trends in theory and research.* New York: Academic Press.

Mandler, G. (1982). Stress and thought process. In L. Goldberger & S. Breznitz (Eds.), *Handbook of stress: Theoretical and clinical aspects.* New York: Free Press/Macmillan.

Malmo, R. B. (1975). *On emotions, needs and our archaic brain.* New York: Holt, Rinehart and Winston.

Malmo, R. B. & Shagass, C. (1949). Physiologic study of symptom mechanisms in psychiatric patients under stress. *Psychosomatic Medicine, 11*, 25–29.

Mason, J. W. (1975). A historical view of the stress field. *Journal of Human Stress, 1*, 22–36.

Murgatroyd, S. (1981). Reversal theory: A new perspective on crisis counselling. *British Journal of Guidance and Counselling, 9*, 180–193.

Murgatroyd, S., Rushton, C., Apter, M. J. & Ray, C. (1978). The development of the Telic Dominance Scale. *Journal of Personality Assessment, 42*, 519–528.

Paster, S. (1948). Psychiatric reactions among soldiers of World War II. *Journal of Nervous and Mental Disease, 108*, 54–66.

Pribram, K. H. & McGuinness, D. (1975). Arousal, activation and effort in the control of attention. *Psychological Review, 82*, 116–149.

Rabkin, J. G. & Struening, E. L. (1976). Life events, stress and illness. *Science, 194*, 1013–1020.

Rahe, R. H., (1969). Multi-cultural correlations of life change scaling: America, Japan, Denmark and Sweden. *Journal of Psychosomatic Research, 13*, 191–195.

Ross, R. & Glomset, J. A. (1976). The pathogenesis of atherosclerosis. *New England Journal of Medicine, 295*, 369–377.

Selye, H. (1956). *The stress of life.* New York: McGraw-Hill.

Selye, H. (1982). History and present status of the stress concept. In L. Goldberger & S. Breznitz (Eds.), *Handbook of stress: Theoretical and clinical aspects.* New York: Free Press/Macmillan.

Sterbach, R. A. (1966). *Principles of psychophysiology.* New York: Academic Press.

Svebak, S. (1982a). The effect of task difficulty and threat of aversive electric shock upon tonic physiological changes. *Biological Psychology, 14*, 113–128.

Svebak, S. (1982b). *The significance of motivation for task-induced tonic physiological changes.* Unpublished doctoral dissertation, University of Bergen, Norway.

Svebak, S. (1983a). The effect of information load, emotional load and motivational state upon tonic physiological activation. In H. Ursin & R. Murison (Eds), *Biological and psychological basis of psychosomatic disease: Advances in the biosciences* (Vol. 42). Oxford: Pergamon.

Svebak, S. (1983b). Personality and cardiovascular risk. *Journal of the Norwegian Psychological Association, 20*, 183–193.

Svenbak, S., & Apter, M. J. (1984). Type A behaviour and its relation to seriousmindedness (Telic Dominance). *Scandinavian Journal of Psychology, 25*, 161–167.

Svebak, S., Storfjell, O. & Dalen, K. (1982). The effect of a threatening context upon motivation and task-induced physiological changes. *British Journal of Psychology, 73*, 505–512.

Svebak, S. & Stoyva, J. (1980). High arousal can be pleasant and exciting: The theory of psychological reversals. *Biofeedback and Self-Regulation, 5*, 439–444.

Swank, R. L. (1949). Combat exhaustion. *Journal of Nervous and Mental Disease, 109*, 475–508.

Ursin, H. & Murison, R. (1983). The stress concept. (1983). In H. Ursin & R. Murison (Eds.), *Biological and psychological basis of psychosomatic disease: Advances in the biosciences* (Vol. 42). Oxford: Pergamon.

Weiner, H. (1977). *Psychobiology and human disease.* New York: Elsevier.

Wilson, G. T. (1982). Alcohol and anxiety: Recent evidence on the tension reduction theory of alcohol use and abuse. In K. R. Blankstein & J. Polivy (Eds.), *Self-control and self-modification of emotional behavior: Advances in the study of communication and affect* (Vol. 7). New York: Plenum.

Wise, R. A. (1982). Neuroleptics and operant behavior: The anhedonia hypothesis. *The Behavioral and Brain Sciences, 5*, 39–87.

Zajonc, R. (1965). Social facilitation. *Science, 149*, 269–274.

4

Cognitive Components of Heterosexual Social Anxiety in Shy Males

Michel Girodo
University of Ottawa

Susan Elizabeth Dotzenroth
Ministry of Correctional Services, Canada

Steven Joel Stein
Thistletown Regional Centre

Social anxiety has long been seen as a potentially disruptive force in interpersonal relations and to individual self-esteem (Sullivan, 1947). In chronic and severe cases, social anxiety can lead to social avoidance and to the kind of isolation which is subsequently accompanied by loneliness and depression. Of particular importance to personal adjustment are social relations involving transactions with members of the opposite sex. For example, among college students, up to 40% admit to some degree of fear of meeting someone of the opposite sex for the first time (Borkovec, Stone, O'Brien, & Kaloupec, 1974). Evidence of the widespread concern over achieving satisfying heterosexual social relations also comes from Martison and Zerface (1970). They found that students were more concerned with learning "how to get along better with the opposite sex" than in receiving guidance on academic programs, career counseling, or in learning about their aptitudes, abilities, and interests. Partly in response to this need, numerous psychological studies have focused on the development of cognitive and behavioral strategies for reducing social anxiety and increasing "minimal dating behavior" in college students (e.g. Christensen, Arkowitz, & Anderson, 1975; Curran & Gilbert, 1975).

While social anxiety has its somatic and physiological components, of particular interest has been the role of cognitive factors in the origin and maintenance of social anxiety. One of these components has been isolated in terms of the evaluation apprehension which accompanies many heterosexual relations (Rehm & Marston, 1968). Watson and Friend (1969) developed the Fear of Negative Evaluation (FNE) scale and concluded from studies with this instrument that the anxiety which prompts people to avoid social situations may originate from an excessive preoccupation with being unfavorably evaluated. From this heightened sensitivity to negative interpersonal cues the socially anxious person is also more likely to arrive at negative self-descriptive inferences about his or her own level of competency and effectiveness. The typical consequence of this cognitive operation is lowered self-esteem that leads to normal depression (Depue & Monroe, 1978).

What is the nature and role of social anxiety which underlies shyness reactions? How do cognitive factors mediate in the maintenance of low frequency social interactions? What can we learn about the relationship between social anxiety and social self-esteem in the successful amelioration of shyness? The following studies summarize some of our attempts at addressing these questions. The first investigation examines cognitive factors associated with social self-esteem, social anxiety and distress, and fear of negative evaluation in shy and nonshy males. Of particular interest are the causal attributions made by subjects in interpreting the cause of past heterosexual social successes and failures. The second study reports on the effectiveness of a composite cognitive-behavioral treatment program in an outclient population wanting to learn how to make new friends and get along better with the opposite sex. The third study outlines the findings obtained from college students who followed this program on their own without therapist assistance. In the fourth study, the relationships between changes in social anxiety and changes in causal attributions for success and failure are examined.

CAUSAL ATTRIBUTIONS IN SHY MALES

The social learning theory assumption is that, because of a history of negative social experiences, shy people not only engage in low frequency dating behavior but report dissatisfaction with opposite sex relations, social anxiety, and low social self-esteem. From this theoretical standpoint it follows that self-perceptions would improve and anxiety levels would abate if shy people were exposed to a series of successful heterosexual social encounters. Based upon causal attribution theory however, successful social experiences might have a beneficial effect only if the person was led to believe that certain factors were responsible for these outcomes. Thus, ascribing the cause of a socially successful transaction to internal factors (ability and effort) would have positive affective consequences, whereas task difficulty (it was easy) or luck attributions would not. The opposite is predicted when social failures are ascribed to internal factors. While the internal-external locus of control dimension governs self-esteem and other affective reactions, confidence in future outcomes and risk taking are linked to the stability-variability dimension of causal attributions. Ability and task difficulty attributions for success are more closely associated with expectancies for future outcomes than are effort and luck attributions.

In the study (cf. Girodo, Dotzenroth, & Stein, 1981) 284 male undergraduates completed the following instruments: The Social Self-Esteem Inventory (SSEI) (Lawson, Marshall, & McGrath, 1979), the Social Avoidance and Distress (SAD) scale, and Fear of Negative Evaluation (FNE) scale (Watson & Friend, 1969). They responded to various questions concerning their dating frequency and their satisfaction with relations with the opposite sex. Subjects also reported on their

Table 1 Modal Attributions of Success and Failure

	Success		Failure	
	High SSEI (N = 36)	Low SSEI (N = 42)	High SSEI (N = 36)	Low SSEI (N = 42)
Ability	55.6	6.0	4.2	47.6
Task difficulty	36.1	37.0	27.8	7.1
Effort	5.6	29.8	43.1	19.0
Luck	2.8	27.4	25.0	26.2

causal attributions for past heterosexual social successes and failures in connection with four kinds of interpersonal transactions with the opposite sex. Finally, subjects indicated their expectancy for success given four additional hypothetical situations involving females.

Following data tabulation, subjects were divided into two groups: those scoring 1 standard deviation above and those scoring one standard deviation below the mean on the SSEI. Compared with subjects with low social self-esteem, high SSEI men had significantly lower SAD and FNE scores; they also dated approximately once a week compared with once a month for the low SSEI subjects. On a 21-point scale high SSEI subjects reported a mean satisfaction with opposite sex relations of 18.25 while low SSEI subjects obtained a mean of 8.44.

In terms of causal attributions for past social successes, approximately 92% of the high SSEI men expressed a modal preference for either ability or ease of the task as a cause for success, in contrast to 43% of the low SSEI subjects. Ability in social interactions with the opposite sex loaded heavily for the high SSEI group (58%) whereas ability as a cause of success was only popular in 6% of the low SSEI men. With respect to interpreting failure experiences, the reverse was found. Failures in social interations with the opposite sex were attributed to lack of ability by only 4% of the high SSEI subjects, in contrast to 55% of the low SSEI subjects. Table 1 summarizes these results.

Thus, men with high social self-esteem tended to give themselves credit for their social successes and to blame their failures on lack of effort (a variable cause). Very few of the low social-self-esteem men gave themselves credit for positive outcomes, and showed a sharp preference for blaming themselves when they failed. Also, when subjects were asked to predict how successful they might be with the opposite sex in a series of hypothetical transactions, high SSEI men showed greater expectancies for success X = 15.72) compared with their low SSEI counterparts (X = 11.61). Moreover, the results of the study illustrated a clear preference for stable attributions (ability and task difficulty) of success to be associated with future anticipations of success, in contrast to variable (effort and luck) attributions (see Girodo et al., 1981).

While we may be accustomed to seeing social anxiety in shy people in terms of a fear of negative evaluation from others, the causal attribution bias found in this study has implications for another anxiety construct. Heckhausen (1967, 1975), working in the achievement motivation area, has found it useful to use the expressions *fear of failure* versus *hope for success* to distinguish between people who show a distinctive causal attribution bias. If interpersonal relations with the opposite sex are seen as achievement-oriented undertakings (as indeed they were presented to subjects), fear of failure in achieving a desired outcome may represent an additional component to the fear of negative evaluation underlying social anxiety.

The statistical relationships extant among measures of dating frequency, satisfaction, social self-esteem, social avoidance and distress, and fear of negative evaluation in shy males point to an interesting syndrome. The causal attribution bias for success and failure has been linked to the esteem component of affective reactions produced by interpersonal outcomes. Although the relationships among variables are based on a correlational methodology, the dynamic and instrumental way in which these factors influence each other, as well as the role of anxiety in modifying shyness reactions, requires a more experimental approach. The following two studies summarize some of the findings obtained in modifying this syndrome.

MODIFYING THE SHYNESS SYNDROME

The literature on minimal dating behavior generally points to some behavioral differences in social competence between shy and nonshy males (e.g. Arkowitz, Lichtenstein, McGovern, & Hines, 1975; Twentyman & McFall, 1975). Also, nondaters often tend to underestimate their true level of social skill and to remember their faults more than nonanxious people (O'Banion & Arkowitz, 1974). Furthermore, while many nondaters have inappropriate fears relating to dating, many also lack information concerning dating behavior such as how and where to go to meet people and how to make arrangements for a future meeting (Martinson & Zerface, 1970).

In developing a treatment program for shyness problems we favored an approach which packaged intervention strategies embodying a wide array of cognitive, emotional, and behavioral problem areas rather than an individual differences approach that targeted specific deficits in certain people. The treatment program for shy males evolved essentially by trial and error over several years. In its final form the composite cognitive-behavioral program consisted of the following five features:

1. An educational phase focused on social skills training. This emphasized balancing verbal, nonverbal, and vocal aspects of communication and self-presentation. Instructions were given on normative rules for beginning, maintaining, and terminating conversations with the opposite sex, as well as how and where to go to meet new people.

2. A Rational-Emotive (e.g. Ellis, 1962) component adapted specifically for challenging irrational beliefs associated with social relations with females is introduced. Instruction is provided in how to reduce defeating self-statements and for altering unrealistic expectations.

3. A causal reattribution component emphasizes appropriate risk taking, measuring success due to ability, and reinterpreting failures in terms of lack of effort, the difficulty of the encounter, or simply bad luck.

4. Homework assignments that ask the person to take part in social interactions

in a wide range of structured contexts outside of the treatment sessions. Tasks assigned involve increasing levels of skill and risk taking.

5. Self-monitoring exercises require the person to attend to and record changing levels of nervousness and tension, and to estimate their degree of success in meeting specified interpersonal objectives.

This program was detailed in a 50-page treatment manual and was accompanied by cassette tapes and self-monitoring sheets. Over the years the program was available for use by trained counselors and therapists in university counseling centers and other public and private mental health facilities. Typically, the treatment program is conducted in groups of 6–8 participants who meet weekly for 3 hours over a period of 6–7 weeks.

The opportunity for evaluating the effectiveness of this program arose in connection with its implementation at a local behavior therapy clinic. Newspaper advertisements solicited participants who "wanted to learn how to make friends more easily and get along better with the opposite sex." Over a period of 6 months, three separate groups of 6–8 male participants ranging in age from 18–40 years completed the 6-week program. Pretest and posttest data were collected on the FNE, SAD, and SSEI scales.

Collapsing across the 3 groups and taking the 21 participants as a whole, 19 males decreased their SAD scores at the end of 6 weeks: pretest = 18.80, posttest = 13.57; ($t = 2.53$, $df = 20$, $p < .02$). On the FNE scale 16 males reported lower scores at posttest: pretest = 20.38, posttest = 15.30; ($t = 2.05$; $df = 20$, $p < .05$). All participants increased their scores on the SSEI from a pretest mean = 82.66 to a posttest mean = 104.61; ($t = 2.80$, $df = 20$, $p < .02$).

While these data point to increases in social self-esteem with accompanying decreases in fear of negative evaluation and tendencies to avoid social situations, the absence of proper controls render the findings far from unequivocal. Nevertheless, some factor or group of factors were producing reliable changes in self-perceptions and social fears. Several observations during the group sessions were particularly noteworthy. The very fact of participating in a group raised anxiety levels considerably. This should not have been so surprising since evaluation apprehension in social contexts is what underscored the very reason for entering into the program. This had several opposing consequences, one of which was a tendency for subjects not to report accurately the extent to which homework assignments were being faithfully carried out. In addition, the group leader's role had been defined in terms of guiding, facilitating, and encouraging participants in becoming more socially active as they progressed through various assignments. Our own perception of the leader and participant interactions eventually led us to conclude that the support and encouragement fostered by the leader promoted a certain dependency which was dramatically opposed to the program's objectives: In order to increase motivation for self-guided risk taking and to profit from social successes shy people would have to learn self-reliance by assuming personal responsibility for overcoming their timidity. With a supportive leader assuming the role of educator it was too easy for participants to transfer responsibility for behavior change on to an external source. These were hardly the conditions under which internal-stable attributions could be orchestrated.

Table 2   Pretest and Posttest Means of Self-Report Measures

	SAD				FNE				SSEI			
	Pre	Post	df	t	Pre	Post	df	t	Pre	Post	df	t
Bibliotherapy	10.05	7.45	15	21.9*	16.0	11.05	15	4.86**	130.05	137.70	15	2.42*
Own resources	15.00	13.50	15	N.S.	15.55	13.45	15	N.S.	139.80	136.45	15	N.S.
Controls	7.40	8.40	17	N.S.	15.65	18.80	17	N.S.	138.80	130.65	17	N.S.

$* = p < .05.$
$** = p < .01.$

Given the importance we placed on self-directed efforts and motivation for gaining social experience, the question of the utility of various components in the program was raised. Do shy people really need this cognitive-behavioral education, or would any sustained effort at increasing social participation succeed in increasing self-confidence and reducing social anxiety? In the next study we were interested in the effects of self-directed efforts at overcoming shyness problems. Also, since the manual had been published in trade book form, it presented a unique opportunity for assessing the effects of what may be termed *bibliotherapy.*

Single males enrolled in undergraduate classes were solicited to participate in an experiment designed to "improve their social relations with members of the opposite sex." Potential participants were told their involvement in the project would be required for a period up to 4 months. Fifty men agreed to participate and these were randomly assigned to one of three conditions. Sixteen men served in the Bibliotherapy group. They were given a copy of the published manual (Girodo, 1978) and instructed to read and carry out all of the exercises and social assignments contained therein. Sixteen additional men were assigned to the Own Resources group. Here, subjects were told that the purpose of the study was to find out about how people can go about making new friends and become more active and comfortable in their relations with women. They were told to use their own imagination, efforts, resources, and skills for increasing social contacts and becoming more sociable. Finally, 18 other subjects served in a control condition. They were told that the study involved becoming more aware of opportunities for social contacts. They were asked to monitor weekly and to report at the end of the study what they had learned about the various opportunities which existed for interacting socially and for making new female friends. Pretest and posttest SAD, FNE, and SSEI scores 4 months later yielded the following results presented in Table 2.

Bibliotherapy subjects who were told to follow through with the instructions in the book significantly decreased their social avoidance and distress and fear of negative evaluation. Their scores measuring social self-esteem also significantly increased. Neither the Own Resources or the Control group changed on these measures. In group comparisons, the SAD and FNE measures discriminated between Bibliotherapy and Control subjects. Postexperimental inquiry revealed that both treatment groups reported an increase in social contacts, in making new friends, and in venturing into different social groups and contexts.

Aside from the obvious differences in treatments given the groups it is possible that the results were due to inadvertent attribution sets. Bibliotherapy subjects were given a manual to follow which clearly specified self-change and self-reference connections between efforts and outcomes. Own Resources subjects, may have been equally active; however, their trying out new behaviors may have been primarily in response to the demands of the experimenter. Social and behavioral compliance may have been at the service of the study rather than in service of the self.

It is interesting to note that in both studies the intervention program succeeded in bringing about changes in all three measures. It may be significant that while SAD, FNE, and SSEI scores are correlated, change scores from pretest to posttest are not statistically related to one another: Conceivably different components of the program impact each measure individually. Notwithstanding, these findings still raise the question of what role causal attributions play in changing these various shyness measures. Although internal attributions of ability and effort have affective consequences with respect to social self-esteem, are they in any way implicated in social anxiety and fear of failure? The following experiment was designed to assess the extent to which changes in causal attributions to social success and failure are related to social avoidance, fear of negative evaluation, and self-esteem.

CHANGING CAUSAL ATTRIBUTIONS

From a pretested sample of 289 male undergraduates 40 subjects scoring 1 standard deviation or more below the mean on the SSEI were asked and agreed to participate in a study involving "improving relations with the opposite sex." Pretest measures included SAD, FNE, and SSEI scores, causal attribution preferences for past social successes and failures with the opposite sex, dating frequency, and reported satisfaction with social relations with the opposite sex.

Thirty males were randomly assigned to the treatment group while ten were randomly chosen to serve as test-retest controls. Subjects in the treatment condition were exposed to the cognitive-behavioral treatment in small groups of four and five. They were provided with the original (unpublished) version of the manual and were guided through its various components in 3-hour weekly sessions spanning a 4-week treatment period. In the hope of isolating the separate contributions made by each component, the initial approach was to give small groups one or a combination of the various treatment components. This, however, proved to be impractical; for all intents and purposes all 30 subjects were exposed to substantially all components of the previously described treatment package. In the 3-hour sessions various components of the treatment were presented and individually tailored homework social assignments were assigned. In subsequent sessions subjects would hand in written reports of their successes, and were urged and coaxed to carry out new tasks that were assigned. In the 6th week all subjects returned to complete all pretest measures.

Table 3 summarizes the results from the main dependent measures. As can be seen, treatment subjects significantly increased their dating frequency, reported satisfaction, and social self-esteem. They also decreased on the SAD and FNE measures.

Table 3   Means and t Values of Pre- and Posttest Scores on the Major Self-Report Measures

	Treatment sample (n = 30)				Test-retest control group (n = 10)			
	Pretest $\bar{X}$	Posttest $\bar{X}$	df	t Value	Pretest $\bar{X}$	Posttest $\bar{X}$	df	t Value
Dating score	3.00	3.55	28	2.29*	3.79	4.00	8	1.70
Satisfaction	10.41	12.85	26	2.65**	12.78	14.44	8	.98
SSEI	111.97	125.37	29	4.22***	114.33	117.89	8	.70
SAD	13.00	7.67	26	5.27***	12.33	12.33	8	.00
FNE	17.96	11.75	27	5.61***	16.44	12.67	8	1.49

*p < .05.
**p < .01.
***p < .001.

In terms of pretest attributional choices the pattern of causal ascriptions mirrored the results obtained in the first study. Briefly, at pretest, ability was chosen by 8% of the treatment subjects as a cause of social success. On the other hand, lack of ability was seen as the major cause of failure in 38% of these same subjects. In tabulating total attribution preferences across the four situations presented, pretest and posttest differences were found. Table 4 shows these differences.

As can be seen, none of the causal attribution choices were changed significantly from pretest to posttest in control subjects. Treatment subjects, however, chose ability as a cause of recent success more often, and saw luck as less important in successful outcomes. In terms of interpreting failure experiences, treatment subjects were significantly less likely to attribute this outcome to a lack of ability. Correlation coefficients computed on attribution change scores revealed a negative

Table 4   Means and t Values of Attributional Preferences from Pre- to Posttesting

	Treatment sample (n = 30)				Test-retest control group (n = 10)			
	Pretest $\bar{X}$	Posttest $\bar{X}$	df	t Value	Pretest $\bar{X}$	Posttest $\bar{X}$	df	t Value
			Success					
Ability	3.11	4.32	27	2.23*	1.77	2.33	8	.71
Task difficulty	8.30	8.04	22	.37	6.78	7.56	8	.86
Effort	6.18	7.27	21	1.34	8.78	8.00	8	.77
Luck	4.74	3.26	26	2.63**	6.67	6.11	8	.51
			Failure					
Ability	7.63	5.33	23	3.37**	6.89	7.00	8	.23
Task difficulty	6.40	7.15	19	1.07	6.44	8.11	8	1.32
Effort	4.89	5.67	26	1.01	4.11	3.11	8	.75
Luck	4.82	4.39	27	.63	5.89	5.11	8	.56

*p < .05.
**p < .01.

correlation ($-.40$, $p < .05$) between ability and luck attributions for social successes. This suggests that the increased tendency to see ability as a cause of success was at the expense of downplaying luck as an explanation. In terms of attribution changes to social failures, a correlation of $-.41$ ($p < .05$) between lack of ability and lack of effort suggests that the less treatment subjects saw lack of ability as a cause for failure the more they tended to blame it on lack of effort.

The relationship between changes in attributional preferences and changes in the other self report measures was also examined. The only significant correlations that emerged were those which implicated changes in the Fear of Negative Evaluation scale. Decreases in FNE scores were associated with the following: (1) increased use of ability as a cause of success ($r = -.42$, $p < .05$); (2) decrease in lack of ability as a source of failure ($r = .43$, $p < .05$); and (3) increase in use of lack of effort as a cause of failure ($r = -.51$, $p < .01$).

These results clearly implicate causal attributions for success and failure with social anxiety that is represented by a fear of negative evaluation. Indeed internal factors (ability and effort) for success are the major participants in anxiety changes. Although our own earlier research had previously favored changes in self-esteem as the major affective component underlying internal versus external factors, these findings suggest that fear of failure and fear of negative evaluation may be similar components of social anxiety in heterosexual transactions.

CONCLUSION

The findings of the present studies and other research (e.g. Girodo et al., 1981) point to a reliable statistical relationship among various components of shyness in males. Low self-esteem in social situations has been consistently associated with social avoidance and a heightened concern over being negatively evaluated. Traditional thinking along lines of causal attribution theory has held that internal attributions for success and external attributions for failure are mediating cognitive processes which serve to increase and preserve self-esteem levels. The results of the last study reported herein showed attributional changes in the predicted direction however with no consequent self-esteem changes on the SSEI scale. Rather, *social anxiety levels, as measured by the FNE scale, are what are associated with causal attribution changes.* We can speculate as to how these measures are dynamically related in the maintenance of shyness behaviors as well as in their modification in response to treatment programs.

On the one hand it might be argued that a certain level of interpersonal skill is required in order to guarantee some modicum of favorable responsiveness in social transactions. On the other hand one can wonder about to what extent behavioral incompetence as opposed to *perceived* incompetence is really at the root of low risk-taking social anxiety, and inhibition in shy males. Expectancies of failure and/or poor social performance follow from the belief that one lacks the skill for promoting a favorable response. In the studies reviewed here it was not possible to ascertain the extent to which behavioral skill did increase as a result of the educational training phase of the treatment program; all we can say is that the treatment was successful in instilling the belief that their successes would be due to their ability or skill. The fact that such changes in perception were associated with a lowering of evaluation anxiety may be the most noteworthy finding. For it may very well be that social anxiety in heterosexual social encounters is not so much the product of not knowing what to do or what to say, but more the result of *not believing* that one has the capacity to effect positive outcomes.

REFERENCES

Arkowitz, H., Lichtenstein, E., McGovern, K., & Hines, P. (1975). The behavioral assessment of social competence in males. *Behavior Therapy, 6,* 3–13.

Borkovec, T., Stone, N., O'Brien, G., & Kaloupec, D. (1974). Evaluation of a clinically relevant target behavior for analog outcome research. *Behavior Therapy, 5,* 503–513.

Christensen, A., Arkowitz, H., & Anderson, J. (1975). Practice dating as treatment for college dating inhibitions. *Behaviour Research and Therapy, 13,* 321–331.

Curran, J., & Gilbert, F. (1975). A test of the relative effectiveness of a systematic desensitization program and an interpersonal skills training program with data anxious subjects. *Behavior Therapy, 6,* 510–521.

Depue, R., & Monroe, S. (1978). Learned helplessness in the perspective of the depressive disorders: Conceptual and definitional issues. *Journal of Abnormal Psychology, 87,* 3–20.

Ellis, A. (1962). *Reason and emotion in psychotherapy.* New York: Lyle Stuart Press.

Girodo, M. (1978). *Shy? (You don't have to be).* New York: Pocket Books.

Girodo, M., Dotzenroth, S., & Stein, S. (1981). Causal attribution bias in shy males. Implications for self-esteem and self-confidence. *Cognitive Therapy and Research, 5,* 325–338.

Heckhausen, H. (1967). *The anatomy of achievement motivation.* New York: Academic Press.

Heckhausen, H. (1975). Fear of failure as a self-reinforcing motive system. In I. G. Sarason and C. Spielberger (Eds.), *Stress and Anxiety* (Vol. 2). Washington, DC: Hemisphere.

Lawson, J., Marshall, W., & McGrath, P. (1979). The social self-esteem inventory. *Educational and Psychological Measurement, 39,* 803–811.

Martinson, W., & Zerface, J. (1970). Comparison of individual counseling and a social program with nondaters. *Journal of Counseling Psychology, 17,* 36–40.

O'Banion, K., & Arkowitz, H. (1974). *Social anxiety and selective memory for affective information about the self.* Unpublished manuscript, Indiana University.

Rehm, L., & Marston, A. (1968). Reduction of social anxiety through modification of self-reinforcement: An instigation therapy technique. *Journal of Consulting Psychology, 32,* 565–574.

Sullivan, H. (1947). *The interpersonal theory of psychiatry.* New York: Norton.

Twentyman, C., & McFall, R. (1975). Behavioral training of social skills in shy males. *Journal of Consulting and Clinical Psychology, 43,* 384–395.

Watson, D., & Friend, R. (1969). Measurement of social-evaluative anxiety. *Journal of Consulting and Clinical Psychology, 33,* 448–457.

II

SITUATIONAL DETERMINANTS OF STRESS AND ANXIETY

5

Development of Test Anxiety in High School Students

Ralf Schwarzer and Matthias Jerusalem
Freie Universität Berlin

This paper examines test anxiety as a situation-specific trait in the school environment. It aims at exploring the antecedents and concomitants of test anxiety in several samples of West German students. The perceived learning environment, together with its associated achievement pressures, is considered as one determinant of test anxiety. Further determinants are the social context of the school environment, which provides relevant reference norms, and self-related cognitions. Therefore, theoretical issues regarding test anxiety, self-concept, self-awareness, and self-efficacy in the school socialization process will be reviewed prior to describing recent research findings.

Test Anxiety

Anxiety has been defined as an unpleasant emotional state or condition characterized not only by subjective feelings of tension, apprehension, nervousness, and worry, but also by activation or arousal of the autonomic nervous system (Spielberger, 1972a, 1972b). Test anxiety is a situation-specific trait which refers to the anxiety states and worry cognitions that are experienced during examinations. However, test anxiety might be confounded with social anxiety when a test is taken in public, or when social interactions are involved in the performance to be evaluated.

Theory concerning test anxiety has a long tradition, which makes this one of the most studied phenomena in the field of psychology (see Sarason, 1980). Cognitive approaches to emotions and actions have given rise to new concepts that contribute to the understanding and explanation of subjective experiences of anxiety as an emotional state (Spielberger, 1972a). With regard to test anxiety, the first six vol-

The research reported herein was supported by Volkswagen Foundation. We are grateful to Wolfgang Dutka, Manfried Kuliga, and Claudia Marggraf, who conducted Study 3.

umes of the book series *Advances in Test Anxiety Research* demonstrate the importance of cognitions for performance and socialization in schools (Schwarzer, van der Ploeg, & Spielberger, 1982, 1987, 1989; van der Ploeg, Schwarzer, & Spielberger, 1983, 1984, 1985).

Tests are regarded as general academic demands in schools or places of higher education, but can also be highly specific demands, as in the case of mathematics anxiety (Hunsley & Flessati, 1988; Richardson & Woolfolk, 1980) or sports anxiety (Hackfort, 1983). Such demands, if personally relevant for the individual, can be challenging, ego threatening, or harmful (Lazarus & Folkman, 1984). The appraisal of a task as ego threatening gives rise to test anxiety if a person perceives a lack of coping ability as well. The latter is most interesting for the study of *self-related cognitions*. The individual searches for information about his or her specific competence to handle the situation. Coping resources include one's ability to solve the kind of problem at hand, the amount of time available, or the existence of a supportive social network (see Sarason & Sarason, 1985; Schwarzer & Leppin, 1988a, 1988b).

Perceiving a contingency between a potential action and a potential outcome, and attributing this contingency to internal factors, is most helpful in developing an adaptive coping strategy. This confidence in one's ability to complete a successful action can be called self-efficacy (Bandura, 1977, 1986, 1988). Lack of self-efficacy expectation leads to an imbalance between appraised task demands and appraised subjective coping resources, which results in test anxiety. Thus ongoing person-environment transactions are inhibited and performance is decreased. This process, which implies cognitive interference (Sarason, 1986), causes the individual's attention to be divided into task-relevant and task-irrelevant aspects.

In some cases, task-irrelevant cognitions can be interpreted as mental withdrawal (Carver & Scheier, 1986). Those who wish to escape from an aversive situation physically, but cannot do so because of social or other constraints, direct their thoughts away from the problem at hand. Task-irrelevant thoughts can be divided into self-related cognitions (such as worry about one's inability or failure) on the one hand, and thoughts which are totally unrelated to the task (such as daydreams) on the other. This mental withdrawal from threatening demands appears to be one component of test anxiety which is debilitating to academic performance. Perceiving discomfort and tension constitutes another component (autonomic arousal may accompany this component, but need not). Mental withdrawal is maladaptive in specific situations because it counteracts problem-centered coping actions. However, in the long run there could also be a certain adaptive value, because a person might learn to distinguish between difficult and easily manageable situations, thus avoiding those which are overtaxing or extremely difficult.

There are many factors that can cause anxiety. A personal history of success and failure, combined with an unfavorable attributional style and lack of supportive feedback from parents, teachers and peers, may become a vicious circle. This would cause an individual to develop a proneness to scan the environment for potential dangers ("sensitizing"), to appraise demands as threatening, and to cope with problems in a maladaptive way.

For the assessment of test anxiety it is necessary to consider these theoretical deliberations, requiring specific measures for each separate component. The Test Anxiety Inventory (TAI) by Spielberger (1980) and the Reactions to Tests Questionnaire (RTT) by Sarason (1984) meet these criteria.

Self-Concept

Generally, self-concept can be conceived of as being the overall sum of self-referent information which an individual has processed, stored, and organized in a systematic manner. Briefly, it is a set of organized knowledge about oneself. For scientific purposes the self-concept can be considered as a hypothetical construct with a multidimensional structure. Shavelson and Marsh (1986) subdivide the general self-concept into academic, social, emotional, and physical categories, each of which can be further subdivided. A relatively stable hierarchy of cognitions represents the perception an individual has of himself, and at the same time provides categories for self-evaluation. Several factors play a role in developing such an image of oneself.

First, direct and indirect information from the social surroundings are relevant. Parents, peers, and teachers provide evaluative performance feedback in a variety of situations. If an individual is praised after having accomplished something, it may lead to feeling competent. However, feedback does not always have such a straightforward effect. Indirect communication, such as critique, can also produce a positive self-concept under certain circumstances (Meyer, 1984). Additionally, perceiving the emotions of others can trigger self-related cognitions. For instance, if the teacher is angry the student may feel lazy (Weiner, 1986). From the communication given by another an individual infers how this other person perceives and attributes causes of behavior.

Second, the person relies on self-perception and self-evaluation by monitoring his or her accomplishments, attributing these either to ability or to other causes. Also, memory scanning provides a selective retrieval of information about the self. The processes involved are self-reflective and comparative. Standards for comparison are based on either social or individual norms, or on absolute criteria (Rheinberg, 1980). The most powerful and efficient way of obtaining information about one's ability is through social comparison, which allows a quick review of one's relative standing with respect to one or more target individuals who are characterized by "related attributes" (Suls & Miller, 1977). In classroom environments and many other settings these social comparison processes yield results about an individual's status within a reference group. A student's self-concept of ability is developed primarily by social comparison within school reference groups (Jerusalem, 1984a, 1984b).

Self-Awareness

Focus of attention is a key variable of information processing. Directing the focus toward the self creates self-preoccupation, which increases self-knowledge on the one hand, but potentially impairs the ongoing action and causes debilitated performance on the other. The theory of objective self-awareness (Wicklund, 1975) states that self-focus makes certain aspects of the self more salient and creates a motivation to reduce discrepancies. In an emotional state, self-awareness leads to more affect. Buss (1980, 1986) distinguishes between private and public self-awareness. Private self-awareness is defined as evaluating oneself, investigating one's own feelings and attitudes, and ruminating about one's identity. Public self-awareness is defined as the feeling of being observed or evaluated by others. In this situation, individuals worry about their public image. Self-awareness as a state is distinguished from self-consciousness as a disposition; both, however, have private and public components. This has implications for self-presentation and for social anxicty (see Asendorf, 1984; Jones & Briggs, 1984).

Self-focus is often contrasted with task-focus, implying that the direction of attention is the major determinant of task persistence and accomplishment. However, studies by Carver and Scheier (1984, 1986) show that this dichotomy is too simple and misleading. High trait self-consciousness makes an individual prone to a high frequency of self-focused attention. A self-focused state can be induced experimentally by the presence of a mirror or a technical device that provides feedback of facial appearance, voice, or behavior. This state can also be induced naturally through arousal of anxiety. The individual perceives bodily changes such as increased pulse rate, blushing, and sweating, which leads to self-focus and interruption of ongoing activity. It remains unclear, however, which occurs first, self-focus or interruption. Self-focus, then, facilitates performance for low-anxiety individuals and debilitates performance for the high-anxiety ones (see also Carver, Scheier, & Klahr, 1987). This important statement in the work of these authors raises the question of how anxiety is defined. If it is equated with perceived arousal, then there would be no disagreement with this observation. But if anxiety is defined as a set of cognitions including worry, self-deprecatory rumination, and negative outcome expectancy, combined with emotionality, then the validity of their statement is questionable.

Carver and Scheier (1984, 1986) define anxiety as a coping process that begins with self-focus. Self-focus leads to an interruption of action and provokes a subjective outcome assessment. At this point the authors claim the existence of a "watershed" with respect to the content of the self-focused attention: For some persons this state of self-awareness leads to favorable outcome expectancies, for others to unfavorable ones. The former will shift to a more task-focused attention, invest more effort, and show more persistence, resulting in more successes. The latter will mentally withdraw from the task and become preoccupied with self-deprecatory ruminations. Therefore, they will be less persistent, invest less effort, and will probably experience failure. The first group can be defined as being low, the second as being high in anxiety. High-anxiety individuals may become more prone to perceived discrepancies and interruption of action by arousal cues. The key variables in this model are self-focus and outcome expectancies. Here worry is not the primary cause of performance decrements, but is only one element in a maladaptive coping process based on mental withdrawal and unfavorable expectancies. Self-focus leads to a cognitive process in which one's own coping ability is under scrutiny.

Self-Efficacy

The notion of outcome expectancy is somewhat different than Bandura's (1977, 1986) concept of self-efficacy. While outcome expectancy is an action-outcome contingency, self-efficacy can be defined as a situation-action contingency. This also could be called *competence expectancy* (Krohne, 1985; Schwarzer, 1987).

Perceived self-efficacy can be acquired by direct, indirect, or symbolic experience (Bandura, 1977). Mastery of tasks provides information about one's capability to handle specific kinds of problems. Observing other persons performing well on a task leads to the conviction of having the same capability. One may also believe oneself to be competent of possessing the necessary coping resources if persuaded by someone else.

Self-efficacy is partly responsible for selection of actions, for mobilization of effort, and for persistence at a task. People who are assured of their capabilities intensify their effort, whereas people who lack self-efficacy may be easily discouraged by failure. Bandura and Cervone (1983) have studied the interplay of goal setting, performance feedback, self-dissatisfaction, and self-efficacy. They found that combining a personal aim with performance feedback of progress toward this goal resulted in increased motivation more often than either goal setting or feedback alone. Subgoals and standards had to be explicitly quantitative, challenging, and temporally proximal in order to serve that purpose. In addition, perceived negative discrepancies between what to do and what to achieve created self-dissatisfaction that served as a motivational incentive for enhanced effort. High self-dissatisfaction with a substandard performance and strong self-efficacy for goal attainment subsequently influenced the intensity of effort. This finding sheds light on the role of self-doubts in motivation, which are induced by a perceived negative discrepancy between the current performance level and the desired goal attainment. In applying acquired skills, goals are more difficult to attain if one is plagued by self-doubts. The acquisition of a new skill, however, is stimulated by self-doubts or by slightly negative self-evaluations. Self-efficacy may be more important in the execution of established skills than in the learning of unfamiliar tasks. "In short, self-doubts create an impetus for learning but hinder adept use of established skills" (Bandura & Cervone, 1983, p. 1027).

The construct of perceived self-efficacy might be defined as a component of anxiety. Bandura, however, postulates an "interactive, though asymmetric, relation between perceived self-efficacy and fear arousal, with self-judged efficacy exerting the greater impact" (1983, p. 464). For Bandura (1988), perceived self-efficacy and anxiety are different concepts, the first exerting more of an influence on performance. However, his definition of anxiety is not a cognitive one. Instead, it is similar to fear or perceived arousal. In other words, he alludes to nothing but the emotionality component when referring to anxiety. Findings indicating a superiority of self-related cognitions over "anxiety" are, therefore, consistent with others who hold similar theoretical views on the worry component of anxiety. The question raised by Bandura's (1988) and Carver and Scheier's (1984) findings, among others, seems to be a matter of definition: Which theoretical concepts described in the coping process should be subsumed under the heading of anxiety? The authors of this chapter prefer a broad conceptualization and suggest the use of variables such as perceived self-efficacy (hope vs. doubt), self-deprecatory rumination (worry), and mental withdrawal (escape cognitions) as constitutive cognitive elements of state and trait anxiety. Subdividing anxiety into more than the usual two components is consistent with the findings of Sarason (1984, 1986), Helmke (1982), Schwarzer and Quast (1985), and Stephan, Fischer, and Stein (1983).

The following three studies were undertaken with this theoretical background in mind. For reasons of brevity, the focus will be on test anxiety, although data on the other related concepts were also obtained. More information about the first two studies has been published by Schwarzer, Jerusalem, and Faulhaber (1984).

STUDY 1: TEST ANXIETY AND SCHOOL SYSTEM CHARACTERISTICS

The West German secondary school system provides three achievement tracks for students who, entering at the age of 10, had spent four years in primary school. Those students at the bottom level of the achievement distribution enter the low track ("Hauptschule"), those at top enter the high track ("Gymnasium"), and all others enter the mid-track ("Realschule") school. In addition, in some communities all three levels of students attend comprehensive schools ("Gesamtschulen"). Reference group theory predicts that those who enter the low track will feel better than they did before, while many entering the high track will have a hard time because they will no longer be favored by social comparison processes (see Levine, 1982; Schwarzer, Jerusalem, & Schwarzer, 1983; Schwarzer & Lange, 1983).

A longitudinal study was conducted with a sample of 622 students. A subsample of 112 students entered fifth grade at the low track level, and 107 entered at the high track level. These students were observed for almost two school years, with data collected at five points in time. The subjects responded to the German form (TAI-G; Hodapp, Laux, & Spielberger, 1982) of the Test Anxiety Inventory (TAI; Spielberger, 1980), an instrument designed to assess both the worry and emotionality components of test anxiety. The psychometric properties of this version were found to be satisfactory (see Schwarzer, 1984).

Figures 1 and 2 show the development of both anxiety components over time. When leaving primary school there is a significant difference between low and high achievers. However, after having adapted to the respective new reference groups, both samples converge with respect to the worry and emotionality grand

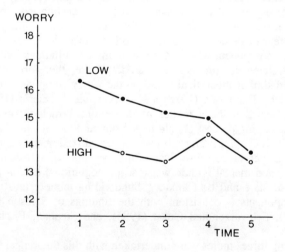

Figure 1 Changes of worry over time.

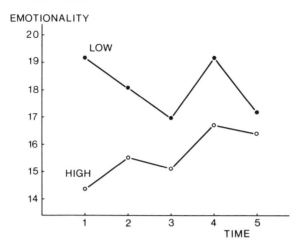

Figure 2 Changes of emotionality over time.

mean. This is consistent with reference group theory: Subjective well-being depends partly on the social context. Students compare their ability and outcomes with that of their peers and establish a within-group rank order for themselves. If their individual position is favorable they may experience "relative gratification." If it is unfavorable they may experience "relative deprivation" because their scope is limited to the immediate reference group instead of to nationwide social standards or to other group norms.

This result was replicated by means of the structural equation approach. (For the application of this method in test anxiety research see Hagtvet, 1983; Hodapp & Henneberger, 1983; Liepmann, Herrmann, & Otto, 1988; Schwarzer, 1983.) The school tracks were specified as a dummy variable (1 = high track, 0 = low track). Test anxiety was specified as a latent variable with two indicators, worry and emotionality, measured at five points in time. The structural model was specified as one independent latent variable (school tracks or reference groups) and five dependent latent variables (anxiety as a repeated construct).

When a structural equation approach (LISREL V; Jöreskog & Sörbom, 1983) was used, the model could not be fitted by the data because a direct impact of school tracks was found only at the first point in time. The respecified model (as shown in Fig. 3) obtained a chi-square of 204.33 (40 *df*). The goodness of fit index provided by the program was .79, the Tucker-Lewis coefficient .78, Bentler's delta .82, and the root mean square residual .065. Therefore, the fit may be regarded as being moderately satisfactory. The results show that there is a strong impact of group differences at the first point in time appearing as a direct causal effect (− .45). At later stages of the development there are only indirect effects of − .31, − .28, − .23, and − .18, respectively. This is a descending order of a reference group effect over time. It quantifies the convergence depicted in Figs. 1 and 2, this time at the level of a latent variable.

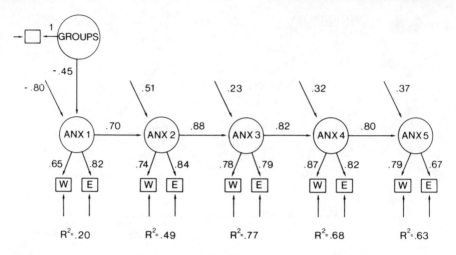

Figure 3 Structural equation model for the development of anxiety.

STUDY 2: TEST ANXIETY, SELF–RELATED COGNITIONS, AND CLASSROOM CLIMATE

Whereas the first study examined the objective school environment, the second dealt with the perceived environment or classroom climate in connection with certain self-related cognitions. Subjects in this study were from the same sample as before, but, in addition, students in the mid-track and in comprehensive schools were included ($N = 287$).

The relationship between test anxiety development and self-concept, self-awareness, and classroom climate was evaluated. Self-concept was assessed using a self-esteem scale (the German form of the Rosenberg Scale, 1979) and a self-concept of ability scale (Meyer, 1972). Self-awareness as a trait (self-consciousness) was assessed by two subscales, private and public self-consciousness (Fenigstein, Scheier, & Buss, 1975; German form by Jerusalem & Schwarzer, 1986). Classroom climate was measured with informal achievement pressure and anonymity scales. Self-concept was measured at the first two points in time, self-awareness at the fourth, and classroom climate at the fifth. A causal model was specified with cross-lagged relationships between self-concept and test anxiety. However, it had to be respecified, as is depicted in Fig. 4.

This final model obtained a chi-square of 426.5 (125 df). The goodness of fit index provided by the LISREL V program was .80, the Tucker-Lewis coefficient .84, Bentler's delta .83, and the root mean square residual .14.

These results may be satisfactory for preliminary interpretation. First, there was no causal relationship between self-concept and test anxiety, only a covariation. Self-awareness had considerable impact on test anxiety: The more the students were aware of themselves, the more they perceived themselves as being anxious. However, this is a controversial issue (see Carver & Scheier, 1984, 1986). The classroom climate also had a strong influence (.67) on anxiety at the last point in time. Those who perceived a great deal of achievement pressure and anonymity in school tended to be more anxious.

STUDY 3: TEST ANXIETY, CLASSROOM CLIMATE, AND TEACHER BEHAVIOR

The last study to be reported here is based on a sample of 808 students (400 female and 408 males) who attended either grade 5 or 6 and were between 10 and 12 years of age. They completed the questionnaires at two points in time. Variables chosen measured several aspects of perceived teacher behavior, classroom climate, and emotions. The following seven teacher behavior scales were used:

1. Reference Norm: Individualized teacher feedback;
2. Fairness: Perceived equity with respect to marks;
3. Support: Perceived individual assistance by teacher;
4. Acceptance: Liberal attitude of teacher, positive appraisals;
5. Relaxed Attitude: Teacher's calm handling of disturbances;
6. Sanctions: negative verbal reactions to students; and
7. Praise: Positive feedback, teacher's attention to student effort.

The Anonymity Scale was used as a classroom climate measure at both points in time. Emotions were assessed by scales for anxiety, dissatisfaction, self-efficacy, and helplessness. Test anxiety was measured by the TAI-G (Hodapp et al., 1982).

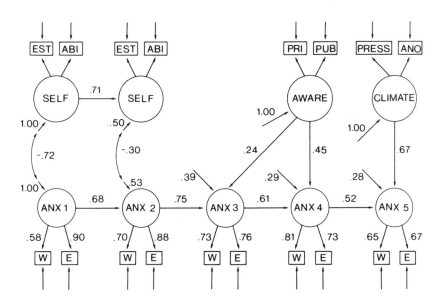

Figure 4 Structural equation model relating anxiety to self-related cognitions and classroom climate.

Table 1 Correlation Matrix of Observed Variables (Study III)

	Self-efficacy	Anonymity	Fairness	Relaxed attitude	Reference norm
Test anxiety	−.44	.38	−.26	−.20	−.22
Self-efficacy	—	−.33	.23	.29	.22
Anonymity	—	—	−.37	−.31	−.35
Fairness	—	—	—	.51	.35
Relaxed attitude	—	—	—	—	.30

Path Analysis with Observed Variables

The previous study dealt with the prediction of test anxiety using characteristics of the learning environment. This prediction is now elaborated as a causal model using the same variables as before.

How can test anxiety variance at point 2 be explained by some antecedents? The variables chosen as precursors were based on theory and on temporal or logical antecedence. It was assumed that self-related cognitions are both antecedents and ingredients of the anxiety experience (Carver & Scheier, 1984, 1986). Previous causal models dealing with this assumption were presented by C. Schwarzer and Cherkes-Julkowski (1982) and by Schwarzer, Jerusalem, and Schwarzer (1983).

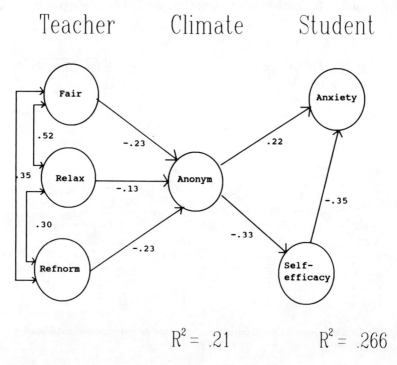

Figure 5 Path model for the impact of teacher behavior and classroom climate on anxiety.

Table 2 Path Analysis with Observed Variables: Decomposition of Causal
Effects (Study III)

From	Total	Direct	Indirect
Fairness	−.18	−.10	−.08
Relaxed attitude	−.07	.04	−.10
Reference norm	−.14	−.05	−.10
Anonymity	.31	.22	.08
Self-efficacy	−.34	−.35	0

Based on these models, the variable *self-efficacy* was used as one of the determinants of test anxiety.

Both anxiety and self-efficacy were specified as being directly determined by the classroom climate, and by all teacher variables indirectly. Classroom climate represented by *anonymity* was seen as a mediator variable connecting the teacher behavior characteristics (fairness, relaxed classroom management, individualized reference norm) with student's cognitions and emotions (self-efficacy and anxiety). The teacher and climate measures were collected at the first point in time. A path analysis for this causal model, based on the correlation matrix shown in Table 1, was computed.

The results are depicted in Fig. 5. The path analysis explains 27% of the anxiety variance. As can be seen, the climate is determined mainly by the perceived reference norm of the teacher. Classes with unfair and overreactive teachers have a high degree of anonymity, which may be reinforced if the classroom management is more tense than relaxed. As expected, a negative climate had a positive impact on test anxiety (.22), whereas high self-efficacy had a negative influence on

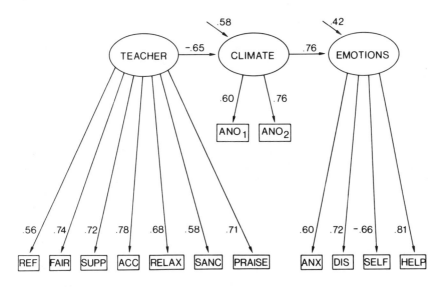

Figure 6 Structural equation model for the impact of teacher behavior and classroom climate on emotions.

test anxiety ($-.35$). In addition to these direct sources of variation, indirect effects have to be taken into account (see Table 2).

Using anxiety as the dependent variable, the direct and indirect effects (which add up to the total effect) of all precursors were decomposed. The three teacher variables had some indirect effects through the climate mediator on anxiety, but in the whole model they were rather remote or distal antecedents. They were too weak to directly determine test anxiety. The climate, however, can be seen as a rather strong situational precursor of anxiety. It provided an indirect effect (through self-efficacy) of .08, which adds up to a total effect of .31. This is a considerable influence of the perceived classroom context on anxiety, especially when taking into account that the time span between both variables is several months.

Path Analysis with Latent Variables

The approach mentioned above was extended to a multiple indicator model in order to consider more relevant variables simultaneously. The basic idea, supported by the results of the path analysis, was a three-step design starting with perceived teacher characteristics, which partly determine the classroom climate. The climate then represents the main cause of student emotions in school.

In order to identify these relationships, a structural equation approach using the LISREL V program was chosen. The causal model was specified in the following way. First, three latent dimensions were established: teacher characteristics, classroom climate, and student emotions. The first is an exogenous variable, the other two are endogenous. Emotions are expected to be caused by teacher characteristics and classroom climate; climate is primarily determined by teacher characteristics. These three dimensions were measured by multiple indicators. For the exogenous variable, the following seven observed variables were measured: individualized reference norm, fairness, support, acceptance, relaxed attitude, sanctions, and praise. All of these measures were collected at the first point in time (as described above). Classroom climate as the mediating dimension was indicated by the observed variable *anonymity,* which was measured at the first point in time and once more at the second. Student emotion as a latent dimension was indicated by four observed variables: anxiety, school dissatisfaction, self-efficacy, and helplessness, all measured at the second point in time.

This model was run by LISREL V, using maximum likelihood estimates, and obtained a good fit. All equations and loadings had significant estimates except one: There was no significant relationship between teacher characteristics and student emotions. Therefore, this causal path was set to zero. The respecified model obtained the same results. The run was then repeated, using unweighted least squares. The goodness of fit index was .99, the adjusted goodness of fit index was .98, and the root mean square residual was .047 (based on 709 observations). The standardized solution is given in Fig. 6.

As a proof of the validity, the two subsamples of girls and boys were run separately. Since there were no important differences between the samples, group-specific findings are not reported here.

CONCLUSION

In conclusion, the results of this study provide insight into the school socialization process. The development of student characteristics such as anxiety, dissatisfaction, self-efficacy, and helplessness depends on the perceived learning environment. Classroom climate itself is strongly influenced by perceived teacher characteristics. Most important is the finding that teacher characteristics do not have a direct influence on the student emotions, but only an indirect one ($-.49$). Further research should focus on the mediating role of classroom climate in school socialization.

These preliminary steps help to clarify the complex relationships involved in the development of trait test anxiety in academic settings. A macroperspective focusing on quasi-experimental field designs was intended. Similar results to those presented here were also found in previous studies (see Schwarzer et al., 1983, 1984; Schwarzer & Lange, 1983).

Test anxiety appears to be an important indicator of an individual's adaptation to the school environment, one's vulnerability toward potentially threatening academic demands, and one's belief in personal competence, self-efficacy, and coping resources. Test anxiety is therefore an important factor in school socialization and deserves to be considered in research on such processes.

REFERENCES

Asendorpf, J. (1984). Shyness, embarrassment, and self-presentation: A control theory approach. In R. Schwarzer (Ed.), *The self in anxiety, stress, and depression* (pp. 109–114). Amsterdam: North-Holland.

Bandura, A. (1977). Self-efficacy: Toward a unifying theory of behavioral change. *Psychological Review, 84,* 191–215.

Bandura, A. (1983). Self-efficacy determinants of anticipated fears and calamities. *Journal of Personality and Social Psychology, 45,* 464–469.

Bandura, A. (1986). *Social foundations of thought and action.* Englewood Cliffs: Prentice-Hall.

Bandura, A. (1988). Self efficacy conception of anxiety. *Anxiety Research. An International Journal, 1* (2), 77–98.

Bandura, A., & Cervone, D. (1983). Self-evaluative and self-efficacy mechanisms governing the motivational effects of goal systems. *Journal of Personality and Social Psychology, 45,* 1017–1028.

Buss, A. H. (1980). *Self-consciousness and social anxiety.* San Francisco: Freeman.

Buss, A. H. (1986). Two kinds of shyness. In R. Schwarzer (Ed.), *Self-related cognitions in anxiety and motivation* (pp. 65–76). Hillsdale, NJ: Erlbaum.

Carver, C. S., & Scheier, M. F. (1984). Self-focused attention in test anxiety: A general theory applied to a specific phenomenon. In H. M. van der Ploeg, R. Schwarzer, & C. D. Spielberger (Eds.), *Advances in test anxiety research* (Vol. 3, pp. 3–20). Hillsdale, NJ: Erlbaum.

Carver, C. S., & Scheier, M. F. (1986). Functional and dysfunctional responses to anxiety: The interaction between expectancies and self-focused attention. In R. Schwarzer (Ed.), *Self-related cognitions in anxiety and motivation* (pp. 111–142). Hillsdale, NJ: Erlbaum.

Carver, C. S., Scheier, M. F., & Klahr, D. (1987). Further explorations of a control-process model of test anxiety research. In R. Schwarzer, H. M. van der Ploeg, & C. D. Spielberger (Eds.), *Advances in test anxiety research* (Vol. 5, pp. 15–22). Lisse, The Netherlands: Swets & Zeitlinger.

Fenigstein, A., Scheier, M. F., & Buss, A. H. (1975). Public and private self-consciousness: Assessment and theory. *Journal of Consulting and Clinical Psychology, 43,* 522–527.

Hackford, D. (1983). *Theorie und Diagnostik sportbezogener Ängstlichkeit.* Köln, West Germany: Deutsche Sporthochschule.

Hagvet, K. V. (1983). A construct validation study of test anxiety: A discriminant validation of fear of failure, worry and emotionality. In R. Schwarzer, H. M. van der Ploeg, & C. D. Spielberger (Eds.), *Advances in test anxiety research* (Vol. 2, pp. 15-34). Hillsdale, NJ: Erlbaum.

Helmke, A. (1982). *Schulische Leistungsangst: Erscheinungsformen und Entstehungsbedingungen.* Unpublished dissertation, Universität Konstanz, West Germany.

Hodapp, V., & Henneberger, A. (1983). Test anxiety, study habits, and academic performance. In R. Schwarzer, H. M. van der Ploeg, & C. D. Spielberger (Eds.), *Advances in test anxiety research* (Vol. 2, pp. 119-127). Hillsdale, NJ: Erlbaum.

Hodapp, V., Laux, L., & Spielberger, C. D. (1982). Theorie und Messung der emotionalen und kognitiven Komponente der Prüfungsangst. *Zeitschrift für Differentielle und Diagnostische Psychologie, 3,* 169-184.

Hunsley, J., & Flessati, S. L. (1988). Gender and mathematics anxiety: The role of math-related experiences and opinions. *Anxiety Research. An International Journal, 1* (3) 215-224.

Jerusalem, M. (1984a). Reference group, learning environment and self-evaluations: A multi-dynamic analysis with latent variables. In R. Schwarzer (Ed.), *The self in anxiety, stress, and depression* (pp. 61-74). Amsterdam: North-Holland.

Jerusalem, M., (1984b). *Selbstbezogene Kognitionen in schulischen Bezugsgruppen. Eine Längsschnittstudie.* Berlin, West Germany: Freie Universität Berlin.

Jerusalem, M. & Schwarzer, R. (1986). Selbstaufmerksamkeit. In R. Schwarzer (Ed.), *Skalen zur Befindlichkeit und Persönlichkeit.* (Forschungsbericht 5, pp. 3-14). Berlin, West Germany: Freie Universität Berlin.

Jöreskog, K., & Sörbom, D. (1983). *LISREL V: Analysis of linear structural relationships by the method of maximum likelihood.* Chicago: International Educational Services.

Jones, W. H., & Briggs, S. R. (1984). The self-other discrepancy in social shyness. In R. Schwarzer (Ed.), *The self in anxiety, stress, and depression* (pp. 93-108). Amsterdam: North-Holland.

Krohne, H. W. (Ed.). (1985). *Angstbewältigung in Leistungssituationen.* Weinheim, West Germany: Edition Psychologie.

Lazarus, R. S., & Folkman, S. (1984). *Stress, appraisal, and coping.* New York: Springer-Verlag.

Levine, J. M. (1982). Social comparison and education. In J. M. Levine & M. C. Wang (Eds.), *Teacher and student perceptions: Implications for learning* (pp. 29-56). Hillsdale, NJ: Erlbaum.

Liepmann, D., Herrmann, C., & Otto., J. (1988). Anxiety and meta-cognitions: A structural analysis. *Anxiety Research. An International Journal, 1*(2) 151-161.

Meyer, W. U. (1972). *Überlegungen zur Konstruktion eines Fragebogens zur Erfassung von Selbstkonzepten der Begabung.* Bochum, West Germany: Ruhr-Universität.

Meyer, W. U. (1984). *Das Konzept von der eigenen Begabung.* Bern, Switzerland: Huber.

Ploeg, H. M. van der, Schwarzer, R., & Spielberger, C. D. (Eds.). (1983). *Advances in test anxiety research* (Vol. 2). Hillsdale, NJ: Erlbaum.

Ploeg, H. M. van der, Schwarzer, R., & Spielberger, C. D. (Eds.). (1984). *Advances in test anxiety research* (Vol. 3). Hillsdale, NJ: Erlbaum.

Ploeg, H. M. van der, Schwarzer, R., & Spielberger, C. D. (Eds.). (1985). *Advances in test anxiety research* (Vol. 4). Lisse, The Netherlands: Swets & Zeitlinger.

Rheinberg, F. (1980). *Leistungsbewertung und Lernmotivation.* Göttingen, West Germany: Hogrefe.

Richardson, F. C., & Woolfolk, R. L. (1980). Mathematics anxiety. In I. G. Sarason (Ed.)., *Test anxiety* (pp. 271-288). Hillsdale, NJ: Erlbaum.

Rosenberg, M. (1979). *Conceiving the self.* New York: Basic Books.

Sarason, I. G. (1980). Life stress, self-preoccupation, and social supports. In I. G. Sarason & C. D. Spielberger (Eds.), *Stress and anxiety* (Vol. 7, pp. 73-91).

Sarason, I. G. (1984). Test anxiety, worry, and cognitive interference. In R. Schwarzer (Ed.)., *Self-related cognitions in anxiety and motivation* (pp. 19-33). Hillsdale, NJ: Erlbaum.

Sarason, I. G., & Sarason, B. R. (Eds.). (1985). *Social Support: Theory, research and applications.* Dordrecht, The Netherlands: Martinus Nijhoff Publishers.

Schwarzer, C., & Cherkes-Julkowski, M. (1982). Determinants of test anxiety and helplessness. In R. Schwarzer, H. M. van der Ploeg, & C. D. Spielberger (Eds.)., *Advances in test anxiety research* (Vol. 1, pp. 33-43). Hillsdale, NJ: Erlbaum.

Schwarzer, R. (1983). Unterrichtsklima als Sozialisationsbedingung für Selbstkonzeptentwicklung. *Unterrichtswissenschaft, 11,* 129-148.

Schwarzer, R. (1984). Worry and emotionality as separate components in test anxiety. *International Review of Applied Psychology, 33,* 205-220.

Schwarzer, R. (1987). *Stress, Angst und Hilflosigkeit* (2d ed.). Stuttgart, West Germany: Kohlhammer.

Schwarzer, R., Jerusalem, M., & Faulhaber, J. (1984). Test anxiety development in West German schools: A structural equation analysis. In R. Schwarzer (Ed.), *The self in anxiety, stress, and depression* (pp. 171–180). Amsterdam: North-Holland.

Schwarzer, R., Jerusalem, M., & Schwarzer, C. (1983). Self-related and situation-related cognitions in test anxiety and helplessness: A longitudinal analysis with structural equations. In R. Schwarzer, H. M. van der Ploeg, & C. D. Spielberger (Eds.), *Advances in test anxiety research* (Vol. 2, pp. 35–43). Hillsdale, NJ: Erlbaum.

Schwarzer, R., & Lange, B. (1983). Test anxiety development from grade 5 to grade 10: A structural equation approach. In R. Schwarzer, H. M. van der Ploeg, & C. D. Spielberger (Eds.), *Advances in test anxiety research* (Vol. 2, pp. 147–157). Hillsdale, NJ: Erlbaum.

Schwarzer, R., & Leppin, A. (1988a). Social Support: The many faces of helpful social interactions. *International Journal of Educational Research, 2,* 333–345.

Schwarzer, R., & Leppin, A. (1988b). *Sozialer Rückhalt und Gesundheit: Eine Meta-Analyse.* Göttingen, West Germany: Hogrefe.

Schwarzer, R., Ploeg, H. M. van der, & Spielberger, C. D. (1982). Test anxiety: An overview of theory and research. In R. Schwarzer, H. M. van der Ploeg, & C. D. Spielberger (Eds.), *Advances in test anxiety research* (Vol. 1, pp. 3–9). Hillsdale, NJ: Erlbaum.

Schwarzer, R., Ploeg, H. M. van der, & Spielberger, C. D. (Eds.). (1982). *Advances in test anxiety research* (Vol. 1). Hillsdale, NJ: Erlbaum.

Schwarzer, R., Ploeg, H. M. van der, & Spielberger, C. D. (Eds.). (1987) *Advances in test anxiety research* (Vol. 5). Lisse, The Netherlands: Swets & Zeitlinger.

Schwarzer, R., Ploeg, H. M. van der, & Spielberger, C. D. (Eds.). (1989). *Advances in test anxiety research* (Vol. 6). Lisse, The Netherlands: Swets & Zeitlinger.

Schwarzer, R., & Quast, H.-H. (1985). Multidimensionality of the anxiety experience: Evidence for additional components. In H. M. van der Ploeg, R. Schwarzer, & C. D. Spielberger (Eds.), *Advances in test anxiety research* (Vol. 4, pp. 3–14). Lisse, The Netherlands: Swets & Zeitlinger.

Shavelson, R. J., & Marsh, H. W. (1986). On the structure of self-concept. In R. Schwarzer (Ed.)., *Self-related cognitions in anxiety and motivation* (pp. 305–330). Hillsdale, NJ: Erlbaum.

Spielberger, C. D. (1972a). Anxiety as an emotional state. In C. D. Spielberger (Ed.), *Anxiety: Current trends in theory and research* (Vol. 1, pp. 23–49). New York: Academic Press.

Spielberger, C. D. (1972b). Conceptual and methodological issues in anxiety research. In C. D. Spielberger (Ed.), *Anxiety: Current trends in theory and research* (Vol. 2, pp. 481–493). New York: Academic Press.

Spielberger, C. D. (1980) *Test Anxiety Inventory.* Palo Alto, CA: Consulting Psychologists Press.

Stephan, E., Fischer, M., & Stein, F. (1983). Self-related cognitions in test anxiety research: An empirical study and critical conclusions. In R. Schwarzer, H. M. van der Ploeg, & C. D. Spielberger (Eds.), *Advances in test anxiety research* (Vol. 2, pp. 45–66). Lisse, The Netherlands: Swets & Zeitlinger.

Suls, J. M., & Miller, R. L. (Eds.). (1977). *Social comparison processes.* New York: Wiley.

Weiner, B. (1986). *An attributional theory of motivation and emotion.* Berlin, West Germany: Springer-Verlag.

Wicklund, R. A. (1975). Objective self-awareness. In L. Berkowitz (Ed.), *Advances in experimental social psychology* (Vol. 8, pp. 233–275). New York, NY: Academic Press.

6

Learned Helplessness: Affective or Cognitive Disturbance?

Miroslaw Kofta and Grzegorz Sedek
University of Warsaw

Level of control has long been recognized as an important factor in theory and in research on stress and anxiety. Two major perspectives can be distinguished in the study of stress-control relationships. The first approaches control as a modifier of the impact of stressful events on anxiety, arousal level, and performance (Glass & Singer, 1972; Averill, 1973; Miller, 1980). Past research strongly suggests that behavioral control over aversive stimuli, that is, effective coping, reduces stress. Conversely, lack of control increases stress, imposing additional psychophysiological costs on the organism (Miller, 1980).

A second approach to stress-control relationships assumes that lack of control itself is the fundamental factor in eliciting stress reactions, regardless of whether control is concerned with aversive or nonaversive events. This assumption is central for the theory of anxiety proposed by Mandler and Watson (1966) and for Lazarus' influential conception of psychological stress. According to Lazarus' (1966; Lazarus & Launier, 1978) two-stage theory of stress, an imbalance between situational requirements (e.g., task demands) and available personal resources (e.g., intellectual capacity) decreases personal control over outcomes. This creates psychological threat which motivates an individual to engage in a variety of coping activities, ranging from direct action to defensive reappraisals. Coping behavior, as described in Lazarus' theory, is essentially an attempt to regain control over the environment via direct action or, if such control is no longer possible, to maintain illusory control via defensive mechanisms. This general approach has been further elaborated by other stress theorists (e.g., McGrath, 1970; Cox, 1978; Schulz & Schönpflug, 1982; Lundberg, 1982).

The impact of loss of control on motivation, affect, and behavior has also become the focus of considerable interest in learned helplessness research. On the basis of behavioral research with animals, Seligman (1975) hypothesized that an organism exposed to a series of uncontrollable outcomes (called helplessness training) learns that outcomes are unrelated to responses. Consequently, expectation of

Preparation of this article was supported by the Central Research Program (CPBP. 0802) of the Polish Academy of Sciences. The authors are grateful to Grace Shugar for checking the English.

no control is formed. Once established, the no control expectation interferes with learning new response-outcome contingencies in subsequent controllable situations, undermines motivation to initiate activity, and produces a depressed mood. Recent developments in learned helplessness theory based on research with human beings have identified additional cognitive mediators that supplement Seligman's model, such as attributions for loss of control (cf., Abramson, Seligman & Teasdale, 1978; Miller & Seligman, 1982). However, such refinements do not alter the theory's core assumption that the cognitive, affective, and motivational deficits in learned helplessness result from the generalization to new situations of no-control expectations learned during helplessness training.

INTEGRATION OF THEORY ON STRESS AND ANXIETY AND LEARNED HELPLESSNESS/DEPRESSION

Following a period of independent development of theory and research on stress and anxiety and learned helplessness/depression, there is now considerable effort to integrate these theories. We will briefly consider two attempts to integrate these fields, one in the clinical domain and the other in the area of individual differences in achievement-related stress.

The belief that negative outcomes are uncontrollable is now seen as a common etiological assumption in theories of clinical anxiety and depression (Garber, Miller, & Abramson, 1980). This belief is held responsible for lowered self-confidence and the behavioral disruption observed in anxiety and depression. In the model proposed by Garber et al. (1980), when anticipation of loss of control is associated with uncertainty about the occurrence of a negative event, anxiety will develop. However, when loss of control is accompanied by strong expectation of the occurrence of undesirable events (i.e., feelings of hopelessness), depression is likely to emerge.

Theoretical integration and empirical convergence of research on stress and learned helplessness is also reflected in recent work by Dweck and Wortman (1982). They compared the cognitive, emotional, and behavioral responses to failure of subjects who were low in achievement need, or high in test anxiety or learned helplessness. An extensive review of the research literature revealed a number of common features in these three personality syndromes, including high self-focus, low self-esteem, low aspiration level, attribution of failure to internal causes, negative attitudes toward problem-solving tasks, and a tendency to atypical expectancy shift following failure experiences. Similarity in the psychological reactions to failure across the three personality types further suggested that the seemingly diverse conceptual frameworks provided by theories of achievement motivation, test anxiety, and learned helplessness are concerned with similar psychological phenomena.

Attempts to integrate stress and anxiety theory with learned helplessness theory are perhaps most cogently reflected in the increased popularity of an affective model of human helplessness. From this perspective, the main causal factor in helplessness is the failure to attain a desirable goal, rather than the independence of behavior and outcome per se. Repeated failure triggers mediating processes, usually described in affective-motivational terms, which produce the behavioral symptoms of learned helplessness. Within this affective model, it is not necessary to postulate any specific cognitive mechanism (e.g., expectation of no control) to account for the emergence of helplessness symptoms. Repeated failure is identified as the source of helplessness (affective factor), and the impact of failure on subsequent performance is explained in affective-motivational terms. This impact has been explained differently, however, depending on the theoretical approach: Helplessness deficits have been attributed to the arousal of egotism motivation (Frankel & Snyder, 1978), evaluation anxiety (Coyne, Metalsky, & Lavelle, 1980), frustration-produced behavioral persistence (Boyd, 1982), or the emergence of degenerated intention (Kuhl, 1984). To illustrate these affective conceptualizations of human helplessness, the egotism explanation is briefly presented (Frankel & Snyder, 1978; Snyder, Smoller, Strenta, & Frankel, 1981).

Repeated failure is a chief aspect of helplessness training for egotism theory. Because failure on easy problems strongly implies lack of problem-solving ability, such failure poses a threat to self-esteem. In order to cope with ego threat, people engage in a least-effort strategy during the test phase of a typical learned helplessness study. They simply try half-heartedly. Thus, those who use this coping strategy can attribute present failure (and, by implication, previous failures) to lack of effort, and this also allows them to deny the ego-threatening attribution of lack of ability. Since impaired task performance is attributable to low motivation, the least-effort strategy is instrumental in maintaining positive self-esteem.

Within the egotism model of helplessness, uncontrollability, which is a central concept of learned helplessness theory (Seligman, 1975; Maier & Seligman, 1976), is generally ignored. The same might be said of the other affective theories mentioned above: In all of these theories helplessness is seen merely as a manifestation of a more general phenomenon (e.g., human attributional egotism, anxiety arousal, or degenerated intention), rather than as a unique phenomenon with idiosyncratic features that requires a special explanation.

An Information-Processing Model of Helplessness

In this chapter, we will endeavor to show that affective theories of human helplessness, as outlined above, do not satisfactorily explain the phenomenon. To this end, findings from our research on learned helplessness (Kofta & Sedek, 1985, 1989; Sedek & Kofta, 1988) will be presented to support a theoretical model in which helplessness is conceptualized in cognitive terms as a disturbance of action-related information processing. From an information processing perspective the essential feature of a state of helplessness is the difficulty experienced by an individual in generating adequate action programs in new problem situations.

A problem situation arises when an individual has an initial set of relevant information (problem data) and some idea about what he or she wants to achieve (goal). Broadly speaking, the subject's task is to fill the gap between the data associated with a problem and the desirable goal, that is to generate a meaningful action program leading to goal attainment (problem solution). To do this, the task data must be processed in such a way as to produce and verify reasonable hypotheses about the problem solution. To solve a new problem, some form of productive (creative) information-processing is necessary. In the context of this model, helpless people demonstrate a problem-solving deficit, in that they cannot adequately integrate task data into reasonable solution ideas. Consequently, the process of developing an effective action program is seriously undermined. This approach does not deny the existence of the affective component in helplessness. Rather, its origin and dynamics are explained within a cognitive framework.

In contrast to the affective theoretical position previously described, the information processing model does *not* consider emotional reactions as causal factors in the induction of helplessness; the *causal status* of emotions in helplessness is questioned, not their presence in the helplessness syndrome. This chapter reports findings from our research program that pertain to the focal issue: Is helplessness primarily an affective or cognitive phenomenon? Before considering this research, the main assumptions of the information-processing model of learned helplessness are briefly reviewed (Kofta & Sedek, 1985; Kofta & Sedek, 1986; Sedek & Kofta, 1988).

The information-processing model assumes that helplessness results from repeatedly experienced inability to integrate task information into reasonable hypotheses that generate an appropriate solution. Two factors must operate together to produce helplessness: (1) The subject must be sequentially exposed to internally inconsistent task information, that is, must be presented with an insoluble problem of a sequential type; and (2) he or she must be cognitively involved, that is, ready to encode and transform task information in order to produce and verify hypotheses about its solution. Cognitive involvement implies a considerable amount of cognitive effort and selective attention, encoding and analysis of relevant data, and a process of hypothesis formation and testing. Given the joint operation of these factors, a person is likely to engage in prolonged and inefficient (futile) cognitive work. Despite persistent effort, the subject is unable to achieve a meaningful solution because the task is insoluble. This futile cognitive activity cannot continue indefinitely. After a period of intense effort, a state of *cognitive exhaustion* is experienced, characterized primarily by difficulty in getting involved in new problem-solving activity and a tendency to avoid cognitive exertion.

Instead of a creative approach to new problems, persons who experience cognitive exhaustion are likely to resort to previously developed, rather automatic ways of thinking and acting. These ineffective problem-solving activities are considered as directly responsible for the helplessness-related performance deficits that are observed on new tasks in the test phase of learned helplessness studies. Helplessness deficits are expected to be most detrimental on relatively complex tasks which require a more creative form of information integration, such as the production of new ideas and/or different kinds of behavior. In contrast, no deterioration would be expected on relatively simple tasks, or on complicated tasks that are soluble by means of previously developed, ready-to-use algorithmic procedures.

RESEARCH ON THE ANTECEDENTS
OF HELPLESSNESS

The studies reported in this section address two questions. First, the role of repeated failure in the development of helplessness is evaluated. Second, the effects of exposure to inconsistent task information on subsequent task performance are analyzed.

Repeated Failure: Relevant or Irrelevant to the Emergence of Helplessness?

Two studies (Kofta & Sedek, 1989) primarily concerned with the egotism explanation of helplessness are described in which the implications of the findings transcend the issue of the adequacy of this theoretical model.* In these experiments, high school students were given five discrimination problems with instructions suggesting that, by paying attention to experimenter feedback, they would be able to solve the problem. On each problem, the participant was shown 10 pairs of geometrical figures in sequence, and asked to designate one figure in each pair as correct for a given trial. Experimental Group 1 (noncontingent feedback, no failure) was given 50% "correct" and 50% "incorrect" feedback in a predetermined random order. Thus, feedback was independent of response. Moreover, subjects were not informed about the results they obtained on the consecutive problems. Experimental Group 2 (noncontingent feedback, repeated failure) was exposed to identically structured noncontingent feedback, but the task was presented as indicative of general intelligence, and after the completion of each problem the subjects were told they had failed. The Control Group received contingent feedback and was veridically informed about the outcome for each consecutive problem.

In the test phase, the participants responded to a soluble avoidance learning task. In a series of trails, they could learn how to avoid, or at least to escape, the aversive stimulus (unpleasant noise delivered through earphone). Mean latency of the coping response (avoidance or escape) and number of failures to avoid were the indices of performance level. Table 1 shows that exposure to noncontingent feedback (Group 1) resulted in performance deficits. Comparisons between Group 1 and the Control Group revealed statistically significant effects for each performance measure in both studies. In contrast, repeated failure did not exert any noticeable effect on subsequent performance. Comparisons of Groups 1 and 2 did not yield any significant differences in either study.

*In describing these and subsequent studies, detailed information about the research design and the experimental results are not reported. A complete description of the studies may be found in Kofta and Sedek (1989) and Sedek and Kofta (1988).

Table 1   Effects of Helplessness Training on Performance

Dependent measure	Control	Group 1 (without failures)	Group 2 (with failures)
Study 1			
Latency (s)	7.15	8.83	9.13
Number of failures to avoid	19.1	26.9	26.2
Study 2			
Latency (s)	7.42	9.32	9.13
Number of failures to avoid	19.2	27.3	25.6

The obtained results are clearly inconsistent with the hypothesis that the experience of repeated failure accounted for the emergence of helplessness. On one hand, it was demonstrated that mere exposure to noncontingent feedback (information on outcome eliminated) resulted in typical helplessness symptoms during performance. On the other hand, supplementing noncontingent feedback during problem performance with ego-involving information about repeated failure did not produce even the slightest change in subsequent performance. Additional analyses showed the effectiveness of the failure-manipulation with ego involvement. In both studies, Group 2 subjects perceived failure in the training phase more strongly, and felt more depressed at the end of the study, than subjects in the other experimental conditions. Subjects who were told they had failed also reported the highest level of self-dissatisfaction with their performance. This effect was revealed in the second study.

Although difficult to explain within the conceptual framework of affective models, the data pattern is readily interpretable from the information-processing perspective which ascribes the effects of noncontingent feedback alone to the fact that this produces a stream of self-contradictory task information. Given cognitive involvement (guaranteed in this procedure by the presentation of the training task as soluble), the information inconsistency made it impossible to derive and verify any meaningful solution idea. This led to futile cognitive work, followed by cognitive exhaustion. The information-processing model further suggests that the subject's knowledge about the final outcome was not directly relevant to the process of developing a useful action program because this information came too late, that is, after action completion. Since difficulties with action programming are considered here to be specifically responsible for helplessness, even repeated failure might appear unrelated to the subsequent helplessness symptoms.

Information Inconsistency and Helplessness Symptoms

While the findings discussed above support the information-processing model, the data cannot be unequivocally interpreted as evidence of its validity. The studies that follow attempted to provide a more direct test of the informational explanation of helplessness in terms of the inconsistency of task information as a critical component of helplessness training. If this approach is valid, then sequential exposure to inconsistent information should result in helplessness symptoms, even for subjects who do not emit overt responses and receive no evaluative feedback with respect to performance.

To further test the information processing theory of helplessness, a new form of helplessness training was developed, called *informational helplessness training*. This procedure was essentially a variation of the insoluble discrimination task utilized in previous studies (e.g., Hiroto & Seligman, 1975; Kofta & Sedek, 1989), which involved sequential exposure to self-contradictory task-related information. However, in contrast to traditional insoluble discrimination tasks, the subjects were *not* behaviorally engaged, that is, they were not required to emit any overt responses, and the experimenter's evaluative behavior was minimized. Instead of positive or negative evaluations of the participants' behavior, only messages about the successively presented geometric figures were given. Information about final outcome on consecutive problems was also eliminated, making this

yes   no   yes   no

Figure 1 Helplessness training through exposure to inconsistent task-information. Each figure had five dimensions; shape (triangle vs. circle), size (big vs. small), surface (plain vs. striped), position of the line (top vs. bottom), and the size of the letter *r* (big vs. small).

aspect of the procedure similar to the task employed in Experimental Group 1 of the studies described earlier.

During helplessness training, the subject's task was to discover the designated feature of a figure (see Fig. 1) by utilizing cues provided by experimenter in a series of trials in which confusing information about the discrimination problem was given. Each problem consisted of 8 or 12 presentations (trials) of figures similar to Fig. 1. For each problem, the subject was shown a sequence of figures (one in each trial) and given inconsistent information about whether the figure contained the feature to be discovered or not. In an exemplary series of trials, the value of each figure feature was paired with one supportive (yes) and one discrepant (no) experimenter information response. Operationally, this procedure creates a maximum level of inconsistency because, for every problem, the specified feature was paired with the same proportions of supportive and discrepant feedback given by the experimenter.

In the test phase of the study, all subjects performed an avoidance learning task. There were two performance measures: Mean latency of coping (avoidance or escape) and number of trials followed by four successful avoidance responses (avoidance criteria). The results of three independent studies (Sedek & Kofta, 1988) revealed a highly consistent pattern: Mere exposure to self-contradictory task information led to substantial performance deficits on both measures. This effect was demonstrated for a 4-problem training task in the first study of the series, in which the control group performed on a similar but soluble discrimination task, see Table 1, Study 1 (Sedek & Kofta, 1988, Experiment 1).

In the second study in this series (Sedek & Kofta, 1988, Experiment 4), for which the results are also reported in Table 2, a significant learned helplessness effect was obtained with an extended informational training task, consisting of 5 problems. Since the control group in this study did not undergo any treatment in the first phase of the study, the demonstrated effect could not be attributed to possible improvement in the control condition. The results of a third study (Sedek

Table 2 Effects of Informational Helplessness Training on Performance

Dependent measure	Study 1		Study 2	
	Control	Helplessness training	Control	Helplessness training
Latency (s)	6.30	7.44	7.78	10.17
Avoidance criterion	27.94	37.22	22.7	31.0

& Kofta, 1988, Experiment 3), which are reported in Table 3, showed that only lengthy exposure to inconsistent task information resulted in manifest helplessness symptoms. The differences between the experimental and control conditions in Study 3 were significant under 5-problem training, but were not significant for 2- and 3-problem training.

In all three studies, it should be noted that information about final failure, which is usually given as feedback on insoluble discrimination tasks in the laboratory, was totally excluded. Thus, the results support the findings in previous studies that the presence or absence of failure information during training is unrelated to the subsequent emergence of helplessness symptoms. However, they tell us something more: The learned helplessness effect can be obtained even when the evaluative component (noncontingent feedback) is totally eliminated from the procedure. Overall, the findings provide direct empirical support for the hypothesis that task information inconsistency is a crucial factor in helplessness training.

MEDIATING PROCESS IN LEARNED HELPLESSNESS

The findings described above identify a purely cognitive factor—inconsistency of task information during problem solving—as the main source of helplessness symptoms. However, the possibility cannot be excluded that affective factors may also influence the internal mediating processes that link exposure to inconsistent information to subsequent performance impairment. Theoretical questions concerning the nature of these mediating processes are far more difficult to clarify than questions about the situational antecedents. Therefore, the findings that are reported here are best seen as suggestive rather than as indisputable evidence of the role of cognitive mediation in helplessness.

Cognitive, Motivational, and Affective Components of Exposure to Informational Helplessness Training

In order to gain insight into the nature of the mediating process in learned helplessness, subjective reports of cognitive functioning during helplessness training were obtained. Participants in two studies (Sedek & Kofta, 1988, Experiments 1 and 2), were asked to respond to a brief 4-item questionnaire after the comple-

Table 3   Effects of Informational Helplessness Training on Performance for Problems of Different Length

Dependent measure	Control condition			Helplessness training		
	2 Problems	3 Problems	5 Problems	2 Problems	3 Problems	5 Problems
Latency (s)	8.66	8.22	7.23	8.48	8.80	9.93
Avoidance criterion	12.62	12.50	11.50	12.96	13.75	16.00

tion of each problem. In the first study, half of the subjects were exposed to informational helplessness training, while the other half performed on a similar but soluble discrimination. In the second study, failure feedback was manipulated independently of task information consistency: Half of the subjects in each condition were repeatedly informed about failure, while the other half were given no information about final outcome.

Table 4 presents the results based on self-reports of cognitive functioning in the two studies. The subjects exposed to informational helplessness training in Study 1 reported that problem solving was "going hard"; they also indicated that they were uncertain whether the hypotheses that they finally produced were right or wrong. Consequently, their expectation (prediction) of subsequent success on the next problem also decreased. Moreover, in both studies intellectual activity appeared to be less pleasant for the helplessness trained than for the controls, and the helplessness trained subjects in Study 2 reported that they were making little progress in understanding the problem despite prolonged contact with it (knowledge increment index in Study 2). All the reported effects were highly significant. Thus, the findings of impaired processing of task-relevant information during exposure to helplessness training support the informational model.

The post-experimental questionnaires (Sedek & Kofta, 1988, Experiments 1, 2, and 3) also revealed that, during exposure to the informational helplessness training, subjects experienced difficulty in concentration, and in generating solution ideas. They also reported feelings of "empty-headedness" and variety of negative emotions, including anxiety, anger, sadness, and self-dissatisfaction (see Sedek & Kofta, 1988, Experiment 2). Because reports of discouragement during training would also seem to reflect a decline in motivation, the findings do not rule out the possibility that affective-motivational dysfunction significantly contributed to the development of the helplessness symptoms.

What Accounts for Helplessness Deficits?

Fortunately, findings in the three independent learned helplessness experiments reviewed above help to clarify this question. The results indicated that preexposure to inconsistent task-information during training resulted in typical helplessness performance deficits in the test phase of these studies (see "Antecedents Helplessness"). The critical question that will now be considered is: Can these deficits be attributed to motivational or affective mediators, or not?

Hypothesis of Motivation Decline

If the behavioral impairment in learned helplessness studies is due to a decrease in motivation produced by uncontrollable preexposure, symptoms of motivational decline should be manifested in the test phase of these studies. Accordingly, a behavioral measure of motivational deficit was included in one of our investigations (Sedek & Kofta, 1988, Experiment 1). Before beginning to work on the avoidance learning task, the subjects performed a much simpler escape-learning task in which they rather quickly and easily mastered the escape response. As can be seen in Table 5, helplessness trained and control subjects did not differ on the escape criterion measure.

Table 4 Subjective Measures Obtained During Informational Helplessness Training

			Study 2			
	Study 1		Control		Helplessness training	
Dependent measure	Control	Helplessness training	No fail.	Failure	No fail.	Failure
Hardgoing	2.60	5.73	0.00	0.00	0.00	0.00
Certainty of good performance	5.75	2.27	4.63	3.44	2.60	1.83
Predictions of future performance	4.94	2.78	4.47	3.83	3.50	2.64
Pleasantness	4.71	3.23	4.71	4.16	4.40	3.54
Knowledge increment	0.00	0.00	4.10	3.52	3.17	2.46

The measure of latency of escape in this study might be interpreted as a "pure" index of motivational deficit, that is, a decreased tendency to initiate voluntary responses (Seligman, 1975). But inspection of Table 5 reveals no slowdown in responding among subjects pretrained with insoluble problems. It may be recalled that these same subjects showed gross impairment on a more complex avoidance-learning task (see Table 2). Clearly, these findings do not support the hypothesis that a simple motivational deficit is responsible for the performance deficits of helplessness-trained subjects.

Verbal reports obtained in another study (Sedek & Kofta, 1988, Experiment 4) also failed to support the motivational deficit hypothesis. Despite substantial performance deficits during the test phase of the study, subjects exposed to helplessness training did not differ from controls on subjective measures of motivation such as self-reports of interest in the task and feelings of discouragement. Thus, the decline in motivation during helplessness training reported in the previous section did not generalize to subsequent tasks. When the subjective data are taken into account, the hypothesis of motivation decline does not appear to offer a satisfactory explanation of the performance deficits of helplessness trained subjects.

Hypothesis of Negative Affect

Another feasible explanation that must be considered is that helplessness deficits result from the affective processes that are triggered by helplessness training.

Table 5 Effects of Informational Helplessness Training on Easy Talk Performance (Escape Learning)

Dependent measure	Control	Helplessness training
Escape criterion	1.56	1.15
Escape latency (s)	7.73	7.67

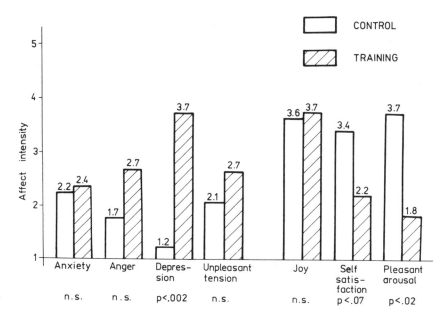

Figure 2 Effects of informational helplessness training on affective measures in the test phase.

Affective change, specifically the emergence of depressive feelings, has long been recognized as an important component of the state (Abramson, Seligman, & Teasdale, 1978; Peterson & Seligman, 1984; Seligman, 1975). Therefore, it is possible that such affective processes are directly responsible for performance deterioration during the test phase of helplessness studies.

An interesting affective reaction to uncontrollability noted in the research previously reviewed was the arousal of negative emotions as a direct response to informational helplessness training (Sedek & Kofta, 1988, Experiment 2). However, when similar measures were collected at the end of the test phase, the whole picture changed markedly (Sedek & Kofta, 1988, Experiment 4): There was a profound increase in feelings of depression accompanied by a decrease in pleasant arousal, but no significant effects were found for other affect measures, as can be seen in Fig. 2.

In order to evaluate whether depressive feelings could account for the performance deficits in the test phase of this study, analyses of covariance (ANCOVA) of the latency and avoidance measures were carried out, with depression as the covariate. After controlling for the effects of depression, the informational helplessness training still had a significant effect on performance. Therefore, the arousal of depressive affect following exposure to the uncontrollable situation did not fully explain the observed performance impairment.

Hypothesis of Cognitive Deterioration

The findings in the learned helplessness studies that have been examined do not support theoretical explanations that attribute the observed performance deficits in these studies to motivational decline or negative affect. There are indications, however, that the processes responsible for these deficits were essentially cognitive in character. In a recent study, subjects exposed to uncontrollable training tasks were questioned concerning their cognitive functioning during the test phase (Sedek & Kofta, 1988, Experiment 4). They reported experiencing difficulty in thinking (it "was hard going"), in getting involved and energized to solve the test task, in focusing their attention on the task, and in evaluating the solutions that came to mind. In keeping with the informational model of learned helplessness, these findings suggest that cognitive disengagement and impediments in selecting and effectively processing task-relevant information emerged after exposure to helplessness training. Given the inadequacy of the motivational and/or affective explanations of helplessness deficits that have been noted, cognitive dysfunction seems to provide the best explanation of the nature of the mediating process in human helplessness. Obviously, a more direct evaluation of cognitive mediation is necessary to establish the validity of predictions from the informational model.

INFORMATIONAL MODEL
AND LEARNED HELPLESSNESS THEORY

The bulk of this chapter has been devoted to examining affective interpretations of learned helplessness. These models assume a critical role of failure, while tending to ignore the influence of uncontrollability per se in the development of helplessness symptoms. On the basis of the available research evidence, however, the affective models do not provide a satisfactory explanation of the learned helplessness phenomenon. The relationship between an informational-processing model and Seligman's (1975) original theory of learned helplessness will now be addressed.

The informational model may be viewed, essentially, as a reformulation of Seligman's (1975) original learned helplessness theory (Maier & Seligman, 1976). Both approaches point to the uncontrollability of events, rather than failure as the critical factor that produces the helplessness effect. Both models also assume that the development of helplessness symptoms results from the exposure of an organism to a problem that it cannot manage. However, only the information-processing model emphasizes the cognitive aspects of an unmanageable situation in which a person is unable to reconcile inconsistent environmental information via covert or overt activity.

Although the informational and classical models both regard the core symptom of human helplessness as cognitive in nature rather than affective or motivational, an important divergence occurs with respect to the nature of the postulated mediation. In the classical view, an expectation of no control—emerging after helplessness training—accounts for helplessness symptoms. In contrast, the informational-processing view points to cognitive exhaustion as the critical mediating process that emerges from prolonged and inefficient cognitive work during helplessness training. Thus, the two models propose quite different conceptions of the nature of the cognitive deficit: The classical approach emphasizes the decreased expectation of response-outcome covariation, whereas the informational approach views helplessness symptoms as resulting from cognitive disengagement, with accompanying deficits in productive problem solving.

Research Implications of the Information Processing Model

The information processing model provides a framework for the integration of learned helplessness theory with a more general theory of action that considers how people organize complex units of behavior, and how they react to difficulties experienced in achieving outcomes they seek to control (see Frese & Sabini, 1985). This model proposes that the repeated experience of difficulty in the generation of action programs results in an altered psychological state in which the production of new action programs is seriously hampered. In emphasizing the cognitive nature of the difficulties encountered by helpless people, the model suggests that helplessness develops as a consequence of impaired processing of task-relevant information, and that subsequent performance deficits reflect qualitative changes in the mode of processing. In essence, productive cognitive involvement is replaced by cognitive disengagement, with increased reliance on automatic forms of information processing.

Despite years of study, knowledge about how an uncontrollable situation is encoded and represented and the nature of this representation is extremely limited. Current knowledge about the performance deficits produced by helplessness is also very limited due, in part, to the tendency among researchers to use an extremely narrow range of tasks in learned helplessness research. For example, a substantial portion of the studies reported in this area have used only one type of problem—the anagram task. Moreover, researchers have focused on performance outcomes and not on the processes leading to problem solution. Process tracing methodology, increasingly popular in research on decision-making and thinking (e.g., Simon, 1978; Svenson, 1979), is virtually absent in the learned helplessness literature.

The information-processing view provides a suitable conceptual context for dealing with these and related problems, using methods of study that are elaborated in cognitive psychology. This framework may also help to overcome present limitations in helplessness research by redirecting attention to the cognitive processes involved in task performance. By framing helplessness in an information-processing perspective, relevant conceptual developments in cognitive psychology may be more readily applied and assimilated.

Informational Helplessness and Stress

The findings reported in this chapter indicate that helplessness phenomena cannot be adequately explained in terms of the emotional or motivational response to repeated failure. Our results point out the inadequacy of theories that conceptualize helplessness training as merely a stressful event that evokes an emotional response. Does this mean that helplessness cannot be encompassed within the broader framework of stress theory? We think that it can, but such an integration may require extension and modification of the concept of stress. In particular, the concept of a stressful situation or event may require further refinement in order to distinguish between two aspects of stressful events, threat value and uncontrollability.

Situations that provoke stress because they directly endanger the fulfillment of human needs have high threat value, that is, they produce an affective overload that is difficult for the organism to manage. Aversive physical stimuli, threats to positive self-esteem, and signs of social rejection all fall into this broad category. Psychologists tend to identify stressful events with this particular class of situations (Laux & Vossel, 1982; McGrath, 1982). Indeed, on the basis of a systematic review of a large number of current stress studies, McGrath (1982) concluded that physical threat, ego threat, and interpersonal threat are the basic types of stressor conditions that have been hitherto investigated in this literature.

There is another broad class of stress-provoking situations that deserves equal attention. The main source of psychological strain in these situations is lack of control, an organism's inability to develop and/or execute an adequate action program to control desirable or undesirable life events. Although such situations may evoke emotional tension that leads to performance deficits, the basic feature that differentiates these situations from the stressful conditions identified by McGrath is the cognitive character of the experienced problem. The organism cannot integrate environmental information received during exposure to uncontrollable events into meaningful cognitive procedures (action programs) that lead to goal attainment. It is this cognitive problem, not just its affective accompaniment, that has a high probability of becoming a major source of behavioral disruption.

The notion that difficulty with action control may be a powerful source of psychological stress, which constituted the core assumption of Mandler and Watson's (1966) theory of anxiety, has recently become increasingly popular (e.g., Glass & Singer, 1972; Schönpflug, 1982; Schulz & Schönpflug, 1982). Lundberg (1982) has proposed that the mental effort invested in task activity be considered as a third important type of coping, along with the direct action tendencies and defensive reappraisals proposed by Lazarus (1966). According to Lundberg (1982), physiological stress in uncontrollable situations may have more adverse effects on health than the stress experienced in controllable situations.

The distinction between threat value (affective overload) and uncontrollability (cognitive overload) can be applied directly to the phenomenon of learned helplessness. The experience of failure belongs to the first class of stressful events: It has high threat value due to its implications for social evaluation and self-esteem. But even repeated failure, experienced on the training problems, appears to be unrelated to the emergence of helplessness symptoms. The critical factor in helplessness seems to be of the second type (cognitive overload), which results from the interaction of cognitive involvement and exposure to inconsistent task information. Threat value and uncontrollability appear to be relatively independent aspects of stressful situations that should be examined in a comprehensive conceptual framework in research on personal control and emotional stress. Such analyses may ultimately lead to new theoretical formulations that will help to integrate these two broad research domains.

SUMMARY

This chapter attempted to clarify the affective and cognitive determinants of helplessness phenomena. The findings obtained in a series of experimental studies argue against purely affective explanations of helplessness, suggesting instead that cognitive factors are critical in the development of helplessness symptoms. An informational helplessness model was proposed which attributes helplessness symptoms to an individual's inability to integrate inconsistent task data into a meaningful solution that is repeatedly experienced during helplessness training. In examining the relationship between helplessness phenomena and stress reactions, it was suggested that threat and uncontrollability should be carefully distinguished as different aspects of stressful events. Threat produces affective overload whereas uncontrollability produces cognitive overload. Human helplessness was attributed to the operation of the latter, but not the former, aspects of stressful events.

REFERENCES

Abramson, L. Y., Seligman, M. E. P., & Teasdale, J. (1978). Learned helplessness in humans: Critique and reformulation. *Journal of Abnormal Psychology, 87*, 49–74.

Averill, J. R. (1973). Personal control over aversive stimuli and its relationship to stress. *Psychological Bulletin, 80*, 286–303.

Boyd, T. L. (1982). Learned helplessness in humans: A frustration-produced response pattern. *Journal of Personality and Social Psychology, 42*, 738–752.

Cox, T. (1978). *Stress.* London: Macmillan.

Coyne, J. C., Metalsky, G. I., & Lavelle, T. L. (1980). Learned helplessness as experimenter-induced failure and its alleviation with attentional redeployment. *Journal of Abnormal Psychology, 89*, 350–357.

Dweck, C. S., & Wortman, C. B. (1982). Learned helplessness, anxiety, and achievement motivation: Neglected parallels in cognitive, affective, and coping responses. In H. W. Krohen and L. Laux (Eds.), *Achievement, stress, and anxiety.* Washington, DC: Hemisphere.

Frankel, A., & Snyder, M. L. (1978). Poor performance following unsolvable problems: Learned helplessness or egotism? *Journal of Personality and Social Psychology, 36*, 1415–1424.

Frese, M., & Sabini, J. (Eds.). (1985). *Goal-directed behavior.* Hillsdale, NJ: Erlbaum.

Garber, J., Miller, S. M., & Abramson, L. Y. (1980). On the distinction between anxiety and depression: Perceived control, certainty, and probability of goal attainment. In J. Garber & M. E. P. Seligman (Eds.), *Human helplessness: theory and applications.* New York: Academic Press.

Glass, D. C., & Singer, J. E. (1972). *Urban stress: Experiments on noise and social stressors.* New York: Academic Press.

Hiroto, D. S., & Seligman, M. E. P. (1975). Generality of learned helplessness in man. *Journal of Personality and Social Psychology, 31*, 311–327.

Kofta, M. (1977). Kontrola psychologiczna nad otoczeniem: Ramy pojeciowe teorii (Psychological control over the environment: The conceptual framework of the theory). *Psychologia Wychowawcza, 2*, 150–167.

Kofta, M., & Sedek, G. (1985). From behavioral to informational helplessness. In J. J. Sanchez-Sosa (Ed.), *Health and clinical psychology.* Amsterdam: North-Holland.

Kofta, M., & Sedek, G. (1989). Repeated failure: A source of helplessness, or a factor irrelevant to its emergence? *Journal of Experimental Psychology: General, 118*, 5–12.

Kofta, M., & Sedek, G. (1986, April). *Learned helplessness in humans: An information-processing view.* Paper presented at the Polish-American Conference on Self and social involvement, Princeton. NJ.

Kuhl, J. (1984). Volitional aspects of achievement motivation and learned helplessness: Toward a comprehensive theory of action control. In B. A. Maher (Ed.), *Progress of Experimental Personality Research.* New York: Academic Press.

Lazarus, R. S. (1966). *Psychological stress and the coping process.* New York: McGraw-Hill.

Lazarus, R. S., & Launier, R. (1978). Stress-related transactions between person and environment. In L. A. Pervin, & M. Lewis (Eds.), *Perspectives in interactional psychology.* New York: Plenum Press.

Laux, L., & Vossel, G. (1982). Theoretical and methodological issues in achievement-related stress and anxiety research. In H. W. Krohen, & L. Laux (Eds.), *Achievement, stress, and anxiety.* Washington, DC: Hemisphere.

Lundberg, U. (1982). Psychophysiological aspects of performance and adjustment to stress. In H. W. Krohne, & L. Laux (Eds.), *Achievement, stress, and anxiety.* Washington, DC: Hemisphere.

Maier, S. F., & Seligman, M. E. P. (1976). Learned helplessness: Theory and evidence. *Journal of Experimental Psychology: General, 105,* 3–46.

Mandler, G., & Watson, D. L. (1966). Anxiety and the interruption of behavior. In C. D. Spielberger (Ed.), *Anxiety and behavior.* New York: Academic Press.

McGrath, J. E. (1970). A conceptual formulation for research on stress. In J. E. McGrath (Ed.), *Social and psychological factors in stress.* New York: Holt, Rinehart and Winston.

McGrath, J. E. (1982). Methodological problems in research on stress. In H. W. Krohne, & L. Laux (Eds.), *Achievement, stress, and anxiety.* Washington, DC: Hemisphere.

Miller, S. M. (1980). Why having control reduces stress: If I can stop the roller coaster, I don't want to get off. In J. Garber & M. E. P. Seligman, (Eds.), *Human helplessness: Theory and applications.* New York: Academic Press.

Miller, S. M., & Seligman, M. E. P. (1982). The reformulated model of helplessness and depression: Evidence and theory. In R. J. Neufeld (Ed.), *Psychological stress and psychopathology.* New York: McGraw-Hill.

Peterson, C., & Seligman, M. E. P. (1984). Causal explanations as a risk factor for depression: Theory and evidence. *Psychological Review, 91,* 347–374.

Schönpflug, W. (1982). Aspiration level and causal attribution under noise stimulation. In H. W. Krohne, & L. Laux (Eds.), *Achievement, stress, and anxiety.* Washington, DC: Hemisphere.

Schulz, P., & Schönpflug, W. (1982). Regulatory activity during states of stress. In H. W. Krohne, & L. Laux (Eds.), *Achievement, stress, and anxiety.* Washington, DC: Hemisphere.

Seligman, M. E. P. (1975) *Helplessness: On depression, development, and death.* San Francisco: Freeman.

Sedek, G., & Kofta, M. (1988). *When cognitive exertion does not yield cognitive gain: Towards an informational explanation of learned helplessness.* Unpublished manuscript.

Simon, H. A. (1978). Information-processing theory of human problem solving. In W. K. Estes (Ed.), *Handbook of learning and cognitive processes* (Vol. 5). Hillsdale, NJ: Erlbaum.

Snyder, M. L., Smoller, B., Strenta, A., & Frankel, A. (1981). A comparison of egotism, negativity, and learned helplessness explanations for poor performance after unsolvable problems. *Journal of Personality and Social Psychology, 40,* 24–30.

Svenson, O. (1979). Process description of decision making. *Organizational Behavior and Human Performance, 23,* 86–112.

7

Stress and Anxiety in a Fast Developing African Country: Zaire

Hugo F. Dries
State University of Ghent

The belief that social and cultural change always leads to some emotional difficulties has been widespread in anthropological and psychiatric literature. In general, the arguments have been that social disorganization, cultural stress, or communal crises act as mediating variables between the variables of social change and *acculturative stress*. This latter term has been employed by Berry (1970, 1978, 1980a,b; Berry & Annis, 1974 a,b) as a general term for referring to those individual states and behaviors that are mildly pathological and disruptive, including those problems of mental health and psychosomatic symptoms so often observed during social change.

This catastrophic, pessimistic view of culture change was primarily associated with and inspired by anthropoligical functionalism. According to this school, individual psychological equilibrium could only be guaranteed in slowly evolving cultures. All external, abrupt change creates incalculable situations, disturbs the existing equilibrium, and is catastrophic for the psychic life of the individual. Mair, who did distinguished fieldwork in Buganda in the 1930s, saw culture contact as inevitably pathological. The primitive society in question might already be pathological at the zero point of contact and change, but further penetration could only dislocate a going system which satisfied needs at least "with a reasonable degree of general satisfaction" (1934). Since that time, and especially after the Second World War, this pessimistic interpretation largely dominated the field of psychological acculturation: the terminology concerning concomitants and consequences of acculturative change and modernization was predominantly drawn on psycho- and sociopathological literature. Terms used in this context are: *frustration* (Doob, 1960, 1967), *identity confusion* (Wintrob & Sindell, 1972), *marginality* (Barry, 1970; Smith, 1974), *personal discomfort* (Cawte, 1968), *lack of personal adjustment* (Chance, 1965), *no psychosocial adjustment* (Barger, 1977), *loss of cognitive control* (Spindler, 1968), *functional breakdown* (Murphy, 1973), *deviant behavior* (Sesay, 1977), *depersonalization* (Kizerbo, 1963), and *homeless mind* (Berger, Berger & Kellner, 1973).

In the same state of mind, to be or to become modern was associated with mental disorder (Eisenstadt, 1966; Wolff & Goodell, 1968; Jaco, 1970; Toffler, 1970), aggressiveness and violence (Borg, 1971) and with stress in general (Lapiere, 1965; Constantini, 1973; Lauer & Thomas, 1976).

On the other hand, some anthropologists and social psychologists accentuated the fact that people generally seem pleased with the change. When Lerner made a study of the process of becoming modern in six countries in the Middle East, he found that the urbanized and modernized man was far more likely to rate himself "happy" than his country cousin. It was those who were loyal to traditional ways and value who were dissatisfied: "those who embody tradition are most unhappy while those seeking to forsake it become increasingly happy in the measure that they succeed" (Lerner, 1958, p. 101).

One of the champions of the optimistic interpretation of culture change undoubtedly is Musgrove, who wrote that "learning to be modern seems generally to have brought satisfaction, pleasure and fulfillment" (1982, p. 108).

Our point of view is that a catastrophic interpretation of culture change is particularly a result of Eurocentric, theoretical considerations. Indeed, if one opposes the characteristics of traditional man and his culture to the requirements of a modern or modernizing society, the adaptation to this changes fatally must get the individual into serious trouble. Such a theoretical approach clearly underrates the adaptative power of the populations concerned.

The rare optimistic interpretations, however, seem even more speculative than the previously reviewed pessimistic standpoints. As far as these interpretations are based on empirical research, they can only be accepted with some reserve, since the methodological purity of these investigations seems to be open to question.

Adaptation to change can give rise to stress and frustration, as well as to pleasure and satisfaction. All depends on the concrete situation. Even in a single society, the processes of acculturation and modernization can draw forth positive and negative psychological responses in different segments of social life. This depends, among other factors, on the compatibility or incompatibility between old and new, traditional and modern, culture traits. We studied this problem in an investigation of modernization in Zaire.

METHOD

Sample

Cross-cultural research implies a number of specific problems as to which subjects have to be involved. Besides a sometimes disturbing lack of sensitivity to this problem, there is an alarming shortage of reliable demographic, statistical information about third world countries (Paden, 1970; Piche, 1976).

The choice of independent variables, relevant for particular research, also needs to involve precautions: too soon we meet an automatic transfer from Western situations to cultural areas in which certain variables do not appear in the same form, or in the case of formal similarities, they differ totally with respect to function or content (Davidson & Thompson, 1980). In most cases such abuses are the consequence of a superficial knowledge and of an insufficient integration in the culture studied (Irvine, 1968). Finally, it needs to be pointed out that there are a number of cultural, administrative, political, or ideological imponderabilities which impose restrictions on researchers in the choice of their samples.

Our sample was composed of 275 adult males from the province of Shaba (formerly Katanga): 70 university students, 70 clerks, 70 workmen, and a group of 65 farmers from Sambwa, a medium-sized village, 40 km south of Lubumbashi, on the right bank of the river Kafubu and predominantly inhabited by members of the Lamba tribe. The average age of our subjects was 29.7 years.

Differentiation according to the educational level shows that the farmers are predominantly illiterate (57%); the workmen are mainly on the level of primary education (50%) and the majority of the clerks have a secondary education (77%). The student group consisted of university-trained subjects of different levels.

Finally, the environment of the subjects (urban-rural) has been taken into account. As for this variable, not only the actual dwelling-place has been taken in account, since (especially in Africa) someone who stays in town is not necessarily a townsman. One of the most important factors, which is at the basis of an urban experience and its psychological concomitants, is the relative duration of the stay in an urban environment. For the total sample, this differentiation showed as follows:

1. U: more than 3/4 of the life spent in town.
2. Ur: between 3/4 and 1/2 of the life spent in town.
3. uR: between 3/4 and 1/2 of the life spent in rural environment.
4. R: more than 3/4 of the life spent in rural environment.

Respectively, 99, 49, 62, and 65 subjects have been placed in these subgroups.

The subjects were split up into two quantitatively equivalent subgroups: 100 moderns and 100 traditionals. The first subgroup contains mainly urban (U, Ur) students (higher education) and employees (higher education or more than 4 years of secondary education). The second subgroup, conventionally called the "traditionals," consists of farmers and workmen who have had almost no education (at the most 6 years of primary education). It is obvious that the farmers in this group are rurals, the workmen belong to the subgroup uR. (In this text, we restrict ourselves to a few generalizations. For more detailed information, see Dries, 1983, 1984a, 1984b).

Instrument

The main instrument of our research was a series of 14 pictures, inspired by the Thematic Apperception Test (TAT). Recognition that pictures and story-telling are highly culture-bound and strongly influenced by situational factors has led to countless adaptations of the TAT. Special forms of the TAT have been developed for a wide variety of different cultures, ages, male and female heterosexuals and homosexuals, and different occupational groups. The effective design and administration of picture stimuli techniques for particular cultures has been developed to a high degree (Holtzman, 1980). However, the most marked trend in the use of the TAT-like picture stimuli techniques is the use of such devices to elicit responses that are relevant to sociopsychological and cultural questions, rather than responses primarily relevant to personality. TAT-like pictures have been found useful in the investigation of attitudes, values, beliefs, and status-role behavior of many sorts, all viewed as social and cultural phenomena, rather than as expressions of individual or group psychodynamics. When picture stimuli are directed to this more social level of inquiry, they are designed to maximize the dramatic impact of realism, as ideally would be provided by a photograph, and they avoid the "projective" ambiguity that is characteristic of traditional TAT-pictures.

Investigators who have employed these techniques have shown unusual regard for research design and objectivity (Edgerton, 1973). Representative realizations in this field can be found in the publications of Parker (1964), Goldschmidt and Edgerton (1961), and Spindler and Spindler (1965).

Our research with thematic pictures started with a series of seven pictures. Based on acculturation research in Africa, on discussions with colleagues and students, and on my own experiences in the field of African social change, I described seven different situations. They were graphically executed as black and white drawings by Mulumba, a Zairian artist. That series was used in an important preliminary investigation on samples of secondary and university students. The results of that preliminary investigation (elaborated in several dissertations) forces me to an adaptation of the first picture-series: new themes, improved identification modalities, and differentiation of situations. The definitive test consists of 14 thematic pictures, containing the following situations and themes:

1. Scholarization of a rural girl: in front, an adolescent girl, some classbooks in her hand. In the rear, a woodcutting man, a woman pounding maize, and two little children. Rural environment (huts, banana tree, etc.).

2. Industrial versus traditional economic activities: a man in a workshop, sitting on a machine. He looks through the window, watching some traditional agricultural laborers. Behind in the workshop, a well-dressed man and two other workmen.

3. A townsman in a rural environment: a modern-dressed man with a briefcase in his hand, standing in a traditional African village. Several villagers (men, women, and children), in different postures observe the "stranger."

4. Biomedicine versus ethnomedicine: a hospital room, with a man in the sickbed, surrounded by a physician (with stethoscope and hypodermic syringe), a nurse, and a nun. The right side of the picture shows a witch doctor in his hut, manipulating magic objects.

5. Family solidarity: a man, two bags in his hands, approaches a small house. In front of the house, a family (man, woman, three children) is watching him.

6. Polygamous family structure: a man, hand in hand with a young, modern-dressed woman, looks at a more traditional looking woman with a child on her back, standing in front of a hut.

7. Villager in an urban environment: an elderly barefoot man (manifestly a villager) walking in a modern city (buildings, cars, etc.).

8. Sorcery and magic: a sorcerer, kneeling on a leopard skin, handling magic objects. Opposite to the sorcerer, a manifestly shabby man.

9. Priorities in consumption: a man, some notes in his hand, facing a bar and a food store.

10. Loneliness: a young, shabby man, sitting in a hut on a tree stump. Outside, two boys playing football.

Figure 1 A townsman in a rural environment.

11. Death: a young dead man, lying on the floor of a modern room. Two men and two women weep for him.

12. Generation conflict: two men, an old one and a young one. They are disputing.

13. Authority: two police officers check a citizen. In the background there are houses, a car, and a man.

14. Partner choice: an elderly man presents a young girl to a boy, and says to him: "this is the girl I did choose for you, my son". Rural environment.

Procedure

The subjects were tested by five competent collaborators, students in anthropology. Sensitive to the problem of culture change from their studies, they were especially prepared to become familiar with the employed techniques by theoretical instruction, model testing, probe testing, and discussion. Testing took place in French (most of the students and clerks) and in Swahili (most of the workmen).

Figure 2 Biomedicine versus ethnomedicine.

The rurals reacted in their own language (Cilamba). All protocols were translated as literally as possible in French.

The test instructions were also translated into these languages. For each picture the subject was invited to produce a story, in which he indicated what happened on the picture, what had happened before, and how the story would finish. The experimenters limited their interventions to encouragements and stimulations, without giving suggestions to the subject. Only in the case where the subject limited himself to a description of the picture did the experimenter insist on story telling.

The data presented and discussed in this report result from content analysis (optimism–pessimism, aggressiveness) and thematic analysis characteristics of the produced stories).

The *content variables* relate to semantic aspects of the reactions and accentuate attitudes and motivations involved. One of the content variables included in our analysis is the degree of optimism and pessimism of the produced stories. Every story was quoted with relation to its emotional tone on a five-point scale, going from extremely pessimistic reactions, dominated by stress and anxiety, to very optimistic ones. To adjust the scores (from 1 to 5 points), we used the following scale:

1. 1 point: very pessimistic, sadness, despair, loneliness, failure, death, illness, boredom, accident, and misfortune.

2. 2 points: pessimistic, displeasure, resentment, fatigue, suspicion, and negative prospects.

3. 3 points: nonemotional situations, equilibrium between positive and negative emotions, and routine activities.

4. 4 points: optimism, hope, hopeful prospects, and optimistic aspirations.

5. 5 points: very optimistic, success, health, gladness, satisfaction, happiness, and wealth.

The results of this quotation are presented in Table 1.

Another content variable studied, is the degree of aggressiveness. This degree was adjusted according to the following criteria:

1. 1 point: no aggressiveness.
2. 2 points: aggressive action without specific orientation; symbolic, innocent aggressiveness.
3. 3 points: oriented oral aggressiveness, challenge, disapproval, accusation.
4. 4 points: aggressive actions with a specific orientation, beating, fighting, and hurting.
5. 5 points: aggressive action with a fatal result; sadism, homicide, divorce, and bewitchment.

The aggressive levels of the produced stories are presented in Table 2.

The *thematic analysis,* is based on procedures used in the analysis of open questionnaires, and more particularly on categorization of reactions and on classification of analogical contents (Bardin, 1977).

Table 1   Optimism–Pessimism: Number of Stories Per Score

					Score									
	1		2		3		4		5		Mean			
						Subgroup								
Picture number	Mod	Trad	Mod	Trad	Mod	Trad	Mod	Trad	Mod	Trad	Mod	Trad	$F(1.198)$	p
1	6	2	50	24	22	35	21	22	2	17	2.61	3.28	22.45	.001
2	5	8	50	14	41	56	4	17	–	5	2.44	2.97	22.15	.001
3	2	–	32	19	23	27	32	39	11	15	3.18	3.50	4.93	.05
4	3	13	35	12	29	27	33	45	–	3	2.92	3.13	2.20	N.S.
5	8	3	71	17	16	29	3	28	2	23	2.20	3.51	98.21	.001
6	16	7	50	38	20	38	9	9	5	8	2.37	2.73	6.32	.05
7	28	16	30	30	28	19	13	24	1	11	2.29	2.84	11.17	.01
8	2	3	18	20	20	30	56	45	4	2	3.42	3.23	2.23	N.S.
9	9	19	23	28	60	30	8	20	–	3	2.67	2.60	0.27	N.S.
10	37	45	37	29	11	18	15	8	–	–	2.04	1.89	1.11	N.S.
11	65	51	23	30	8	15	4	4	–	–	1.51	1.72	3.14	N.S.
12	12	15	79	54	6	13	3	14	–	4	2.00	2.38	10.55	.01
13	4	9	55	35	33	40	8	16	–	–	2.45	2.63	2.63	N.S.
14	10	2	73	35	15	20	2	27	–	16	2.09	3.20	75.21	.001
Total	207	193	626	385	332	397	211	318	24	107	2.44	2.83	68.52	.001

Table 2 Aggressiveness: Number of Stories Per Score

Picture number	Score													
	1		2		3		4		5		Mean			
	Subgroup													
	Mod	Trad	Mod	Trad	Mod	Trad	Mod	Trad	Mod	Trad	Mod	Trad	$F(1.198)$	p
1	44	77	11	9	41	14	2	–	2	–	2.07	1.37	29.98	.001
2	35	74	23	10	38	14	4	2	–	–	2.11	1.44	29.16	.001
3	56	72	22	17	20	11	2	–	–	–	1.68	1.39	6.96	.01
4	61	76	4	7	21	2	13	10	1	5	1.89	1.61	2.68	N.S.
5	18	77	21	11	53	9	5	2	3	1	2.54	1.39	84.67	.01
6	29	42	8	26	31	27	17	4	15	1	2.81	1.96	24.56	.001
7	83	76	7	7	7	6	1	11	2	–	1.32	1.52	2.35	N.S.
8	75	58	5	27	–	4	18	7	2	4	1.67	1.72	0.09	N.S.
9	92	67	3	12	3	14	2	6	–	1	1.15	1.62	16.78	.001
10	76	77	11	9	8	10	5	4	–	–	1.42	1.41	0.01	N.S.
11	57	57	4	12	8	4	21	18	10	9	2.23	2.10	0.37	N.S.
12	4	19	3	16	80	52	10	11	3	2	3.05	2.61	14.04	.001
13	13	15	20	36	61	45	4	3	2	1	2.62	2.39	3.87	.05
14	8	48	3	15	72	32	12	4	5	1	3.03	1.95	67.27	.001
Total	651	835	145	214	443	244	116	82	45	25	2.11	1.75	57.86	.001

RESULTS

Content Variables

Optimism–Pessimism

The results show a clear preponderance of optimistic reactions in the more traditional group. For eight pictures we find significant differences between the two subgroups, and in all these cases, traditionals produce more optimistic stories than moderns (see Table 1). Without wanting to go further into the too often stereotyped description of the optimism of Africans, we do point out that an engagement into the modernizing society and a partial interiorization of its rules lead to tensions and frustrations which, in the group that is becoming modern, are necessarily projected in a number of pessimistically experienced situations. It is striking that the most important differences between the two subgroups are noted in the areas that are complicated by the modern attitudes of life and it is there that conflicts arise with the tradition. This is clearly the case for pictures 5 and 14. The family solidarity creates enormous problems for the modernizing African. On the one hand, he feels committed to the strength of his traditional values, and on the other hand, material and other circumstances prevent him from actualizing these values.

In the traditional context, the "partner choice" which was more or less forced or oriented by the family was not felt to be frustrating. Yet, in this case, the modern attitudes of life lead to extremely ambivalent situations, with frustrating competition between the need for a personal choice and the securing fidelity to the tradition.

Aggressiveness

In general, we find that modern Zairians apparently have more aggressive attitudes and reactions than their traditional brothers (see Table 2). Moderns produce the most aggressive reactions to pictures 5, 6, 12, 13, and 14. It is worth mentioning that four of these pictures directly relate to family life. This phenomenon possibly refers to an interiorization or a desocialization of aggressiveness, resulting from the social repression and social depreciation of aggressiveness in traditional Bantu societies (Erny, 1972; Maquet, 1967). Aggressive character of these situations will be partially related to the fact that our subjects are males, who in many cases can only realize their authority, power, and dignity in a family environment, in which they find compensation for the frustrations, stress, and anxiety they experience in the quickly and incoherently changing African societies.

Striking too is the high aggressiveness level in the reactions to picture 11 (death). Death, which in our society is predominantly associated with grief, often evokes, in a context of magical interpretation, very aggressive reactions in Bantu cultures. In magical thinking, death is rarely interpreted as a natural phenomenon. Except in the case of old age, one dies by magical intervention of others. Such conceptions naturally lead to aggressive reactions to the supposedly responsible individuals or groups.

The most important differences between the two subgroups are found on pictures 5 and 14. These divergent reaction-patterns could be explained by the fact that both pictures concern situations that were perfectly integrated in the traditional way of life. The incompatibility of family solidarity and traditional partner choice with the changed society places the modernized individual in a very delicate position and frequently brings him to aggressive attitudes and reactions.

Thematic Variables

Scholarization of a Rural Girl (Picture 1)

In the stories of the moderns, we find more girls who continue their scholarization against the will of their parents. Conflict and stress dominate these situations. In more than 40% of the stories of moderns, we find a conflict between the girl and her parents. In the traditionals' stories, conflict occurs only in 15% of the reactions.

Industrial versus Traditional Economic Activities (Picture 2)

It is striking that we find no significant differences between the reactions of moderns and traditionals. Almost 50% of both subgroups prefer a traditional activity, especially for reasons of freedom, and by the fact that the salary for industrial work is hardly at the survival minimum. This picture puts down at the same time the obstinate view as if Africans would be blindly enthusiastic for every form of modern work. Beyond material and financial aspects, moderns stress with surprising emphasis the psychological factors which make modern activities unattractive.

Stress, frustration, antitraditional human relations, and imposed work rhythm are the most mentioned sources of displeasure (62% of the negative characteristics of modern work given by the modern subgroup).

A Townsman in a Rural Environment (Picture 3)

This picture shows an important alienation from the rural environment and from traditional culture. Moderns and traditionals each live in different worlds, behave differently, and they become more and more aware of these differences. This frequently leads to mutual misunderstanding, frustration, and stress, especially on the side of the moderns. More than 40% of the stories produced by the moderns characterize the confrontation between rural and urban Africans as a negative experience; in the stories of the traditionals, we only find 15% of such reactions.

Biomedicine versus Ethnomedicine (Picture 4)

Both subgroups, but moderns more than traditionals (respectively 95% and 74%), prefer biomedicine to ethnomedicine. In the two groups we find typical syncretic reactions: after a treatment in the hospital, one goes to visit the medicine man, since modern scientific medicine can only treat the external symptoms of the disease. The real origin of illness is magic, and can only be approached by a traditional healer.

Family Solidarity (Picture 5)

The traditional value of mutual help between the members of an extended family is degraded by modernization to an unilateral parasitism, in this sense that the urban members of the family are supposed to provide financial help for their rural relatives. This creates enormous problems, both for the rurals, who stay unsatisfied, and for the citizens, who feel themselves exploited by this traditional value. More than 90% of the moderns tell a story which refers to a negative reception of the visitor (vs. 35% of the traditionals).

Polygamous Family Structure (Picture 6)

Polygamy (or more exactly polygyny) was the traditional African family structure. Acculturation and modernization have profoundly disturbed this structure, especially through the influence of Christianization and urbanization. Nonetheless, the situation remains very ambiguous, and becomes extremely stressful, because almost all men continue to see plural marriage as an ideal, but this ideal becomes more and more difficult to realize. The progressive emancipation of the African girls and women further complicates this situation. The reactions on picture 6 clearly indicate the crisis African marriage goes through. Almost 75% of the moderns interpret the portrayed situation in terms of conflict and dispute. The traditional subgroup, on the contrary, refers to problems in the family in only 30% of the stories.

Villager in an Urban Environment (Picture 7)

What could be remarked on picture 3 (a townsman in a rural environment) is also valid for this situation. The villager gets lost in the city, literally as well as psychologically. A first contact with the town is a very terrifying and stressful experience for many Africans (more than 60% for both subgroups). For a townsman, rural population becomes more and more a real out-group, in spite of the persisting covering clan structures and tribal ties. The formation of new urban subcultures is attended with the creation of stereotyped characterizations of the others. In the townsman's eyes, rural are dirty, naive, mistrusting, greedy figures. The villagers describe citizens as showy, indifferent, and selfish.

Magic and Sorcery (Picture 8)

Magic and sorcery still occupy a central place in modern Africa, and are firmly integrated in the daily life of modern Africans. The reasons to make appeal to these forces are very divergent. On the one hand, the more traditional situations persist: disease, family problems, problems of hunting and fishing. On the other hand, the sorcerer is contacted for help in case of unemployment, school problems, and he can help a football team win an important match. Partially, this magic world view is for the African an important source of security, because it offers him a satisfying explanation of the phenomena, and gives him the idea that he can solve all kinds of problems in this way. Yet, it also creates a permanent state of latent anxiety, since he can always become a victim of sorcery.

Priorities in Consumption (Picture 9)

How shall the man on picture 9 spend his money: by buying food, or by drinking a bottle of beer and having a good time with one of the nice girls at the bar? Consumption patterns often lead to enormous problems due to the manipulation of money. African culture is hardly anticipatory, and often the salary of the month is used up in a few days. Yet, moderns seem to have adapted more realistic consumption patterns. In more than 50% of their stories the man in the picture spent his money exclusively to buy food (traditionals: 22%).

Loneliness (Picture 10)

Modern and traditional Africans interpret this situation differently. For the traditionals, the melancholy of the portrayed person is predominantly explained by sickness or by a specific socioethnic situation (67%). The moderns, on the contrary, refer to their material problems (76%). In the first place, they apprehend unemployment. It is striking that in their stories unemployment is neither brought about by conjunctural nor structural lack of work, but as a result of dismissal. The reasons for dismissal are predominantly situated in the victim himself, and in his problematic adaptation to modern professional activities. Other financial problems also result from the well-known acculturative stumbling blocks.

Death (Picture 11)

To die was and still is for the African a magical phenomenon. More than 85% of all our subjects, moderns as well as traditionals, put the deceased in a magical framework. One dies because magical forces kill. It is clear that such an attitude is frequently at the origin of stress and anxiety.

Generation Conflict (Picture 12)

Generation gaps and conflicts are quite universal phenomena. Especially in quickly developing cultures, the problem becomes catastrophic because the distance between generations increases spectacularly. The lack of mutual comprehension and the reactive attitudes of the younger generation often create very stressful relationships. Like all other forms of behavior, relations between generations are largely influenced by culture. Generation conflict in Africa seems to be dominated by a social dimension: the reputation of the group (family, clan, etc.). That social background of conflict is present with moderns as well as with traditionals, but the latter more often comply with the remarks of the father: 60% of their stories revolve on obedience to the father (moderns: less than 10%).

Authority (Picture 13)

In contrast to traditional authority, modern administration and authority are cold, anonymous and often incomprehensible for modernizing Africans. The confrontation with a police officer is always a potentially dangerous and terrifying event. The stories on picture 13 clearly show that traditional reaction patterns are no longer functional. The traditionals particularly suffer from the confrontation with modern authority: only 39% of their stories have a happy ending (moderns 65%).

Partner Choice (Picture 14)

Modern young Africans, more and more want to choose their partner on their own. Traditionally it was the father or the family who arranged marriage. In quite 90% of the stories of the modern subgroup, this forced-partner choice creates a conflict situation between the boy and his father. The traditionals generally identify this picture as a normal, neutral situation.

DISCUSSION

We did find more stress, frustration, anxiety, and aggressiveness in modern than in traditional Africans. Although the reactions of our subjects do not urge us to pathological interpretations, modernization often faces Africans with serious psychological problems. This was clearly manifested by the more aggressive and more pessimistic nature of the reactions of the modern subgroup: their global mean scores were significantly higher than those of the traditionals. Thematic analysis also confirmed these findings.

Yet interpretation of the results must be done very carefully. The stimuli we presented related to contrasts between traditional and modern African culture, and the moderns are much more involved in these contrasts. Therefore, it is normal that their reactions were more explicitly aggressive and pessimistic. In other words, modern Africans are obliged to take a view of the changing culture with which they are confronted, as well as of the tradition that still makes demands on them. In this respect, the traditionals are in a more comfortable situation: their way of life remains oriented to traditional norms and values; the confrontation with modern culture is very dilapidated and they do not have to engage in a new style of life.

This is clearly the case in a number of situations. Picture 14 (partner choice), for instance, depicts a situation that corresponds perfectly to the traditional norms, but is contested by modernization. For the traditionals, this situation does not pose any problem and it does not imply conflicts in their daily life. The modern African, however, finds himself faced with a very delicate choice: according to his status as modern man, he is required to choose his own partner, but such a choice often gives rise to conflicts with his family. The aggressiveness, stress, and pessimism that characterize this situation should not be regarded as intrinsic personality traits of modern Africans. On the contrary, they inevitably accompany conflict and compromise.

Theoretically, the modernization of society puts an enormous psychological pressure upon the African individual: his traditionally inculturated and socialized personality cannot effectively react to the requirements of his modified society, but at the same time, the confrontation with modernity opens new perspectives, satisfies the fundamental human need for exploration, and enables an optimal actualization of behavioral creativity.

Sometimes, one compares the situation of the modernizing individual with puberty. Indeed, both situations entail a difficulty. But, as the unilateral accentuation of the crises in puberty is partially a fiction of developmental psychologists (Bandura, 1964), the question is raised whether frustration and anxiety (characterizing the processes of acculturation and modernization) do not find their origin in the minds of anthropologists and cross-cultural psychologists.

In a number of cases, stories of moderns evidence a high adaptation level to modern situations and problems. In spite of their often precarious financial and material situation, consumption behavior (Picture 9) of the moderns is apparently so purified by urban experience that they are infrequent victims of the classic acculturative monetary dangers. In the traditionals' stories, we find more indications of thoughtlessness and of a lack of farsighted money manipulation.

Relations with modern authority (concreted in Picture 13) arise in modern Africa in a specific manner. Formally, this authority is modernly structured and organized, but in reality it does not appear to function in such a way, and it largely remains traditionally oriented. Based on classic modern attitudes, effective adaptation to this hybrid institution is quite difficult. The way modern or modernizing Africans face authority does not seem very orthodox from an eurocentric point of view, but it actually works in these specific circumstances.

CONCLUSIONS

The image of the modern African as it is expressed in the results of our research is rather chaotic. It is characterized by coexistence of divergent and apparently incompatible forms of action and reaction, and seemingly forms a catalogue of all possible psychological consequences of acculturation. It consists of both purely traditional and purely modern elements, as well as a more dominating syncretic combination of these basic forms. That mixture shapes the African personality. In this context, terms such as *chaotic, incompatible,* and *disintegration* have a very ethnocentric connotation. So-called "incompatible" behaviors, found in an efficiently functioning personality, can hardly be seen as incompatible!

Methodologically, psychological research in non-Western cultures remains a delicate issue. Most instruments and techniques of our psychological machinery are not directly useful in cross-cultural research, particularly when the subjects are traditionals or illiterates. "Objective" methods often provide very subjective, superficial information. When one asks an African if he believes in magic and sorcery, chances for a positive answer are small. Yet in a story about illness or misfortune, magic regularly plays a fundamental role.

The lack of adaptation to non-Western situations is not limited to methodology. Even most of the basic psychological concepts must be overhauled in the light of third world data. Terms such as *personality, individual, integration, normality, activity, efficiency, intelligence,* and *pathology,* become extremely relative in a cross-cultural context.

All this implies that the results of our research (and of all cross-cultural research) must be interpreted very prudently. It is beyond doubt, however, that modern Africans are neither (and will probably never be) comfortable copies of the Westerners, nor defenseless victims of their acculturated society. Despite serious adaptative difficulties and problems, they succeed with startling plasticity in developing original behavior patterns, which enable them to face pragmatically a syncretic, complex reality.

REFERENCES

Bandura, A. (1964). The stormy decade: fact or fiction. *Psychology in Schools, 1,* 224–231.
Bardin, L. (1977). *L'analyse du contenu.* Paris: P.U.F.
Barger, W. K. (1977). Culture change and psychosocial adjustment. *American Ethnology, 2,* 471–495.
Berger, P. L., Berger, B., & Kellner, H. (1973). *The homeless mind: modernization and consciousness.* Harmondsworth: Penguin.
Berry, J. W. (1970). Marginality, stress and ethnic identification in an acculturated aboriginal community. *Journal of Cross-Cultural Psychology, 1,* 239–252.
Berry, J. W. (1978). Acculturative stress among the James Bay Cree: prelude to a hydro-electric project. In L. Muller-Will (Ed.), *Unexpected consequences of economic change in circumpolar regions.* Edmonton: Boreal Institute.
Berry, J. W. (1980a). Ecological analyses for cross-cultural psychology. In N. Warren (Ed.), *Studies in cross-cultural psychology* (Vol. 2). New York: Academic Press.
Berry, J. W. (1980b). Social and cultural change. In H. C. Triandis and R. W. Brislin (Eds.), *Handbook of cross-cultural psychology* (Vol. 5). Boston: Allyn and Bacon.
Berry, J. W., & Annis, R. C. (1974a). Acculturative stress; the role of ecology, culture and differentiation. *Journal of Cross-Cultural Psychology, 5,* 382–406.
Berry, J. W., & Annis, R. C. (1974b). Ecology, culture and psychological differentiation. *International Journal of Psychology, 9,* 173–193.
Borg, M. (1971). *Conflict and social change.* Minneapolis: Augsburg Publishing.
Cawte, J., Bianchi, G. N., & Kiloh, L. G. (1968). Personal discomfort in Australian aborigines. *Journal of Psychiatry, 2,* 69–79.
Chance, N. A. (1965). Acculturation, self-identification and personality adjustment. *American Anthropologist, 67,* 372–393.
Constantini, P. (1973). Personality and mood correlates of schedule of recent experience scores. *Psychological Reports, 32,* 1143–1150.
Davidson, A. R., & Thomson, E. (1980). Cross-cultural studies of attitudes and beliefs. In H. C. Triandis & R. Brislin (Eds.), *Handbook of cross-cultural psychology* (Vol. 5). London: Allyn and Bacon.

Doob, L. W. (1960). *Becoming more civilized; a psychological exploration.* New Haven: Yale University Press.

Doob, L. W. (1967). The psychological pressure upon modern Africans. In J. M. McEwan and R. B. Sutcliffe (Eds.), *Modern Africa.* New York: Thomas Y. Crowell.

Dries, H. (1983). Psychologische aspecten van modernisatie. *Aviag. Bulletin, 10,* 43–50.

Dries, H. (1984a). Acculturation and psychological modernisation. In R. Pinxten (Ed.), *New perspectives in Belgian anthropology, or the postcolonial awakening.* Göttingen: Herodot.

Dries, H. (1984b). *De psychologie van de moderne Afrikaan. Een psycho-anthropologische benadering van het modernisatieprobleem in Zaire.* Lisse: Swets & Zeitlinger.

Egerton, R. B. (1973). Method in cultural anthropology. In R. Narrol & R. Cohen (Eds.), *A handbook of method in cultural anthropology.* New York: Columbia University Press.

Eisenstadt, S. N. (1966). *Modernization: protest and change.* Englewood Cliffs: Prentice-Hall.

Erny, P. (1972). *L'efant et son milieu en Afrique Noire.* Paris: Payot.

Goldschmidt, W., & Edgerton, R. B. (1961). A picture technique for the study of values. *American Anthropologist, 63,* 26–47.

Holtzman, W. H. (1980). Projective techniques. In H. C. Triandis & J. W. Berry (Eds.), *Handbook of cross-cultural psychology* (Vol. 2). Boston: Allyn and Bacon.

Irvine, S. H. (1968). *Human behavior in Africa; some research problems noted while compiling source materials.* Paper presented at the East African Institute of Social Research Workshop in Social Psychology in Africa, New York.

Jaco, E. (1970). Mental illness in response to stress. In S. Levine & N. Scotch (Eds.), *Social stress.* Chicago: Aldine Publishing Company.

Kizerbo, J. (1963). Y-a-t-il crise de la civilisation Africaine? *Afrique Documents, 66,* 51–70.

Lapiere, R. (1965). *Social change.* New York: McGraw-Hill.

Lauer, R. H., & Thomas, R. (1976). A comparative analysis of the psychological consequences of change. *Human Relations, 29,* 239–248.

Lerner, D. (1958). *The passing of traditional society; modernizing the Middle East.* New York: Free Press.

Mair, L. P. (1934). The study of culture contact as a practical problem. *Africa, 7,* 112–134.

Maquet, J. (1967). *Africanité traditionnelle et moderne.* Paris: Présence Africaine.

Murphy, J. M. (1973). Sociocultural change and psychiatric disorder amdong rural Yorubas in Nigeria. *Ethos, 1,* 239–262.

Musgrove, F. (1982). *Education and anthropology: other cultures and the teacher.* New York: Wiley.

Paden, J. N., & Soja, E. W. (Eds.). (1970). *The African experience* (Vol. 1). Evanston, IL: Northwestern University Press.

Parker, S. (1964). Ethnic identity and acculturation in two Eskimo villages. *American Anthropologist, 66,* 325–340.

Piche, V. (1976). Les enquêtes de fécondité en Afrique Tropicale ou le principe du double standard. *Population et Famille, 37,* 143–164.

Sesay, L. (1977). Crime and development in Africa. *Annals of the American Academy of Political and Social Science, 432,* 42–51.

Smith, P. (1974). Kultuurkonflik en misdaad by kleurlinge. *Suid-Afrikaanse Tydskrif vir Sosiologie, 9,* 44–47.

Spindler, G. D. (1968). Psychocultural adaptation. In E. Norbeck, D. Price-Williams, & W. M. McCord (Eds.), *The study of personality; an interdisciplinary appraisal.* New York: Holt, Rinehart and Winston.

Spindler, G. D., & Spindler, L. (1965a). The Instrumental Activities Inventory: a technique for the study of the psychology of acculturation. *Southwestern Journal of Anthropology, 21,* 1–23.

Spindler, G. D., & Spindler, L. (1965b). Researching the perception of cultural alternatives: the Instrumental Activities Inventory. In. M. E. Spiro (Ed.), *Context and meaning in cultural anthropology. In honour of A. Irving Hallowell.* New York: Free Press.

Toffler, A. (1970). *Future shock.* New York: Random House.

Wintrob, R. M., & Sindel, P. S. (1972) Culture change and psychopathology: the case of Cree adolescent students in Quebec. In J. W. Berry & G. J. S. Wilde (Eds.), *Social psychology: the Canadian context.* Toronto: McClell & Stewart.

Wolff, S., & Goodell, H. (1968). *Stress and disease.* Springfield, IL: Charles Thomas.

8

Type A, Anger and Performance in a Stressful Noise Situation

C. Levy-Leboyer, N. Girault, and G. Moser
Université René Descartes

The Type A behavior pattern is now a widely used and well-known psychological construct. This construct has been used extensively both in basic and applied research (Matthews, 1982), and in epidemiological studies (Rosenman et al., 1964). It first emerged from Friedman and Rosenman's (1959, 1969) studies of patients who suffered from coronary heart disease, but did not present any of the traditional risk factors associated with these disorders. Only a set of behavioral characteristics differentiated these patients from noncardiac ones.

Friedman and Rosenman (1974) give the following definition of Pattern A: "an action-emotion complex that can be observed in any person who is aggressively involved in a chronic, incessant struggle to achieve more and more in less and less time, and if required to do so, against the opposing efforts of other things or other persons" (p. 67). Since the Type A construct was introduced, much effort has been devoted to identifying and describing precisely the psychological and behavioral characters common to all persons who may be labeled "Type A", and that are less often observed among "non-A" persons (Jenkins, 1975 & Matthews 1982).

Correlations between Type A assessment, measured by either the Jenkins Activity Survey (JAS) or the Bortner scale, and other personality inventories indicate rather weak relationships, even though significant differences are generally found (e.g. Glass, 1977; Matthews & Krantz, 1976) between A's and B's on such measures as the Thurstone Temperament Survey Activity, Impulsivity, and Dominance scales. For a French-speaking sample, a weak relationship was observed between scores on a translation of the Bortner scale and the Eysenck Personality Inventory (Pichot et al., 1977). However, self-report and survey data about anger, impatience, and achievement striving give interesting results. For example, Dimsdale, Hackett, Block and Hutter (1978), in a study of cardiac patients, report that Type A subjects showed a high level of anger, tension, and depression; a comparison with healthy persons showed the same trend (Suls, Gastorf & Wittenberg 1979).

Achievement striving is better documented in its relation with Type A behavior. In her review of the literature, Matthews (1982) notes that "Type A adults . . . both men and women . . . report rapid career advancement . . . , attain a higher occupational status . . . , and receive more rewards from their

113

work. . . . Similarly, Type A undergraduate men and women [state] that they study and work more hours for paid employment and sleep less than do Type B's. . . . In addition, Type A undergraduate men . . . have higher resultant need achievement scores than do Type B's" (p. 302).

The results of behavioral observations are consistent with what has been previously summarized. Type A individuals outperform Type B's in situations which are challenging because of the task requirements (speed, persistence), work conditions, or risks of failure. Again, Matthew's survey of available evidence shows that behavior and performance of Type A subjects is generally consistent with the self-report results described above. Moreover, Type A's seem more likely to exhibit angry, hostile and aggressive behavior when placed in adverse work situations, or when confronted with pressure to maintain their performance level.

In the research work described thus far, the focus has been either on self-reports, such as anger or achievement striving, or on performance observed in specific laboratory situations. Therefore, there is as yet no clear evidence on the following questions:

1. Do Type A people experience more anger than Type B people when placed in difficult or stressful situations?

2. Do Type A people perceive work conditions as more challenging than Type B?

3. Are self-reports of emotions during the experimental situations significantly linked with behavior, and more specifically, with the quality of performance?

RESEARCH PROCEDURES

The present research investigates behavior in an experimental situation planned to provide answers concerning the above questions. The research procedures are designed (1) to study carefully selected Type A and Type B young men; (2) to expose subjects to a standardized work situation that consists of an information processing task with uncomfortable acoustic conditions; (3) to have subjects answer specific questions about their performance after the completion of the task; (4) to measure state and trait anger before and after the task itself.

Data for other physiological and biological measures taken during the same experiment have been reported elsewhere. A first account of these results is reported in a paper by Henrotte et al. (1983).

The research was organized in two phases. The first phase was devoted to developing French adaptations for the JAS (Jenkins, Zyzansky & Rosenman, 1979) and the Bortner scale (Bortner, 1969; Bortner & Rosenman, 1967). Norms for these adaptations were then established for a sample of 204 students. To recruit subjects, a note was posted at the university, asking for male volunteers who would be paid for their participation in a psychology experiment. Every candidate filled out both the JAS and the Bortner scales, and a short medical screening questionnaire aimed at eliminating potential subjects with chronic diseases. Only subjects with scores on the JAS Type A/B Subscale of one standard deviation above the mean ("Type A") or one standard deviation below the mean ("Type B") were selected for the experiment. Twenty Type A and twenty Type B subjects completed the entire experiment.

In the second phase of the experiment, the subjects had to perform a task developed by Bakan (1959) and adapted as auditory task by Jones (Jones, Smith, & Broadbent, 1979) which required information processing of auditory cues (72-76 dBA) under difficult conditions. The auditory stimuli, presented through earphones, were accompanied by a background noise (85 dBA), which made the task stressful. It should be emphasized, however, that the auditory stimuli were audible for normal ears, and that all subjects had normal hearing.

The subjects heard a series of digits, one per second. Their task was to write down the digits each time three different odd digits followed one another. Thus, it was necessary to memorize the last two digits, while listening to a new one. Subjects recorded the digits they detected on a sheet of paper. The task lasted 20 minutes, following a learning phase of 2 minutes. Performance was assessed by the number of correct answers and by the number of false alarms.

Before performing the task itself, the subjects were asked to fill out the French version of the Spielberger Trait Anger Scale (Spielberger, Jacobs, Russell & Crane, 1983). After the task was completed they then filled out the Spielberger Trait Anger Scale and gave their evaluation of:

- their own performance: with their answer sheets in front of them, the subjects reported on the number of false alarms and digits missed
- the annoyance caused by the noise
- the annoyance which they thought would be caused by the noise if it occurred on its own
- the performance they expected to achieve on the task without the noise (See the Scales in Appendix)

Each of the three annoyance scales consisted of a straight line, 10 cm in length, on which a cross could be marked at any point between the two poles, from "not annoying at all" to "extremely annoying" or between the two poles "much better"–"much worse".

After a period of rest, the subjects were asked to fill out the JAS and Bortner scale again before they left the laboratory. This was to enable us to check the reliability of a French translation of these two scales. In this restricted sample, the correlations between the test-retest trials of the JAS and the Bortner scale are very high: $r : .93$ in both cases.

The results are presented in three sections. First, the A/B differences on the scales filled out before the experiment are examined. Second, the performance by A and B subjects on the task is described and compared. Third, there is an analysis of the subjects' self-reports after the task and of the exposure to the stressful situation, measured on both the Spielberger State Anger Scale and the annoyance and performance evaluation scales.

SELF–REPORT DIFFERENCES BETWEEN A AND B SUBJECTS

We studied the differences between Type A and Type B subjects for the Bortner Scale and the two Spielberger Anger Scales.

In order to calculate the scores on the Bortner scale, items 1, 12 and 13 were discarded: items 1 and 12 bear no relationship with the total score (cf. Pichot et al., 1977), while item 13, which reads "Few interests outside work–many interests," raises problems with regard to its real meaning. The pole attributed to Type A people is "Few interests outside work," to indicate a high concentration on work as a central interest in life. However, it is possible to have interests both inside and outside work. The correlation between the total score and this item was, in fact, negative for the French sample.

A study of the 11 remaining items reveals that the difference between the means for the Type A and the Type B subjects is very high: 79.8 for the A's ($\sigma = 12.8$); 41.3 for the B's ($\sigma = 16.6$). For the total reference population, the mean for the Bortner is between these two values (i.e. 59.27) with a similar standard deviation ($\sigma : 15.5$). Bearing in mind that the subjects selected for the experiment were those with scores of one standard deviation above or below the mean on the JAS subscale, their scores on the Bortner scale were also found to one standard deviation above or below the mean.

Do Type A and Type B subjects give different answers on the two Spielberger Scales? Let us first look at the relationships between the Trait Anger Scale, and both the Bortner and the JAS, since these questionnaires were all completed before the experimental session. Figures 1 and 2 describe the entire network of relationships. Taking into account the above comparisons of A and B subjects' group means for the Bortner scale, it is not surprising to see that the relationships between the JAS and the Bortner are high and significant for the A and the B subjects. Although a somewhat different picture emerges with the Spielberger, there is still a similar relationship, whichever scale is applied to identify Type A and Type B.

For the Type A subjects, the correlations between the Spielberger Trait Anger Scale and either the JAS or the Bortner are significant and near .50. The correlations are lower (.40) and not significant, for the same instruments in the case of the Type B subjects.

How is this to be explained? It must be remembered that the group of Type A subjects was clearly defined by a proneness to cardiovascular diseases but the Type B subjects were less clearly defined simply as subjects not belonging to the A group. The results presented suggest, therefore, that one characteristic common to all the A's is their disposition to anger, but that the B's are not necessarily characterized by a quiet temperament and an absence of anger.

In fact, Type A subjects reported that they became angry more easily and more

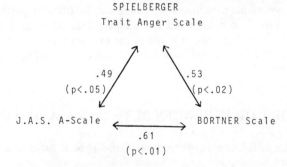

Figure 1 Type A subjects.

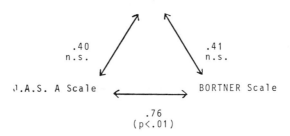

Figure 2 Type B subjects.

often than Type B: the mean scores on the Anger Trait Scale were 2.19 for the Type A ($\sigma = 0.48$) and 1.57 for the Type B ($\sigma = 0.24$). The difference is highly significant ($t = 5.03$; $p < .001$).

Looking at the scales in more detail, we can see that some items play a decisive role in this difference. The answers of the two groups were very different for items 17 (" I get annoyed when I am singled out for correction"), 18 ("I am a hotheaded person") and 22 ("I get angry when I am slowed down by others' mistakes"). They were also different but to a lesser degree, on items 28 ("I feel infuriated when I do a good job and get a poor evaluation"), 29 ("It makes my blood boil when I am pressured") and 30 ("It makes me furious when I am criticized in front of others").

It must be noted that nearly all these items are linked to social situations. This would suggest that Type A subjects are more disposed to react with anger to annoying or frustrating situations in which other people play an instrumental role, either because they criticize or undervalue the subjects' behavior, or because their own behavior is, from the subject's point of view, inadequate.

The fact that these items are grouped together in our results is not surprising. The Angry Reaction subscale (Spielberger, 1980) consists, in fact, of the same items. This subscale is made up of 4 items taken from the Trait scale, in the same way as the subscale Anger Temperament is made up of a further 4 items from this scale. These two subscales are arrived at as the result of a factor analysis showing two independent dimensions: dealing with the temperament (items 16, 18, 19 and 24), and with the reactions themselves (items 22, 23, 28 and 30).

Moreover, comparing a sample of hypertensive and normal subjects, Spielberger (1980) found a significant difference on the Angry Reaction subscale. In the case of our sample, all hypertensive subjects were discarded. However, we asked our normal subjects different questions about the health characteristics of their parents. It is interesting to note that many more A subjects reported having at least one hypertensive parent (58%) than did the B subjects (16%; $x^2 = 7.23$; $p < .01$). In view of this, we thought it would be interesting to use the same procedure as Spielberger and examine the two subscales he described.

Table 1 presents the mean scores for both subscales, calculated separately for

Table 1 Trait Anger Scale (Means and standard deviations for the two subscales)

	Type A		Type B	
Subscale	m	σ	m	σ
Anger Temperament*	2.02	0.96	1.31	0.49
Angry Reaction**	2.75	0.99	1.79	0.62

*Student t = 2.55 (p < .02);
**Student t = 3.26 (p < .01).

Type A and Type B subjects. We found a significant difference on both subscales, the difference being greater on the Angry Reaction subscale.

DIFFERENCES IN PERFORMANCE FOR A AND B SUBJECTS

Previous research data (Matthews, 1982) bears out the fact that Type A subjects outperform Type B's, especially in a difficult situation. This is usually explained in terms of motivation, whereby A's are stimulated by challenging or provoking situations.

Our results are less clear-cut than expected on this point, as the A subjects did not give significantly more correct answers than the B subjects (see Table 2). However, another performance index was collected, in the form of the total number of false alarms, that is where the subjects reacted mistakenly to what was not a succession of three different odd digits; the difference between A and B, as shown in this index, is clear. Type A subjects gave four times as many false alarms as Type B (see Table 2). It is also interesting to note that group A results showed a much greater dispersion than group B results. This requires further investigation, particularly as there is also a wide dispersion of the biological and physiological data in group A. We had expected the group B results to be more scattered because of the empirical nature of the A and B constructs, but this is not the case.

When the ratio of correct answers to the total number of answers is computed, it is evident that the performance of Type B subjects seems more efficient than Type A's (see Table 2). This is due to the fact that the A subjects were more active,

Table 2 Task performance indices

	Type A		Type B	
Answers	m	σ	m	σ
Correct answers*	6.25	3.25	5.42	2.46
False alarms**	5.20	6.46	1.42	1.27
% of correct answers***	0.61	0.29	0.81	0.15

*Student t = .87 (n.s.);
**Student t = 2.43 (p < .02);
***Student t = 2.58 (p < .01).

Table 3 Evaluation of noise annoyance and performance

Level of noise annoyance	Type A		Type B	
	m	σ	m	σ
Noise annoyance	65.1	28	64.6	19.8
Noise annoyance without the task	74.5	22.3	75.3	17.6
Performance without noise	71.0	16.8	68.8	15.6

tried more possible answers and reacted more often to false digits than the Type B subjects.

At this point, it is interesting to look at the subjects' own perception of the situation and of their performance. In spite of behavioral differences, A and B subjects evaluated the situation in exactly the same way (Table 3). Their assessment of the noise annoyance during the task or of the noise without the task was also the same (see Annoyance Scales in the Appendix). Furthermore, the two groups correctly evaluated their performance in the same way. This would seem to mean that Type A subjects do not have a stronger emotional reaction when faced with a difficult task, even though they actively try to cope with the stress and strain of the task.

The picture is slightly different when we look at another index, namely (S − 0)-FA, where S is the sum of all the reactions (good or bad), 0 the number of omissions as evaluated by the subjects, and FA the number of evaluated false alarms. When they made these evaluations, the subjects could see from their sheets how many answers they had given. Thus, the index reflects their evaluation of the number of digits that they should have detected. The A subjects' mean index is higher than that for the B subjects to a significant degree ($MA:13.9$; $\sigma A = 7.7$; $MB = 8.2$; $\sigma B = 4.2$; Student t: 2.02; $p < .05$). One can say that the A subjects do not overestimate the difficulty of the task itself but rather the amount of work to be done. This evaluation is consistent with the behavior of the A's, since they did indeed give more answers.

SELF–REPORT AFTER THE TASK

The experimental procedure used here seems aimed at studying the relationships between the Spielberger Trait and State scales in a standardized stressful situation. These scales measure anger as a permanent trait and as a reaction to specific situation respectively. Each scale has 15 items (in the original form used here), the first scale indicating the subject's general disposition, and the second scale eliciting a self-report of the subject's present reaction.

We have seen that there is a clear difference between A and B subjects on the Trait Scale. A reports more anger and is more frequently angry. Let us now examine the State Scale that was filled out at the end of a task in which A subjects were more active and evaluated the amount of work involved as greater but were finally proved to have been less efficient than the Type B subjects.

The total scores reveal no difference between A's and B's on the State Anger

Table 4   Positions on the State Anger Scale: A and B subjects' answers for the different positions of the State Anger Scale (15 items summed up)

Type	1	2	3	4	Total
A	214	51	25	10	300
B	247	47	1	5	300

scale (MA = 21.8; σA = 8.1; MB = 18.7; σB = 4.2) but a more detailed look at the data shows a difference in the way subjects used the scales. A breakdown of the A and B subjects' answers marked on the different positions of the scales, including a sum for all the items, is given in Tables 4 and 5. For instance, Table 4 shows that, for the 15 items on the State Scale, the 20 A subjects used "position 1" 214 times.

As the distribution of results was not normal, we calculated a chi 2 which is statistically significant: on the State Anger scale, A subjects used "position 3" five times more often than the B subjects; similarly, the A's used "position 4" ten times more often than the B's (x^2 = 25.1; p < .001).

It is interesting to note (in Table 5) that the same is true for the Trait Anger scale. It is possible, therefore, to speak of a general tendency among the Type A subjects to adopt high positions (x^2 = 78.1; p < .001) when expressing their feelings.

DISCUSSION

In summarizing the differences observed among two groups of Type A and Type B subjects, four points can be noted:

1. The relationship between the Spielberger State-Trait Anger scale, the JAS, and the Bortner scale is fairly high for the Type A subjects and very weak for the Type B subjects. This could be interpreted as indicating that one of the strongest characteristics common to all Type A individuals has to do with extreme reactions, including anger, as they mobilize their energy in order to deal with adverse situations. Such an interpretation follows logically from the overactivity observed during the work phase of the experiment. Thus, A's behavior could be described as an example of instrumental aggressivity.

2. Type A subjects are not more efficient in a stressful work situation but they "try more" than Type B subjects, and perceive the situation as more demanding.

Table 5   Positions on the Trait Anger Scale: A and B subjects' answers for the different positions of the Trait Anger Scale (15 items summed up)

Type	1	2	3	4	Total
A	99	84	77	40	300
B	154	123	22	1	300

However, the annoying characteristics of the situation do not elicit different emotional verbal reactions from the A's and the B's. These observations lead one to question what has been called the achievement motivation of Type A subjects. Is it, perhaps, more true to say that they are hyperactive in difficult situations rather than being motivated by challenge and stress?

3. Type A seems to constitute a less homogeneous group than usually described. As will be shown in a future publication, this observation is also true for the physiological and biological data. This heterogeneity has not yet been explored because research has focused on the characteristics that are common to a population presenting a proneness to coronary heart disease. It is quite possible that both the actual behavior and the self-report description of Type A subjects could, after thorough analysis, give way to meaningful subclassification.

4. Type A subjects report a disposition to reacting angrily but do not describe themselves as being more angry than B Types after exposure to a stressful task. This is open to various interpretations. One such interpretation is that A subjects overact during the work situation and return to a quiet level of activity and emotion as soon as the task is over. This could be tested in further experimentation by introducing the Spielberger State Anger scale during the course of the task.

REFERENCES

Bakan, P. (1959). Extroversion-introversion and improvement in auditory vigilance task. *British Journal of Psychology, 50*, 325–332.

Bortner, R. W. (1969). A short rating scale as a potential measure of Pattern A Behavior. *Journal of Chronic Disease, 22*, 87–91.

Bortner, R. W., & Rosenman, R. H. (1967). The measurement of Pattern A Behavior. *Journal of Chronic Disease, 20*, 525–533.

Dimsdale, J. E., Hackett, T. P., Block, P. C., & Hutter, A. M. (1978). Emotional correlates of the Type A Behavior Pattern. *Psychosomatic Medicine, 40*, 580–583.

Friedman, M., & Rosenman, R. H. (1959). Association of specific overt behavior pattern with blood and cartiovascular findings. *Journal of the American Medical Association, 169*, 1286–1296.

Friedman, M., & Rosenman, R.H. (1969). The possible general causes of coronary artery disease. In M. Friedman (Ed.), *Pathogenesis of coronary artery disease.* New York: McGraw-Hill.

Friedman, M. & Rosenman, R. H. (1974). *Type A behavior and your heart.* New York: Knopf.

Glass, D. C. (1977). *Behavior patterns, stress and coronary disease.* Hillsdale, NJ: Erlbaum.

Henrotte, J. G., Plouin, P. F., Levy-Leboyer, C., Moser, G., Girault, N., & Pineau, M. (1983). Blood magnesium, zinc, free fatty acid levels and catecholamine excretion in Type A and Type B subjects. *Journal of the American College of Nutrition, 2*, 294 (Abstract).

Jenkins, C. D. (1975). The coronary prone personality. In W. D. Gentry & R. B. Williams, Jr. (Eds.), *Psychological aspects of myocardial infarction and coronary care.* St. Louis: Mosby.

Jenkins, C. D., Zyzanski, S. J., & Rosenman, R. H. (1979). *Jenkins' Activity Survey Manual.* The Psychological Corporation, New York: Harcourt, Brace, Jovanovich.

Jones, D. M., Smith, A. P., & Broadbent, D. E. (1979). Effects of moderate intensity noise on the Bakan 18. vigilance task. *Journal of Applied Psychology, 64*, 627–634.

Matthews, K. A., & Krantz, D. S. (1976). *Psychosomatic Medicine, 28*,140–144.

Matthews, K. A. (1982). Psychological perspectives on the Type A Behavior Pattern. *Psychological Bulletin, 91*, 293–323.

Pichot, P., De Bonis, M., Somogyi, M., Degre-Coustry, C., Kittel-Bousuit, F., Rustin-Vandenhende, R. M., Dramaix, M., & Bernet, A. (1977). Etude métrologique d'une batterie de tests destinée à l'étude des facteurs psychologiques en épidémiologie cardio-vasculaire. *International Review of Applied Psychology, 26*, 11–19.

Rosenman, R. H., Friedman, M., Strauss, R., Wurm, M., Kositchek, R., Hahn, W., & Werthessen, N. T. (1964). A predictive study of coronary heart disease: The Western Collaborative Group Study. *Journal of the American Medical Association, 189*,15–22.

Spielberger, C. D. (1980). *Preliminary Manual for the STAS.* Unpublished manuscript, University of South Florida, Tampa.

Spielberger, C. D., Jacobs, G., Russell, S., & Crane, R. S. (1983). Assessment of anger: The State-Trait Anger Scale. In J. N. Butcher & C. D. Spielberger, (Eds.), *Advances, in Personality Assessment* (Vol. 2). Hillsdale, NJ: LEA.

Suls, J. M., Gastorf, J. W., & Wittenberg, S. II. (1979). Life events, psychological distress and the Type A coronary prone behavior pattern. *Journal of Psychosomatic Research, 23,* 315–319.

APPENDIX: NOISE ANNOYANCE
SCALES AFTER THE TASK

Was the noise you heard during the task:

    not annoying at all _____ extremely annoying

If you were sitting quietly without anything specific to do, would you find this same noise:

    not annoying at all _____ extremely annoying

For this same task, what performance would you expect to achieve without noise:

    much better _____ much worse

9

Reactivity, Experience, and Response to Noise

Tatiana Klonowicz
University of Warsaw

In the mid-1970s Strelau presented a theory of temperament which empasizes its regulatory role in behavior. Temperament has been defined as a "relatively stable feature of the organism, primarily biologically determined, revealing itself in the formal traits of reactions that account for the energetic level and temporal characteristics of behavior (Strelau, 1983). One particular dimension of temperament—reactivity—evoked much interest and has had more experimental work done on it than the other dimensions of activity and mobility.

Reactivity has been defined as a feature "which determines a relatively stable and characteristic intensity (magnitude) of reactions for a given individual . . . crucial to our understanding of reactivity is the fact that it co-determines the sensitivity (sensory and emotional) . . . and the organism's capacity to work" (Strelau, 1983, p. 177).* The two extremes of the reactivity dimension are high reactivity (R; high sensitivity, low endurance) and low reactivity (r; low sensitivity, high endurance). A continuing interest in the problem of the regulatory role for reactivity may foster an erroneous impression that temperament and reactivity are almost synonymous. However, it is true that reactivity holds a central position in Strelau's model. The reason for this is that the reactivity mechanism is directly responsible for the stimulation processing: its "program" either enhances (R) or attenuates (r) the intensity of the incoming stimuli.

For a detailed discussion see Strelau, (1983) and Klonowicz (1982, 1984). A similar explanatory model has been proposed by Sales, Guydosh, & Iacomo (1974). It should be emphasized that different theories of personality and/or temperament make explicit or implicit claims to be concerned with this model (e.g. extra- or introversion, stimulation-seeking, field-dependency/independency, the

This chapter is based on T. Klonowicz's *Reactivity, Experience and Capacity. Experiments with Stimulation Load,* Warszawa, University of Warsaw Press, in press. Research supported by the Grant MR-I-29 and Grant 0.6.7.7.5.

*Strelau makes reference to the Law of Strength that postulates a direct relation between the intensity of stimulus and intensity of reaction.

neo-Pavlovians). Thus, the model permits a systematic survey and integration of data.

It has been hypothesized that the higher the reactivity, the smaller the preferences for more stimulating situations, the lower the reactivity, the stronger the preferences for more stimulating situations. Research work on reactivity has largely been directed to two general paradigms defined by the following operations: (a) recording the occurrence, type and temporal structure of behaviors (actions) in subjects with different reactivity levels performing a given task in a laboratory and/or real-life situations; and (b) comparison of the psychophysiological and/or behavioral responses under different stimulation load and in subjects with different reactivity levels (Klonowicz, 1984; Strelau, 1983). An assessment of the data dervied from these paradigms, in approximately 50 experiments dealing directly with reactivity and even a greater number of studies on comparable variables, has led us to identify the basic regulatory processes accounted for by reactivity.

One aspect controls the preparatory activation or anticipation. The higher the reactivity, the higher the anticipatory arousal and the more salient its negative emotion tone (Klonowicz, 1984). A second regulates the task performance under a given stimulation load. The higher the reactivity, the bigger the deficits in performance with the increase in either the background stimulation load or in the task demands, the lower the reactivity, the greater the deficits with a decrease in the stimulation load (Klonowicz, 1984; Strelau, 1983). A third aspect of the regulatory role of reactivity concerns either short- or long-term side effects such as those induced by exposure to a given stimulation load (task) and recorded changes in the organism's state during and/or after the main task. The higher the reactivity, the bigger the state changes with the increase in the stimulation load. However, a very severe reduction of stimulation inputs is necessary to obtain the postulated reverse relation according to which the lower the reactivity, the bigger the changes with the decrease in the stimulation load (Klonowicz, 1974, 1984).

Gradually it became clear that the general model of the role of reactivity became too narrow to explain the empirical findings. The reactivity mechanism controls reactions to unspecific stimulation loads which may be represented with a series of inverted U-curves along a stimulation dimension; the two poles of this dimension are described in terms of under- and overload or weak and strong stimulation. It has been hypothesized (Eliasz, 1981) that reactivity determines both the localization of an inverted-U curve for performance and general well-being as well as the width of an optimal zone under the curve. Our recent data (Klonowicz, 1984) seem to corroborate this hypothesis.

Thus, reactivity is an important variable in both predicting and explaining the overload and underload stress. Behavioral studies generally show that the higher the reactivity, the lesser the tolerance to the overload and that an incrementing of psychophysiological or behavioral indices over a baseline is produced by a relatively weak input change. The lower the reactivity, the lesser the tolerance to the underload, although a considerable input change is necessary to deregulate the output measures and even if the performance suffers, at the psychophysiological and posttask behavioral levels the results indicate a relatively high tolerance to the stress of underload.

How can an organism compensate for deficits resulting from the inappropriate environmental or task demand (stimulation supply) and its own capacity as determined by the level of reactivity? Two possibilities of adaptational changes have been demonstrated.[†] A prolonged exposure to the environmental stimulation may change the program stimulation processing, that is, the mechanism of reactivity (Eliasz, 1981). The level of reactivity in urban dwellers exposed to sociospatial density and noise is significantly lower than in their counterparts from the less dense and calmer city areas. This phenomenon may be qualified as a "structural change" or the "end result" of the process of adaptation (Martin, 1964). Another type of adaptation to the stimulation load is functional sensitization/desensitization, that is, task-induced temporary sensory threshold shifts (Eliasz, 1979, 1981; Klonowicz, 1974). A question arises whether more stable new adjustments are possible as a result of the individual learning (e.g. the acquisition of appropriate coping strategies) or experience (Zuckerman, 1979, postulate 3) or both.

Earlier in this chapter it was proposed that the capacity to function under a different stimulation load or adaptability to the environment is determined, and limited, by reactivity. Presumably *experience* defined here is gained through frequent and/or long exposure with the typical environmental stimulation load, and will interact with reactivity in determining the human capacity to cope with the stimulation load. A logical basis for this assumption may be found in different theories, and both behavioral as well as psychophysiological studies imply that people tend to adapt to their environment and to disregard its invariant characteristics (Helson, 1959; Kagan, 1970; Sokolov, 1964; Thompson, 1975; Zuckerman, 1979).

The study reported below was designed to determine whether experience with street noise—considered here as belonging to the group of overload stressors most frequently encountered in urban life—modifies the effect of this environmental stressor on people with different reactivity levels. It has been hypothesized that in persons with a similar urban level of adaptation (adaptation to street noise), the modifying role of reactivity will be attenuated. The effect of noise on people lacking the urban experience will depend on reactivity as postulated above. The higher the reactivity, the bigger the deficits in performance and the bigger the aftereffects with the increase in the stimulation load (noise); the lower the reactivity, the bigger the deficits in performance and the bigger the aftereffects with the decrease in the stimulation load.

At the present stage no specific hypotheses are advanced to explain how our experience with noise variable acts. It is my intuition that it involves some sort of filtering. As postulated above, it may lead to the acquisition of coping strategies, such as ability to concentrate on the main task while neglecting the secondary inputs. It seems likely, too, that experience with noise is an important factor in establishing the range of the optimal level of stimulation which determines the "wakefulness of choice" and thus affects the overall level of cortical arousal. These two possibilities are complementary rather than antithetical, yet it is worth noting that although the neglection hypothesis necessitates the cortical mechanism, the substrate for the second type of filtering may be localized either in the cortex or in the lower portions of the brain.

[†]The present study is focused on the role of reactivity; the discussion on the active coping strategies is not included here, since they involve the different temperamental dimension of activity.

METHOD

Subjects

The subjects were 10th and 11th grade secondary school female students aged 16–18. They consented to participate in the experiment and were told it dealt with the effect of working conditions.

Design

The experiment consisted of two parts. The aim of Part 1 was to select the groups with equal IQ and different reactivity and experience with noise levels. Part 2 was the experiment proper for which 8 independent groups were formed: 2 levels of experience times 2 levels of reactivity times 2 levels of stimulation load (experimental conditions). The experiment included a one hour performance test (proofreading) under a given experimental condition (stimulation load), and a pre- and posttest measure of aftereffects.

Independent Variables

Reactivity

Reactivity was measured by Strelau's Temperament Inventory (STI, Strelau, 1983) and the two levels of this factor were provided by the selection of the extreme groups (25 upper and lower % of the sample tested in Part 1).

Experience with Noise

The experience of noise is equated with the level of adaptation. Unfortunately, there is no general rule that says when an adaptation level (AL) has been fixed or shifted. Helson's (1959, 1964) experiments in psychophysics (e.g. weight evaluation) as well as the evidence on habituation and other forms of learning clearly demonstrate that this process depends on a wide variety of factors. A rule of thumb for solving this problem would be to aim at a sufficiently long exposure time. The Cohen, Evans, Krantz, Stokols, & Kelly, (1981) study suggests that the nonauditory noise effects are quite plain in children and students attending a noisy school for about 2 years. The authors found, too, that the effect of the stimulation prevailing in a school setting is not neutralized by a quiet residence. Heft (1979) and Cohen et al. (1981) reported that children from a noisy school or home, when tested in a quiet atmosphere, performed poorer than those from quiet schools or homes. This evidence suggests that the AL has already been fixed.

It has been assumed that a 2 year exposure to noise in a school setting will be effective in shaping individual experience, that is, a characteristic AL. In order to meet this assumption two different—quiet (small town) and noisy—schools were selected. The choice was next verified by the sound measures inside the classrooms (without students). Monitoring of noise level with a decibel meter yielded values fluctuating from 40–43 dBA in one school and 64–68 dBA in the other. The noise measures were taken on several occasions, covering a 1.5 hour period each. However, due to the limitation of the equipment, these averaged measures represent only relative—yet believed to be sufficiently illustrative—differences between the two settings.

Stimulation Load

The two levels of stimulation load were provided by the manipulation of the background stimulation imposed over the task. Under the No Load ($\sim L$) condition all the subjects, (regardless of the original school setting), were tested in a room with a noise level of about 42–44 dBA (no background stimulation was used). It should be noted that for the noisy school subjects the level of sound under this condition was below their adaptation level (64–68 dBA). This measure was necessary to assure the comparable $\sim L$ conditions as well as equal magnitude of change for both settings. Under the Load (L) condition a continuous background acoustic stimulation—80–85 dBA street noise—was delivered through the loudspeakers. The street noise recording consisted of superimposed sounds of urban traffic, unintelligible bits of speech, occasional bursts of construction noise, distress sounds (sudden braking, ambulance siren) and so forth. The stimulation lasted throughout the main task (proofreading), that is, for one hour.

Criterion and Intermediate Variables

It is worth noting that Part One provides the criterion (reactivity and experience) as well as the intermediate (IQ) variables. The proofreading measure was proved to be highly variable and IQ was used as a precaution against the errors attributable to the variation among subjects' comprehension of the test and short-term memory. Raven Progressive Matrices were used to this effect.

Dependent Variables

Level of Performance

This includes productivity and quality of work. The productivity measure is the total number of misprints that could have been detected at the point the subject was told to stop. The quality of work was measured in terms of the errors of omission (misprints not corrected). The subjects were given erratum forms and were required to indicate the misprints, that is, locate them by the page and the line as well as to correct the misprints. As a control for learning, the proof marks were not introduced.

Aftereffects

The aftereffects were measured by the means of Thayer's Activation-Deactivation Adjective Check List (AD ACL, short form; Thayer, 1967). Thayer has formulated a four-dimensional activation model and succeeded in measuring the experience of activation by self-report. The AD ACL measures four states of activation[‡] identified by the model:

1. General Activation (GA): most relevant to cognitive and physical effort, denotes the readiness to work;
2. Deactivation (OSL): Sleep, tiredness;
3. High Activation (HA): tension, anxiety; and
4. General Deactivation (GD): most unspecific changes in the level of activa-

---

[‡]Four scales emerged in factor-analytic studies. Their psychological content is inferred from the adjectives with the highest loadings on each scale as well as from the empirical data (Thayer, 1978).

tion, interpreted along three other AD ACL scales. Appears as a common pole for several kinds of activation identified by the AD model.

The reliability (test-retest) estimates of AD ACL range from .79 to .93. Although use of self-report measures of activation has been much debated and often the preference will be given to the objective methods of assessment, at least arguments support strongly the use of AD ACL:

1. A self-report provides a central measure of a given state of activation, a measure of different physiological systems' reactivity integrated on the cortical level (Eysenck, 1975), whereas at the physiological level the results are conflicting due to the response specifity (Lacey, 1967).
2. In contrast to the other activation models the AD promotes the measurement of qualitatively different activation-emotion states and their quantification.
3. The correlations obtained between the AD factors and composites of physiological variables (skin conductance, heart rate, muscle action potentials, and a finger blood volume) range from .68 to .60 (Thayer, 1970).

The latter findings justify the interpretation of data in terms of levels (states) of activation. Activation scores were calculated separately for each scale (state) as a sum of ratings on all five adjectives within the scale. A measure of the aftereffect was a difference score (a comparison of pre- and posttest measures of activation).

Group-Matching Manipulation Check

257 subjects from both settings completed the STI and Raven's Progressive Matrices. The results of 104 of them were taken into account after forming the independent experimental groups (13 subjects each) with different experience with noise and reactivity levels, equal IQ, and exclusion of extras (Random Numbers Table).

The mean IQ score was 49.97 (SD = 7.82) ranging in the eight groups from 48.77 to 52.00 (the group means). No significant effects were found in the analysis of variance check of the groups' assignment with respect to this criterion ($F < 1$).

The mean reactivity score was 33.85 (SD = 5.69) in high reactive subjects (the mean scores for four experimental groups ranging from 32.54 to 35) and 66.56 (SD = 5.31) in low reactive subjects (65.92 − 67.31). The analysis of variance revealed only one significant effect: Reactivity ($F_{1,96}$ = 879.860, $p < .0001$). Five other F ratios were negligible ($Fs < 1$).

Therefore it may be concluded that the two assumptions (similar IQ in all eight groups and equal reactivity level in the groups with different experience assigned to the one or the other experimental condition) were met.

RESULTS

The presentation of data (Zawadzka, 1979) is subdivided into two parts corresponding to the two categories of dependent variables: task performance and aftereffects. This procedure is believed to better serve the purposes of a systematic analysis of findings, yet it requires an additional effort; the hypothesis was formulated in a general manner and as concerns the urban dwellers, no separate predictions were offered with regard to either of the dependent measures. To avoid repetition, suffice it to say here that the modifying effect of experience with noise is expected with regard to both classes of variables.

Three-way analyses of variance were applied to the scores on both classes of dependent variables. The first step of the analysis, an estimate of the three main effects, bears no relevant information, as the research interests are placed elsewhere. Therefore the discussion of these data is not included here. The estimate of the Stimulation Load by Reactivity interaction effect may be viewed as an approximate replication of the earlier research focused on the role of reactivity. At the same time this interaction constitutes the first step toward answering the question whether the experience modifies this general relation. The two other interaction effects, that is, the experience by the other factor interactions, are a test of specific assumptions as to the role of experience, whereas the three-way interactions estimate is the criterion of the hypothesis verification and accomplishes the analysis.

Task Performance

Table 1 shows the means and standard deviations of the dependent measures of productivity of work and proportion of errors. The proportion of errors measure has been used because of a large variance among subject productivity (an approximate estimate of variance may be inferred from the SD values in Table 1). The summaries of the analyses of variance are presented in Table 2.

As previously mentioned, the attention will be focused on the interaction effects (Table 2).

The analysis of variance for productivity indicated that out of the four interaction F ratios only two were statistically signficiant: the Stimulation Load by Reactivity (Fig. 1) and the three-way interaction effect.

As indicated in Fig. 1, only for r subjects was the effect of the background stimulation as predicted by the general hypothesis concerning the role of reactivity in functioning under different stimulation load. A contrast t test of productivity was highly signficant ($t = 3.71, p < .0005$). For R subjects there was no significant difference between the two stimulation conditions ($t = .45$). The latter result may seem surprising, as the theory predicts the opposite outcome for high as

Table 1 Average productivity (P) and proportion of errors (E) in two experimental conditions

Variable			Noise-school[a]		Quiet-school[a]	
			R	r	R	r
~L	P	$\bar{x}$	125.85	138.38	107.15	105.23
		SD	19.01	17.11	15.23	13.41
	E	$\bar{x}$	.09	.16	.11	.14
		SD	.04	.04	.05	.04
L	P	$\bar{x}$	130.85	148.00	98.23	128.23
		SD	15.93	18.12	14.56	12.04
	E	$\bar{x}$	.09	.06	.19	.10
		SD	.05	.03	.04	.05

[a]Terms denote the two levels of experience (independent variable).

Table 2 Analyses of variance for productivity and proportion of errors

		Productivity		Proportion of errors	
Variable	df	ms	F	ms	F
Load L	1	1.337.78	5.338***	.006	3.000*****
Reactivity R	1	5.423.09	21.638*	.001	.500
Experience E	1	17.564.09	70.439*	.032	16.000*
L × R	1	2.169.47	8.656*	.079	39.500*
L × E	1	.47	.002	.018	9.000*
E × R	1	4.23	.017	.016	8.000**
E × L × R	1	1.211.77	4.835****	.014	7.000**
Residual	96	250.63		.002	

*p < .001.
**p < .01.
***p < .02.
****p < .05.
*****p < .10.

compared to low reactive persons, that is a significant decrease with the increase in the stimulation load.

One possible explanation of this phenomenon is based on the twofold effect of reactivity: (a) usually acts as a natural braking system in order to reduce the stimulation fed back by a person's own activity; (b) R is associated with a higher

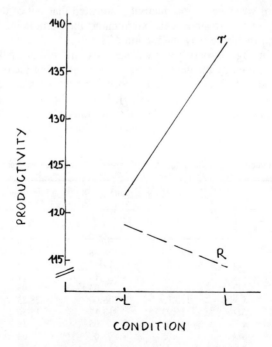

Figure 1 Stimulation load by reactivity interaction effect
on productivity.

sensitivity to the external social demands and forbids lowering the standards of excellence (Eliasz, 1981; Klonowicz, 1984). Yet it seems that at least partially it can be explained by the effect of the experience with noise.

The individual comparisons were carried away in order to examine the three-way interaction effect (for the means see Table 1). The outcome of contrast t tests shows clearly that the differential effect of the background stimulation on R and r subjects, that is, the Stimulation Load by Reactivity interaction effect holds true with regard to the quiet-school subjects only.

The quiet-school highs were marginally less productive under the $\sim L$ as compared to the $\sim L$ condition ($t = 1.44$, $p < .10$). The quiet-school lows were significantly more productive under the $\sim L$ than under L ($t = 3.70$, $p < .005$).

In the noisy school groups, irrespective of their level of reactivity, the productivity always increased under the L as compared to the $\sim L$ condition, however, the effect attributable to the change in background stimulation load was only marginally signficiant ($ts \leqslant 1.55$, $p < .10$).

Thus, the same general pattern of response—a rise in productivity with the increased background stimulation load—was found in all r subjects, regardless of their experience, as well as in the R subjects with urban experience.

The second measure of task performance—proportion of errors—was sensitive to all two-factor interaction effects. This is illustrated in Fig. 2 in which a, b, and c show the different two-factor interaction effects. A significant three-way interaction effect emerged as well.

The Stimulation Load by Reactivity Interaction Effect

The data presented in Fig. 2a fully corroborate our general hypothesis as to the role of reactivity. In R subjects the proportion of errors increased with the increase in the stimulation load ($t = 3.22$, $p < .005$), whereas r subjects were significantly more reliable under increased stimulation load ($t = 5.64$, $p < .0005$).

The Stimulation Load by Experience Interaction Effect

The data are shown in Fig. 2b. In the noise school group there was a marked decline in the proportion of errors from the $\sim L$ to the L condition ($t = 4.03$, $p < .0005$). In the quiet-school group the proportion of error scores under the two conditions were not significantly different, but there was, in fact, a tendency towards a greater performance deficit under L ($t = 1.61$, $p < .10$).

This interaction effect yields still another interesting fact. The analysis of variance indicated the Experience main effect on the proportion of errors (see Table 2); proportion of errors was significantly lower in the noisy school students than in their counterparts from the quiet setting. As the data in Fig. 2b show, this effect is limited to the groups working under L ($t = 5.64$, $p < .0005$). The means for the $\sim L$ condition were identical. Thus, it seems that experience is triggered in the relevant conditions only, in the presence of the specific stressor (street noise).

Seeing that the comparisons were carried away on the scores aggregated for the groups with different reactivity levels, the decisive test of this conclusion is deferred until later, when the individual comparisons will permit the separation of the postulated effect of experience from that already described of low reactivity.

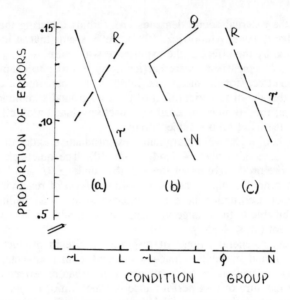

Figure 2 Two-factor interaction effects on proportion of
errors: *a*) Stimulation load by reactivity; *b*) Stimulation load by experience; *c*) Experience by
reactivity; N = noisy school students, Q =
quiet-school students.

The Experience by Reactivity Interaction Effect

The significance of this interaction effect (see Figure 2*c*) indicates that when the
stimulation load is not taken into account, experience acts differently for the two
reactivity levels. Indeed, only the highs made use of their experience with street
noise, as shown by a signficant difference between R subjects from the two settings (t = 4.84, p < .0005). The scores in r subjects from the two settings were
almost identical. This conclusion needs a more detailed examination, too; the
aggregated data may be misleading as they do not differentiate between the possibility of the beneficial effect of lowering the noise intensity for the urban highs
under the ~L condition and the beneficial effect of the experience as such.

Most pertinent to the topic is the significance of the three-way interaction effect. The individual comparisons bring out its meaning and dissect what could be a
source of confounding in the analyses of the two-factor interaction effects.

As the data in Table 1 indicate, the noisy school R subjects were equally reliable
under either experimental condition. The noisy school r subjects were more reliable under the L as compared to the ~L condition (t = 5.70, p < .0005)The
quiet-school R subjects worked significantly less accurately under the L as compared to the ~L (t = 4.56, p < .0005). Finally, in the quiet-school r subjects the
proportion of errors was significantly smaller under the L than under the ~L
condition (t = 2.28, p < .02).

It may be concluded that regardless of their experience the lows do better on the
task under the L as compared to the ~L condition. Experience with noise is of

particular value for the highs; those acquainted with noise maintain the standard of accuracy despite the additional stimulation load, while the accuracy of work in the subjects lacking the urban experience with noise drops with the increase in the background stimulation load.

It seems of interest, too, to change the focus of attention and to examine the data from a different angle. A tentative proposition has been advanced above that the subjects make use of their experience only in the presence of the specific stressor (see the Load by Experience interaction effect) and that experience with noise is of importance to R subjects only (see the Experience by Reactivity interaction effect). Yet at this point there was a strong possibility of an error due to the aggregation of the data. The following individual comparisons permit a better test of these propositions.

The outcome of the contrast t tests indicate that the $\sim L$ condition experience has no effect on the accuracy of performance; the differences between the groups with the same reactivity level but with a different experience failed to reach the critical level ($ts \leqslant 1.14, p \geqslant .20$). Under the L condition the effect of experience with noise was quite distinct. Out of the r groups the one acquainted with noise was more accurate ($t = 2.28, p < .05$). The same was true for R groups ($t = 5.70, p < .001$).

Thus, the proposition concerning the situational trigger of experience seems fully justified. There is apparently a situational specificity of action of the experience factor; it helps in coping with an overload context. It appears, too, that experience with noise may be useful regardless of the level of reactivity.

Aftereffects

Table 3 shows the means and standard deviations on all four measures (states) of activation. Within each group an estimate of magnitude of change from pre- to poststimulation measure was calculated (t test). These data, being secondary to the main problem, are not discussed further. The summaries of the analyses of variance are presented in Table 4.

As in the previous section, I will move directly to the interaction effects. The outcome of the analyses of variance bears out the general hypothesis as to the relationship among reactivity, stimulation load, and the magnitude of aftereffects. Figure 3 summarizes the evidence on the Load by Reactivity interaction effect on the changes in activation.

In the R subjects the aftereffects increase with the increase in the background stimulation load. In low r subjects the decrease in the background stimulation load produced changes on sleep deactivation and regular deactivation only.

The mirror-like effect produced by the Stimulation Load by Reactivity interaction on GD seems of interest, too. R subjects are "deactivated" (low arousal) under $\sim L$ and respond to the L condition with the decrease in deactivation (increase in arousal); most probably this is a response to the activating effect of noise. The reverse pattern of change was found in r subjects who were significantly more activated under $\sim L$ (lower GD score) than under the L condition. The latter change reflects the functional shift in reactivity; one possible response to underload is lowering the sensory threshold or searching for intenal sources of stimulation in order to maintain the level of activation within the acceptable range. While the highs are relaxed under the $\sim L$ condition, the lows are forced to make some

Table 3 Average poststimulation effects: AD ACL difference scores

Measure group		Noise-school		Quiet-school	
		R	r	R	r
GA	$\bar{x}$ ~L	-1.54^a	-1.31^b	-1.00^b	-1.38^a
	SD	1.71	1.82	1.26	1.68
	$\bar{x}$ L	-2.92^a	-1.08^b	-3.23^a	-2.31^a
	SD	2.00	1.75	2.07	1.95
DSL	$\bar{x}$ ~L	$+1.62^a$	$+2.54^a$	$+2.08^a$	$+2.31^a$
	SD	1.39	2.03	1.35	1.97
	$\bar{x}$ L	$+1.92^a$	$+1.46^a$	$+4.23^a$	$+1.77^a$
	SD	1.44	1.09	1.69	1.59
HA	$\bar{x}$ ~L	$+1.54^a$	$+2.38^a$	$+2.54^a$	$+2.31^a$
	SD	1.45	2.02	1.27	2.27
	$\bar{x}$ L	$+2.08^a$	$+1.54^a$	$+4.69^a$	$+1.92^a$
	SD	1.82	1.30	2.06	2.12
GD	$\bar{x}$ ~L	$+2.08^a$	-2.31^a	$+1.23^a$	-1.77^a
	SD	1.93	2.07	1.89	2.14
	$\bar{x}$ L	$-.54$	$+.46$	-2.92^a	-1.54^a
	SD	1.68	1.49	1.63	1.82

[a]Significantly different from zero at .01 level (lower limit).
[b]Significantly different from zero at .05 level.

adaptational effort. The additional stimulation seems to fulfill the low reactive persons' need for stimulation, hence their relaxation under the *L* condition.

As Table 4 shows, none of the three-way interaction *F* ratios reached the significant level. Thus the data do not confirm the hypothesis as to the role of experience with regard to the aftereffects' magnitude. However, it seems of interest to note that the analyses of variance yielded significant two-factor interaction effects involving the Experience factor (Table 4). A detailed discussion of these effects seems superfluous; the aggregated scores inevitably mask the information most relevant to the purposes of the present study. Yet these data prompt the analysis of the specific means on the involved AD scales: D-SL, HA, and GD.

Lowering the noise intensity (Table 3, No Load) had a marginal effect, limited to highly reactive students and to the two scales only: HA and GD. On these two scales the urban highs had lower ratings ($ts \leqslant 1.40$, $p \geqslant .20$) than the quiet setting-high reactive group for whom the $\sim L$ condition equaled the AL. When exposed to the street noise (Table 3, Load), the urban highs—as compared to their counterparts from the quiet school—responded with significantly smaller changes on D-SL ($t = 3.68$, $p < .005$), HA ($t = 3.65$, $p < .005$), and GD ($t = 3.18$, $p < .005$). The urban lows were considerably more deactivated (GD) than the lowly reactive students from the quiet setting ($t = 2.67$, $p < .02$).

Thus, if the results failed to support the general hypothesis as to the attenuated role of reactivity in the urban dwellers, the revealed mediating effect of experience was as expected.

Table 4 Summary of analyses of variance for productivity and proportion of errors

Variable	df	General activation		Deactivation-sleep		High activation		General deactivation	
		ms	F	ms	F	ms	F	ms	F
Load L	1	30.16	9.336*	1.16	.455	3.47	1.042	23.09	.323***
Reactivity R	1	11.12	3.443******	5.09	1.996	11.78	3.538******	40.63	11.132*
Experience E	1	.89	.503	13.16	5.161****	25.01	7.511**	35.78	9.803*
L × R	1	13.88	4.297*****	27.01	10.592*	25.01	7.511**	155.09	42.490*
L × E	1	6.50	2.012	9.24	3.624******	7.01	2.105	27.01	7.400**
E × R	1	3.85	1.192	11.78	4.620*****	17.78	5.339****	5.09	1.395
E × L × R	1	.16	.050	2.78	1.090	2.16	.649	1.61	.441
Residual	96	3.23		2.55		3.33		3.65	

*p < .001.
**p < .01.
***p < .02.
****p < .05.
*****p < .10.

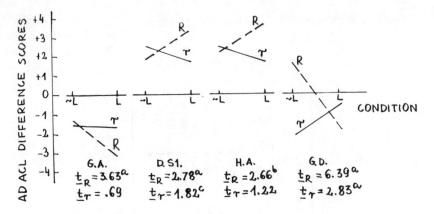

Figure 3 Stimulation load by reactivity interaction effect on activation state changes.

DISCUSSION

The study provided the data on two general problems: (a) the role of the level of reactivity as a codeterminant of human capacity to cope with the stimulation load, and (b) the role of the individual experience as a variable that interacts with and moderates the steering role of the reactivity mechanisms in behavior.

As concerns the role of reactivity, the results support and extend those obtained in the previous studies (Eliasz, 1981; Strelau, 1983) and summarized above. However, the aim of the present study goes beyond this replication. Rather, it should be regarded as tentative to enlarge the regulative net and as a search of the effect of other factors' interactions with the reactivity mechanism. It has been predicted that the capacity to cope with the stimulation load is shaped by experience which pools with reactivity. The evidence gives only partial credence to the idea. Experience has been shown to moderate the effect of the change in the stimulation load on task performance, but it failed to change substantially the relationship among stimulation load, reactivity, and the aftereffects among stimulation load, reactivity, and the aftereffects magnitude.

As expected, task performance in the groups familiar with and accustomed to work in noise was not sensitive to the change in the background stimulation load imposed over the main task. An interesting pattern emerged from the analysis of the data on task performance. R persons from both settings profit from the additional stimulation load, as evidenced by the increase in the productivity and the improvement of their quality of work. This is a clear case of the Broadbent's (1963) "two stressors' interactions", that is, the interaction of noise (an activating stressor) with a relatively monotonous task, where the background stimulation imposed over the main task helps to maintain the level of activation within the optimal range. However, as might be predicted on the basis of the Helson's AL theory, the effect produced by noise on the urban lows' productivity was marginal. Apparently, the differences in the stimulation load between the two conditions just meets their demand for the stimulation which is necessary to maintain an optimal level of activation for the task at hand, but it does not result in a more productive behavior than that customarily displayed. In the r persons from the quiet setting noise produces an environment which is more than usually stimulating and this is clearly reflected by the changes in their task performance; a significant increase in both the productivity and the accuracy of work. Quite unexpectedly, noise produced a marginal increase in the urban highs' productivity. As for the quality of work, they maintain the standard of performance despite the increase in the stimulation load. R persons from the quiet setting slightly decrease their activity on the task when confronted with the more stimulating environment; the decrease in the productivity is paralleled by the poorer quality of work.

Thus, the contribution of the experience factor is the variation in the previously described "order of groups" along the stimulation dimension. It has been demonstrated that the higher the reactivity, the closer the optimal zone to the "weak stimulation intensity" pole of the stimulation dimension (Klonowicz, 1984). Insofar as performance is considered, the urban highs almost level with the lows and if they do not profit from the increase in the stimulation load, their performance is not deregulated.

The second fact brought out in the analysis of the data is the absence of the effect of experience when no additional stimulation is imposed. The relationship between the task performance and the experience with noise has been demonstrated only for the context which involved the specific stressor; the differences between the groups from the quiet and noisy settings are visible under street noise only. Apparently, experience with noise is a compensating mechanism triggered off by the environmental demand. Experience with noise enlarges capacity to cope with the overload, but it has almost no effect on the capacity to cope with underload. The latter conclusion, based on the above presented comparisons of task performance under the $\sim L$ condition, will be best visualized with a deformed, asymetrical inverted-U curve: the area under the curve representing effective performance under increased stimulation load is broader, while the area below the optimal remains unchanged.

As previously mentioned, the evidence on the aftereffects discards the theoretical prediction as to the moderatory effect of experience on the stimulation induced state changes in persons with different reactivity levels. However, a limited effect of reactivity with experience has been demonstrated. The comparisons of the aftereffects' magnitude in R persons from the two settings show that for the urban group the test under noise is less demanding. Experience with noise seems to protect the high reactive persons, but the immunization has not been achieved. It is worth noting, too, that just as for the task performance, the "shield" becomes operative only in the relevant context.

The evidence clearly shows that the experience with noise is of particular importance to R persons. However, it seems quite probable that the experimental manipulation failed to disclose the effect of familiarity with noise on the lows. In fact, the proportion of errors under noise is higher in the lows from quiet setting than in their urban counterparts; street noise has a bigger activating effect on this group, too. Viewing the general beneficial effect of the increase in the stimulation load on persons, of low reactivity, one possible explanation is that the effect of noise on the lows from the quiet setting is twofold. The unspecific activating influence helps to maintain the optimal CNS tonus, but the cue function of street noise demands attention and appraisal.

At this point a tentative explanatory model may be proposed to tie together the data on the task performance and aftereffects. To produce arousal a danger signal or a stressor must not only be physically present, but psychologically present as well. When in the physical presence of a stressor people can adopt a strategy which psychologically removes them from the danger. Experience tells one to disregard street noise, qualified as an irrelevant typical input, and a person has more available capacity to be allocated to the main task. Most probably, this indifference to environmental events is a learned strategy which helps one to cope with an overload. The absence of experience requires an allocation of attention (capacity) to both the task and peripheral events. This explanation accounts for the so called "direct" effect of experience and is in line with the Cohen's (1978, 1980) model of aftereffects which implies lesser aftereffects with lesser demands.

Both the objective (task performance) and subjective (AD ratings) changes recorded in the high reactive groups from the two settings tested under noise allow for still another, concurrent explanation which suggests the possibility for the indirect effect of experience. When a person disregards the invariant habitual environment, cognitive and emotional appraisals do not occur. It may be assumed that discrepancies in the provided and needed stimulation load are noted in the course of scanning. The process of scanning is imperative in an unknown environment, but it will be inhibited under typical and/or invariant conditions. When no discrepancies are noted, the appearance of signals to counteract or withdraw, such as tiredness and tension, will be delayed or they may not appear at all. This delay or decrease in the changes of state increases capacity; the vicious circle (negative emotions–efficiency) is broken. As a result, R urban dwellers behave like r persons.

In sum, having effective, learned strategies psychologically removes one from danger cues and helps to maintain behavioral standards, although the reactions that occur after the stressor termination are only slightly reduced. The occurrence of strong aftereffects despite the familiarity with street noise suggests that experience should be visualized as a central (cortical) mechanism; the cortical pattern which develops through experiencing stimulation regulates the competition between the inputs, but does not lead to indifference to external stimuli.

CONCLUSIONS

Two themes recur throughout this chapter and deserve some additional emphasis. The first theme has to do with the importance of reactivity in mediating the relationship between noise and human response. The results of this study confirm those obtained in an earlier research. Reactivity appears as a final common path which controls not only the localization of the comfort/discomfort areas along the stimulation dimension, but also the range within which the regulation of stimulation is still possible.

The second theme involves the possibility that the role of reactivity in behavior may be modified by the individual experience. It seems likely that experience with noise results in learning of effective coping strategies which serve to counteract the stress of stimulation overload; regardless of their level of reactivity the urban dwellers were able to maintain the standard of performance. Although, the data suggest that experiencing a situation leads to the learning of strategies which reduce the effect of overload on performance, the present study confirms that the mediating effect of experience with noise on the relationship among reactivity, aftereffects, and stimulation load is not significant. It may be concluded that exposure to noise in community or work settings remains harmful to the general well-being of highly reactive persons.

REFERENCES

Broadbent, D. E. (1963). Differences and interactions between stresses. *Quarterly Journal of Experimental Psychology, 15*, 205–211.

Cohen, S. (1978) Environmental load and the allocation of attention. In A. Baum, J. E. Singer & S. Wallins (Eds.), *Advances in environmental psychology* (Vol. 1). Hillsdale, NJ: Erlbaum. 1978.

Cohen, S. (1980). Aftereffects of stress on human performance and social behavior: A review of research and theory. *Psychological Bulletin, 88*, 82–108.

Cohen, S., Evans, G. W., Krantz, D. S., Stokols, D. & Kelly, S. (1981). Aircraft noise and children: Longitudinal and cross-sectional evidence on adaptation to noise and the effectiveness of noise abatement. *Journal of Personality and Social Psychology, 40*, 331–345.

Eliasz, A. (1979). Temporal stability of reactivity. *Polish Psychological Bulletin, 10*, 187–198.

Eliasz, A. (1981). Temperament a system regulacji stymulacji. Warszawa: PWN.

Eysenck, H. J. (1975). The measurement of emotion: Psychological parameters and methods. In. L. Levi (Ed.), *Emotions, their parameters and measurement.* New York: Raven Press.

Heft, H. (1979). Background and focal environmental conditions of the home and attention in young children. *Journal of Applied Social Psychology, 9*, 47–69.

Helson, H. (1959). Adaptation level theory. In S. Koch (Ed.), *Psychology a study of science.* New York: McGraw Hill.

Helson, H. (1964). *Adaptation level theory.* New York: Harper & Row.

Kagan, J. (1970). Attention and psychological change in young children. *Science, 170*, 826–832.

Klonowicz, T. (1974). Reactivity fitness for the occupation of operator. *Polish Psychological Bulletin, 5*, 129–136.

Klonowicz, T. Potrzeba stymulacji: Analiza pojecia. In J. Strelau (Ed.) *Regulacyjne funkcje temperamentu.* Warsaw: Ossolineum, 1982.

Klonowicz, T. (1984). *Reaktywność a funkcjonowanie człowieka w różnych warunkach stymulacyjnych.* Wroclaw: Ossilineum.

Lacey, J. I. (1967). Somatic response patterning and stress: Some revision of activation theory. In M. H. Appley & R. Trumbull (Eds.), *Psychological stress.* New York: Appleton-Century-Crofts.

Martin, I. (1964). Adaptation. *Psychological Bulletin, 61*, 35–44.

Sales, S., Guydosh, R., & Iacomo, W. (1974). Relationship between "strength of the nervous system" and the need for stimulation. *Journal of Personality and Social Psychology, 1*, 16–32.

Sokolov, E. N. (1964). *Perception and the conditioned reflex.* Oxford: Pergamon Press.

Strelau, J. (1983). *Temperament—personality—activity.* London: Academic Press.

Thayer, R. E. (1967). Measurement of activation through self-report. *Psychological Reports, 20*, 663–678.

Thayer, R. E. (1970). Activation states as assessed by verbal report and four physiological variables. *Psychophysiology, 7*, 86–94.

Thayer, R. E. (1978). Toward a psychophysiological theory of multidimensionsl activation (arousal). *Motivation and Emotion, 2*, 1–34.

Thompson, R. E. (1975). *Introduction to physiological psychology.* New York: Harper & Row.

Zawadzka, G. (1979). *Wpływ miejsca zamieszkania i cech temperamental-nych na poziom wykonania monotonnej pracy umysłowej w warunkach obciazenia hałasem ulicznym.* Unpublished master's thesis, University of Warsaw.

Zuckerman, M. (1979). *Sensation seeking. Beyond the optimal level of arousal.* Hillsdale, NJ: Erlbaum.

10

Circadian Variation in Stress: The Effects of Noise at Different Times of the Day

Andrew P. Smith
University of Sussex, Brighton

Two major occupational health problems are noise and shiftwork. Both have been studied a great deal (see Folkard, 1981, for a review of shiftwork and performance; see Broadbent, 1979, for a review of the effects of noise on performance) but there has been little attempt to look at the interactions of the two factors, except for the study of the effects of noise on daytime sleep of nightworkers. Studies from the field suggest that the effects of noise and shiftwork are different. For example, Cesana et al. (1982) studied the effects of noise and shiftwork on the excretion of adrenalin and noradrenalin. Both noise and shiftwork increased noradrenalin excretion but shiftwork also changed the circadian pattern of adrenalin excretion. Cohen (1973) studied the effects of noise and shiftwork on health and industrial accidents. He concluded that workers subjected to noise showed greater numbers of diagnosed medical problems, absences for illness and job-related accidents than workers in the quieter area of the same plant. No consistent differences emerged in the number of recorded accidents, medical problems, or amounts of sick leave as a function of the work shift.

This paper is concerned with laboratory studies of the effects of noise at different times of day on performance. Most of the previous studies that have investigated this have only used short noise exposures and a limited range of testing times. My colleagues and I hope to remedy this weakness by examining the effects of an 8-hour noise exposure starting at 8:00, 16:00, or 24:00. However, I have no data from this type of study at the moment and the present discussion is restricted to laboratory studies using short noise exposures at a limited number of different times.

Certain theoretical approaches suggest that noise and time of day will interact. It has frequently been assumed that arousal increases over the day (Colquhoun, 1971) and it has also been assumed that noise increases arousal level (Broadbent, 1971). The Yerkes-Dodson law states that there is an optimum level of arousal for

I would like to thank Angus Craig and Ruth Condon for allowing me to include their unpublished data, shown in Fig. 1, in this paper. I would also like to thank Ruth Condon for her help in testing the subjects.

efficient performance and one would predict, therefore, that noise would improve performance when arousal level is low (e.g. early in the morning) but have little effect or even impair performance when circadian arousal is higher. Such results have in fact been obtained. For example, Blake (1971) found that noise improved performance on a letter cancellation task carried out at 8:00 a.m. but did not affect performance at 10:30 a.m. Similarly, Mullin and Corcoran (1977) found that detection rate on a vigilance task improved from morning to evening when the noise was low but not when the noise level was higher.

However, recent approaches have suggested that a unidimensional concept of arousal is inadequate (Broadbent, 1971; Folkard & Monk, 1980, 1982; and Hamilton, Hockey, & Rejman, 1977). Broadbent (1971) suggested that some variables produce a change in the average speed of performance whereas others primarily affect the proportion of errors or blocks in performance. This distinction was based largely on studies using the five-choice serial reaction time task and included in the first class of variables are alcohol, time of day, barbiturates and the personality dimension of introversion-extraversion. The second class of variables includes sleeplessness, noise, amphetamine and chlorpromazine. In each class there are some variables which might be regarded as 'stimulant' and others 'depressant'. The former will reduce or cancel out the effect of the latter provided they are from the same class. For example, the effect of sleeplessness is reduced by noise, and introverts are less impaired than extraverts when testing is in the early morning. A variable from one class has no consistent effect upon variables in the other. Thus, on the basis of Broadbent's classification, one would expect that time of testing would have little influence upon the effects of noise on performance.

Recently, it has been possible to classify variables according to their effects on semantic memory and working memory tasks (Baddeley, 1981). Folkard (1975) showed that performance on a syntactic reasoning task, which has a large working memory component, is at a peak in the late morning. Smith (1987) has shown that performance on a semantic processing test also varies over the day and this is shown in Table 1.

In contrast to these results Smith (1985) has shown that both the syntactic reasoning test and semantic processing test are not influenced by 85dB continuous noise.

Another series of experimental studies suggests that one should consider other variables when studying the effects of noise and time of day. Loeb, Holding and Baker (1982) and Baker, Holding and Loeb (in press) have found that noise × time of testing interactions differ for male and female subjects. Similarly, Davies and Davies (1975) found an interaction between noise, time of day, and age of the subject.

Table 1 Effect of time of testing on
number completed on the
semantic processing test

Time	Number completed
9:00	98.2
12:00	107.4
18:00	117.7

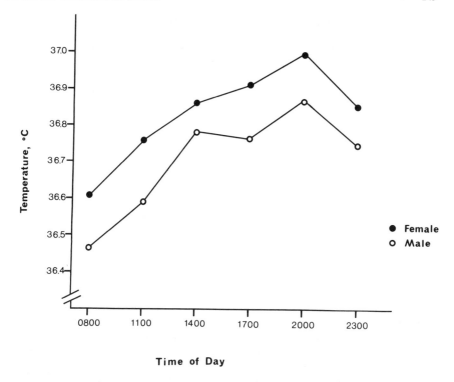

Figure 1 Mean temperature for male and female subjects at different times of the day.

Baker and Pangburn (1982) have presented data which show that males and females have different circadian temperature rhythms. Changes in temperature have often been equated with changes in arousal and Baker and Pangburn found that female subjects had a higher temperature than males in the early morning whereas males had a higher temperature in the late afternoon and evening. Unfortunately, there is other data which does not agree with that reported by Baker and Pangburn. Craig and Condon (unpublished study) have found that females have a higher mean temperature than males but the shape of the circadian temperature rhythm is the same for the two sexes. This is shown in Figure 1.

However, there is some other evidence which suggests that males and females may have a different pattern of circadian arousal. This is based on subjective reports of arousal level (Smith, unpublished) and the Thayer scores for male and female subjects at different times of day are shown in Table 2.

This shows that males increase in arousal from 9:00 to 12:00 to 18:00, whereas females show a peak at 12:00 and are then less aroused at 18:00.

All of the previous studies which have looked at the interaction between noise and time of testing have used very loud noise (90dB or over). However, recent studies of the effect of noise on performance have concentrated on moderate intensity noise (80–85dB) where there is little risk to hearing. Many of the theoretical views which have already been discussed were based on studies using high intensity noise and may not be applicable to the effects of lower intensity noise. For example, Broadbent's (1971) classification of noise was based on studies using

Table 2   Thayer scores for male and female subjects at different times
of day

Sex	General activation		
	9:00	12:00	18:00
Females (N = 20)	10.0	13.7	10.3
Males (N = 24)	8.5	11.4	12.3
	Deactivation-sleep		
Females (N = 20)	12.1	8.7	11.5
Males (N = 24)	13.4	9.0	9.2

95dB noise or above and lower intensity noise does not have any effect on the task which formed the basis of his classification. The first aim of the present study was to examine whether the effects of moderate intensity noise differed as time of testing was varied. The noise exposures were also fairly short and this meant that any findings could be related to studies already reported in the literature. Loeb and others (1982) showed that sex of subject interacted with noise and time of day and this was also examined in the present experiments.

EXPERIMENT 1

Frankenhauser and Lundberg (1977) showed that a certain type of mental arithmetic task (the Norinder mental arithmetic task) was performed more slowly in noise than in quiet. Loeb, Holding and Blake (1982) found that this result was only true for male subjects in the morning. When male subjects were tested in noise in the late afternoon, they completed more items than subjects tested in the quiet in the afternoon. Female subjects did not show the noise induced impairment in the morning. The first experiment was a modified replication of the Loeb study.

Method

A between-subject design was used and subjects were assigned to one of the groups formed by combining the following factors: time of testing, noise conditions, and sex of subject. Subjects were tested at 9:00, 12:00, or 18:00. Details of the noise and quiet conditions are given below. The subjects were tested in small groups and there were male and female subjects in each group. Separate groups were tested by male and female experimenters to control for any effects being due to a sex of subject-sex of experimenter interaction.

Subjects

The subjects were 77 male and female students from the University of Sussex. They were paid for participating in the experiment.

Nature of the Noise

Continuous free-field noise was used and the sound level of the noise condition was 85dB(C), with equal levels per octave ($\pm$1dB) from 125–400Hz. In the quiet condition the same noise was used as a level of 60dB(C).

Norinder Mental Arithmetic Task

The instructions and examples of this task are shown below.

> *You are to work as accurately and rapidly as you can. The rules for each item are as follows: If the sum or difference in the upper row is greater than that in the lower one, the lower result is subtracted from the upper one. However, if the lower result is the same as or greater than the upper one, the two results are added. In both cases all calculations are made in the head, and only the final answer is written below each problem. Three examples are worked out for you immediately below. If you have any questions regarding the procedure ask me before beginning.*

$$
\begin{array}{ccc}
8 + 4 & 9 + 5 & 6 + 9 \\
7 + 3 & 7 + 7 & 8 + 8 \\
\hline
2 & 28 & 31
\end{array}
$$

Each subject performed the task for 20 minutes. After 10 minutes the noise was switched off briefly and the subjects put a cross by the problem they were attempting at this time. The noise was then switched on again. This meant that performance on two 10-minute blocks could be examined.

Results

No evidence was obtained for interactions between time of day and noise or between time of day, noise, and sex of subject. However, there was a significant main effect of time of day ($F(2,65) = 5.30$, $p < 0.01$) with more problems being completed at 12:00 than 9:00 or 18:00. This is what one would expect for a task with a large working memory component. There was a significant main effect of sex ($F(1,65) = 5.61$, $p < 0.05$), the males completing more items than the females. Both of these significant effects are shown in Table 3.

The other significant effect was that of blocks ($F(1,65) = 16.29$, $p = 0.001$), subjects completing more items in the second 10-minute block than the first.

Discussion

The results of the first experiment failed to confirm the findings of Loeb and co-workers. This could be due to several factors, the most likely being the different noise levels in the two studies. As pointed out earlier it was not intended to use noise above 95dB and the next step was, therefore, to see whether there was any evidence for interacting between noise of this intensity and time of testing in other tasks.

Table 3   Effect of time of testing on number completed
on the Norinder Arithmetic Test[a]

Time	Number completed per 10 min. block
9:00	72.3
12:00	95.0
18:00	72.5

[a]Effect of sex on number completed: males = 89.5;
females = 72.0.

EXPERIMENT 2

Method

This experiment was similar in design to the previous one except that subjects
carried out a battery of tasks rather than the Norinder task. The noise levels and
times of testing were identical to those in Experiment 1.

Subjects

The subjects were 69 male and female students from Sussex University. They
were paid for participating in the experiment.

Battery of Tests

The tests used were (a) a syntactic reasoning test, (b) a semantic processing
test, (c) a digit symbol substitution test, and (d) a category clustering memory test.
Details of the tests are given below.

A syntactic reasoning test developed by Baddeley (1968) was used. The test
involves verifying statements ranging in complexity from simple active to passive
negative. Each statement relates the order of the letters A and B (e.g. 'A follows
B') and is followed by either the letters AB or the letters BA. The subject has to
read the statement, look at the order of the letters, and then decide whether the
statement is true or false. Each subject was given five practice statements prior to a
3-minute test session.

The semantic processing test, created by Baddeley and Thomson (Baddeley,
1981) consists of a large number of sentences typed on sheets of paper. The subject
ticks the ones they regard as correct and places a cross by the ones that are wrong.
The subjects worked at the test for 3 minutes. The instructions given to the subjects, and some example sentences, are shown below.

> Many of the things we do rely on common sense, a knowledge of the world and an ability to
> make use of such knowledge. The present test looks at the speed and accuracy with which people
> can use such information. It consists of a series of sentences, about half of which are true and
> half false. The true sentences are all obviously true, for example, "dogs have four legs", or
> "birds have wings". The false sentences are made up by combining two true sentences, such as
> "dogs have wings", or "birds have four legs". While the true sentences may not be all quite as
> obvious as this, there are no trick questions. The only slight exceptions to this are: (1) the term
> "edible" applies to anything that is normally eaten or drunk. Hence the statement "brandy is

edible" should be marked "true", while the statement "newspapers are edible" should not, despite the fact that some people nibble the odd newspaper from time to time. (2) the term "feet" refers to animals as well as people, despite the fact that the term "paws" or "hooves" might be more usual in some cases. Hence the sentence "A horse has feet" should be marked "true". (3) if you find a question that you really cannot answer, mark it with a ?

Work as quickly as you can without making errors, and put a tick against sentences which are true and a cross against those which are false. Are there any questions?

For the digit symbol substitution test, subjects were shown a sheet which consisted of random sequences of the numbers 0–9. At the top of the sheet were the numbers 0–9 and underneath each number was a symbol. The subjects had to work through the sheet drawing the appropriate symbol under each number. They had to complete as many items as possible in three minutes.

For clustering in free recall, subjects were shown a list of words and instructed that they were going to have to recall the list. They were told that they could write down the words in any order. The list consisted of 32 words and there were eight words from four different categories. The subjects were given 1 1/2 minutes to write down as many words as possible. Further details of this task are given in Smith, Jones and Broadbent (1981).

Results

There was no evidence of noise × time of day interactions nor noise × time of day × sex of subject interactions for the syntactic reasoning test and the digit symbol substitution test. However, there were significant interactions between noise × time of day × sex of subject for both the semantic processing test ($F(2,57) = 3.99$, $p < 0.05$) and the clustering test ($F(2,57) = 5.10$, $p < 0.01$). These results are shown in Table 4.

If one initially considers only the 9:00 and 18:00 scores, one can see that the semantic processing results resemble those obtained by Loeb and co-workers

Table 4 Interactions between noise, time of testing, and sex of subject

| | Semantic Processing Test[a] | | | | | |
| | Males | | | Females | | |
Noise level	9:00	12:00	18:00	9:00	12:00	18:00
Quiet (60dBC)	109.4	106.0	98.0	91.5	98.3	131.7
Noise (85dBC)	90.6	110.5	124.4	101.2	115.2	116.7
	Clustering in Free Recall[b]					
Quiet (60dBC)	0.62	0.75	0.79	0.89	0.67	0.90
Noise (85dBC)	0.84	0.61	0.73	0.77	0.90	0.60

[a]Number completed;
[b]The higher the C score, the more organized the recall.

(1982): males impaired by noise in the morning but better in noise than quiet in the evening; females better in noise than quiet in the morning but better in quiet in the evening. At 12:00 both males and females were better in noise.

However, the interaction found for the clustering test is produced by a different pattern of results. Clustering scores (*C* scores) were calculated using the following formula (Dalrymple-Alford, 1970).

$$C = \frac{R - \text{Min } R}{\text{Max } R - \text{Min } R}$$

where *R* = Numbers of words recalled − number of runs
  Max *R* = Number of words recalled − number of categories
  Min *R* = 0 if number recalled + 1 ⩾ 2 × largest category recalled, otherwise
       = 2 × (largest category recalled − 1).

Scores range from 0, no clustering, to 1, perfect clustering. The results showed that males clustered to a greater extent in noise in the morning whereas they clustered more in quiet in the evening. Females were better in the quiet in both the morning and the evening. At 12:00 males were better in quiet than noise whereas females showed the reverse pattern of results.

Discussion

The results of this experiment provide some support for an interaction between noise, time of testing, and sex of subject. However, they also show that this interaction is only obtained with certain tasks. The results also suggest that the interaction may also arise from different pattern of results for different tasks. The next experiment examined the reliability of the interaction obtained for the semantic processing test.

EXPERIMENT 3

Method

In this experiment time of testing was a between-subject variable but noise became a within-subject variable. Each subject carried out the semantic processing task in both noise and quiet at one of the times of testing. Subjects were tested in the order quiet-noise or in the order noise-quiet.

The times of testing and noise levels were the same as in the previous experiment.

Subjects

The subjects were 43 male and female students from Sussex University. They were paid for participating in the experiment.

Table 5 Effects of noise, time of testing and sex of subject on the semantic processing task: An attempt to replicate

Noise level	Males			Females		
	9:00	12:00	18:00	9:00	12:00	18:00
Quiet (55dBC)	105.6	115.0	105.0	112.1	114.4	118.2
Noise (85dBC)	105.5	111.7	109.0	116.5	113.0	127.8

Results

The results from this study are shown in Table 5.

An analysis of variance showed that the interaction between noise, time of testing, and sex failed to reach significance ($F < 1$).

GENERAL DISCUSSION

It has often been assumed that noise increases arousal and, if one adheres to the Yerkes-Dodson law, which states that there is an inverted-U relationship between arousal and performance, noise should improve performance when circadian arousal is low (e.g. in the early morning) but have little effect or even impair performance at later times of day. However, the results from a series of laboratory studies showed no interaction between noise and time of testing. This argues against interpreting the effects of noise and time of day in terms of a single dimension of arousal. The present results also conflict with findings reported by Blake (1971) and Mullin and Corcoran (1977), which showed an interaction between noise and time of day. The conflicting results could be due to the different noise levels used; Blake used very loud noise (100dB) and Mullin and Corcoran used 90dB noise whereas the noise level in the present studies was 85dBC. It is still possible, therefore, to maintain the view that noise and time of day interact but one must qualify this statement and say that such an interaction may depend on a very high noise intensity.

In the present studies there were some interactions between noise, time of day, and sex of subject. However, these interactions were only obtained in certain tasks (the semantic processing and clustering tasks) and the pattern of results producing the interaction varied with the task. The interaction found in the semantic processing task reflected the same pattern of results as those obtained by Loeb and others (1982): males being impaired by noise in the morning but better in noise in the evening, females being better in noise than quiet in the morning, but better in quiet in the evening. Unfortunately, this effect was not very reliable and could not be replicated in Experiment 3. In the clustering task males were better in noise in the morning but better in quiet in the evening, whereas females were better in the quiet in both the morning and evening. It appears, therefore, that the interaction between noise, time of testing, and sex of subject does not depend on the noise level being 95dB or higher. Unfortunately, the interaction is very variable and is task-dependent. It is possible that the poor reliability of the interaction reflects the experimental design used in these studies. The between-subject design employed eliminates the possibility of asymmetric transfer. However, one will not obtain main effects using such a design if the size of the effect is smaller than the individual differences in the task. Sampling biases may produce higher order interactions and it is essential to replicate any study showing such interactions to determine whether they are reliable or whether they may be due, at least in part, to biases in subject sampling.

Although the results reported here have been negative or variable one should not take this to mean that there is little or no circadian variation in stress. They do suggest that it may be more profitable to study this in other ways. It has already been pointed out that there is a need to look at longer noise exposures at a wider range of times. It may also be better to take tasks where there is a reliable circadian rhythm (e.g. letter cancellation) and have subjects perform the task for several days at different times of day. The subjects would then be aided by developing more adequate models of how noise and time of day influence performance. In the area of circadian rhythms it has been traditional to explain variation in performance in terms of changes in arousal. A unidimensional view of arousal has now been replaced by more sophisticated multidimensional models, but there is still a need to examine performance in detail to see which aspects actually change over the day. A change in performance over the day may reflect several things. For example, subjects may carry out the task in the same way throughout the day but may do this more or less efficiently at different times. Alternatively, subjects may carry out the task in different ways at different times and some strategies may be more efficient than others. Finally, circadian variation may be due to changes in the subjects' motivation and not reflect any variation in the more mechanistic aspects of performance. Such an approach has already been applied to the effects of noise on performance (Smith, 1983) and noise appears to influence the choice of strategy, the efficiency of the control processes, and it also changes the motivation of the subjects. Preliminary studies suggest that the effects of noise and time of day often differ and this supports Broadbent's (1971) classification. Broadbent distinguished an upper level which controls performance of lower levels of processing. Variables such as noise and sleep loss were assumed to influence the lower level directly whereas others, such as time of day, changed the efficiency of the upper level. Recent results suggest that Broadbent may have linked the variables to the wrong levels, for noise appears to alter the efficiency of the control processes rather than the lower levels of performance. However, there is strong evidence, including the results reported in this paper, supporting Broadbent's view that variables which have often been related to a single dimension of arousal should be classified into at least two distinct groups.

CONCLUSION

Shiftwork and noise exposure have been recognized as important factors in producing occupational stress. Both of these factors have been studied a great deal but there have been few studies which have examined the effects of noise on performance at different times of day. The results of a series of laboratory studies on the effect of moderately intense noise on various tasks at different times of day showed no evidence of an interaction between noise and time of day. There was some evidence that circadian variation in the effects of noise differed for male and female subjects but these effects were confined to certain tasks and were not very reliable. Future studies will examine the effects of prolonged noise exposure around the clock and this may yield interactions which will be of interest from a practical and theoretical point of view.

REFERENCES

Baddeley, A. D. (1968). A three-minute reasoning test based on grammatical transformations. *Psychonomic Science, 10,* 341–342.

Baddeley, A. D. (1981). The cognitive psychology of everyday life. *British Journal of Psychology, 72,* 257–269.

Baker, M. A. & Pangburn, K. (1982, July). *Female temperature cycles and their relationship to performance.* Paper presented at the 20th Congress of the International Association of Applied Psychology, Edinburgh, Scotland.

Baker, M. A., Holding, D. H. & Loeb, M. (1984). Noise, sex and time of day effects in a mathematics task. *Ergonomics, 27,* 67–80.

Blake, M. (1971). Temperament and time of day. In W. P. Colquhoun (Ed.), *Biological rhythms and human performance.* London: Academic Press.

Broadbent, D. E. (1971). *Decision and stress.* London: Academic Press.

Broadbent, D. E. (1979). Human performance and noise. In C. M. Harris (Ed.), *Handbook of noise control.* New York: McGraw-Hill.

Cesana, G. C., Ferrario, M., Curti, R., Zanettini, R., Grieco, A., Sega, R., Palermo, A., Hara, G., Libretti, A. & Algeri, S. (1982). Work stress and urinary catecholamines excretion in shift workers exposed to noise. *La Medicina del Lavero, 2,* 99–109.

Cohen, A. (1973). Industrial noise, medical absence, and accident record data on exposed workers. In *Proceedings of International Congress on Noise as a Public Health Problem.* (pp. 441–454). Washington, DC: U.S. EPA.

Colquhoun, W. P. (Ed.). (1971). *Biological rhythms and human performance.* London: Academic Press.

Dalrymple-Alford, E. C. (1970). Measurement of clustering in free recall. *Psychological Bulletin, 74,* 32–34.

Davies, A. & Davies, D. R. (1975). The effects of noise and time of day upon age differences in performance at two checking tasks. *Ergonomics, 18,* 321–336.

Folkard, S. (1975). Diurnal variation in logical reasoning. *British Journal of Psychology, 66,* 1–8.

Folkard, S. (1981). Shiftwork and Performance. In L. C. Johnson, W. P. Colquhoun, D. I. Tepas and M. J. Colligan (Eds), *Biological rhythms, sleep and shiftwork: Advances in sleep research* (Vol. 7). New York: Spectrum.

Folkard, S. & Monk, T. H. (1980). Circadian rhythms in human memory. *British Journal of Psychology, 71,* 295–307.

Folkard, S. & Monk, T. H. (1982). Circadian rhythms in performance: one or more oscillators. In R. Sinz and M. R. Rosenzweig (Eds.), *Psychophysiology 1980.* Elsevier: Amsterdam.

Frankenhauser, M. & Lundberg, U. (1977). The influence of cognitive set on performance and arousal under different noise loads. *Motivation and Emotion, 1,* 139–149.

Hamilton, P., Hockey, G. R. J. & Rejman, M. (1977). The place of the concept of activation in human information processing theory: An integrative approach. In S. Dornic (Ed.), *Attention and performance VI.* Hillsdale, NJ: Erlbaum.

Loeb, M., Holding, D. H. & Baker, M. A. (1982). Noise stress and circadian arousal in self-paced computation. *Motivation and Emotion, 6,* 43–48.

Mullin, J. & Corcoran, D. W. J. (1977). Interaction of task amplitude with circadian variation in auditory vigilance performance. *Ergonomics, 20,* 193–200.

Smith, A. P. (1983). The effects of noise on strategies of human performance. In G. Rossi (Ed.), *Proceedings of Fourth International Congress on Noise as a Public Health Problem* (pp. 797–807). Turin, Italy, Centro Ricerche e Studi Amplifon.

Smith, A. P. (1985). The effects of different types of noise on semantic processing and syntactic reasoning. *Acta Psychologica, 58,* 263–273.

Smith, A. P. (1987). Activation states and semantic processing: A comparison of the effects of noise and time of day. *Acta Psychologica, 64,* 271–288.

Smith, A. P., Jones, D. M. & Broadbent, D. E. (1981). The effects of noise on recall of categorised lists. *British Journal of Psychology, 72,* 299–316.

III

PHYSIOLOGICAL ASPECTS OF STRESS

11

Individual Differences
in Tolerance to Stress: The Role of Reactivity

Jan Strelau
University of Warsaw

Since the beginning of the 1950's, especially under the influence of H. Selye's two most popular monographs (1950, 1956), hundreds, if not thousands, of books and papers have been published with the aim of presenting different aspects of psychological stress. These earlier studies paid little attention, if any at all, to the individual differences in stress. Indeed, these were regarded more as sources of error variance as was the case at the beginning of experimental psychology.

Among the pioneers who advocated the individual differences approach in the study of stress, one should mention E. A. Haggard, who wrote in 1949, among other things, that: "some of the factors which influence an individual's ability to tolerate and master stress include: the nature of his early identifications and his present *character structure*, and their relation to the demands and gratifications of the present stress-producing situation" (Haggard, 1949, p. 458). The idiosyncratic approach to the study of different aspects of stress has been systematically developed by Lazarus (1966; Opton & Lazarus, 1967), and for several years it has been accepted by many psychologists involved in stress research (e.g. Appley & Trumbull, 1967; Chan, 1977; Krohne & Rogner, 1982; Lacey, 1967; Magnusson, 1982; McGrath, 1970b; Schulz & Schönpflug, 1982).

The significance of individual differences in approaching stress differs depending on the understanding of the nature of stress. Without going into details, one should agree with J. E. McGrath (1970a) who argues that there is almost no place for individual differences if stress is regarded as an external factor, as a stress-inducing situation (see e.g., Weick, 1970). The same is true if one regards stress as the response (reaction) to given stressors, which is in line with Selye's understanding of stress (1956, 1975).

The importance of individual differences in research on stress has become clear since stress began to be regarded as a state which is the outcome of interaction between the stress-inducing environment (stressor) and the individual, including his physical, as well as psychological, characteristics (Magnusson, 1982; McGrath, 1970a). "What becomes a stressor is not determined solely by the nature of

Preparation of the manuscript was carried out during the author's fellowship (1983–84) at the Netherlands Institute for Advanced Study in the Humanities and Social Sciences (N.I.A.S.). The author is in debt to Mrs. Saskia Lepelaar for the preparation of the manuscript.

the situation or by the individual and his disposition. A stress reaction in an individual is the joint effect of his psychic and somatic dispositions *and* the stress-provoking quality of situational conditions, the stressors" (Magnusson, 1982, p. 234).

Most psychologists involved in stress research undertaken at the interactional level agree with R. S. Lazarus (1966) that appraisal of the perceived situation should be treated as an important variable in determining psychological stress, the latter being regarded as threat (see also, Appley & Trumbull, 1967; Magnusson, 1982; McGrath, 1982). The process of appraisal which takes place in the individual is always a subjective one, and this means, among other things, that it runs differently in different people. If we take this understanding of stress as a point of departure, then the conclusion must be that the individual differences approach should be considered as one of the most important paradigms in the study of stress. "Individual differences, styles, patterns or response, and prepotent tendencies appear to be the rule rather than the exception in studies of psychological stress" (Appley & Trumbull, 1967, p. 4).

SOURCES OF INDIVIDUAL DIFFERENCES IN STUDYING STRESS

I do not pretend to be presenting a taxonomy of all possible sources of the individual differences which should be taken into account when studying stress. However, I would like to make a preliminary list of those factors which might be regarded as sources of individual differences within the different aspects of studying stress, including the perception of stress-inducing situations, the reactions to stress, as well as coping with stress.

Differences in Appraising a Threatening Situation

What is regarded as threatening for one individual may be treated as less threatening, or not at all threatening for another (Lazarus 1966; McGrath, 1970b). The differences in perceiving given situations as being threatening may also be considered within one individual only. What he or she perceives as a source of threat at a given moment may not be appraised as threatening in another period of life, or when situated in another place. Thus inter- as well as intraindividual differences exist in objectively appraising the same situation as a stressor. Allow me to mention several sources for these differences.

The Individual's History of Life

No two people exist who may be considered to be equal from this point of view, and even the same person, under successive experiences in the ontogenetic development, changes permanently in this respect (Tyler, 1978). Appley & Trumbull (1967) pay much attention to the history of life as one of the determinants of the individual's vulnerability to different types of stressors. The history of life seems to be the most general factor which has several aspects and some of these are of special importance in determining whether or not a given situation is appraised as threatening. These factors will be mentioned below.

The Cognitive Map (Network)

Appraising a given situation as being threatening or not should first be regarded as a cognitive process (Lazarus, 1966, 1967). The outcome of this process depends on the situation being analyzed, and the knowledge stored by the individual during his or her lifetime. People differ significantly in cognitive maps, the network of which also undergoes strong developmental changes.

Experience with Stress-Inducing Situations

Of special importance is the knowledge of the consequences of stress-inducing situations as well as the acquired experience to cope with them. Knowledge and experience are different in different people and they change during the individual's lifetime.

System of Motivation and the Accepted System of Values

A situation which is important to the individual for some reasons, may be regarded as more threatening than the same situation to which he or she pays little attention. Depending on different peoples' systems of values, the same situation may be treated as either threatening or not threatening. For instance, some people may be particularly sensitive to threats of a physical nature, whereas others are more sensitive to a threat to their ego, or interpersonal threats (see McGrath, 1970c).

The Structure and Sensitivity of the Receptor

The stress-inducing situation, where it is determined by its physical properties, may change according to the sensitivity and structure of the individual's receptors. In this respect inter- as well as intraindividual differences have been recorded (see Nebylitsyn, 1972; Strelau, 1983). Also strongly expressed developmental changes may be observed. For example, noise of high frequency may not be perceived at all by old people because of changes in the structure of the auditory receptor. Auditory stimuli of moderate intensity will be perceived as such by individuals of average age, whereas the same stimuli may be perceived as very strong in both young and old people because of developmental changes in the sensitivity of the auditory receptor.

The Actual (Physical and Psychic) State of the Individual

Individuals with a high level of arousal (activation) react to objectively the same stressors differently than individuals characterized by a low level of arousal. The appraisal of stress will be different, depending on whether the individual, at the very moment the stressful situation appears, experiences anger, pleasure, or fear. Many other stages in which people differ, and which may be different even within the same individual, might be mentioned here as codeterminers of the appraisal of the perceived situations as being threatening.

Individual Differences in Reactions to Stressors

The variety of reactions to stressors, independent of whether the former will be regarded as consequences of stress, as stress itself, or as indicators of the state of stress, depends not only on the kind of stress-inducing situations, but also on the individual himself or herself, and here again, exist strongly expressed as inter- and intraindividual differences. These may be considered at least from the following points of view.

Preferences in Response to Stress

Reactions to stressors may be considered on three different levels of human activity—physiological, psychological and behavioral (McGrath, 1970c). People differ where the kind of activity which might be considered as dominant to stress-inducing situations is concerned. Some individuals express the state of stress in physiological reactions, whereas others respond at the psychological or behavioral level. But also within the same individual some stressors evoke psychological reactions whereas in other situations the behavioral component of stress will be dominant.

Individual Differences in Behavior

During the state of stress the motor reactions of some individuals are dominant, whereas others tend to expose verbal behavior. When considering motor reactions it is highly probable that, depending on the specificity of the effector(s) being held under control, the expressiveness of behavior, treated as the response to stress-inducing situations, may be different. Inter- and intraindividual differences in this respect seem to be of special importance in all experiments where decrement of performance has been regarded as an indicator of the state of stress (e.g., Lundberg, 1982; McGrath, 1982).

Individual Differences in Psychic States

Where psychological reactions to stressors are concerned, it is known that people may differ in whether they react to stressors with anger rather than fear. In some people the changes in the mental processes which are being regarded as a response to stress may appear especially strong in the thinking processes, whereas in others perception is greatly influenced. These differences may also be considered as intraindividual ones.

Individual Differences in Physiological Reactions

Many data have been collected which show that the pattern of physiological changes depends not only on the specificity of stressors under which they have been evoked, but also on the individual (e.g., Cox, 1978). In some individuals the cardiovascular system reacts strongly to stressors, in others the electrodermal activity is especially sensitive to these stimuli. The estimation of resistance to stress may completely change when electrocortical activity is taken into account. Classical experiments which show that there exist intraindividual differences in physiological reaction patterns to stress have been conducted by Lacey (1967; Lacey & VanLehn, 1952; see also Fahrenberg et al., 1983).

Individual Differences in Coping with Stress

The state of stress in itself may occur or not, the stressors may be perceived as more or less threatening, depending on the degree to which the individual is able to cope with stress, or what is the repertoire of coping mechanisms being activated during stress. The importance of coping with stress in human behavior has been exposed by Lazarus (1966, 1967), who distinguishes two main coping mechanisms with stress—direct actions and defense mechanisms, Schultz & Schönpflug (1982) have regarded the inadequate coping behavior as the main condition for the occurrence of stress. It is not possible here to go into the details of the nature of coping mechanisms for stress and the role they play in human behavior which have been discussed by many authors (e.g., Cox, 1978; Fenz, 1975; Lazarus, 1966, 1967; Meichenbaum, 1977). However, it should be mentioned that the individual differences approach in studying these mechanisms may help in their proper understanding. Individual differences in coping with stress may have different aspects; let me discuss some of these.

Direct Actions Versus Defense Mechanisms

Whether direct actions or defense mechanisms will be preferred as main ways of coping with stress largely depends on the system of reinforcement used by parents and other important persons in case of successful or unsuccessful behavior in stress-inducing situations thus leading to individual differences in this respect. Many other factors could be mentioned here as determining differences in the preferences mentioned above.

Differences in Defense Mechanisms

If defense mechanisms are taken into account we should be aware that different people may use different defense mechanisms as successful means by which the state of stress may be avoided or lowered. At the same time the same individual may use different defense mechanisms in different periods of time and in different situations in order to lower the stimulative value of stressors. The significance of defense mechanisms in regulating the stimulative value of situations has been explored in our laboratory by H. Grzegolowska-Klarkowska (1980).

Differences in Direct Actions

If we consider direct actions, people may prefer actions which are aimed at removing or lowering the state of stress by approaching the given situation (approaching reactions to stress), or they may prefer to undertake actions which allow escape or withdrawal from stress-inducing situations so as to avoid stress reactions. These differences may be regarded as inter- and intraindividual ones.

Differences in Repertoire, Capacities, and Acquired Skills

Depending on the level of knowledge, experience in coping with stress, and also on some psychophysiological features of the organism (being inherited as well as developed in ontogenesis), individuals differ in their ability to cope with stress. This ability also undergoes developmental changes.

ROLE OF PERSONALITY DIMENSIONS IN CODETERMINING THE STATE OF STRESS

In any discussion of the individual differences approach in studies on stress, a special place should be given to personality and temperament traits. As has been stressed by Lazarus ". . . the objective stimulus situation is appraised on the basis of its characteristics as well as traits of personality . . ." (1967, p. 164). The impact of personality dimensions in codetermining the state of stress differs according to the type of situation regarded as being stress-inducing, the individual, and on the specificity of the personality trait being taken into account (see Chan, 1977; Cox, 1978).

Personality Traits with Limited Contribution in Codetermining the Tolerance to Stress

One may assume that in many stress-inducing situations some personality dimensions may not be at all important in determining the state of stress, or their importance is low or limited in scope; for example, a high position on the dimension of sociability probably does not influence the individual's reactions and behavior when he or she is attacked by an aggressive and dangerous dog. If we take another personality dimension into account, level of aspiration, then it might be assumed that for individuals with a high level of aspiration, an examination situation or a situation of competition will be perceived as more threatening than for individuals with low level of aspiration. This personality dimension may at the same time have no influence on perceiving other situations as being threatening.

Let us take another example which illustrates a broader scope of influence in codetermining the state of stress. Depending upon the position the person shares on the repression-sensitization dimension of personality, he or she may appraise many situations as being threatening (sensitizer), or the opposite may occur, that is, the individual may reveal a tendency not to appraise situations as being threatening (repressor) (Krohne & Rogner, 1982).

The impact of this personality trait in codetermining the state of stress is much broader as compared with the personality dimensions discussed above, because it influences the appraisal of all, or almost all, perceived stimuli (situations).

Many personality dimensions may be mentioned here as examples of traits which may codetermine to some degree whether or not a situation is appraised as being threatening. They may also codetermine the type of reaction in which the state of stress might be expressed as well as the way in which the individual copes with stress.

Personality Traits with High Impact on Determining the State of Stress

Special attention should be paid to such personality and temperament dimensions which, because of their specific nature, have a high impact in determining whether the joint effect of the interaction between the perceived situation and the individual results in the state of stress or not. I would like to mention three dimensions: anxiety, extraversion-introversion, and reactivity. These should, however, be treated more as examples than as full list of this type of dimension (also important is neuroticism or strength of the nervous system).

Because the perception of a situation as being threatening is generally expressed as being typical for the state of stress* (e.g., Lazarus, 1966; McGrath, 1970a;

---

*It should be emphasized that this understanding of stress is in contradiction to the classical understanding of stress introduced by Selye (1956, 1975).

Spielberger, 1972), it may be assumed that individuals with a high level of trait-anxiety—who are especially prone to developing the state of anxiety (Spielberger, 1976)—will suffer a greater amount of stress, and intensity of stress, than individuals in a low-anxiety group. This regularity depends, of course, on the specificity of the stress-inducing situation.

Many studies are to be found in the literature on stress which refer to resistance to stress (and coping with it) being related to the individual's trait-anxiety. The eight volumes edited by Spielberger and his joint editors from 1975 until 1982, under the title of *Stress and Anxiety,* may serve as the best example of this. In fact, this personality dimension does influence to some degree the type of reaction taken here as an indicator of the state of stress. It also influences the level of performance regarded as one of the most popular indices of resistance to stress as well as the way of coping with it (e.g., approaching vs. avoiding behavior).

As regards the extraversion-introversion aspect, one may look at this dimension as a codeterminer of the state of stress at least from two different points of view. Taking into account the specificity (content) of this dimension it could be said that extraverts are more externally and socially oriented and would therefore regard situations of social deprivation as being stressful, which is unlikely to be the case for introverts, who are more likely to regard extensive and intensive interpersonal contacts as being stressful.

The extraversion-introversion dimension may also be considered as related to stress from another point of view, taking into account the physiological mechanism underlying this dimension. Thus I would like to discuss the nonspecific aspect of this dimension as being especially important in determining stress. As is already well known, the reticulocortical arousal loop has been regarded by Eysenck (1967, 1970) as the physiological mechanism of extraversion-introversion. Extraverts should be characterized as having a generally lower level of arousal compared with introverts for whom a high level of arousal is rather typical. It can be learned from the literature devoted to stress (e.g., Lazarus, 1966; Lundberg, 1982; Selye, 1974) that there is a close relationship between the individual's level of arousal, the stimulative value of the threatening situation, and the state of stress.

The physiological mechanism which takes part in regulating the stimulative value of the perceived situation should be regarded as an important factor in codetermining whether a situation is appraised as being threatening. Referring to Wundt (1874), Eysenck looks at the fact that extraversion-introversion codetermines whether a stimulation of given intensity should be regarded as evoking a positive hedonic tone or a negative hedonic tone (Eysenck, 1981a). By taking Selye's position we could say that both extremes (high positive and high negative hedonistic tones) have much in common with stress, whereas regarding stress as a state evoked by threatening situations, the negative hedonistic tone may be considered as synonymous with stress. Where introverts are concerned, stimuli of lower intensity evoke a hedonistic negative tone (the state of stress) as compared with extraverts, and the range of stimuli which evoke this state will be broader where introverts are concerned.

A great deal of evidence has been collected by H. J. Eysenck (1981b) and his students, which shows that specific interrelation exists between level of performance and the stimulative value of situations, depending on whether we are dealing with extraverts or introverts. From those regularities which can be found in this respect, it should be clear that so far as the state of stress in relation to level of performance is concerned—and this is one of the most common approaches in stress research (e.g., Broverman et al., 1974; Lundberg, 1982; McGrath, 1970a)—we have to consider extraversion-introversion as one of the individual's most important traits which take part in the interplay between the stimulative value of the situation regarded as being threatening, and the individual's level of performance.

Extraversion-introversion, because of its physiological mechanism, has been regarded by many psychologists as an especially important personality trait for codetermining whether or not a situation might be regarded as threatening. It is also this mechanism which forces us to consider it as a dimension which influences the individual's type of reaction, and his or her level of performance during the state of stress (e.g., Eysenck, 1981b; Morris, 1979; Schalling, 1976; Schönpflug, 1982; Schulz & Schönpflug, 1982).

It would require a longer paper than this to draw the whole picture for an understanding of the interaction between extraversion-introversion and stress. One of the main purposes here is to indicate the place of reactivity, which is regarded as a temperament dimension in codetermining the resistance to stress.

REACTIVITY AS CODETERMINER OF THE STATE OF STRESS

Discussing the relation between the state of stress and reactivity I would like to refer to the understanding of stress as a state caused by the lack of equilibrium (imbalance) between environmental demands and the individual's capability to cope with them (see McGrath, 1970a; Schultz & Schönpflug, 1982; Laux & Vossel, 1982).

The Concept of Stress

Instead of limiting the cognitive appraisal of the demand-capability imbalance almost to threat regarded as the synonym of psychological stress (Lazarus, 1966; McGrath, 1970a, 1982) let us pay attention to the understanding of stress proposed by Selye (1956), who considers the nonspecificity of demands (stressors) and the nonspecific response to these demands (stress) as the essence of his theory. As Selye writes: *"it is immaterial whether the agent or situation we face is pleasant or unpleasant;* all that counts is the intensity of the demand for readjustment or adaptation" (1975, p. 15). Thus the intensity of demand (stimuli) is the crucial factor (stressor) causing stress. The stress response will be stronger the more extreme (on both directions on the intensity dimension of demands) the stimuli are. "Deprivation of stimuli and excessive stimulation are both accompanied by an increase in stress, sometimes to the point of distress" (Selye, 1975, p. 21).

Selye regards his concept of stress as a response-based one being in essence a biological phenomenon, although produced by environmental factors. This is often described as systemic stress (see Appley & Trumbull, 1967). If we take into account, however, that the intensity of agents causing stress depends not only on the agents themselves but above all on the individual's cognitive appraisal of these agents and on his or her tolerability (Lazarus, 1966) or vulnerability (Appley & Trumbull, 1967) to stressors, in which individuals differ, then we have a psychological concept of stress based on an interactional paradigm. The essence of this concept consists of paying attention to the intensity of stimulation (determined by the stimuli themselves as well as by the individual's cognitive appraisal), and to the capacity of the individual to cope with stimuli of extreme value, both deprivation and strong stimuli.

The state of stress is caused by the imbalance between the individual's capacity (determined by external and internal conditions) to respond to stimuli of different intensities and the stimulation value of the situation; the stimulative value being determined by its objectively existing features (intensity, complexity, etc.) as well as by the subjective process of appraisal undertaken.

The intensity of stimulation (stressor) has been regarded by Selye (1956,1975) as a nonspecific agent causing stress. Also authors discussing the concept of psychological stress consider the intensity of stimulation as a source of stress (see McGrath, 1970c; Lundberg, 1982; Weick, 1970), which allows us to relate the concept of stress to the level of arousal (activation) theory. Taking as point of departure the Yerkes-Dodson (1908) law and Hebb's (1955) concept of arousal, one may conclude that stimulation above as well as below the individual's need evokes a state of discomfort; this is the state of stress, which leads to changes in physiological, psychological and behavioral reactions as well as in the level of performance (see Lundberg, 1982).

The Understanding of Reactivity

In accordance with our theory of temperament, reactivity is regarded as a trait that is primarily biologically determined and should be considered an important variable in codetermining the stimulation value of situations as well as the individual's capacity to respond to stimuli of given intensity. Thus reactivity has an influence in developing the state of stress. It is impossible to discuss the concept of reactivity, in detail here.[†] Reactivity is considered in our theory as one of the two main temperament traits related to the energetic characteristics of behavior. It is regarded as a feature of the organism which codetermines individuals' sensitivity and their capacity to work (endurance) under strong or prolonged stimulation. Understood in this way reactivity reveals itself in the intensity (magnitude) of reactions. The higher the reactivity, the larger (stronger) the reactions to stimuli of a given intensity caused by high sensitivity. In individuals characterized by high level of reactivity the capability to work under strong stimulation is lower than in individuals having low level of reactivity. The decrement in the working capacity (endurance) reveals itself in a breakdown of the law of strength, which means that increasing stimulation causes a decrease in the intensity (magnitude) of reaction or even some disturbances in reactions to strong or long lasting stimuli.

Interrelations Between Reactivity and Stress

In high-reactive individuals, whose physiological mechanism intensifies stimulation (with low sensory sensitivity threshold and low endurance) a given situation has higher stimulative value in comparison with low-reactive individuals. The

---

[†]The concept of reactivity as well as other aspects of our theory which might be regarded as important for better understanding of the relation between stress and reactivity have been presented in details elsewhere (Strelau, 1983).

latter are characterized by a physiological mechanism which suppresses stimulation (high sensory threshold and high endurance). Hence it appears that situations of high-stimulative value which do not evoke stress in low-reactive individuals (who have a high need for stimulation) evoke the state of stress in high-reactive individuals (who have a low need for stimulation). The opposite may be said to be true in case of situations characterized by a low stimulative value. A situation of deprivation which may evoke a state of discomfort (stress) in low-reactive individuals may be perceived as adequate for individuals with a high level of reactivity, because in this case the same situation has a higher stimulation value.

We may look at the reactivity dimension as a factor modulating the intensity of objectively acting and/or perceived stimuli, as has been argued above. Yet this temperament trait might be also regarded as a feature of the organism which codetermines the individual's sensitivity and endurance, considering both these phenomena as dependent on each other and sharing a relatively stable ratio between them (see Nebylitsyn, 1972; Strelau 1983). Reactivity, being one of the internal conditions of the capacity to respond to stimuli of different intensity, should be regarded as codetermining tolerability to stressors. In high-reactive individuals the tolerability to stressors, defined as situations of high stimulative value, is low because of their low endurance, whereas the tolerability of high reactives to situations of low stimulative value (stimulus deprivation) is high because of their high sensitivity. The opposite is true in case of low-reactive individuals. They reveal a high tolerability under highly stimulating situations whereas their tolerability to stressors characterized by extremely weak stimulation is low.

All the described relations between the state of stress and reactivity should only be given the status of hypotheses built first of all upon theoretical considerations. During the last few years, however, several sets of data have been collected in our laboratory which make us convinced (see e.g., Eliasz, 1981; Klonowicz, 1974; Strelau, 1983) that the way we built our hypotheses is fruitful and promising.

CONCLUSIONS

The understanding of stress as an outcome of the interaction between the individual and the stress-inducing environment implicates the importance of individual differences in research on stress. The process of appraisal of the perceived situation, treated as the most important factor in determining stress, is always a subjective one, thus being different in different people. Individual differences in perceiving a situation as threatening (stress) should be considered only as one aspect of the differential approach to stress. There exist also individual differences in reactions to stress as well as in coping with stress.

A special place in codetermining the state of stress should be given to personality dimensions in which individuals differ. It has been suggested by the author that some of these dimensions have a particular impact in determining whether a situation will be perceived as being threatening or not. This impact may be seen also if one takes into account reactions to stress or performance under stress-inducing situations.

Special attention has been payed to reactivity. This temperament dimension, codetermining the stimulative value of situations and the individual's capacity to respond to stimulation of given intensity, should be regarded as an important source of variance in most of the aspects of stress under investigation.

REFERENCES

Appley, M. H., & Trumbull, R. (1967). On the concept of psychological stress. In M. H. Appley & R. Trumbull (Eds.), *Psychological stress. Issues in research.* New York: Appleton-Century-Crofts.

Broverman, D. M., Klaiber, E. L., Vogel, W., & Kobayashi, Y. (1974). Short-term versus long-term effects of adrenal hormones on behavior. *Psychological Bulletin, 81,* 672–694.

Chan, K. B. (1977). Individual differences in reactions to stress and their personality and situational determinants: Some implications for community mental health. *Social Science and Medicine, 11,* 89–103.

Cox, T. (1978). *Stress.* London: Macmillan Press.

Eliasz, A. (1981). *Temperament a system regulacji stymulacji.* Warszawa: Panstwowe Wydawnictwo Naukowe.

Eysenck, H. J. (1967). *The biological basis of personality.* Springfield, IL: Thomas.

Eysenck, H. J. (1970). *The structure of human personality.* London: Methuen.

Eysenck, H. J. (1981a). General features of the model. In H. J. Eysenck (Ed.), *A model for personality.* New York: Springer-Verlag.

Eysenck, H. J. (Ed.) (1981b). *A model for personality.* New York: Springer-Verlag.

Fahrenberg, J., Walschburger, P., Foerster, F., Myrtek, M., & Müller, W. (1983). An evaluation of trait, state and reaction aspects of activation processes. *Psychophysiology, 20,* 188–195.

Fenz, W. (1975). Strategies for coping with stress. In I. G. Sarason & C. D. Spielberger (Eds.), *Stress and anxiety* (Vol. 2). Washington, DC: Hemisphere.

Grzegolowska-Klarkowska, H. (1980). Use of defence mechanisms as determined by reactivity and situational level of activation. *Polish Psychological Bulletin, 11,* 155–168.

Haggard, E. A. (1949). Psychological causes and results of stress. In D. B. Lindsley et al. (Eds.), *Human factors in undersea warfare.* Washington, DC: National Research Council.

Hebb, D. O. (1955). Drives and the C.N.S. (conceptual nervous system). *Psychological Review, 62,* 243–254.

Klonowicz, T. (1974). Reactivity and fitness for the occupation of operator. *Polish Psychological Bulletin, 5,* 129–136.

Krohne, H. W., & Rogner, J. (1982). Repression-Sensitization as a central construct in coping research. In H. W. Krohne & L. Laux (Eds.), *Achievement, stress, and anxiety.* New York: Hemisphere/McGraw-Hill.

Lacey, J. I. (1967). Somatic response patterning and stress: Some revisions of activation theory. In M. H. Appley & R. Trumbull (Eds.), *Psychological stress. Issues in research.* New York: Appleton-Century-Crofts.

Lacey, J. I., & VanLehn, R. (1952). Differential emphasis in somatic response to stress. *Psychosomatic Medicine, 14,* 73–81.

Laux, L., & Vossel, G. (1982). Theoretical and methodological issues in achievement-related stress and anxiety research. In H. W. Kohne & L. Laux (Eds.), *Achievement, stress, and anxiety.* New York: Hemisphere/McGraw-Hill.

Lazarus, R. S. (1966). *Psychological stress and the coping process.* New York: McGraw-Hill.

Lazarus, R. S. (1967). Cognitive and personality factors underlying threat and coping. In M. H. Appley & R. Trumbull (Eds.), *Psychological stress. Issues in research.* New York: Appleton-Century-Crofts.

Lundberg, U. (1982). Psychophysiological aspects of performance and adjustment to stress. In H. W. Krohne & L. Laux (Eds.), *Achievement, stress, and anxiety.* New York: Hemisphere/McGraw-Hill.

Magnusson, D. (1982). Situational determinants of stress: An interactional perspective. In L. Goldberg & S. Breznitz (Eds.), *Handbook of stress.* New York: The Free Press.

McGrath, J. E. (1970a). A conceptual formulation for research on stress. In J. E. McGrath (Ed.), *Social and psychological factors in stress.* New York: Holt, Rinehart and Winston.

McGrath, J. E. (1970b). Major methodological issues. In J. E. McGrath (Ed.), *Social and psychological factors in stress.* New York: Holt, Rinehart and Winston.

McGrath, J. E. (1970c). Settings, measures, and themes: An integrative review of some research on social-psychological factors in stress. In J. E. McGrath (Ed.), *Social and psychological factors in stress.* New York: Holt, Rinehart and Winston.

McGrath, J. E. (1982). Methodological problems in research on stress. In H. W. Krohne & L. Laux (Eds.), *Achievement, stress, and anxiety.* New York: Hemisphere/McGraw-Hill.

Meichenbaum, D. (1977). *Cognitive-behavior modification: An integrative approach.* New York: Plenum.

Morris, L. W. (1979). *Extraversion and introversion. An interactional perspective.* Washington, DC: Hemisphere.

Nebylitsyn, V. D. (1972). *Fundamental properties of the human nervous system.* New York: Plenum Press.

Opton, E. M., & Lazarus, R. S. (1967). Personality determinants of psychophysiological response to stress: A theoretical analysis and an experiment. *Journal of Personality and Social Psychology, 6,* 291–303.

Schalling, D. (1976). Anxiety, pain, and coping. In I. G. Sarason & C. D. Spielberger (Eds.), *Stress and anxiety* (Vol. 3). Washington: Hemisphere.

Schönpflug, W. (1982). Aspiration level and causal attribution. In H. W. Krohne & L. Laux (Eds.), *Achievement, stress, and anxiety.* New York: Hemisphere/McGraw-Hill.

Schulz, P., & Schönpflug, W. (1982). Regulatory activity during states of stress. In H. W. Krohne & L. Laux (Eds.), *Achievement, stress, and anxiety.* New York: Hemisphere/McGraw-Hill.

Selye, H. (1950). *Stress.* Montreal: Acta.

Selye, H. (1956). *The stress of life.* New York: McGraw-Hill.

Selye, H. (1975). *Stress without distress.* New York: New American Library.

Spielberger, C. D. (1972). Anxiety as an emotional state. In C. D. Spielberger (Ed.), *Anxiety: Current trends in theory and research* (Vol. 1). New York: Academic Press.

Spielberger, C. D. (1976). The nature and measurement of anxiety. In C. D. Spielberger & R. Diaz-Guerrero (Eds.), *Cross-cultural anxiety.* Washington, DC: Hemisphere.

Strelau, J. (1983). *Temperament–personality–activity.* London: Academic Press.

Tyler, L. E. (1978). *Individuality. Human possibilities and personal choice in the psychological development of men and women.* San Francisco: Jossey-Bass.

Weick, K. E. (1970). The "ess" in stress. Some conceptual and methodological problems. In J. E. McGrath (Ed.), *Social and psychological factors in stress.* New York: Holt, Rinehart and Winston.

Wundt, W. (1874). *Grundzuge der physiologischen Psychologie.* Leipzig: Engelmann.

Yerkes, R., & Dodson, J. D. (1908). The relation of strength of stimulus to rapidity of habit-formation. *Journal of Comparative and Neurological Psychology, 18,* 459–482.

12

Reaction to Perceptual Ambiguity and Psychophysiological Changes During Anticipatory Stress

Tytus Sosnowski and Ewa Karczykowska
University of Warsaw

Situations of anticipated stress are usually accompanied by greater or lesser degrees of cognitive uncertainty as to expected stressors. This uncertainty can have at least two sources. First, the individual may perceive the outcome of the situation as unpredictable and independent of any influence of his or her own (e.g., as depending on change). Second, the individual may find it difficult to develop a sufficiently consistent image (cognitive representation) of the situation which would allow a generation of subjectively certain predictions. These two different perceptions of the situation are probably contingent upon different location of the source of uncertainty, that is, either external, resulting from specific characteristics of the situation itself, or internal, resulting from own capability to cognitively cope with the situation. In laboratory settings the first source of uncertainty is usually manipulated. A typical example of such manipulation is the setting in which subjects are informed that they will not know exactly whether a given stressor will appear with such and such probability (other than one or zero) (Bowers, 1971; Epstein and Roupenian, 1970; Jennings, Averill, Opton, and Lazarus, 1971; Monat, Averill, and Lazarus, 1972).

Such instructions, however, though relatively effective as far as generation of uncertainty as to anticipated stressor, at the same time explicitly define the stress situation itself. In natural situations this is seldom the case. Here subjects must usually generate an image of the situation themselves on the basis of the available data.

One of the main difficulties in doing so lies in the ambiguity of the information which an individual has at his or her disposal. As Folkman, Schaefer, and Lazarus (1979) have underlined, "in stressful transactions, especially in those that are interpersonal, ambiguity and uncertainty are the rule rather than the exception" (p. 277).

In the psychological literature various effects of information ambiguity are discussed. Two of them call for special attention in the context of our study. First, ambiguity can lead to increased tension, arousal and, under certain circumstances, to anxiety (Budner, 1962; Epstein, 1972; Frenkel-Brunswick, 1949; McReynolds,

1976). Second, ambiguity usually leads to increased overt or intrapsychic activity of the subject (cf. Berlyne, 1960, 1965). This activity, as stated by Folkman, Schaefer, and Lazarus (1979) may serve various functions, that is, it may be aimed at solving the task situation (problem-solving function) or it may be aimed at minimization of the emotion consequences of the ambiguity (palliative function).

At the same time attention is drawn to the fact that people differ in their reactions to ambiguity. Frenkel-Brunswick (1949) was the first to draw attention to this problem at the end of 1940s, when she formulated her conception of tolerance-intolerance of ambiguity. This conception did not, however, have much influence on experimental studies of stress despite the fact that many ideas put forward by Frenkel-Brunswick, both methodological and theoretical, definitely deserve attention.

The investigation presented in this paper are concerned with relationships between reaction to perceptual ambiguity and psychophysiological changes (more precisely, changes in tonic level of skin resistance and heart rate) in ambiguous-stress situations. By ambiguity we will understand here such features of the message which make it impossible to "adequately structure or categorize it because of lack of sufficient cues" (Budner, 1962, p. 30). Reaction to ambiguity is measured using Berlyne's (1957) paradigm consisting of arranging conditions in which subjects are free to repetitively self-expose perceptual material but with fixed and relatively short single exposure duration. It is assumed that the time necessary for recognition of the perceptual material is the index of assimilation facility, that is, facility to incorporate it into subjects cognitive structures (cf. McReynolds, 1976). Number of expositions is taken as the measure of activity directed at resolving the perceptual task.

The results of our previous investigations and data from the literature (sec Discussion) show that confrontation with ambiguity leads, at least in some conditions, to an increase in electrodermal activity. We may thus predict that, on one hand, those individuals who manifest stronger reactions to perceptual ambiguity (as regards the indices used in our studies) will also show greater tonic changes in skin resistance in an ambiguous-stress situation. On the other hand, we know that situations requiring greater activity or effort on behalf of the subject cause cardiovascular change including increase in heart rate. This suggests that those individuals who show greater activity in resolving ambiguous perceptual tasks will show also greater increase in heart rate in ambiguous stress situations. The study presented below was an attempt to verify these hypotheses.

METHOD

Subjects

Thirty-five active male soldiers aged 19 to 26 were studied. Participation was voluntary. Each subject was offered reimbursement (150 zl.) for his participation.

Procedure and Material

The experiment consisted of two sessions. The first measured reactions to perceptual ambiguity, the second psychophysiological changes in an ambiguous-stress situation.

In session 1 subjects were presented with three series of slides, each of which consisted of three unambiguous slides and three ambiguous ones, presented alternately (see Fig. 1). Each series was preceded by one additional buffer slide (unambiguous), not analyzed. The slides in series 1 were drawings of animals which were either congruous (unambiguous) or incongruous (ambiguous). In series 2 the slides contained words printed correctly (unambiguous) or incorrectly (ambiguous). In both series the subjects were asked to report exactly what was on the slide. The material in series 3 consisted of four stripes: one horizontal (the standard) and three perpendicular. The subjects were to point to the perpendicular stripe most resembling in length the standard stripe. On some of the slides (unambiguous) one of the perpendicular stripes was identical with the standard, the remaining two were clearly different. On the ambiguous slides two or even three perpendicular stripes were the same length and were identical to the standard. Subjects were instructed that the perpendicular stripes, although sometimes very similar in length, are never identical.

Subjects were free to self-expose each slide as often as they like by pressing a lever they held in their hand. Duration of expositions was fixed and was 20 ms for series 1 and 2 and 300 ms for series 3.

The instruction stressed that accuracy of recognition of perceptual material was important whereas time needed for correct recognition and number of expositions was irrelevant. Actually, the number of expositions of each slide and the time lapse between first exposition and response were measured.

Subjects sat in a soundproof chamber. Slides were presented on a screen 1×1 m, set at about 2 m from the subject. Reactions were registered in a separate room

Figure 1 Examples of perceptual material presented during session 1: ambiguous (left) and unambiguous (right), (the word "srsrebro" is written incorrectly, correct form is "srebro".)

unseen by the subject. The subject responded through a microphone. Slide expositions were observed through a TV camera.

Session 2 of the experiment consisted of five trials during which subjects awaited a potential electric shock. The shock was signaled each time by means of a special message. This message was a pair of slides presented for 5 seconds each with a 5-second interval between slides. Each slide consisted of one black circle on a white background. The first circle was always the same size (the standard) whereas the size of the second circle could vary from trial to trial. Subjects were instructed that the shock would always be delivered when the second circle was bigger than the standard, whereas no shock would be delivered when it was smaller. Actually in the three test trials (2, 3, and 4) both circles were identical (ambiguous message) and the stimulus was exposed according to a prefixed schedule, always in trial 2. Trial 1 was a buffer. Here an ambiguous message announcing lack of exposition of shock was presented (the second circle was much smaller than the first). In trial 5 various messages were presented randomly and shocks were given or not, respectively. This was done in order to prevent the subjects from recognizing the experimental design (one shock, always in trial 2) and communicating it to other subjects awaiting their turn.

At the beginning of the session subjects were generally informed that the study was concerned with how people react when they know something unpleasant can happen but are unable to predict it exactly. Next, the exact experimental procedure was presented, exemplary slides were demonstrated, and the electric shock was given. Finally, one instructory trial was given with identical procedure as in the test trials with the exception that no electric shock was delivered. When the instruction was completed subjects were asked whether they agreed to participate in the experiment—nobody refused. Electrodes were then attached and the experiment proper began. Each trial was identical and proceeded as follows. First, after the experimenter's introduction, the message consisting of two slides was presented. Immediately after the second slide disappeared from the screen a digital clock standing opposite the subject was switched on. This clock measured the duration of waiting for the potential stimulus exposition (60 seconds). When the clock was switched off the subject had a 2 minute interval before the next trial began.

The experiment was run in the same chamber as session 1. The subject was alone in the chamber. Monitoring of the apparatus and psychophysiological recording was performed in an adjacent room, unseen by the subject.

Psychophysiological Recording

In session 2 two psychophysiological indices were continuously recorded: heart rate (HR) and skin resistance (SR).

SR was measured with a recorder (Janmaz) measuring skin resistance level (in KΩ) and its momentary fluctuations (in %). Dry, silvered, disc electrodes, 1 cm in diameter, placed on the medial phalanx of fingers 2 and 3 of the left hand were used. Before each trial (i.e., before the experimenter's introduction) initial level of SR was established and then its maximal decrease in successive 15-second intervals was recorded: measure 1 during exposition of the message, measures 2 through 5 during the waiting period for the potential shock, measures 6 through 9 during successive 60-second periods following switching off of the clock. Aggregated mean changes in trials 2, 3, and 4 were analyzed.

HR was measured continuously by means of an E-30 electrocardiograph with bipolar extremity outputs. The recording was divided into 15-second segments, analogous to SR measurement. For each segment mean heart rate in beats/min was computed and then these results were transformed into size of HR change, as compared to initial level registered during the last 20 seconds before the onset of a given trial. Aggregated changes for trials 2, 3, and 4 were analyzed.

Electric Shock

The electric shock was a single bidirectional impulse of constant intensity about 1 mA and 20 ms duration. The stimulus was delivered by means of a pair of disc electrodes, 1 cm in diameter, attached to the middle phalanx of fingers 2 and 3 of the subject's right hand.

Data Reduction and Analysis

Data analysis was carried out in two stages. First, the results of both experimental sessions were correlated. Next, changes in psychophysiological variables in groups differing in reaction to the perceptual material were compared.

For the correlational analysis the results of session 1 were reduced to six indices. For each subject mean time necessary for recognition of ambiguous slides (RT_a), unambiguous slides (RT_u) and the ratio $RT_r = RT_a/RT_u$ were computed. Three analogous indices: NE_a, NE_u and NE_r were computed for number of expositions. These indices were first computed separately for each series of slides. Because there was a large positive correlation between series, the final analysis was performed on aggregated means for the three series.

The results of session 2 were reduced to three indices for SR and three for HR. These indices were to characterize psychophysiological changes caused by: (a) exposition of the message; (b) awaiting the stimulus; and (c) the stimulus itself. Regarding the SR changes, analysis was carried out using the results of measurement 1 (SR_a), the mean from measurements 2 through 5 (SR_b), and the results of measurement 6 (SR_c). Regarding the HR changes, which had different dynamics (Figs. 2 and 3), slightly different indices were selected for analysis, that is, results of measurement 2 (HR_a), the mean from measurements 2 through 5 (HR_b), and results of measurement 5 (HR_c).

Because many of the indices of reaction to ambiguity had a clearly skewed distribution (to the right), Kendall's rank correlation coefficient (τ) was used in analysis of all data.

State two consisted of the comparison of the curves portraying changes in SR and HR between groups differing in type of reaction to perceptual material presented in session 1. Selection of groups was done ex post, on the basis of the median of that index which was most strongly correlated with a given psychophysiological variable. In order to obtain groups of equal size (i.e. $N = 17$) the results of the subject in the middle of each distribution were discarded. The results of the groups thus selected were analyzed by means of two-factor ANOVA (group time-within-trial, design 2×9) with repeated measures on the last factor (Winner, 1971).

Table 1 Correlations (Kendall's τ) between indices of reaction to perceptual material (N = 35)

Indices	Number of expositions		Recognition time		
	NF$_u$	NE$_a$	NE$_r$	RT$_u$	RT$_a$
NE$_a$	.555***				
NE$_r$	.113	.569***			
RT$_u$	.619***	.341**	−.008		
RT$_a$	.335**	.498***	.415***	.449***	
RT$_r$	−.083	.232*	.479***	.099	.452***

*$p < .05$.
**$p < .01$.
***$p < .001$.

RESULTS

Analysis of results for session 1 reveals very large differences between reactions to unambiguous and ambiguous material. The medians of recognition times for these two types of slides are, respectively, 1.60 and 4.73 seconds for the animal series, 2.20 and 14.53 seconds for the word series, 3.70 and 13.63 seconds for the stripe series, and 2.66 and 12.33 for all three series together. Analogous indices for number of expositions are: animals, 1.00 and 2.33; words, 1.33 and 5.00; stripes, 2.33 and 5.33; and all three series together, 1.67 and 4.78 (in the case of tied ranks median values were interpolated). Only three times within the whole empirical data was a result incongruent with the tendencies presented above—twice in the animal series and once in the word series the number of expositions was the same for unambiguous and ambiguous slides. In all the remaining cases recognition time was longer and the number of expositions larger for ambiguous slides.

Table 1 presents correlation coefficients between six indices of reactions to perceptual material. All coefficients except those between both ratios (RT$_r$ and NE$_r$) on the one hand and indices RT$_u$ and NE$_u$ on the other are positive, moderately high, and significant at at least $p < .001$.* The four exceptions mentioned above are not surprising since indices RT$_u$ and NE$_u$ are the denominators of the respective ratio indices.

Table 2 presents correlation coefficients between six indices of psychophysiological changes. As can be seen from the table, significant correlations appear between indices of SR changes, and between indices of HR changes. No significant correlation was found, however, between the SR and HR changes indices. It is also noteworthy that the extent of change when waiting for the stimulus (index b) correlates more highly with changes caused by exposition of the message (index a) than by those evoked by exposition of the stimulus itself (index c).

Table 3 presents correlation coefficients between indices of reaction to perceptual material and indices of psychophysiological changes. Two facts are noteworthy here. First of all, SR changes correlate only with time of recognition of slides

*Note that Kendall's τ was used which gives considerably lower estimation of the correlation magnitude than for Spearman's ρ (cf. Jule & Kendall, 1958).

Table 2 Correlations (Kendall's τ) between indices of psychophysiological changes (N = 35)

Indices	SR changes			HR changes	
	SR_a	SR_b	SR_c	HR_a	HR_b
SR_b	.727*				
SR_c	.397*	.447*			
HR_a	−.138	−.155	−.111		
HR_b	−.024	−0.010	−.057	.686*	
HR_c	.103	.091	−.027	.392*	.511*

*$p < .001$.

and do not correlate with number of expositions of slides. HR changes, however, correlate only with number of expositions of slides but do not correlate with temporal indices. Second, SR changes correlate with time of recognition of ambiguous material (i.e. with RT_a and RT_r indices) but not with time of recognition of unambiguous material. HR changes, however, correlate both with number of expositions of ambiguous slides (NE_a index) and unambiguous ones (NE_u index).

In Fig. 2 we see the curves for SR changes for two groups differing in time of recognition of ambiguous slides as compared to unambiguous ones (i.e., in the size of RT_r index, which was most strongly correlated with the size of SR changes). Both curves have similar shapes, that is, show rapid increase (drop in SR) at the moment of exposition of the message and a maximum in measurement 6, directly after stimulus exposition. The compared groups differ, however, as concerns the height of the curves: SR changes are greater in the group with higher RT_r index (HRT_r) than in the group with lower one (LRT_r). These differences, it is worth pointing out here, are clear at the moment of exposition of the message and remain more or less stable up to the last measurement.

Analysis of variance (group × time-within-trial) revealed significant main effect of the group factor ($F(1,32) = 7.38$, $p < .05$), time-within-trial factor

Table 3 Correlations (Kendall's τ) between indices of reaction to perceptual material and indices of psychophysiological changes (N = 35)

Indices	Number of expositions			Recognition time		
	NE_u	NE_a	NE_r	RT_u	RT_a	RT_r
SR changes						
SR_a	−.002	.108	.130	.103	.278*	.266*
SR_b	−.052	.050	.220	.015	.207	.313**
SR_c	.032	.158	.193	.059	.267*	.404***
HR changes						
HR_a	.383**	.239*	.029	.190	.069	.195
HR_b	.326**	.256*	.086	.123	−.012	−.097
HR_c	.167	.286*	.261*	.029	.089	.071

*$p < .05$.
**$p < .01$.
***$p < .001$.

($F(8,256)$ = 46.24, p < .001), as well as group × time-within-trial interaction ($F(8,256)$ = 2.13, p < .05). Analysis of simple effect of the group factor revealed that it is significant for measurement 5 (F = 9.46, p < .01), measurement 6 (F = 15.80, p < .001), and measurement 7 (F = 7.90, p < .01). In measurements 1 (F = 2.96) and 2 (F = 3.70) the significance of between group differences is only p < .10 (for all simple effects df = 1,288). The simple effect of time-within-trial factor was significant both in group HRT$_r$ ($F(8,256)$ = 32.63, p < .001) and group LRT$_r$ ($F(8,256)$ = 15.74, p < .001). It was also found that the variance of means from successive measurements is greater in group HRT$_r$ than in group LRT$_r$. The ratio of both variances ($F(8,8)$ = 2.07) was insignificant, however.

Figure 3 presents the curves for HR changes in two groups. Because these changes correlated both with number of expositions of ambiguous and unambiguous slides, the selection into groups was made on the basis of joint number of expositions of both types of perceptual material (index NE$_j$). As can be seen, HR changes in the group with higher NE$_j$ (HNE$_j$ group) are larger than in the group with lower one (LNE$_j$ group).

Both curves also differ in shape. Analysis of the curve for the whole sample studied (N = 35) revealed that the greatest increase in HR appeared in measurement 2, that is, directly after exposition of the message. This increase, connected with cognitive elaboration of the presented message, is exactly as predicted, as is the drop in HR at the moment of exposition of the stimulus (Lacey, 1967). However, the shape of the curve changed when the sample was divided into two groups. In group HNE$_j$ we still see an increase of HR in measurement 2 as com-

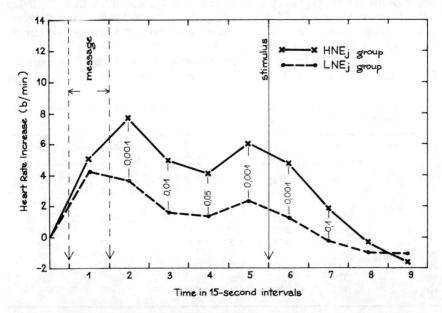

Figure 2 Skin resistance changes in the group with higher (H) and lower (L) RT$_r$ index (time of recognition of ambiguous to unambiguous perceptual material ratio); marked values indicated significance of simple effects between groups.

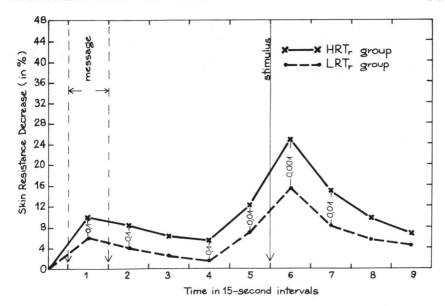

Figure 3 Heart rate changes in the group with higher (H) and lower (L) NE$_j$ index (number of expositions of ambiguous and unambiguous perceptual material taken jointly); marked values indicate significance of simple effects between groups.

pared with measurement 1, whereas in group LNE$_j$ we find a slight drop in HR in the same time sequence.

Analysis of variance revealed a significant main effect of the group factor ($F(1,32)$ = 8.12, $p < .01$) and the time-within-trial factor ($F(8,256)$ = 24.09, $p < .001$) as well as the group × time-within-trial interaction ($F(8,256)$ = 2.77, $p < .01$). Simple effects for the group factor were significant for measurement 2 (F = 11.06, $p < .001$), measurement 3 (F = 7.64, $p < .01$), measurement 4 (F = 5.11, $p < .05$), measurement 5 (F = 9.47, $p < .001$), and measurement 6 (F = 8.26, $p < .001$). For measurement 7 the significance of the simple effect (F = 3.14) amounts to only $p < .10$ (for all above simple effects df = 1,288). Simple effects for the time-within-trial factor were significant both in group HNE$_j$ ($F(8,256)$ = 19.38, $p < .001$) and group LNE$_j$ ($F(8,256)$ = 7.48, $p < .001$). It was also found that the variance of means for the time-within-trial factor is higher in group HNE$_j$ than in group LNE$_j$ but the $F(8,8)$ = 2.59 is significant only at $p < .10$.

DISCUSSION

The results presents above, though partly corroborating our expectations, are far from unequivocal and require detailed discussion.

The results show that those individuals who have more difficulty assimilating ambiguous perceptual material, that is, require more time to recognize it, react with more skin resistance tonic changes in the ambiguous-stress situation than individuals who easily assimilate such material.

Many researchers have drawn attention to the relationship between information ambiguity (or other similar factors) and electrodermal changes. Elliott (1969), on the basis of his own studies and that of others, says, "among the factors that are distinctively effective in controlling increases in PC [palmar conductance—T.S.] are the collative properties of stimulus situations—that is novelty, complexity, and the like" (p. 225).

We may ask, however, whether such collative stimulus properties are sufficient in themselves to evoke electrodermal changes. Berlyne, Craw, Salapatek, and Lewis (1963), presenting subjects with various perceptual material differing in degree of "irregularity", found that more irregular material caused a greater number of GSRs than more regular material only when the subjects were additionally motivated by the experimenter to recognize the presented slides. No differences appeared, however, when such extrinsic motivation was lacking. This result implies that the effects of the collative properties of the stimulus on electrodermal activity depend on the meaning of the stimulus for the individual.

In our earlier study (Sosnowski, 1983) we found that the size of tonic changes (decrease) in SR during anticipation of an electric shock was significantly greater when the message announcing the stimulus was ambiguous (insoluble) than when it was unambiguous. We also found that both curves had an almost identical shape (similar to that in the present experiment) differing only in height. This suggests that ambiguity of message announcing the stimulus is rather a factor modulating the size of electrodermal arousal evoked by the anticipated stressor than an independent source of such arousal.

The basic problem of this study is, however, the relationship between individual differences in reactions to perceptual ambiguity and electrodermal changes in ambiguous-stress situations. According to Frenkel-Brunswick (1949; cf. also Budner, 1962), intolerance of ambiguity is contingent upon perception of the ambiguous situation as threatening and reacting to it with anxiety. Intolerant people also tend to react with defensive denial of external ambiguity. In laboratory experiments led by Frenkel-Brunswick this was manifest among others in the longer recognition times for perceptual material, that is, in indices similar to those we used in our study. If we assume, then, that the variable we measured and tolerance of ambiguity as understood by Frenkel-Brunswick are largely similar constructs, then the individual differences in SR reactivity to an ambiguous-stress situation analyzed by us should be interpreted as manifestations of different levels of anxiety evoked in such a situation in the subjects—higher in those who have greater difficulty assimilating ambiguous material and lower in those who assimilate with ease.

This conclusion, reducing the relationship between facility of assimilation of ambiguous material and electrodermal reactivity in ambiguous-stress situations exclusively to the effects of anxiety as an intervening variable, does not seem, however, directly apparent. We have so far been unable to show unequivocally any relation between the state of anxiety and level of skin resistance or changes in it (Edelberg, 1972; Stern and Janes, 1973). Thus, other alternative hypotheses must be considered which may explain the intergroup differences reported. Data in the literature (Raskin, 1973) suggest in particular that these differences may be caused by the different intensity of such processes as attention of (tonic) orienting reflex. The fact that differences between both groups appear at the moment of exposition of the perceptual material would be consistent with such hypotheses although of course they are no proof of their validity.

The HR changes registered in the second part of the experiment were not correlated with time of recognition of the presented perceptual material. They did correlate, on the other hand, with the number of expositions of slides, both ambituous and unambiguous. These findings suggest that individual differences in HR reactivity during an ambiguous-stress situation are related to the degree of activity of the subject when solving perceptual tasks, irrespective of the degree of ambiguity of these tasks.

The relationship between HR changes and individual activity has been stressed in many sources. Elliott (1969) states, for example, that "the factors that are distinctively effective in controlling increases in tonic HR . . . are primarily the instigation, anticipation, and initiation of responses" (p. 225).

Roberts and Young (1971) obtained spectacular data showing the existence of a very strong relationship between heart rate and movement in rats during aversive classical conditioning. They refer to the results of many other experiments, carried out in various conditions, and state that "somatic arousal was a major determinant of heart rate in each" whereas "relationships between heart rate and nonsomatic processes, such as attention . . . , fear . . . , and hunger motivation . . . , may be secondary to an effect of these processes on skeletal-motor behavior" (p. 509).

The relationship between heart rate changes and somatomotor activity seems to be, however, more complex. Obrist and co-workers (see Obrist, 1976; Obrist, Light, Langer, Grignolo and Koepke, 1982; Obrist, Grignolo Hastrup, Koepke, Langer, Light, McCubbin and Pollak, 1983) showed that phasic HR changes are directionally consistent with nonextensive or striate muscle activity during classical aversive conditioning when these changes are under parasympathetic (vagal) control. Tonic changes, on the other hand, influenced by sympathetic (beta-adrenergic) control, are independent of concurrent somatomotor activity.

The studies of Obrist and Light (1984), and other co-workers, also show that there is one more important relationship, very interesting in the context of our own experiment. They found that HR tonic changes under beta-adrenergic control are most evident during shock-avoidance tasks. The same situation also evoked the strongest individual differences in heart rate reactivity to the experimental condition. These differences generalized on several other situations such as viewing of an erotic film, cold pressor, or pretask rest, although in these conditions, requiring merely passive coping, they were not so large as during the shock-avoidance task.

Our results seem to correspond to a certain degree with the above findings. Obrist and his co-workers maintain that individual differences in HR reactivity are most conspicuous in those conditions which need active coping on behalf of the subject whereas our study shows that individuals with greater HR reactivity to the experimental condition (ambiguous-stress situation) also tend to cope more actively with the task situation (i.e., during the recognition of perceptual material). This contention can also be supported by the fact that differences between the curves of HR changes in both analyzed groups appear not at the moment of exposition of the perceptual communication (as was the case in the curves of SR changes) but only after it had disappeared, that is, when its alleged cognitive elaboration took place.

One more fact is also worth paying attention to here. The task presented in session 2 of our experiment (recognition and elaboration of the message about the stimulus), as opposed to that presented in session 1, did not require any motoric activity on behalf of the subjects. Both tasks did require cognitive activity. The correlations between the results of both sessions show that differences in HR reactivity to the experimental conditions are rather the effect of various degrees of engagement and mental effort to cope with the task situation and need not be correlates of motor activity.

CONCLUSIONS

The studies presented here have yielded a number of positive findings on the relationships between individual reaction to ambiguous perceptual material and the degree of psychophysiological changes (tonic changes in SR and HR) in an ambiguous-stress situation (i.e., a situation in which the anticipated stressor is announced by an ambiguous communication). These results show, among others, that the changes in SR and HR, observed in such a situation, are completely uncorrelated with each other and have different psychophysiological significance.

Individual difference in electrodermal reactivity to an ambiguous-stress situation seem related mainly to the individual's perception and assimilation of incoming ambiguous communications. Those subjects who had more difficulty assimilating ambiguous perceptual material (i.e., needed more time for recognition) also revealed greater tonic changes (decrease) in skin resistance in the ambiguous-stress condition.

The HR changes observed in the same condition seem related to individual differences on the active-passive coping with task situation dimension. These changes were greater in those subjects who exposed the perceptual material (both ambiguous and unambiguous) more frequently. Analysis of the experimental situation suggests, moreover, that the differences in HR reactivity to the experimental condition are related rather to different degrees of engagement and/or mental effort put into resolving the task situation than to motor activity.

The results presented here need, of course, support by further studies (they are now under way in our laboratory). These studies seem to us important as far as they can throw more light on the problem of individual differences in SR and HR activity. At the moment we know incomparably more about the situational determinants of such activity than the factors determining individual differences in it.

REFERENCES

Berlyne, D. E. (1957). Conflict and information-theory variables as determinants of human perceptual curiosity. *Journal of Experimental Psychology, 53*, 399–404.
Berlyne, D. E. (1960). *Conflict, arousal, and curiosity.* New York: McGraw-Hill.
Berlyne, D. E. (1965). *Structure and direction in thinking.* New York: Wiley.
Berlyne, D. E., Craw, M. A., Salapatek, P. H., & Lewis, J. L. (1963). Novelty, complexity, incongruity, extrinsic motivation and the GSR. *Journal of Experimental Psychology, 66*, 560–567.
Bowers, K. S. (1971). Heart rate and GSR concomitants of vigilance and arousal. *Canadian Journal of Psychology, 25*, 175–184.
Budner, S. (1962). Intolerance of ambiguity as a personality variable. *Journal of Personality, 30*, 29–50.
Edelberg, R. (1972). Electrical activity of the skin: Its measurement and uses in psychophysiology. In N. S. Greenfield & R. A. Sternback (Eds). *Handbook of psychophysiology.* New York: Holt.
Elliott, R. (1969). Tonic heart rate: Experiments on the effects of collative variables lead to a hypothesis about its motivational significance. *Journal of Personality and Social Psychology, 12*, 211–228.
Epstein, S. (1972). The nature of anxiety with emphasis upon its relationship to expectancy. In C. D. Spielberger (Ed.), *Anxiety: Current trends in theory and research.* New York: Academic Press.
Epstein, S., & Roupenian, A. (1970). Heart rate and skin conductance during experimentally induced

anxiety: The effect of uncertainty about receiving noxious stimulus. *Journal of Personality and Social Psychology, 16,* 20–28.

Folkman, S., Schaefer, C., & Lazarus, R. S. (1979). Cognitive processes as mediators of stress and coping. In V. Hamilton, & D. M. Warburton (Eds.), *Human stress and cognition.* Chichester: Wiley.

Frenkel-Brunswick, E. (1949). Intolerance of ambiguity as a emotional and perceptual personality variable. *Journal of Personality, 18,* 108–143.

Jennings, J. K., Averill, J. R., Opton, E. M., & Lazarus, R. S. (1971). Some parameters of heart rate change: Perceptual versus motor task requirements, noxiousness, and uncertainty. *Psychophysiology, 7,* 194–212.

Jule, G. U., & Kendell, H. G. (1958). *An introduction to the theory of statistics.* London: Griffin.

Lacey, J. I. (1967). Somatic response patterning and stress: Some revisions of activation theory. In M. H. Appley & R. Trumbull (Eds.), *Psychological stress: Issues in research.* New York: Appleton-Century-Crofts.

McReynolds, P. (1976). Assimilation and anxiety. In M. Zuckerman & C. D. Spielberger (Eds.), *Emotion and anxiety, new concepts, methods, and applications.* Hillsdale: Erlbaum.

Monat, A., Averill, J. R., & Lazarus, R. S. (1972). Anticipatory stress and coping reactions under various conditions of uncertainty. *Journal of Personality and Social Psychology, 24,* 237–253.

Obrist, P. A. (1976). The cardiovascular-behavior interaction—As it appears today. *Psychophysiology, 13,* 95–107.

Obrist, P. A., Grignolo, A., Hastrup, J. L., Koepke, J. P., Langer, A. W., Light, K. C., McCubbin, J. A., & Pollak, M. H. (1983) Behavioral-cardiac interactions in hypertension. In D. S. Krantz, A. Baum, & J. E. Singer (Eds.), *Handbook of psychology and health, Vol. III: Cardiovascular disorders and behavior.* Hillsdale, NJ: Erlbaum.

Obrist, P. A., & Light, K. C. (1984). Active-passive coping and cardiovascular reactivity: Interaction with individual differences and types of baseline. In A. Baum, W. Gordon & J. A. Herd (Eds.), *Proceedings of the Academy of Behavioral Medicine Research, 1981–1982.* New York: Academic Press.

Obrist, P. A., Light, K. C., Langer, A. W., Grignolo, A., & Koepke, J. P. (1982). Behavioral-cardiovascular interaction. In O. A. Smith, R. A. Galosy, & M. Weiss (Eds.), *Proceedings of working conference on circulation, neurophysiology and behavior.* New York: Elsevier.

Raskin, D. (1973). Attention and arousal. In W. F. Prokasy & D. C. Raskin (Eds.), *Electrodermal activity in psychological research.* New York: Academic Press.

Roberts, L. E., & Young, R. (1971). Electrodermal responses are independent of movement during aversive conditioning in rats, but heart rate is not. *Journal of Comparative and Physiological Psychology, 77,* 495–512.

Sosnowski, T. (1983). Sources of uncertainty and psychophysiological state changes under conditions of noxious stimulus anticipation. *Biological Psychology, 17,* 297–309.

Stern, J. A. & Janes, C. L. (1973). Personality and psychopathology. In W. F. Prokasy & D. C. Raskin (Eds.), *Electrodermal activity in psychological research.* New York: Academic Press.

Winner, B. J. (1971). *Statistical principles in experimental design.* Tokyo: McGraw-Hill/Kogakusha.

13

Emotional Fainting: Its Physiological and Psychological Aspects

A. J. J. M. Vingerhoets
Free University of Amsterdam

L. R. B. Schomaker
University of Nijmegen

INTRODUCTION

Fainting or syncope refers to the collapse of a person followed by a relatively quick recovery. Therefore, vasodepressor or vasovagal syncope generally is considered as a relatively benign disorder, mostly not associated with life threatening diseases. In common language vasodepressor syncope sometimes is referred to as "emotional fainting." This seems to point to the relevance of psychological factors involved in the onset of the syncope. Edmondson, Gordon, Lloyd, Meeson and Whitehead (1978) provide data that, in dental surgery, about 60% both of the operators and patients gave emotion as the cause of this episode. In addition, fainting can result from other causes. Engel (1962) provided a clinical classification of all kinds of fainting, based on etiology. In this paper, we want to restrict ourselves to a more rough subdivision:

1. emotional fainting (vasovagal syncope);
2. fainting due to physical or physiological stress in its widest meaning (e.g. drugs, excessive blood loss, standing still for a long time etc.);
3. fainting as a symptom of cerebral or cardiovascular pathophysiology; and
4. hysterical fainting.

The vasovagal syncope is the most common type of fainting. Knowledge of the incidence of fainting mainly results from a restricted number of studies with blood

This manuscript was prepared when both authors worked as Research-Associates at Tilburg University, The Netherlands. Preparation was supported by the Netherlands Foundation for Pure Research (ZWO) (grant 58-61).

donors as subjects. Of course, because blood donors cannot be considered as a select sample from the population, care should be taken in generalizing to the whole population. For an impression of the general incidence of reactors in blood donors, one is referred to Callahan, Edelman, Smith and Smith (1963). In their study a donor reaction rate of 4.5 percent was found on the total of nearly 140,000 donations. The severity of the reactions was, somewhat arbitrarily, classified as mild, moderate or severe. Mild reactions were those characterized by weakness and sweating; moderate reactions involved dizziness, nausea or vomiting and in severe cases there was loss of consciousness and/or convulsions. Mild reactions clearly predominated (65.2%), followed by the moderate category (29.1%) and, at last, the severe cases with an incidence of 5.7%. Another important finding in the Callahan, Edelman, Smith and Smith study was the clear tendency of one-time reactors to have a second reaction. This result suggests that independent of extrinsic or stress factors, in some individuals a clear predisposition toward syncope exists. These special characteristics make fainting an interesting phenomenon for students of psychosomatic medicine. In the first place, the existence of a clear syncope-prone group of people allows for the study of their personality and psychosocial antecedents as well as their physiological makeup. (Ruetz, Johnson, Callahan, Meade & Smith 1967; Sledge & Boydstun, 1979). In addition, because fainting is mostly an immediate response to a particular psychosocial context, this offers a unique opportunity to study both the foregoing psychological responses (e.g. Graham, 1961; Sledge, 1978; Sledge & Boydstun, 1979) and the specific characteristics of the situation (Sledge, 1978). Engel (1978) occupies an extreme position by his conviction that sudden cardiac death in fact results from physiological processes set in motion by very similar psychological processes conducive to vasodepressor syncope. The same opinion was proclaimed by Weiss (1940) who once referred to sudden death as irreversible syncope. The aim of the present paper is to provide a review of some important physiological mechanisms relevant to the vasodepressor syncope, the personal characteristics of the fainters and their psychological responses to the psychosocial context just before the onset of the symptoms. At last, we want to deal with the psychophysiological hypotheses put forward with respect to fainting. We want to conclude this section with a description of fainting according to Weissler and Warren (1959):

> Most often one first observes the occurrence of pallor, usually accompanied by beaded
> perspiration. The subject soon experiences epigastric discomfort which is frequently likened to
> nausea but often distinguished as a separate sensation. There is associated yawning and sigh-
> ing, leading to frank hyperventilation and accompanied by pupillary dilatation and blurring of
> vision which precedes loss of hearing. There is often deterioration in the ability to concentrate.
> Little anxiety is usually remembered by the subject, who may volunteer that he almost preferred
> the anticipated unconsciousness to the uncomfortable premonitory phase. (p. 788)

PHYSIOLOGICAL MECHANISMS OF VASOVAGAL SYNCOPE

The direct physiological cause of syncope is a rapid reduction of the blood supply to the brain. This is due to a critical discrepancy between the capacity of the vascular system and the amount of blood contained in it. In genuine (emotional) vasovagal fainting this discrepancy is the result of strong local or general vasodilatation (decreased peripheral resistance) while compensatory adjustments fail, or are absent. Blood flow becomes inadequate to maintain cerebral metabolism, especially in the erect position. The symptoms, described earlier, are indicative of a complex interaction between processes of the autonomous nervous system (ANS) (see Table 1).

In general there are no adverse effects of fainting, although sometimes there may be injuries resulting from the collapse, such as rib fractures (Goldstein, Spanarkel, Pitterman, Toltzis, Gratz, Epstein & Keiser, 1982). Data on cardiovascular and other physiological changes are scarce, and many aspects remain obscure because it is not feasible to study emotional faint under rigid experimental conditions, using a sufficiently large number of subjects to provide statistical reliability. Apart from the evident ethical objections, the use of emotional stimuli often produces unpredictable results. Subjects know that the experimenters will not inflict life-endangering harm upon them (Roddie, 1977). Therefore, many students of syncope have used physical and pharmacological manipulations to induce syncope. Examples are: tilting, prolonged standing, Valsalva maneuver, venesection, rising after squatting for a long time, inducing hypoxia, and injection of sodium nitrite, nitroprusside or apomorphine. Care should be exercised in comparing the results of these experiments to physiological changes in the naturally occurring vasovagal faint. On the one hand, it is evident that in vasovagal syncope many physical factors (prolonged standing, ambient temperature) may play a contributory role. On the other hand, emotional factors cannot always be disregarded totally in experiments inducing faint via physical and pharmacological manipulation. The following description is an attempt to integrate findings of several studies.

Shortly before the onset of the reaction, there is a rise in heart rate and blood pressure (Engel, 1962; Roddie, 1977), often coinciding with increased anxiousness (Graham, 1961; Graham, Kabler & Lundsford, 1961). Then, the arterial blood pressure begins to fall, however. This lowering of the blood pressure may be accompanied by a (lagging) compensatory increase in heart rate, sometimes attributed to a lessening of the baroreceptor reflexes (Gellhorn & Loofbourrow, 1963). This rise in heart rate apparently has not enough effect to overcome the continuous fall in blood pressure. Then, just before the critical systolic blood pressure (60 mmHg, Engel, 1962) is reached, both heart rate and blood pressure fall sharply. Heart rate may reach values varying from 30 to 60 beats per minute. Mean arterial pressure may reach values between 20 to 50 mmHg. Loss of consciousness and a decrease in muscle tone result in a collapse. Temporary asystole is possible at this stage. It should be noted that syncope is a diphasic phenomenon (Graham et al., 1961), the turning point being the sharp fall in blood pressure.

While it is generally accepted that it is the reduction in cerebral blood flow caused by a decrease in arterial blood pressure that triggers the collapse, there is considerable controversy about the exact mechanisms involved and the role of the sympathetic and parasympathetic components of the autonomous nervous system. The symptoms just preceding the sudden, critical drop in blood pressure are part of the first phase of syncope and can be attributed to sympathetic activity well exceeding the baseline level. The evidence for sympathetic activity resides in increased heart rate (Engel & Romano, 1947), vasodilatation in skeletal muscles (Barcroft & Edholm, 1945; Barcroft & Swan, 1953) and in reduction of

Table 1 Symptoms experienced by fainters, related process and systems involved

Process/system	Nausea	Pale skin	Sweating	Transient blushing	Lightheadedness	Loss of muscle tone	Postsyncopal oliguria
Process	Unknown	Cutaneous vascoconstriction	Exocrine glands secretion	Cutaneous vasodilatation	Disturbed cerebral metabolism	Unknown[c]	ADH secretion
System	PNS[a] and/or posterior pituitary are assumed to be involved	SNS[b] circulating catecholamines	SNS cholinergic glandular activation, noradrenergal myoepithelium cells are not involved (Roddie, 1977)	PNS	Many cardiovascular systems are involved	Unkown[d]	Posterior pituitary

[a]Parasympathetic Nervous System = PNS.
[b]Sympathetic Nervous System = SNS.
[c]Possibly this symptom can be placed under lightheadedness but many processes other than disturbed cerebral metabolism are capable of inducing inhibition of striated muscle activity.
[d]Recording of EMG of posture maintaining muscles during faint is necessary to gain insight into the timing of the symptom.

splanchnic blood flow (Weissler & Warren, 1959). These physiological changes all are indicative of the fight-flight response (Cannon, 1929). The vasodilatation in skeletal muscle was shown to be caused mainly by sympathetic, cholinergic vasodilators; circulating adrenaline or inhibition of vasoconstrictors exerts only a minor influence on blood flow during emotional stress (Roddie, 1977). The second phase of syncope, notably the precipitous fall in blood pressure, is not easy to explain in terms of increasing or decreasing sympathetic activity.

It has long been known that several symptoms of vasovagal syncope, especially bradycardia, nausea, abdominal discomfort, desire to defecate and vomiting, are typical signs of increased parasympathetic activity. Early writers on the mechanism of fainting envisioned all circulatory changes as occurring secondary to failure of the heart: bradycardia caused by vagal activity. Therefore, in spite of its somewhat different origin (Weissler & Warren, 1959), the term "vasovagal attack" was associated with syncope. In 1932 however, Lewis found that administration of atropine (a blocker of cholinergic receptors) removed the vagal bradycardia, but did not prevent the occurrence of syncope. Consequently, the role of the parasympathetic system was assumed to be of much less importance.

When it was discovered that the strong fall in blood pressure was caused by peripheral pooling of the blood (Barcroft & Edholm, 1945), investigators tried to explain decelerating heart rate as a secondary phenomenon, caused by (a) central depletion of blood (Weissler & Warren, 1959), (b) breakdown of baroreceptor reflexes that normally counteract blood pressure variations (Sharpey-Schafer, 1956), and (c) strong reduction in venous return which would act on (left) ventricular receptors (Weissler & Warren, 1959; Sharpey-Schafer, 1956), and inhibit cardiac activity to be adapted to the reduced venous return.

Meanwhile the work of Cannon (1929) had directed attention more and more to sympathetic patterns of ANS activity accompanying the fight-flight response, and to the relation of adrenaline and noradrenaline to emotions. Only occasionally the unexplained parasympathetic symptoms were noted (Edholm, 1952). The concept of perfect reciprocity and balance of sympathetic and parasympathetic nervous systems was difficult to reconcile with the existence of parasympathetic activity in the face of strong sympathetic activation. It was recommended to replace the term *vasovagal syncope* by *vasodepressor syncope* (Engel, 1962) in order to stress the reflex-like lowering of blood pressure.

It became evident, however, that theory did not account for all characteristic phenomena of syncope. Even inconsistencies can be noted. If vasodilatation in skeletal muscle preceding and during faint is cholinergic, then one would have expected a neat reversal of syncope symptoms in the study of Lewis (1932): not only blocking of vagal (parasympathetic) bradycardia, but also reversal of the cholinergic vasodilatation by administration of atropine. Blood pressure should have been restored in such conditions. What exactly happens after administration of atropine is still unknown.

It is remarkable that the parasympathetic symptoms of fainting obtained so little attention for some time. In this connection it is worth noting that Taggart, Hedworth-Whitty, Carruthers, and Gordon (1976) speak of "the forgotten vagus," and make the following remark: "Interest in equating different emotions with a differential secretion of adrenaline and noradrenaline may have diverted attention from the parasympathetic system" (p. 789). Or, as Roddie (1977) formulated it:

Cannon (1929) attempted to unify bodily responses in a frightening situation. The responses are attributed to activity of the sympathetic nervous system to prepare the person for fight-flight. This is an attractive hypothesis and one which is popular with teachers since it is readily understood by students, makes good teleological sense and suggests that the reactions to stressful situations are predictable. It ignores, however, the contributions that the somatic and parasympathetic systems undoubtedly make in the responses to fear.

Roddie (1977) continues with an enumeration of two possible opposite reactions to fear of a great number of physiological systems: (a) a sympathicoadrenal response that prepares the organism for fight-flight and (b) a mainly parasympathetic response with effects which seem to be much less adaptive to the threatening situation (see Table 2). The problem with vasovagal syncope is, then, that physiological responses of both types occur.

The studies by Hess (1957) and Gellhorn and associates (Gellhorn, 1965; Gellhorn & Loofbourrow, 1963) also describe the sympathetic (ergotropic) and parasympathetic (trophotropic) systems as both being related to emotional functioning. According to these authors, the ergotropic system is activated in fight-flight and rage situations whereas the trophotropic system is activated during fear. The ergotropic and trophotropic systems are working in a reciprocal fashion in normal circumstances. Gellhorn contends, however, that there are situations in which the reciprocity of the ergotropic and trophotropic systems breaks down. Two types of breakdown are possible. The first type is a state of concurrent elevated activity of both systems as in chronic anxiety (Gellhorn, 1965). The second type is a state in which alternations or rebounds occur in the activity of the ergotropic and trophotropic systems. Rebound phenomena can be expected when after a period of strong sympathetic activity a rapid decay occurs. The result is an overshoot of trophotropic activity (Gellhorn & Loofbourrow, 1963). This could be what happens in vasovagal faint.

However, the shortcoming of a theory which calls for rebound as the mechanism of syncope is that the moment of overshoot is made dependent on decreasing sympathetic activity. But what causes this decrease in ergotropic activity? The sudden and critical decrease of heart rate and blood pressure in the face of previously increased sympathetic activation is unlikely to be an emergency response to extremely high heart rate or blood pressure. Heart rate is somewhat elevated just preceding the collapse, while blood pressure is slowly decreasing, but all within the normal range. It seems likely that an active central nervous system (CNS) process is involved.

Before continuing, let us look at the first phase of syncope more closely. Due to strong sympathetic activation in the first phase of vasovagal syncope there is an increase in heart rate and an increase in cholinergic vasodilatation in skeletal muscle. These changes occur in the form of feedforward control which prepares the body for massive motor action that is to be expected in the normal fight-flight situation. The physiological state of the organism is fully adapted for energy consuming action. The peripheral vasodilatation provided expansion facilities for increasing cardiac activity. The absence of these expansion facilities would lead to a critical increase in blood pressure (Roddie, 1977). This vasodilatation also may have some function in facilitating metabolism. Since this state is accomplished mainly in a feedforward manner, there is no tendency to return to an equilibrium when disturbing factors arise. The state of system components

Table 2 Two possible physiological reactions to threat (Roddie, 1977)

Effects	Respiration	Muscle tone	Cutaneous reactions	Cardiac output	Peripheral resistance	Pupils	Blood characteristics	Alimentary tract
Sympathico-adrenal	Increased respiration, dilated bronchi, constricted nasal mucosae	Increased by removal of central inhibition	Vasoconstriction: paleness; lowered skin temperature; increased exocrine secretion; sweating; piloerection	Increased	Lowered (by vasodilatation in striated muscle)	Dilated	Increased clotting tendency due to circulating catecholamines and corticosteroids	Reduced salivation; loss of appetite; decreased gastric and intestine secretion and motility; decreased blood flow in splanchnic area; increased ADH release
Parasympathetic	Impaired respiration; release of acetylcholine causes constriction of bronchial smooth muscle	Strong loss caused by central inhibition	Vasodilatation: blushing; increased skin temperature	Decreased (by vagal inhibition)	Increased	Constricted	Blood becomes incoagulable due to activated fibrinolytic system	Salivation; vomiting due to strongly increased gastric motility; (involuntary) defecation; (involuntary) micturition

that are part of feedback loops is at the edge of the working range. Lessening vasodilator action due to reduced baroreceptor activity would have only marginal effect when strong sympathetic, cholinergic vasodilator action prevails.

Three possible processes that can introduce a disturbance at this stage and are likely to be involved in causing the collapse in syncope are considered here: (1) willed inhibition of skeletal motor activity; (2) a general and acute trophotropic response to a threat that cannot be overcome; and (3) the relaxation response.

Syncope Triggered by Willed Inhibition

Willed inhibition of skeletal motor activity should not be confounded with the symptom "loss of muscle tone". Loss of muscle tone is a secondary effect, due to disturbed cerebral metabolism or to central inhibition (see the next two sections). Loss of muscle tone may or may not be reported before the patient actually faints. Willed inhibition means that the victim of syncope is consciously restraining himself from action in the threatening situation. Willed inhibition of the skeletal muscle action, for which the autonomous nervous system (ANS) has prepared, in the threatening situation will result in an extremely unadapted state, that is, peripheral pooling of blood, accompanied by a level of cardiac activity that is too low to maintain an acceptable level of blood pressure (Engel, 1962; Engel & Romano, 1947). When skeletal motor activity actually takes place, the intensity and abruptness of the sympathetic discharges is enhanced through proprioceptive feedback on the hypothalamic system (Gellhorn & Loofbourrow, 1963). Heart rate increases and muscles act as a venous pump because blood is pushed out of the muscles in the direction of the heart via valved veins (Engel, 1962). In that case blood pressure is restored to normal levels. Experimental evidence comes from Engel and Romano (1947) who showed that when the patient with imminent faint performs physical exercise, blood pressure rises to normal levels. Unfortunately this is not the whole story: stopping the exercise caused an immediate fall in blood pressure. Apparently there is a concurrent (most likely parasympathetic) process that counteracts the sympathetic discharges that are triggered by the physical exercise. According to our opinion, willed inhibition of skeletal motor action is an important factor in critically reducing blood pressure. It causes a mismatch between autonomous state and actual energy consumption.

But what about the parasympathetic symptoms? Gellhorn (1965) predicts parasympathetic rebound when motor activity during sympathetic activation is followed abruptly by muscular relaxation. The essential feature of the precollapse phase in vasovagal syncope is, however, that no strong overt action of the fight-flight type occurs. It could be that the first phase of syncope is also characterized by general increased muscle tones of sufficient level to keep the blood pressure within normal range. Measurement of the EMG of posture-maintaining muscles during faint is necessary to solve this question. The sequence of processes leading to vasovagal syncope according to the willed motor inhibition hypothesis is as follows:

1. Threat leading to increased sympathetic activity.
2. Sudden inhibition of skeletal muscle activity caused by psychological factors: giving up.
3. Parasympathetic rebound caused by the combined effect of the two preceding conditions.
4. Circulatory collapse caused by incompatibility of physiological states.

The shortcoming of the motor inhibition hypothesis is that it cannot account for the persistence of parasympathetic activity, which continues in spite of physical exercise. Note that parasympathetic rebound is expected only to be a short-term effect (Gellhorn & Loofbourrow, 1963, p. 252).

In addition, more recently Engel (1978) made the following statement with respect to this hypothesis: "Since this formulation was put forward we have come to appreciate that it fails to account for important aspects of the reaction, notably the prominence of vagal and other parasympathetic activities" (p. 405).

Syncope Triggered by General and Acute Trophotropic Response

It is evident that both absence of strong skeletal muscle contractions and increased parasympathetic activity are strongly conducive to circulatory collapse in case of peripheral pooling of the blood. According to the following hypothesis, parasympathetic discharges and (involuntary) motor inhibition are components of a generalized trophotropic response to threat: the "conservation-withdrawal" response (Engel, & Schmale, 1972; Henry, 1976, 1980; Henry & Stephens, 1977). The concept of trophotropic and ergotropic divisions of the autonomous nervous system originates from the studies of Hess (1957) and Gellhorn and associates (Gellhorn, 1965; Gellhorn & Loofbourrow, 1963). Activation of the ergotropic branch, in general, points to increased sympathetic activity. Activation of the trophotropic system, on the other hand, reflects enhanced parasympathetic activity. The occurrence of the conservation-withdrawal response depends on the physiological/metabolic state and on psychological evaluation of the threatening situation. Note the difference with the willed inhibition hypothesis previously mentioned. Skeletal muscle inhibition in case of the withdrawal response is beyond conscious control of the subject; it is part of a general response of the organism. Characteristics are increased ACTH and cortisol levels and increased vagal activity. At the behavioral level, inhibition of ongoing behaviors, restricted mobility, and low sex and maternal drives are essential features. Its counterpart is the fight-flight reaction, which is characterized by increased sympathetic activity, at the behavioral level being attended with behavioral arousal, display and aggression. The sequence of processes that occur when syncope is caused by the withdrawal response is as follows:

1. Threat leading to increased sympathetic activity, fight-flight.
2. Cognitive processes leading to feelings of helplessness accompanied by char-

acteristic parasympathetic and motor inhibition reactions of the withdrawal response.

3. Circulatory collapse caused by incompatibility of physiological states.

The hypothesis of conservation-withdrawal as a trigger of syncope will be worked out later.

Syncope Triggered by the Relaxation Response

Graham, Kabler, and Lunsford (1961) list several objections to the willed inhibition theory of Engel and Romano (1947). In the first place, they consider the presence of bradycardia to be in contradiction with preparation to flight. Second, they note that vasovagal syncope often occurs after a threat has either been carried out or has disappeared. Third, they contend that blood flow is not necessarily increased in the tense muscles preparing for, but not carrying out action. Their hypothesis states that in the first phase of syncope, anxiety predominates and is accompanied by increased sympathetic activity. According to Graham and his co-workers this increase in sympathetic activity calls forth antagonistic reflexes which act to prevent the heart rate and blood pressure from rising without control. Then, in the second phase, because of relief of anxiety, the increased sympathetic activity suddenly disappears. As a consequence, the opposing (vagal) reflex mechanisms are left unopposed, resulting in an exaggerated parasympathetic activity, leading to syncope. However, their psychological interpretation is not firmly supported by clinical findings. Although there are examples of people who develop symptoms in situations characterized by relief, there are a lot of other situations in which there surely is no question of fainting to occur as soon as people overcome their anxiety.

A theory on emotional syncope should, however, account for those occurrences of syncope where psychological relief is the trigger of the reaction. Contrary to Graham and others (1961) who assume that the mere withdrawal of sympathetic activity (due to relief of anxiety) is a sufficient condition to provoke fainting, we feel that a (second) active process must be involved. In case of relief, a serious candidate could be the so-called "relaxation-response" (Benson, 1983; Benson, Beary & Carol, 1974). The physiological changes, constituting the relaxation response, are very similar to the trophotropic response discovered by Hess (1957). Hess electrically stimulated anterior hypothalamic areas of the cat brain and in this way he induced physiological changes opposite to those of the fight-flight reaction first described by Cannon (1927). Benson (1983) states that "the relaxation response appears to be a basic bodily reaction that may have significance in countering overactivity of the sympathetic nervous system in man and other animals" (p. 283). The parasympathetic discharges of the relaxation response may facilitate occurrence of syncope when the cardiovascular system is still preparing for flight-fight. In spite of the fact that Graham, Kabler and Lunsford (1961) preferred one explanation on the grounds of parsimony, they also realized their hypothesis did not capture all cases; witness their statement: "one could, therefore, invoke two different explanations, one for the apparently aberrant cases and another for the majority" (p. 504).

It should be noted that, in spite of the trophotropic reactions that they have in common, there is a clear conceptual difference between the withdrawal response and the relaxation response. The relaxation response is related to positive experiences (such as relief), whereas the withdrawal response should be considered a mechanism with life saving functions. The sequence of events in case of syncope, triggered by the relaxation response is as follows:

1. Threat leading to increased sympathetic activity.
2. Cognitive process leading to 'relief' accompanied by the parasympathetic and motor inhibition reactions of the relaxation response.
3. Circulatory collapse caused by incompatibility of states.

Biochemical Changes During Fainting

In addition to the above mentioned mainly cardiovascular data, there are also some data available on biochemical changes during syncope, although they are scarce. For example, Chosy and Graham (1965), Goldstein and co-workers (1982) and Vingerhoets (1984) provide evidence pointing to enhanced catecholamines, both adrenaline and noradrenaline, just before the onset of the symptoms. This, just like the increased heart rate and blood pressure, suggests increased activity of the sympathetic system. In the second phase, a large decrease of adrenaline but especially of noradrenaline has been reported (Goldstein et al., 1982; Vingerhoets, 1984), favoring the conclusion of withdrawal of sympathetic activity. At the same time, however, plasma levels of both cortisol, human growth hormone, and antidiuretic hormone have been found to be elevated (Edholm, 1952; Vingerhoets, 1984; Weissler & Warren, 1959). The same holds for glucose and lactic acid (Vingerhoets, 1984; Weissler & Warren 1959). On the contrary, eosinophil counts have been reported to decrease after the syncope (Vingerhoets, 1984; Weissler & Warren, 1959). Summarizing, while in the first phase endocrine changes seem to point to enhanced catabolic action, the second phase is characterized by increased levels of the anabolic hormones.

Intermediate Resume

Motor inhibition (sec) and the combined physiological reactions of the withdrawal response or the relaxation response are possible moments of disturbance of a physiological state that is characterized by a feedforward preparation to fight-flight. Cardiovascular homeostasis is disturbed by the uninterrupted peripheral pooling of blood as well as by vagal inhibition of cardiac functioning. When the blood pressure has reached critically low levels, central depletion of blood and reduced venous return will have an additional deteriorating effect on heart action. The temporary asystole (chronic asystole in case of sudden death) is more likely to be produced by these factors than by vagal inhibition of the heart alone.

Very little is known about other disturbing factors of cardiovascular homeostasis. An example is the degree of vasoconstriction/vasodilatation in the splanchnic area. Vasoconstriction in the first phase of syncope can be explained as part of the fight-flight response. What happens in the second phase is unclear. It is evident that sudden vasodilatation of splanchnic blood vessels by parasympathetic activity will lead to a strong decrease in blood pressure, superposed on the already existing lowered level due to peripheral pooling. The recovery phase, however, seems to be characterized by vasoconstriction in the splanchnic area (Edholm, 1952). Below is a list of relevant processes in emotional syncope.

1. Sympathetic vasoconstriction.
2. Sympathetic vasodilatation.
3. Sympathetic acceleration of heart rate.
4. Sympathetic cutaneous vasoconstriction.
5. Parasympathetic deceleration of heart rate via the nervous vagus.
7. Baroreceptor induced inhibition of sympathetic vasoconstrictors.
8. Deceleration of heart rate and stroke volume caused by reduced central blood supply.
9. Deceleration of heart rate via (left) ventricular receptors that inhibit heart activity on reduced venous return.
10. Inhibition of skeletal motor activity.

It should be clear now that physiological activity during faint cannot be explained solely in terms of sympathetic activity and breakdown of cardiovascular feedback systems. There are many changes during faint that can only be attributed to parasympathetic and/or endocrine processes.

Increased parasympathetic activity as a response to threat is probably as common as the well-known fight-flight response. Both types of activity may occur (a) at the same moment in time or (b) in rapid succession. Some occurrences of syncope are likely to be triggered by the relaxation response.

A theory of emotional vasovagal syncope should account for the following phenomena: (a) syncope is a biphasic phenomenon, (b) the first phase is characterized by strong sympathetic discharges, (c) the second phase is characterized by strong sympathetic and parasympathetic discharges, or by parasympathetic discharges and sympathetic peripheral aftereffects, (d) metabolic changes during syncope are necessarily related to autonomous nervous system action in the two phases, and (e) vasovagal syncope is sensitive to physical factors such as posture and ambient temperature but should not be equated with orthostatic faint. Theory has to explain in what way psychological factors are involved, and via which anatomical structures the autonomous nervous system is influenced.

Research, therefore, should be directed at the following:

• heart rate
• blood pressure
• skeletal muscle blood flow
• EMG of muscles that are active in maintaining posture
• cutaneous blood flow
• splanchnic blood flow
• endocrine changes

- psychosocial context
- individual appraisal of the psychosocial context
- personality factors

PERSON CHARACTERISTICS OF FAINTERS

According to Engel (1962, 1978) vasodepressor syncope occurs more commonly among men than women. This seems to hold especially for settings in which men feel the ambience to be one of strong social disapproval of any display of weakness. This conviction leads to the following description:

> *Neurotically determined vasodepressor syncope is more common among men characterized by considerable concern about the integrity of their bodies. Any cut, bruise or injury, real or threatened, however trivial, appears to mobilize an exaggerated degree of anxiety. The primitive flight from injury seems to be overdetermined. Usually these men show considerable attention to the body and pride in muscle mass and athletic endeavor (Engel, 1962, p. 17).*

At first glance this phrase seems to be based more on clinical intuition than on thorough investigations. In the already mentioned Callahan, Edelman, Smith, and Smith (1963) study, reaction rates were higher in women. The same result has been reported by Greenbury (1942), Moloney, Lonnergan, and McClintock (1946), and Williams (1942). Nevertheless, three other studies (Graham, 1961; Hasse, 1956; Poles & Boycott, 1942) do not report sex to differentiate between fainters and nonfainters. However, once again, it has to be noted that in most cases blood donation occurs on a voluntary basis, so the populations in such studies cannot be considered to be an aselect sample of the total population. In the only study on the incidence of vasovagal episodes during simple surgical treatment (Edmondson et al., 1978) the investigators concluded that such reactions indeed were particularly common among young adult males. More consensus exists with respect to the age of the reactors. Several studies (Graham, 1961; Greenbury, 1942; Hasse, 1956; Moloney et al., 1946; Poles & Boycott, 1942; Sledge & Boydstun, 1979; Williams, 1942) suggest that fainting occurs more frequently in the younger age groups. With respect to race, as yet, there are no conclusive data.

More interesting for psychologists is the question whether there are any systematic differences in personality between fainters and nonfainters. To put it another way, does there exist a "syncope-prone" personality? In spite of the eagerness of psychologists to study personality differences between patients with psychosomatic complaints and other patients or healthy controls, until now, fainters not frequently were the prey of psychologists. Ruetz, Johnson, Callahan, Meade, and Smith (1967) undertook, besides hematological and physiological examination, also clinical psychological testing of blood donors with a history of fainting. Few differences were found between these fainters and matched controls. Most striking were the higher scores of the fainters on the depression and hypochondriasis scales of the Minnesota Multiphasic Personality Inventory (MMPI). This result means that the reactors appear to have a heightened awareness and overconcern with bodily functions, much the same as stated by Engel (1962, 1978). In addition, among fainters there was a greater proneness to feelings of inadequacy and depression.

Schmidt (1975) also investigated personality differences between fainters and non-fainters. Not only did this researcher replicate the findings of Ruetz and co-workers (1967); he also found fainters to have higher scores on the neuroticism dimension as measured by the Maudsley Personality Inventory (MPI). It was also found that the Hysteria, Psychopathic Deviate, Paranoia, Psychasthenia, and Schizophrenia scales yielded elevated scores for the fainters. However, cross validation of the 28 MMPI items, which in the Ruetz and co-workers' (1967) study discriminated between the reactor and the nonreactor group, did not yield positive results. Sledge and Boydstun (1982, 1979) compared aircrew members with the diagnosis of vasovagal syncope to controls on variables of personality characteristics, psychosocial antecedents to the onset of their conditions, and hyperventilation experience. For psychological testing they used Cattell's 16 Personality Factors, form A (16 PF), the Cornell Index (CI), the Fear Survey (FS) and the Revised Willoughby Questionnaire (RWQ). No statistically significant total score differences between groups on the FS and RWQ were found. On the CI the syncope group averaged 2.71, while the controls averaged 0.81. These very low scores (also for the fainters) again clearly show that caution is needed to generalize beyond a particular sample. In this case these aircrew members all had passed a very extensive medical examination during the selection procedures for the USAF school of aerospace medicine. Nevertheless, the difference again indicates that fainters are more preoccupied with somatic and psychosomatic symptoms. The 16 PF scores, at last, suggested that the control group tended to be more venturesome, more imaginative and more controlled than the syncope group. Taken together,these findings and the ratings obtained during a psychiatric interview, Sledge and Boydstun (1979) conclude that vasovagal fainters differed from controls along nonspecific psychological factors. These authors believe that the development of the specific autonomic pattern necessary to produce fainting is a combination of several factors including biological patterns and dispositions, personality factors, broad psychosocial elements, and immediate situational variables.

THE CONTEXT OF SYNCOPE

More impressive are the results of Sledge (1978) and Sledge and Boydstun (1979) of their analysis of the specific context in which the syncope occurs, especially the thoughts, fantasies, and feelings of the fainters just before the onset of the symptoms. It appeared that the fainters uniformly reported a fantasy of threat (bodily or psychological) to which they felt they had to submit. In nearly all cases there was a perceived threat emanating from a real figure in the patient's immediate social context. These persons in most cases occupied or represented a position of authority in relation to the patient. Sledge (1978) suggests that perhaps this perception of a threat from a greater authority, often seen as incompetent or inconfident, constrained these people from taking action and led to feelings of helplessness. Ranking the events immediately prior to onset of syncope yields the following results (Sledge & Boydstun, 1979):

- 75% perceived inability to act
- 50% medical procedure

- 46% fantasy of bodily harm or mutilation
- 25% pain
- 25% sight of blood, injury or mutilation

Engel (1978) postulates that physiological processes accompanying psychological "giving up" in the face of increased emotionality and psychological uncertainty may cumulate in vasodepressor syncope in the healthy person. However, in the person with defective cardiovascular homeostatic systems (of whatever origin) the outcome could be sudden death. If this statement can be taken as valid, studies on the psychosocial context in which sudden death occurs also may contribute to our understanding about the psychological mechanisms that play an important role in the onset of fainting. Engel (1978) gives the following enumeration of circumstances surrounding sudden death (N = 275):

- 21% died during the first three weeks of acute grief;
- 9% died on the threat of imminent loss of a close person;
- 7% died after a danger has passed;
- 6% died during public humiliation and loss of self-esteem or upon threat of injury;
- 3% died during mourning or upon an anniversary of a death.

To summarize, these situations range from overwhelming catastrophe to relatively ordinary everyday upsets to trivial circumstances having the characteristics of conditioned stimuli. For the victims, however, the situations were impossible to ignore and evoked intense emotions. Sadness, depression, helplessness, and, on the other hand, relief and elation are most frequently observed immediately before the collapse. The occurrence of fainting in situations characterized by relief, because the threat either has been carried out or has passed, also attracted the attention of other scientists (Graham et al., 1961). Taking into account both these psychological results, the endocrine data and the already mentioned physiological hypotheses, this allows for a critical evaluation of these psychophysiological hypotheses. This will be done in the next section, after having presented more general speculations on the adaptation value of syncope.

HYPOTHESES ON FAINTING

Theorizing about fainting has been done by scholars of many disciplines, and from many points of view. Several speculations on fainting have been put forward within the framework of evolution theory stressing the adaptive elements in it. For example, Engel and Romano (1947) considered this type of response as adaptive when the threatening situation is too great for the organism to meet. For if one has to be killed, it might be more palatable to be killed in unconsciousness. Engel and Schmale (1972), on the contrary, emphasize the similarity between such responses and phenomena in the animal kingdom as "playing dead" reaction, "animal hyponsis," "cataplexy," and "death feint." This kind of reaction can be especially seen in young animals when confronted with a dangerous situation. The animal suddenly falls to the ground as if dead. All its muscles are relaxed, breathing is inhibited and heart rate and blood pressure are depressed. This immobility makes the animal less conspicious to its predators and, as a consequence, in this way they enhance the probability to survive.

More physiologically oriented scientists point to the specific physiological changes during syncope such as low heart rate and low blood pressure. It is suggested that these changes are adaptive when there is a threat of bodily harm, because these changes guard the organism against excessive blood loss.

Still another suggestion stems from Hess (cf. Engel & Schmale, 1972). This postulates that the loss of consciousness protects the nervous system against overload, by blocking all input systems.

Obviously, all these speculations share the influence of the Darwinian point of view, which means that simply because the phenomenon still exists, it has to serve an adaptational objective. Of course, these formulations do not lend themselves for objective testing, and are speculations on the meaning of fainting. Let us now return to psychophysiological hypotheses. To summarize:

1. Fainting occurs when the circulatory preparation for overt action (fight or flight) is persisting at the same time that psychological inhibition of motor activity ("giving up") has developed (Engel, 1962; Engel & Romano, 1947).

2. Fainting results when, because of relief of anxiety, increased sympathetic activity suddenly disappears. This means that the opposing (vagal) reflex mechanisms are left unopposed (Graham et al., 1961).

3. Fainting is the consequence of a very strong excitation of the ergotropic system which, when it continues to mount, rcsults in a "spillover" into the trophotropic system (Gellhorn, 1965).

4. Fainting occurs, when in case of relief, the relaxation-response has been triggered, after strong sympathetic activation.

5. Fainting occurs when there is a rapid succession or alternation of the acute manifestations of two stress reactions: the fight-flight reaction and the conservation-withdrawal response, as described by Henry (1976, 1980) and Henry and Stephens (1977) (Engel, 1978; Vingerhoets, 1984).

This last hypothesis, until now, seems most attractive because it still involves the element of preparation for action followed by inhibition (Engel & Romano, 1947; Engel, 1962). It also is in agreement with psychological findings (Sledge, 1978; Engel & Romano, 1947) that, at first, fainters want to escape from the situation but then feelings of helplessness and hopelessness develop just before the onset of the symptoms. Finally, the pattern of biochemical and cardiovascular changes, generally, seems to correspond nicely to the description given by Henry (1976, 1980) and Henry and Stephens (1977). We would like to conclude by expressing the hope the these conceptions will stimulate further research in this area. For, due to its unique features already mentioned in the introduction, fainting maybe can provide a model for the development of psychosomatic disturbances, which is of interest for students of many disciplines.

SUMMARY

Fainting can be considered a psychosomatic phenomenon. Because of the short time delay between the evoking stimulus and the response, there is a good opportunity to study the psychological aspects of this phenomenon. This may contribute to the understanding of psychosomatic phenomena in general. With respect to the physiological aspects of fainting, it was concluded that, theoretically, there are three mechanisms, each of which may evoke fainting. These are (1) willed inhibition of skeletal motor activity, (2) the conservation-withdrawal reaction, and (3) the relaxation response. Characteristic for the psychosocial context are the presence of emotions, either negative ones such as feelings of helplessness or positive ones, for example, relief. Taking into account these results the conclusion is that fainting occurs when either the conservation-withdrawal reaction or the relaxation-response, both accompanied by parasympathetic overreactivity, is triggered. In addition, results are reported, pointing to the existence of a syncope-prone personality. Most important features of these persons appear to be young age, overconcern with bodily functioning (hypochondria), and depression. It is concluded that much research is needed to complete the picture of this very interesting phenomenon.

REFERENCES

Barcroft, H. & Edholm, O. G. (1945). On the vasodilatation in human skeletal muscle during post-haemorrhagic fainting. *Journal of Physiology, 104*, 161–175.

Barcroft, H. & Swan, H. J. C. (1953). *Sympathetic control of human blood vessels*. London: Edward Arnold Ltd.

Benson, H., (1983). The relaxation response: Its subjective and objective historical precedents and physiology. *Trends in Neuroscience, 6* (7) 281–284.

Benson, H., Beary, J., & Carol, M. P. (1974). The relaxation response. *Psychiatry, 37*, 37–46.

Callahan, R., Edelman, E. B., Smith, M. S. & Smith, J. J. (1963). Study on the incidence and characteristics of blood donor reactors. *Transfusion, 3*, 76–82.

Cannon, W. B. (1927). The James-Lange theory of emotions: A critical examination and an alternative theory. *American Journal of Psychology, 39*, 106–124.

Cannon, W. B. (1929). *Bodily changes in pain, hunger, fear and rage (2nd ed.)*. New York: Appleton Century.

Chosy, J. J. & Graham, D. T. (1965). Catecholamines in vasovagal fainting. *Journal of Psychosomatic Research, 9*, 189–194.

Edholm, O. G. (1952). Physiological changes during fainting. In: G. E. W. Wolstenholme (Ed.), *Visceral Circulation*, Ciba Foundation Symposium, London: Churchill Ltd.

Edmondson, H. D., Gordon, P. H., Lloyd, J. M., Meeson, J. E. and Whitehead, F. I. H. (1978). Vasovagal episodes in the dental surgery. *Journal of Dentistry, 6*, 189–195.

Engel, G. L. (1962). *Fainting*. Springfield, IL: Thomas.

Engel, G. L. (1978). Psychologic stress, vasodepressor (vasovagal) syncope, and sudden death. *Annals of Internal Medicine, 89*, 403–412.

Engel, G. L. & Romano, J. (1947). Studies of syncope: IV Biological interpretation of vasodepressor syncope. *Psychosomatic Medicine, 9*, 288–294.

Engel, G. L. & Schmale, A. H. (1972). Conservation-withdrawal: A primary regulatory process for organismic homeostasis. In CIBA Foundation Symposium 8: *Physiology, Emotion and Psychosomatic Illness.* Amsterdam: Elsevier.

Gellhorn, E. (1965). Neurophysiological basis of anxiety. *Perspectives in Biology and Medicine, 8*, 488–515.

Gellhorn, E. & Loofbourrow, G. N. (1963). *Emotions and emotional disorders, a neurophysiological study.* New York: Harper and Row.

Goldstein, D. S. Spanarkel, M., Pitterman, A., Toltzis, R., Gratz, E., Epstein, S. & Keiser, H. R. (1982). Circulatory control mechanisms in vasodepressor syncope. *American Heart Journal, 104,* 1071–1075.

Graham, D. T. (1961). Prediction of fainting in blood donors. *Circulation, 23,* 901–906.

Graham, D. T., Kabler, J. D. & Lunsford, L. (1961). Vasovagal fainting: A diphasic response. *Psychosomatic Medicine, 23,* 493–507.

Greenbury, C. L. (1942). Analysis of incidence of "fainting" in 5,897 unselected blood donors. *British Medical Journal, 1,* 253–255.

Hasse, W. (1956). Vorkommnisse beim Blutspender während und nach der Blutentnahme. *Bibliotheca Haematologica, 5,* 151–156.

Henry, J. P. (1976). Understanding the early pathophysiology of essential hypertension. *Geriatrics, 30,* 59–72.

Henry, J. P. (1980). Present concept of stress theory. In E. Usdin, R. Kvetnansky & I. J. Kopin (Eds.), *Catecholamines and stress: Recent advances.* Amsterdam: Elsevier.

Henry, J. P. & Stephenes, P. M. (1977). *Stress, health and the social environment: A sociobiologic approach to medicine.* New York: Springer-Verlag.

Hess, W. R. (1957). *Functional organization of the diencephalon,* New York: Grune and Statton.

Lewis, T. (1932). Lecture on vasovagal syncope and the carotid sinus mechanism, with comments on Gowers' and Nothnagel's syndrome. *British Medical Journal, 1,* 873–876.

Moloney, W. C., Lonnergan, I. R. & McClintock, J. K. (1946). Syncope in blood donors. *New England Journal of Medicine, 234,* 114–118.

Poles, F. C. & Boycott, M. (1942). Syncope in blood donors. *The Lancet, 2,* 531–535.

Roddie, I. C. (1977). Human responses to emotional stress. *Irish Journal of Medical Sciences, 4,* 395–417.

Ruetz, P. P. Johnson, S. A., Callahan, R., Meade, R. C. & Smith, J. J. (1967). Fainting: A review of its mechanisms and a study in blood donors. *Medicine* (Baltimore), *46,* 363–384.

Schmidt, R. T. (1975). Personality and fainting. *Journal of Psychosomatic Research, 19,* 21–25.

Sharpey-Shafer, E. P. (1956). Emergencies in general practice: Syncope. *British Medical Journal, 1,* 506–509.

Sledge, W. H. (1978). Antecedent psychological factors in the onset of vasovagal syncope. *Psychosomatic Medicine, 40,* 568–579.

Sledge, W. H. & Boydstun, J. A. (1979) Vasovagal syncope in aircrew: Psychosocial aspects. *The Journal of Nervous and Mental Disease, 167,* 114–124.

Sledge, W. H. & Boydstun, J. A. (1982). Syncope in aircrew. *Aviation, Space and Environmental Medicine, 53,* 258–265.

Taggart, P., Hedworth-Whitty, R., Carruthers, M. & Gordon, P. D. (1976). Observations on electrocardiogram and plasma catecholamines during dental procedures: The forgotten vagus. *British Medical Journal, 2,* 787–789.

Vingerhoets, A. J. J. M. (1984) Biochemical changes in two subjects succumbing to syncope. *Psychosomatic Medicine, 46,* 95–103.

Weiss, S. (1940). Instantaneous "physiologic" death. *New England Journal of Medicine, 233,* 793–799.

Weissler, A. M. & Warren, J. V. Vasodepressor syncope. *American Heart Journal, 57,* 786–794.

Williams, G. E. O. (1942). Syncopal reactions in blood donors: Investigation of 222 cases. *British Medical Journal, 1,* 783–786.

14

The Interaction Between Anxiety State and Performance Efficiency: Application of Psychophysiology

John W. Hinton
University of Glasgow

INTRODUCTION

A review is given of some of the main studies on the correlation between anxiety and nonspecific skin conductance response rate (nonspec SCR rate). The conclusion is that this relationship is well established in regard to pathological conditions and anxiety state (A-STATE). However, most of the evidence points to a cognitive interpretation of nonspecific electrodermal activity. It is proposed that this nonspec SCR rate monitors the rate of switching of "emotionally charged" thoughts. It is argued that this index relates to the control of selective attention—to the degree of intrusion of "task-irrelevant internal stimuli"—when focusing on an externally controlled mental task. A recent study is outlined with results supporting the hypothesis that high nonspec SCR rate relates to increased difficulty in understanding sentences as they become more syntactically complex. The problems of fitting anxiety into an interactional model of stress are examined. Also, a speculative model is presented where anxiety trait (A-TRAIT) and A-STATE can be conceptualized as both "feedforward" and "feedback", in the control of selective attention during the performance of mental tasks. The potential usefulness of physiological measures for tapping psychological functions in this model is outlined, and problems of experimenting in this area are examined.

In this chapter there is an outline and discussion of some of the ongoing research in our Glasgow University laboratory on the psychophysiological correlates of anxiety state and performance on mental tests. Consideration is given of how psychophysiological measures might fit into a model of "Stress." The first question to be dealt with is whether A-STATE can be assessed psychophysiologically. A positive answer to this is derived from an analysis of the experimental data available. Second, there is an examination of research on nonspecific electrodermal activity in relation to anxiety. This research is analyzed in an attempt to elucidate the psychological functions underlying this psychophysiological index. Specifically I will consider whether nonspecific skin conductance response rate is primarily an index of cognitive activity or of autonomic/emotional activity related to anxiety (Hinton, 1983). The third question is on the relationship between psychophysiological indices of anxiety state and performance on mental tasks: in particular, does increasing the mental load of each task lead to a significant differentiation between high and low anxiety state scorers, as assessed psychophysiologically? My fourth consideration will be of some theoretical models relating to stress, anxiety, and mental task performance efficiency. Finally, I will deal with some of the main problems arising in research on test performance efficiency and anxiety state, with particular reference to my own studies and theoretical speculations. Problems considered here are, for instance, due to individual differences in motivation, ability, knowledge, prior conditioning, and personality.

ANXIETY TRAIT, STATE, AND PSYCHOPATHOLOGY: RELEVANCE OF PSYCHOPHYSIOLOGICAL MEASUREMENT

Eysenck (1957) proposed that anxiety is a compound of both introverted and neurotic tendencies. Self-report inventory questions on introversion cover social inhibition and control, while neuroticism questions involve, to a large extent, self-awareness of autonomic activity, moods, and somatic complaints such as tenseness. So from this viewpoint, anxiety has cognitive (introverted) and autonomic/emotional (neurotic) components. Gray (1971), in his modified approach to Eysenck's dimensional scheme, sees anxiety as an amplified "sensitivity to punishment": high introversion relates to increased responsivity to signals of punishment, while high neuroticism relates to a magnified amplitude of autonomic/emotional responses. Thus, people high on E and N could be expected to experience greater fear of failure.

From the cognitive veiwpoint, one might expect that imagination (or high generalization of S-S connections in the brain) would be an essential prerequisite for anxiety development in any psychological test situation. This would be linked to high interference by irrelevant stimulation, that is, stimuli due to conditioned emotional responses would interfere with focusing of attention on a task. Both attention and memory interference could be expected, and this will be discussed later in relation to mental task performance and the development of a model.

Insofar as state or test anxiety is conditioned fear, then the immediate specific environment is the trigger, but proneness and magnitude of response should be dependent on extraversion and neuroticism, respectively. While this has not been investigated specifically, it has been shown that there is a correlation between A-STATE and A-TRAIT especially when A-STATE is measured under "failure feed-back" conditions (McAdoo, 1969). In psychophysiological research in particular, the laboratory and the procedures may be particularly threatening to testees. Also, I think it is reasonable to assume that mental testing is perceived as "ego-threatening" by most university student subjects, especially when there is no guarantee of anonymity and the results are being clearly recorded. This point

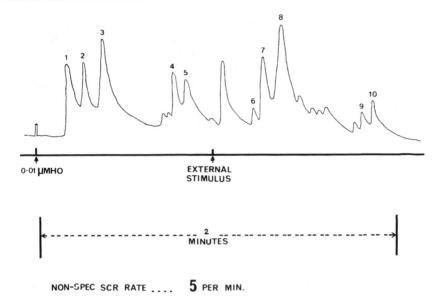

Figure 1 An example of a record of nonspecific skin conductance recording.

must be taken into account, and indeed may be used, in psychophysiological research on anxiety and performance.

The psychophysiological measure which I will consider here in detail is non-specific skin conductance response rate (nonspec SCR rate). This is simply a measure of the rate of occurrence of skin conductance responses which are not produced directly by external stimuli. Figure 1 shows the sort of record that might be obtained. It is usual to record the number of responses per minute in excess of 0.01 μmhos. (To normalize the data we, in this laboratory, now take the log of the measure.) The nonspec SCR has the same general characteristics as the skin conductance orienting response. I suggest that each nonspec SCR should be considered as an orienting response to an internally generated stimulus change (viz a "switch of thoughts").

Lader (1975), in a number of studies summarized in his book *The Psychophysiology of Mental Illness*, indicates that anxiety patients (high trait anxiety?) show higher rates of nonspecific electrodermal activity than nonanxiety subjects under passive test conditions. Under passive conditions (listening to an intermittent signal) anxiety patients show significantly higher levels of nonspec SCR responding compared to normals as shown by Bond, James, and Lader (1974). However, these investigators report that under so-called "active" conditions, that is, having reaction time tested in response to the signal, the rate of nonspec SC responding in normals rises to the same level as that of anxiety patients. Can we assume from this that the psychophysiological measure is indicating an increase in autonomic arousal, that is, emotional reaction of anxiety state? Alternatively, does the increased rate of nonspecific electrodermal responding in normals indicate a rise in some cortical activity connected with attention —linked to a raised level of motivation or test anxiety?

Research by Kilpatrick (1972) indicates that telling people that a mental I.Q.-type test relates to "brain damage" causes an increase in nonspecific electrodermal acitivity, whereas the tonic level of skin conductance relates simply to being put "on test." Kilpatrick believed that his results showed that raised nonspec SCR rate indicates a heightened emotional state, whereas increased skin conductance level indicates cognitive activation. However, the raised nonspecific activity in Kilpatrick's study could be showing increases in interfering thoughts relating to fear of possible findings on the "brain damage" test.

It is worth noting that both Kilpatrick (1972) and Bond, James, and Lader (1974) recorded nonspec SCR rate while the subject was not actually occupied mentally on any externally controlled task: in other words, during waiting periods. These are periods of maximum apprehension, when one would reasonably expect an increase in cognitive activity related to emotional response conditioned to the stimuli in the testing situation.

Hypothesizing from Eysenck's theory, one would predict that if nonspec SCR rate is an index of cognitive function, rather than simply of autonomic activity, then this index should correlate inversely with extraversion and not with neuroticism. This has in fact been found to be the case in a study by Coles, Gale, and Kline (1971) and in a study of 74 security hospital patients (Burke, Hinton, & O'Neill, 1978). In the latter study, extraversion correlated negatively with nonspecific electrodermal activity on two consecutive test sessions ($r = -0.38$, $p < 0.01$; $r = -0.33$, $p < 0.01$).

After an extensive review and discussion of the literature, Schalling (1978) proposes that nonspecific electrodermal fluctuation rate relates to "imaginativeness" and that this explains why, during periods of test anticipation, primary psychopaths show lower levels of electrodermal fluctuations than nonpsychopaths. That is, the primary psychopaths have a reduced imaginative capacity, a defect in cognitive functioning. Further research relevant to this has been published by Hinton, O'Neill, Dishman, and Webster (1979). The hypothesis was tested that primary psychopaths (with multiple types of offense against strangers) would show less indication of anticipatory anxiety than domestic offenders with only one or two types of offense. Psychopathic type offenders did in fact differ from domestic offenders in having lower rates of nonspecific electrodermal responding before testing. The domestic offenders showed a marked drop in nonspecific electrodermal response rate on retesting on a subsequent day, while the psychopathic types did not show a drop. This is illustrated in Fig. 2. It suggests that the difference between the groups was on test anxiety, or A-STATE, rather than trait anxiety. (In fact we found no correlation between A-TRAIT as measured on The Spielberger STAI and nonspec SCR rate.)

Over the past few years, my students and I have carried out a number of tests on the manipulation of text anxiety in the laboratory, with monitoring by the Spielberger A-STATE Inventory and recording of nonspec SCR rate. McCormick (unpublished study, 1981) found a clear relationship between level of ego-threat and nonspec SCR rate during test anticipation. The mean changes in the Spielberger A-STATE score corresponded with the changes in nonspec SCR rate. Figures 3 and 4 give the results of this small study which was carried out on two groups of seven male subjects. Each subject was tested by a young efficient female experimenter on three consecutive days. The test consisted of relaxing while listening to 1000 Hz, 1-second tone bursts of 90 db intensity. These oc-

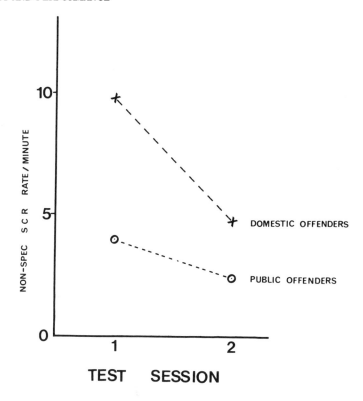

Figure 2 Nonspecific skin conductance response mean rate (pretesting) in
domestic offenders and public offenders (primary psychopaths) on
two consecutive test days.

curred at approximately 30-second intervals. The nonstimulus-bound SC responses were recorded during this period. All subjects were expecting the same
procedures on each occasion, but on the second session the experimental group
was given a mental test ("count backwards out loud, in sevens, from one hundred. This is being recorded"). This unexpected test was given before the passive, tone listening period. The experimental subjects were also told that a similar test would be given to them afterwards. The Spielberger A-STATE inventory
was administered directly before and directly after passive listening periods on
all test sessions. After the experimental group's second test session, the subjects
were informed that the third and final session would definitely be as innocuous
as the first one. The group mean changes in nonspec SCR rate and in A-STATE
scores, relating to the stressor, were significant statistically (especially with posttest   A-STATE scores, with the subject expecting a repeat of the stressor): see
Figs. 3 and 4.

Several studies in my laboratory have checked for correlations between the
Spielberger A-STATE score and psychophysiological indices. These indices have
included heart rate change on mental testing, finger pulse volume and percentage
change in pulse volume on mental testing, skin conductance orienting response
amplitude, and nonspec SCR rate. Only the latter has shown significant correla-

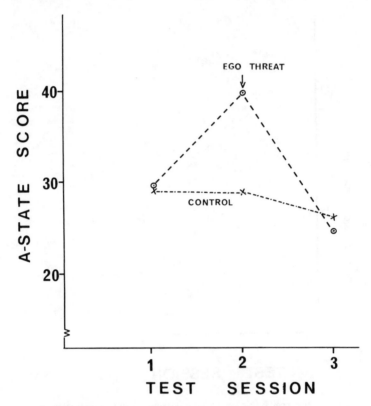

Figure 3 The effect of ego-threat on the Spielberger A-STATE score: group mean data for three consecutive test days.

tions with the Spielberger A-STATE Inventory score. These correlations were found to be significant only under fairly casual test conditions with minimal ego-threat. Under relaxing test conditions, where the subject was made totally aware that his test responses were not being observed by the experimenter, and where the experimenter was a fellow student of the testee, then a significant correlation of 0.85 was obtained. This fell to a nonsignificant correlation of 0.34 under ego-threatening test conditions (the opposite of those described above). These changes in correlation could not be accounted for by any difference in the variance of scores between the two testing conditions. It is possible, that under very ego-threatening conditions there is an increase in defensiveness and dissimulation in some subjects and maybe this could provide an explanation of the results obtained.

Overall, the evidence reviewed here does seem to suggest a strong relationship between nonspec SCR rate and A-STATE. It is important to ask what the functional significance of nonspecific electrodermal activity is, in relation to A-STATE. Is it an indication of autonomic activity related to anxiety, or is it monitoring cognitive activity which leads to and maintains the autonomic activity connected with A-STATE?

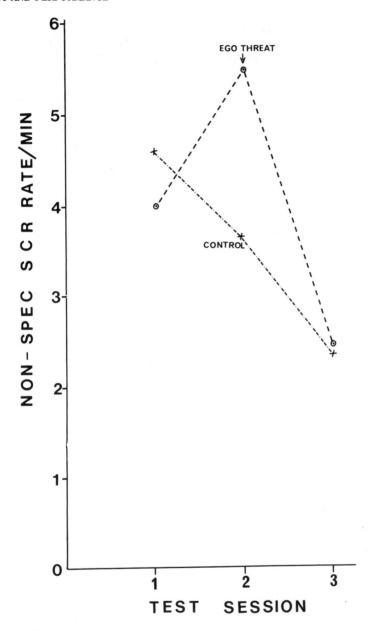

Figure 4 The effect of ego-threat on nonspecific skin conductance response rate: group mean data for three consecutive test days.

EVIDENCE FOR A COGNITIVE
INTERPRETATION OF NONSPECIFIC SKIN
CONDUCTANCE RESPONDING

The first point to notice has already been mentioned: It is that the form of each nonspec SCR is like an SC orienting response produced by an external stimulus. In other words, it is like an elementary attentional response. It occurs when the subject has his eyes closed and is in a silent room. The stimulus for the nonspecific response must therefore be internal.

If rate of nonspecific responding is due to the switching of thoughts as internal stimuli, then one could predict that thought-disordered schizophrenics, who are prone to hallucinations, would show higher nonspecific electrodermal response rate. This has indeed been found to be the case in a number of studies reviewed by Hinton, O'Neill, Hamilton, and Burke (1980). These latter investigators also report a significantly higher rate of nonspecific electrodermal responding in a group of thought-disordered security hospital patients, compared to a group of these patients rated as exhibiting low schizophrenic disorientation.

Nonspecific electrodermal fluctuation rate has been found to correlate significantly with the recovery time of the skin conductance orienting response (Martin & Rust, 1976; Hinton, O'Neill, Dishman, & Webster, 1979). It has been suggested by Venables (1974) that SCR half recovery time relates to the balance between inhibitory hippocampal function and excitatory amygdaloid function connected with the ability to "gate out" stimuli. It is important to note that nonspec SCR rate correlates significantly with SC orienting response half recovery time only under conditions of apprehension (i.e. before a first laboratory test, but not a second one). This was shown by Hinton, O'Neill, Dishman, and Webster (1979) and in the unpublished study by McCormick, to which I already referred. It seems reasonable to assume that, on the second testing session, anxiety state is reduced. So concordance between the two electrodermal indices could be due to mental activity associated with test apprehension.

There seems no doubt that nonspec SCR rate correlates positively with the rate of orienting response habituation. This in turn relates to degree of anxiety (both with anxiety patients and specific phobics). The evidence for these conclusions is effectively reviewed by Sartory and Lader (1981, pp. 174–175). The theoretical basis of habituation has been reviewed by Walrath and Stern (1980, pp. 15–19). There seems to be a strong argument for the view that habituation is an active inhibitory process necessary in the first stage of selective attention. It may be argued that the correlation of electrodermal orienting response habituation with nonspec SCR rate is consistent with the view that nonspecific electrodermal activity is related to efficiency of the selective attention process.

Very recently, a number of studies have been conducted in this laboratory, in which electrodermal activity is recorded while subjects are involved in continuous mental tasks. It seems apparent from this work that nonspec SCR rate can change up or down very rapidly depending on the degree of successful task involvement. We consistently find an overall drop in nonspec SCR rate from the pretest (apprehension) condition to the ontest (task coping) condition. This may reflect a drop in anxiety when focusing on task activity and a realization that the simple tasks are well within the subject's capability. The fact that the nonspecific response rate drops *rapidly* (within a few seconds) is not consistent with the view that it reflects autonomic activation: the metabolizing of circulating adrenaline after an anxiety provoking experience is relatively slow. In this connection, it is interesting to note that Hinton and Woodman (unpublished data, 1977) found almost zero correlation between nonspecific electrodermal response rate and levels of adrenaline in urine, whereas a relatively low but statistically significant correlation with noradrenaline was found. (These urine samples were taken just before psychophysiological testing, and the nonspecific responses were recorded during the pretest anticipation period.)

As already mentioned in relation to Eysenck's theory of personality, and consistent with the view that extraversion relates to cerebral/cognitive function rather than autonomic activation, it has been found that nonspecific electrodermal response rate correlates negatively with extraversion (Burke, Hinton, & O'Neill, 1978; Coles, Gale, & Kline, 1971). There is no correlation with Eysenck's neuroticism dimension, which he claims relates to autonomic functioning.

Lader (1965) suggested that nonspecific electrodermal activity indicates the functioning of a mechanism of internal arousal. This view is consistent with that of Venables (1967) who suggested that nonspecific electrodermal activity could indicate the operating of a subcortical/cortical system of regulation, which assists in maintaining optimum tonic arousal. It may be suggested that nonspecific electrodermal response rate does relate to arousal, insofar as arousal is dependent on cognitive functioning: switching of anxiety provoking thoughts. Nevertheless, the resulting sympathetic activation and adrenaline secretion could feed back, resulting in increase of cortical arousal and a further increase in rate of switching of thoughts.

It is concluded here that nonspec SCR rate is an index relating to cognitive attentional processes. It may be affected by a number of factors relating to internally generated stimuli, for example, the conditioned emotional significance (intensity), the variety (generalization), and the rate of switching. These stimuli are irrelevant to externally controlled tasks, and interfere with, or disrupt, focused attention on the relevant aspects of external stimuli and learned task-relevant stimuli and schemas.

From the viewpoint of nonspec SCR rate, it may be predicted that high rates of nonspec SCR would relate to impairment of functioning as mental task difficulty is increased. This problem was examined by Hinton (1982) and the study is briefly outlined in the following section.

A STUDY OF CHANGES IN EFFICIENCY OF VERBAL UNDERSTANDING AS A FUNCTION OF ANXIETY STATE

A computer literature search indicated that no studies had been conducted on the problem of how anxiety state affects verbal understanding, as complexity of the sentence syntax is increased. The test we used for this was a modification of that presented by Baddeley (1978). This was based on grammatical transformation as shown in Table 1. By prior experimentation we established three difficulty levels which are separated in this table. We studied actual performance level and

Table 1 Test of semantic understanding with varied syntactic complexity[a]

Difficulty level 1	Difficulty level 2	Difficulty level 3
Positive/precedes/active, "* precedes 0" Positive/follows/active, "* follows 0"	Negative/precedes/active, "* does not precede 0" Negative/follows/active, "* does not follow 0" Positive/precedes/passive, "* is preceded by 0" Positive/follows/passive, "* is followed by 0"	Negative/precedes/passive, "* is not preceded by 0" Negative/follows/passive, "* is not followed by 0"

[a]Example of what the subject sees on the monitor:
(1)* 0
0 is not preceded by *
(response by pressing button either true or false).

changes in performance as the difficulty was increased from level 1 to level 3. The subject simply sat at a computer monitor and observed, for example, an asterisk followed by a zero. Secondly, he received a statement in one of the various grammatical forms. He then had to press a button marked "true" or "false" which indicated his judgment. The order of the symbols and the presentation of the eight statements was randomized. Each sentence was presented 16 times. Scores were taken of the percentage correct and the average response time for each level of difficulty. Two groups of 11 male subjects were tested by two 20-year-old female students. One group (the *stressed* group) was tested very formally with their name conspicuously recorded. These subjects were also informed that the test related to intelligence. Subjects in the other group (the *relaxed* group) were treated very informally and were told they were simply subject numbers.

In view of the individual differences in verbal ability, it is not surprising that we found almost zero correlations between the A-STATE score and actual performance level and between psychophysiological indices and the actual performance level. However, we decided that a hypothesis could be made about the relationship between the *degree of deterioration* in performance as task difficulty was increased, and measures of anxiety state. It was hypothesized that the higher the state of anxiety, the greater would be the deterioration in performance as the tasks became more difficult. This hypothesis is consistent with the findings of O'Neill, Spielberger, and Hanson (1969), who showed that on a computer assisted mathematical learning task, students with high anxiety state made more errors on difficult materials and fewer errors on easy materials than the low A-STATE subjects. We investigated change in accuracy of performance as syntax difficulty increased, and found that significant correlations occurred with the nonspec SCR rate taken *during* the test period as a whole (ignoring electrodermal responses relating to button pressing). This correlation was most significant in the stressed group of subjects ($r = -0.63$, $p < 0.05$, as shown in Fig. 5): the greater the electrodermal activity, the greater the increase in errors of judgment. Does this simply mean that people with high apprehension have more selective attention problems as levels of task difficulty increase? Or vice versa: do those people with difficulties in selective attention suffer more from high A-STATE?

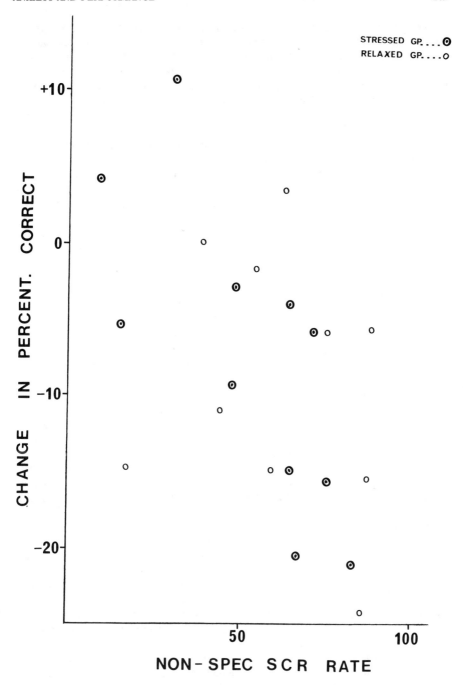

Figure 5 The change in percentage accuracy with increase of syntactic complexity (level 1 to level 3) as a function of log nonspecific skin conductance response rate (per minute × 100), during testing. (For the stressed group, $r = -0.63$, $p < 0.05$.)

Tonic heart rate was also investigated in relation to performance. While the stressed group showed a significantly larger increase in mean heart rate than the relaxed group (13 beats per minute compared to 6.5 beats per minute) there were no significant differences between the groups on performance level, or performance deterioration as the task difficulty increased. There was also no correlation between either the mean heart rate or heart rate change and performance criteria.

Two subjects showed a paradoxically large increase in finger pulse volume when put "on test." These two individuals exhibited by far the worst performance deterioration generally and very long response times compared to other subjects. Clearly increase in skin blood flow is a maladaptive stress response from the point of view of mental test efficiency, when blood should be shunted to the brain. This finding has been replicated, but again with only two subjects out of 20 showing this "abnormality." It should perhaps be seriously investigated as a possible hysterical type of reaction to this situation (the opposite of an anxiety reaction). Early work by Van der Merwe (1948) suggested that finger blood flow could be used to distinguish anxiety patients from hysterics, and this may be of relevance here.

THEORETICAL MODELS RELATING TO STRESS, ANXIETY, AND MENTAL TASK PERFORMANCE EFFICIENCY

It may be useful to employ a stress model in looking at theoretical problems in the psychophysiological assessment of anxiety. The model to be considered here is the transactional one given by Cox and Mackay (Cox, 1978), shown in Fig. 6. Anxiety state, considered as an anticipatory fear response, has cognitive and emotional aspects. This is a feedforward process. As such, how does it fit into the stress model? There appears to be no clear provision for it. There are cognitive and emotional aspects to consider, which surely affect the cognitive appraisal stage through changes in the perceived capability of coping with the perceived demand.

There is another important and potentially overriding factor affecting anxiety state, namely the perceived importance of the situation to the testee: for example, the degree of ego-threat. Relevance of this to anxiety comes after experiencing (and/or imagining) failure or cognitive or behavioral coping difficulties. This negative feedback (and feedforward) to the perceived capability stage would then increase stress responses as shown in the model.

Most anxiety questionnaires appear to assume that emotional response should be assessed: questions, for the most part, tend to deal with subjective cognitive appraisal of emotional responses and also physiological responses. One is aware of emotional responses, so in Cox and Mackay's model it would be advisable to include a feedback from "emotional response" to the "cognitive appraisal" phase. Perception of physiological responses associated with anxiety (e.g. heart stroke volume) must also feedback to this phase.

Perhaps a useful simplification would be to consider A-TRAIT as "providing" the initial feedforward: a function of "actual capability"; while A-STATE might then relate to the feedback: a function of the "stress response."

As Cox and Mackay's model stands, there is no logical reason why there should be a correlation between the four outputs (emotional, cognitive, behavioral, and physiological) except via the operation of feedback to the cognitive appraisal stage.

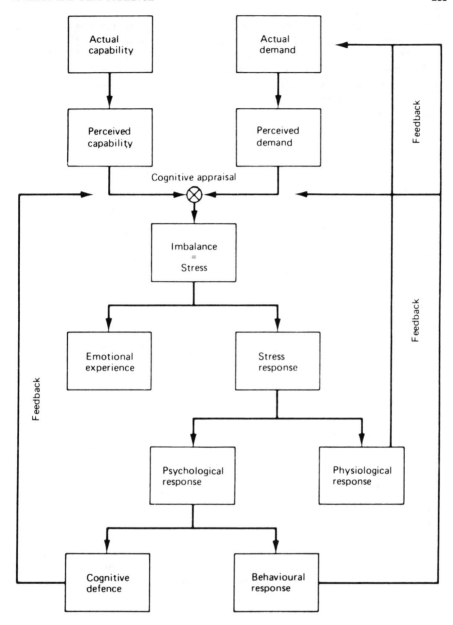

Transactional Model of Stress (Cox and Mackay)

Figure 6 Cox and Mackay's stress model (1978) (reproduced with permission).

Does this explain the correlation between the physiological measure of nonspec SCR rate and the behavioral measure of changes in accuracy of performance on the sentence recognition tasks, described in the previous section? It has been argued earlier that nonspec SCR rate probably indicates some attentional aspect of cognitive functioning. So, in this way, an aspect of actual capability may be monitored psychophysiologically.

A distinction should perhaps be made, in the model, between physiological indices which tap cognitive function and those which do not. The latter could be in the "physiological response" category of the interactional model of stress. Responses in this category would be the more basic ones of the autonomic and endocrine systems. A number of these responses will, of course, affect cognitive functioning. For instance, increased release of adrenaline not only raises heart rate, but it can also promote general arousal of the cerebral cortex, via activation of the brain stem reticular system. In this instance, the physiological response stage should feed back to the actual capability stage, rather than to the demand side of the model.

As already argued, the evidence suggests that nonspec SCR rate relates to cognitive attentional functioning—an indication of interfering internal stimuli which are irrelevant to the task. The effectiveness of these interfering stimuli in disrupting attention will no doubt depend on the intensity of conditioned emotional reactions associated with them and the level of general arousal, both of which should be reflected in A-STATE questionnaire scores. These factors are taken into account in Fig. 7 which attempts to illustrate how mental task performance efficiency may be controlled by interacting psychological and physiological processes.

In carrying out a mental task as in a psychophysiological laboratory, we can consider the external stimulus input under two categories (left-hand side of the model). These are stimuli relevant to the task such as words and sentence structure, and stimuli which are irrelevant to the task, such as the experimenter's manner, the appearance of the laboratory, the feel of the earphones, and the like. There are probably many more "task irrelevant" stimuli than there are "task relevant" ones. This sensory input (1 on Fig.7) must feed into a "selective attention process." The initial outcomes of this process (2) would be conditioned and unconditioned reactions. Skeletal muscle responses leading back to the sensory input (3A) may provide stimuli which are irrelevant to the task, such as due to tensing of the neck muscles, and also stimuli which are relevant, for instance due to placing the fingers over a keyboard. Sensory input from muscle tensing can also lead to an increase in general CNS arousal (3A) both directly from input to the reticular system of the brain stem ("General CNS Arousal Mechanism"), and perhaps indirectly via sympathetic adrenal reactions conditioned to the specific muscle tension stimuli (3A). Direct autonomic reactions to the attended sensory input (2) might include an increase in adrenaline output which again would feed to the arousal system of the brain stem (3B). Stimuli from skeletal muscle responses (e.g. muscle tension) and autonomic responses (e.g. pounding heart, sweaty palms) would add to the bank of internal stimuli which are irrelevant to the task (inputs 3A and 3B). Initial nonspecific arousal (input 4) would affect memory banks of both task-relevant and task-irrelevant internal stimuli. Task-irrelevant internal stimuli associated with the inputs from autonomic/emotional reactions, would feed into the selective attention process (5). It may now be suggested that the initial anxiety state reaction is due to the functioning of this procrress, involving

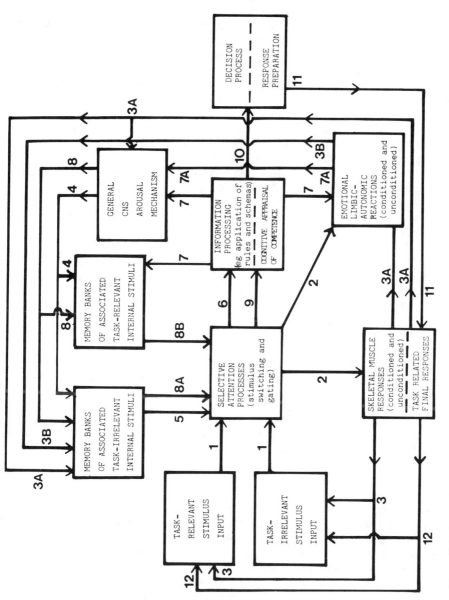

Figure 7 An interactive model of some of the main factors affecting efficiency of cognitive functioning and mental task performance.

the effect of skeletal muscle responses and autonomic reactions, CNS arousal, and ultimately selective attention to internally generated task-irrelevant stimuli. This may be termed *imagination* and constitutes a feedforward aspect in the stress model.

So much then for the first stage. The selected task-relevant and task-irrelevant stimuli are next fed into an "information processing" stage (6). It is here that "cognitive appraisal of competence" ("stress" in Cox and Mackay's model) occurs. If the perceived demands are high, relative to perceived capability, then output (7) activates emotional reactions associated with limbic/autonomic functioning (e.g. fear of failure). Again this feeds into the general CNS arousal mechanism (7A). The emotional and autonomic reactions again feed into the task-irrelevant stimuli (8) increasing further the pressure on the selective attention process (8A).

The efficient processing of "task-relevant external stimuli" involves signals passing through the "selective attention process," which then lead via (6) and (7) to the activation of "memory banks of task-relevant internal stimuli." These relevant signals are then fed again into the "selective attention process" via (8B): an information processing loop is thus formed.

To avoid complicating the figure excessively, the all-important factor of motivation has been omitted. Clearly the initial stages of information processing concerning the nature of the task would have an output to activate a "task-relevant conditioned drive state" (such as need for achievement, need for approval). This task-relevant drive would then have a general activating effect on the CNS arousal mechanism, and also influence direction of "information processing" and the later "decision process." Antagonistic to this, task-irrelevant drive states (perhaps activated by a negative cognitive appraisal of competence at the information processing stage) would have negative effects on the efficiency of information processing and response preparation stages. The final output from the information processing stage (10) would feed into the final decision process and response preparation (e.g. selection of the appropriate button to press). The output (11) would then activate the appropriate skeletal muscle responses related to the task, and this output (12) would then effect changes in the stimulus input (e.g. feedback or delivery of the next task).

In the context of the interactive model I have presented here, nonspec SCR rate would reflect the rate of switching in the selective attention process which, given a relatively invariant external task and a limited number of relevant internal stimuli (8B) would be largely dependent on the extent to which the more extensive task-irrelevant internal stimuli (5) (8A) impinge on the selective attention process. Physiologically, there would be individual differences in the efficiency of gating-out irrelevant stimuli, but this would depend also on the intensity of emotional input (3B) (8), that is, A-STATE. In completing the A-STATE Inventory, the selective attention process is actually directed to what would normally be the task-irrelevant internal stimuli (which include emotional, autonomic, and skeletal muscle responses generated by the total test situation).

Assuming no inhibitory motivational effects on information processes and decision-making (defensiveness), there should be a high correlation between nonspec SCR rate and A-STATE score. As reported earlier, this correlation is in fact high under conditions of non-ego-threat. With advancing research in recording of slow electrocortical changes it may prove possible to objectively assess various aspects of selective attention, information processing, decision-making, and response preparation, while general CNS arousal can be monitored by EEG. There is a wide range of direct autonomic responses which can be used to monitor the intensity of emotional/ arousal reactions, such as changes in salivary response, pupil diameter, blood pressure, vasoconstriction; also indirect measures should be included such as estimates of adrenaline and noradrenaline output from the excretion in urine. The response preparation phase may be reflected in increase of EMG, and this index may be useful as a way of quantifying drive state or effort (Eason & White, 1961).

Although the model cannot claim to be unique or all inclusive, it does perhaps give a framework within which to consider the concept of anxiety state. It may also help in conceptualizing the factors affecting the efficiency of performance on mental tasks, and provide a system for analyzing the interaction of psychophysiological variables which are relevant in the study of the relationship between anxiety and the performance of mental tasks.

PROBLEMS IN EXPERIMENTING ON ANXIETY STATE AND MENTAL TASK PERFORMANCE, WITH SPECULATION ON FUTURE STUDIES

There are a large number of individual factors which can make nonsense of research on the relationship between anxiety and test performance efficiency, if they are not taken into account.

A major factor is degree of motivation. This is not only affected by the social norms and prior conditioning in relation to the particular task, but also to the type of interaction between the experimenter and the subject and the way the subjects are selected, that is, whether it is obligatory or voluntary to take part in the study. Furthermore, whether the experimenter is the same sex as the subject or perceived as attractive or not, can also affect motivation and effort. As discussed earlier, it may be possible to monitor effort, or at least changes in effort, by using integrated EMG.

Clearly, the extent of knowledge and prior practice on similar tasks must be taken into account as much as ability and specific strategies used for tackling tasks. To overcome the problems of prior knowledge and ability, it may be necessary to reject some subjects and to pilot and train those selected. Then for the test proper, the level of task difficulty may be adjusted to suit the individual (e.g. speed of test item presentation). This sort of manipulation could be particularly important where the effect on performance efficiency of various stressors, and drugs, is being tested.

It is impossible to measure objectively how a testee assesses his coping ability in the face of a particular demand. This assessment of "confidence" (perceived demand minus perceived capability) may, however, be scored crudely with rating scales completed by the subject himself.

It cannot be assumed that a high A-STATE at the beginning of a test relates to A-STATE score in the middle or at the end of a test session. Subjects may differ in their rate of habituation to anxiety provoking task-irrelevant stimuli. Furthermore, anxiety during a test may drop fairly rapidly with rise of confidence if the subject changes to a more effective strategy of test performance. Alternatively, the development of fatigue may have a negative feedback effect on confidence. Individuals will of course differ in their rates of practice and fatigue effects. According to Eysenck (1957) extroverts would develop fatigue (reactive inhibition) most rapidly, but these types would have no predisposition to anxiety.

Tiredness, and the intake of drugs, such as nicotine, alcohol, and caffeine as well as common medications may affect cortical arousal and the development of fatigue.

A final important factor affecting the replicability of experiments is the perception of anxiety-provoking stimuli in the test situation. These include the appearance of the lab (does the subject see the control room bristling with electronic equipment?), the approach of the experimenter (is he authoritarian?) and the age, sex, and appearance of the experimenter (does he or she wear a white coat?). In experiments in which an attempt is made to manipulate ego-threat by giving particular information about the significance of test results vis-à-vis the subjects themselves, all the above-mentioned factors must be controlled and specified.

In order to overcome many of these difficulties, it may be preferable to use within-subject designs. We are currently doing this in our laboratory in a number of studies: (1) examining the effects of caffeine on A-STATE and mental task performance efficiency; (2) assessing the effects of beta blockers, and (3) analyzing the relationships between perceived coping ability, effort, and anxiety state. Our research is continuing with nonspec SCR rate as a cognitive index of anxiety. In our studies, we are also looking at the relationship between anxiety change and performance change in an attempt to validate further the usefulness of nonspecific electrodermal response rate as a measure of irrelevant cognitive activity, relating to anxiety, in the selective attention process. An attempt is being made to monitor "effort" using change in integrated EMG. We are also making further evaluations of how the direction of change in finger blood volume pulse (when put "on test") relates to task performance efficiency. What is lacking is a direct measure of CNS arousal and a wide range of autonomic arousal indices. Clearly, in this type of research one ideally needs to monitor a wide range of psychophysiological variables as proposed in relation to the interactional model (Fig. 7).

On the basis of the model, a number of hypotheses can be made and tested, making assumptions about the psychological significance of the psychophysiological indices employed.

REFERENCES

Baddeley, A. D.(1978). A three minute reasoning test based on grammatical transformation. *Psychonomic Science, 10,* 341–342.

Bond, A. J., James, D. C. & Lader, M. H. (1974). Physiological and psychological measures in anxious patients. *Psychological Medicine, 4,* 364–373.

Burke, M., Hinton, J. W. & O'Neill, M. (1978, December). The relationships of some electrodermal indices to extraversion and psychopathic behavior. Paper presented at The Psychophysiology Society Sixth Annual Scientific Meeting, Institute of Psychiatry, London.

Coles, M. G. H., Gale, A. & Kline, P. (1971). Personality and habituation of the orienting reaction: tonic and response measures of electrodermal activity. *Psychophysiology, 8,* 54–63.

Cox, T. (1978). *Stress.* London: Macmillan.

Eason, R. G. & White, C. T. (1961). Muscular tension, effort and tracking difficulty: Studies of parameters which affect tension level and performance efficiency. *Perceptual and Motor Skills, 12,* 331–372.

Eysenck, H. J. (1957). *The Dynamics of Anxiety and Hysteria.* London: Routledge & Kegan Paul.

Gray, J. A. (1971). *The Psychology of Fear and Stress.* London: Weidenfeld & Nicholson.

Hinton, J. W., O'Neill, M., Dishman, J. & Webster, S. (1979). Electrodermal indices of public offending and recidivism. *Biological Psychology, 9,* 151–154.

Hinton, J. W., O'Neill, M., Hamiltion, S. & Burke, M. (1980). Psychophysiological differentiation between psychopathic and schizophrenic abnormal offenders. *British Journal of Social & Clinical Psychology, 19,* 257–269.

Hinton, J. W. (1982, September). The relationship between stress, anxiety and sentence comprehension at differing syntax complexities. *4th international symposium on industrial and organisational psychology.* In Symposium conducted at Dresden University.

Hinton, J. W. (1983, December). *Relationships between psychophysiological indices of anxiety state and changes in efficiency of performance with increasing difficulty of mental tasks.* Paper presented at *The psychophysiological society eleventh annual scientific meeting,* Charing Cross and Westminster Medical Schools, London.

Kilpatrick, D. G. (1972), Differential responsiveness of two electrodermal indices to psychological stress and performance of a complex cognitive task. *Psychophysiology, 9,* 218–226.

Lader, M. (1965). The effects of cyclobarbitone on spontaneous autonomic activity. *Journal of Psychosomatic Research, 9,* 201–207.

Lader, M. (1975). *The psychophysiology of mental illness.* London: Routledge & Kegan Paul.

Martin, I. & Rust, J. (1976).Habituation and the structure of the electrodermal system. *Psychophysiology, 13,* 554–562.

McAdoo, W. G. (1969). *The effects of success and failure feedback on A-STATE for subjects who differ in A-TRAIT.* Unpublished Doctoral Dissertation, Florida State University.

O'Neill, H. F., Spielberger, C. D. & Hansen, D. N. (1969). The effects of state-anxiety and task difficulty on computer-assisted learning. *Journal of Educational Psychology, 60,* 343–350.

Sartory, G. & Lader, M. (1981). Psychophysiology and drugs in anxiety and phobias. In M. J. Christie & P. G. Mellett (Eds.), *Foundations of psychosomatics.* Chichester: Wiley.

Schalling, D. (1978). Psychopath-related personality variables and the psychophysiology of socialization. In R. D. Hare & D. Schalling (Eds.), *Psychopathic behavior: Approaches to research,* Chichester: Wiley.

Walrath, L. C. & Stern, J. A. (1980). General considerations. In H. M. Van Praag (Ed.), *Handbook of biological psychiatry. Pt. 2: Brain mechanisms and abnormal behavior: Psychophysiology.* New York: Marcel Dekker.

Van der Merwe, A. B. (1948). The diagnostic value of peripheral vasomotor reactions in psychoneuroses. *Psychosomatic Medicine, 10,* 347–354.

Venables, P. H. (1967). Partial failure of cortical-subcortical integration as a factor underlying schizophrenic behavior. In J. Romano (Ed.), *The origins of schizophrenia.* Amsterdam: Excerpta Media.

15

Heart-Rate Changes in Sensory Overload (Optokinetic Stimulation) as a Function of Sensation-Seeking Types

Zsuzsanna Kulcsár
Eötvös Loránd University

László Kutor
Kandó Kálmán College of Electrical Engineering

György Bagdy
National Institute for Nervous & Mental Diseases

János Geier
Eötvös Loránd University

INTRODUCTION

This chapter examines cardiovascular reactions as a function of sensation-seeking as a personality trait. More specifically, heart-rate changes in stressful situations involving sensory overload are investigated as a function of two major components of sensation seeking: Thrill and Adventure Seeking (TAS) and Disinhibition (Dis). A critical assumption that has guided our research is that sensory integrative capacity, or capacity for sensory intake, is one of the major determinants of sensation seeking. If sensory intake capacity is dependent on cardiovascular regulation, then the investigation of cardiovascular reactions as a function of the sensation-seeking trait seems to be justified.

Prior to presenting our research findings, the literature on the relevance of cardiovascular psychophysiology for sensation-seeking research will be reviewed. Several hypotheses concerning the characteristic cardiovascular reactions of thrill and adventure seekers and disinhibitors will then be proposed.

Heart Rate and Stimulus Control

Since the early observations of Lacey and his co-workers (Lacey, Kagan, Lacey, & Moss, 1963), substantial evidence has accumulated that demonstrates a close connection between cardiovascular reactions and two diverse attitudes towards stimulation: intake and rejection. It is now well known that stimulus intake is associated with lower heart rate (HR) and the diastolic phase of the cardiac cycle, whereas stimulus rejection is associated with higher HR and the systolic phase (Lacey & Lacey, 1977, 1978; Walker & Sandman, 1982). These phenomena have been observed in the preparatory intervals of reaction time tasks, in classical conditioning paradigms (Obrist, 1981), in evoked potential studies (Sandman, Walker & Berka, 1982; Walker & Sandman, 1982), and on mental tasks of the type that Pribram and McGuinnes (1975) have called "categorization" or "reasoning" (Lacey et al., 1963; Lacey, 1967). There are currently two somewhat contradictory interpretations of these data: Lacey's baroreceptor control hypothesis and Obrist's cardiac-somatic coupling hypothesis.

According to Lacey, heart-rate acceleration and deceleration are controlled by central baroreceptor mechanisms, more precisely, by the function of the nucleus tractus solitarii (NTS) in the brainstem. If stimulated, this autonomic control device not only exerts negative feedback control over cardiovascular functions, but also has a simultaneous inhibitory effect on cortical arousal (Hugelin & Bonvallet, 1957). Consequently, Lacey suggests that the stimulus intake attitude is associated with a lack of baroreceptor stimulation, and low heart rate and blood pressure. This explanation, which assigns an instrumental role to cardiovascular events, has been strongly criticized (Hahn, 1973).

Evidence in favor of Lacey's view has been reported in several studies. For example, the cardiac cycle P-wave, whose effect on the baroreceptors is similar to that of low HR (i.e., NTS is deprived of stimulation), is associated with better perceptual acuity than the R-T interval (Sandman et al., 1982). Curiously, Sandman, Walker, and Berka (1982) observed a "virtual absence of evoked potential during systole . . . in a patient suffering essential hypertension" (p. 213). Thus, baroreceptor mechanisms may play a decisive role in stimulus control, and can therefore be considered as part of a more extensive input control or sensory integrative mechanism.

Additional examples of this peculiar role of the baroreceptor system have been noted. In psychosomatic research, essential hypertension has been linked traditionally with "excessive sensitivity" to environmental stimulation and, as a consequence of this sensitivity, to behavioral introversion and stimulation avoidance (see Julius, 1981). Dworkin, Filewich, Miller, Craigmyle, and Pickering (1979) propose that hypertension may result from the instrumental role of baroreceptor stimulation in reducing reactivity to noxious stimulation. On the other hand, Reis (1981) attributes stimulus avoidance in hypertension to a deficient function of the baroreceptor center. He suggests that "impaired NTS function results in an amplification of the action of the environment and emotions on blood pressure" (Reis, 1981, p. 253), thus contributing to stimulus avoiding behavior. These seemingly contradictory viewpoints may actually characterize two different forms of essential hypertension, one with high and one with low NTS sensitivity. If the malfunction of the baroreceptor center, whether increased or deficient, interferes with normal control of environmental stimulation, this would have extremely important implications for theory and research on sensation-seeking behavior.

An alternative explanation of the HR correlates on certain kinds of tasks was offered by Obrist (1918) and his co-workers. Obrist's "cardiac-somatic hypothesis" states: "When heart rate is primarily under vagal control (whether through increases or decreases in vagal restraint) heart rate changes parallel somatomotor activity. The intergration of cardiac and somatomotor events originates within the central nervous system . . . any event that initiates an alteration in somatomotor activity perforce initiates an alteration in vagal tone" (1981, p. 73). Based on a wealth of experimental data, this explanation connects HR deceleration with immobility, and thus avoids the potential trap of assigning a causal role to HR in explaining psychological phenomena such as intake attitude. However, this explanation fails to clarify the source of the vagal control of HR. Since Obrist's explanation cannot account for HR deceleration with improved perceptual functions, it must consider the cardiovascular effects on perception as by-products. On the basis of the considerations mentioned above, Obrist's explanation of the HR correlates found in sensory overload situations does not seem to be supported.

Neurotransmitter and Hypothalamic Control of the Baroreceptor Center

Even if we suppose (as we do) that central baroreceptor mechanisms are directly involved in input control of perceptual processes, it would be premature to suggest that improved perceptual functions are invariably associated with HR deceleration. Several additional brain mechanisms are involved in the control of cardiovascular activity besides those dealt with by Lacey and Obrist. Two of them are pertinent to this discussion.

First, as Svensson and Thorèn (1979) have shown, the locus coeruleus (LC) exerts an inhibitory effect on the NTS. Since the LC is one of the main noradrenergic centers of the brain, neurotransmitter control of baroreceptor functions seems likely. The LC might modify, for example, the setpoint, or more precisely, the range within which heart rate and blood pressure vary. It is also important to recognize that the pressosensitive receptors of the carotid sinus are themselves under neurotransmitter control, as Lacey has noted: "Acetylcholine applied directly to the wall of the carotid sinus produces enlargement of the sinus (increased strain); norepinephrine produces a smaller carotid sinus, which stretches less during the systole of the cardiac cycle. . . . The effect of these changes is either to augment or diminish the effectiveness of incoming pressure waves as stimuli to the baroreceptors" (Lacey, 1967, p. 29). Thus, even peripheral neurotransmitter effects may modify central baroreceptor functions and HR variability.

A second brain structure involved in cardiovascular control is the hypothalamus. Hypothalamic modulation of baroreceptor activity has been found by Adair and Manning (1975), who called attention to the effect of motivational phenomena on HR. It has been shown that hypothalamic self-stimulation is accompanied by an acceleration in HR and an increase in blood pressure, and that these changes are largely indepdendent of somatomotor activity. This was verified by Angyán who found that HR and blood pressure values "return to near control levels during extinction, when the cat presses the lever without receiving electrical stimulation" (Angyán, 1978, p. 224). Since there is reason to suppose that cardiovascular changes are related to the reward value of self-stimulation (Angyán, 1978), the neurophysiological effects on HR of incentive and reward can be localized in hypothalamic self-stimulation sites. Fowles and his colleagues found a consistent cardiac acceleratory effect for incentives, even monetary rewards (Fowles, 1982; Fowles, Fisher & Tranel, 1982; Tranel, Fisher & Fowles, 1982). However, Fowles, Fisher, and Tranel (1982) fail to comment on the apparent contradiction of their results with Lacey's finding that stimulus intake, as opposed to "sensory dislike" (Lacey, 1967, p. 34), was accompanied by HR deceleration.

There is some evidence in the neurophysiological literature on self-stimulation that may help to resolve this contradiction. Malmo (1961) found that "stimulation of the lateral septal area produced slowing of heart rate" (cited by Angyán, 1978, p. 223), which suggests that this area, together with central baroreceptor effects, may be involved in the HR deceleration associated with rewarding stimulation. In contrast, the hypothalamus causes an opposite HR reaction if incentives are present, the latter being more "motivational."

Fowles (1982, pp. 120-122) is certainly correct when he states that HR responses should be investigated as a function of reward-seeking behavior. Such behaviors appear to be one of the characteristics of sensation seekers, at least those who are high in disinhibition (Zuckerman, 1979), which suggests that research investigating cardiovascular psychophysiology may contribute to understanding the biological bases of disinhibition as a trait. We share this opinion, and have endeavored to take it a bit further. Besides the self-stimulation sites of the hypothalamus, there is evidence that baroreflexes may be reset by the hypothalamic defense area, and that the NTS is inhibited during defense reactions (see Pickering & Sleight, 1977).

Research Relating Cardiovascular Psychophysiology to Sensation Seeking

The concepts of stimulus intake and rejection bear considerable resemblance to the extremes of a sensation-seeking dimension. It has been observed that stimulus rejection or avoidance arises from any dysfunction of the central baroreceptor mechanism. Therefore, optimal NTS sensitivity appears to be a prerequisite for sensation-seeking behavior. In addressing the question of a causal connection between sensory integration and cardiovascular control, it is important to keep in mind that intergration always involves postural and vestibular mechanisms, at least in real life situations where one's sensation seeking capacity is exercised (Miura, & Reis, 1969). Doba and Reis (1974) have reported that the orthostatic reflex, and most probably all the cardiovascular reactions elicited by movement and changes in posture, are regulated by a common, vistubulo-cerebellar and baroreceptor mechanism.

Sensory integrative capacity is usually thought to be related to the thrill- and adventure-seeking aspect of sensation seeking. Indeed, it is impossible to imagine thrill and adventure seeking without sensory integration, that is, a high degree of postural, vertibular and cardiovascular control. In the case of disinhibition, the other main factor of sensation seeking, quite different questions arise. Nevertheless, cardiovascular psychophysiology also seems important for this factor as well, given the cardiovascular reactions associated with reward and incentive motivation.

To the best of our knowledge, HR has not been previously investigated in research on stimulus intake and rejection as a function of sensation-seeking behavior. However, HR measures of high and low sensation seekers have been obtained in the context of orienting versus defensive reactions. Feij, Orlebeke, Gazendam and van Zuilen (in press; cited by Zuckerman, Buchsbaum & Murphy, 1980, and Ridgeway & Hare, 1981), who used auditory stimulation at a level of stimulus intensity "at which OR's shift to DR's in some subjects," found that "high disinhibitors reacted with heart rate deceleration (OR) . . . whereas low disinhibitors reacted with heart rate acceleration (DR). There was no difference between these groups on prestimulus heart rate level" (Zuckerman et al., 1980, p. 195).

Ridgeway and Hare (1981) compared HR reactions to auditory stimulation in high and low sensation seekers (SS) and in subjects with high or low score on the Disinhibition (Dis) scale. For both low SS and low Dis subjects, they found in the first trial, "a brief period of acceleration during the first 4 sec after tone onset" (p. 616). In contrast, high SS and high Dis SS showed deceleration. Moreover, the prestimulus HR in the low SS group was significantly higher than in the high SS group. The short latency acceleration was interpreted as reflecting a startle response. No explanation of the increased tonic HR of the low SS groups was offered, but Ridgeway and Hare noted that Cox (1977) found no difference in tonic HR of high and low SS groups.

On the basis of the finding of the studies reviewed above, disinhibition appears to be a consistent factor in heart rate experiments. The "intake" attitude, or "cardiac somatic coupling" in Obrist's terms, seems to be more easily elicited in high disinhibitors, suggesting that the heart is primarily under vagal control in this group. The contradictory results in the tonic HR data might be explained if it is assumed that low SSs, as compared to high SSs, experienced both increased and decreased HR. In the case of heightened blood pressure, as seen earlier, a dysfunction of the central baroreceptor mechanism may occur together with associated stimulus avoidance, that is, low sensation-seeking. On the other hand, "passive coping" may be the dominant behavioral strategy in the case of low HR (Obrist, 1981). "Passive coping" is characterized by dominant vagal influences on the heart and a general attitude of "giving up" or "helplessness," which is manifested at the behavioral level in low sensation-seeking. Accordingly, the existence of different forms of sensation-seeking would explain the wide range of HR events for the low SSs and the complicated correlations between cardiovascular events and the sensation-seeking trait.

The cardiovascular regulation of disinhibitors is thought to be quite different from that of thrill and adventure seekers. In high disinhibitors, a general tendency for increased HR might be expected on the basis of a reward-seeking attitude, without, however, an increase in the level of circulating catecholamines. Circulating catecholamine levels are connected to tyrosine-catecholamine reactions of the sympathetic nerves in stressful situations (Elödi, 1981). If there is no excess in peripheral (circulating) catecholamines, vagus control of the cardiovascular system can be maintained together with the phasic deceleratory capacity manifested in new stimulus situations. This set of conditions could explain the superior deceleratory reactions of high disinhibitors reported in two studies.

A different pattern of cardiovascular reactivity has been predicted for high thrill and adventure seekers with low disinhibition scores, namely, superior cardiovascular regulation even under strain. On the basis of the theoretical considerations and empirical findings reviewed above, sensory overload was assumed to exert a considerable strain on the cardiovascular system. The following study was designed to address this issue within the context of an experimental program in which optokinetic stimulation was administered and optokinetic nystagmus was recorded, along with heart rate. HR data and interbeat interval, compared to a resting baseline, will be reported in this paper. The aim of the experiment was to describe HR changes that accompany optokinetic stimulation, and to test the hypotheses discussed above.

Vagal influences on tonic heart rate can be tracked by specification of respiratory sinus arrhythmia (RSA) (Chess, Tam, & Calaresu, 1975; Katona & Jih, 1975; Porges, 1976; Porges, McCabe, & Yongue, 1982). According to Katona and Jih (1975), "the degree of respiratory sinus arrhythmia may be used as a noninvasive indicator of the degree of parasympathetic cardiac control" (p. 801). Citing a number of relevant studies, Porges, McCabe, and Yongue (1982) concluded that "the amplitude of RSA is related to background vagal tone, and RSA can be virtually eliminated by atropine administration or vagotomy" (p. 234). Because the degree of vagal control of the heart is a crucial issue in cardiac psychophysiology, specification of the RSA seemed to be imperative.

METHOD

Subjects

A total of 33 paid volunteers participated in the experiment. These included 21 male students between the ages of 21 and 29 from a technical college, and 12 parachutists (9 males, 3 females) between 17 and 25 years of age, with the exception of one male, who was 36. All of the students had participated in a previous experiment (Kulcsár, Kutor, & Arató, 1984) and were selected on the basis of Sensation Seeking Scale scores collected earlier. The student group included 9 high TAS/low Dis (HTLD), 8 high TAS/high Dis (HTHD), and 4 low TAS/low Dis (LTLD) subjects (Ss).

All but one of the parachutists had high scores on the TAS subscale of the SSS Form V. Five parachutists (3 males, 2 females) obtained low Dis scores, and seven (6 males, 1 female) had high Dis scores. Thus the parachutist group consisted of 7 HTHD, 4 HTLD and 1 LTLD subjects. The HTLD and LTLD parachutists were grouped with the corresponding student groups. Because of their peculiar HR measures, a separate group was formed from the HTHD parachutists (HTHD-P).

Procedure

Two versions of the experiment were conducted, one with and one without pre- and postexperimental biochemical tests. Nearly half of the subjects (8 HTLD, 6 HTHD students) took part in the first version of the experiment, in which platelet MAO (from platelet rich plasma; PRP), serum DBH, plasma cortisol and nor-adrenalin (NA) were determined from blood samples taken at the beginning and at the end of the experiment.

The experiment itself consisted of three phases. In the first phase, the subjects lay on a tilting table that produced vestibular stimulation. HR and EEG were recorded simultaneously on an 8 channel EEG and magnetic tape for off-line computer analysis. This part of the experiment lasted for about 20 minutes with a 5 minute rest at the beginning. Baseline heart rate (BLHR) data were collected dur-ing this period. In the second phase, optokinetic nystagmus (OKN) was elicited by a full cylinder with vertical stripes rotated at a 60°/s speed (for the details see Kulcsar et al., 1984). OKN was recorded by the EEG with a "stare" instruction (Honrubia, Downey, Mitchell, & Ward, 1968), but these measures will not be discussed. To record EKG, electrodes were placed above the sternum and below the shoulder of each subject.

During the third phase, a coriolis test was conducted: Subjects were rotated in a chair with headtilts for a maximum of 2 minutes, or until signs of motion sickness were observed. The purpose of this procedure was to increase vestibular stimula-tion before the second blood test.

Analysis

A computer program determined the intervals between two consecutive R waves, with 100-microseconds precision in an off-line analysis of the original records. Statistical analyses were carried out on the data for HR and interbeat interval (IBIs). First, mean HRs in beats/minutes (b/m) were calculated for each subject, at five-second intervals for the entire experimental (OKN) period. The 20 to 40 means that were obtained in this manner were plotted as histograms, with HRs in b/m against interval numbers (using BMDP 6D computer program), and polynomial regressions (0–5 degree) were determined (BMDP 5R).

Next, two sets of 100 IBI data, one from the middle of a 5-minute resting baseline and the other from the first IBIs of the experimental (OKN) period were used for computing the basis statistics (means and SDs), and for a fast Fourier transformation (FFT) which was carried out by an EMG 666 programmable calcu-lator. These analyses were based on only 30 Ss because the starting point of the OKN period for three subjects could not be identified from the printouts due to technical difficulties. In the FFT, both power and amplitude spectra were obtained for the first 40 components of the spectrum. Spectral power density functions were plotted in order to make the main spectral components more salient. However, further statistical analyses were based on the amplitude measures (Sayers, 1980).*

The 0.125-0.42 Hz frequency region associated with respiratory activity (Porges et al., 1982, p. 243) was determined as follows: individual frequency measures were transformed into Hz, taking into account duration measures for the whole period (100 beats). For example, in the case of a 900 ms mean IBI, in which the whole period duration was 90 s, the critical region was between the 11th and the 33th frequencies in the Fourier spectrum. The Respiratory Sinus Arrhythmia (RSA) was then defined as the sum of the amplitudes within the respiratory region, transformed into a percentage of the total amplitude.

RESULTS

Biochemical Measures

Intra-group comparisons of pre- and postexperimental measures (one tailed t-tests) gave two remarkable results: (1) The postexperimental DBH values of the HTLD Ss were significantly higher than the preexperimental measures ($t = 3.65$, $N = 8$, $p < .01$); (2) pre- and postexperimental plasma NA levels also tended to differ in the HTLD group. The preexperimental value was higher, but this difference only approached significance ($t = 2.3$, $N = 8$, $p < .10$).

In the case of the HTHD subjects, DBH and NA levels did not change during the experiment, and neither cortisol (CS) or PRP MAO values differentiated between the two situations in either group. Intergroup comparisons yielded differences in PRP MAO, which tended to be higher in the HTLD as compared to the HTHD group in both the pre- and postexperimental comparisons (2-tailed t-tests; preexperimental comparisons: $t = 2.03$, $df = 12$, $p < .10$; postexperimental comparisons: $t = 2.93$, $p < .02$).

Interbeat Intervals (IBIs) and Heart Rates (HRs)

Three sets of results will be summarized here: (1) means and variances; (2) results of the spectral analysis; and (3) findings of the histogram analysis and polynomial regressions. Means calculated from the 100-item data sets of the OKN and baseline periods changed from BL to OKN as follows. In 21 out of 30 cases, IBIs were lower during OKN as compared to the BL, that is, the majority of subjects evidenced increased heart rates as a consequence of the optokinetic stimulation. Of the 9 subjects who did not show this pattern, it is interesting to note that 7 were parachutists.

The only significant difference between groups in mean IBIs was that the interbeat intervals of the low sensation seekers (LTLD) and, interestingly, those of the

---

*Power spectra, or more expicitly the distribution of total record variance among the available spectral components emphasize the large-amplitude components at the expense of small-amplitude components and may therefore produce an unrealistic picture. So amplitude spectra may be preferred to power spectra in the analyses of interbeat interval records (Sayers, 1980, p. 202).

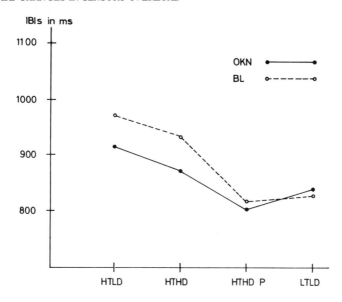

Figure 1 Mean interbeat intervals (IBIs) of extreme scorers on TAS and Dis scales on baseline (BL) and during optokinetic nystagmus (OKN) (HTLD = high TAS, low Dis; HTHD = high TAS, high Dis; P = parachutist, etc.).

HTHD parachutists were lower (i.e., their HR was higher) in the baseline resting situation, as compared to the baseline data of the HTHD and HTLD groups (see Fig. 1).

In the HTHD and HTLD groups, the reaction to the OKN experimental sensory overload situation was a lowering of heart rate variability. The opposite was found for the HTHD parachutists, for whom optokinetic stimulation increased heart rate variance. The subjects in the LTLD group could not be characterized by the variance measure. In the intergroup comparisons, two significant differences were found in the variances: the BL variance of the HTHD parachutist group was lower than the same measure in the HTHD and HTLD groups (see Fig. 2).

Respiratory Sinus Arrhythmia (RSA)

No group differences were found in the RSA measure during BL. Three of the four groups, HTLD, HTHD-P and LTLD, had significantly higher RSA in the baseline as compared to the OKN situation, but this was not found for the HTHD group (see Fig. 3). However, in the OKN condition, the respiratory region of the IBI spectra proved to be significantly higher for the HTHD group as compared to the HTLD group. Although the RSA of the HTHD group was also higher than the same measure for the HTHD-P and LTLD groups (see Fig. 3), the differences for these comparisons were not statistically significant (2-tailed t-tests, $p < .10$).

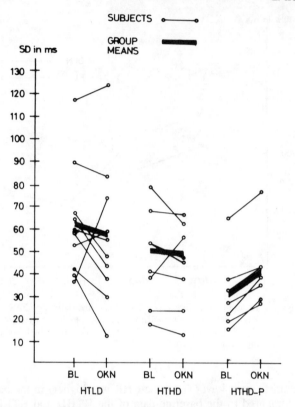

Figure 2 Standard deviations of interbeat intervals (IBIs) by
subjects and groups (extreme scorers on TAS and
Dis scales) in baseline (BL) and during optokinetic
nystagmus (OKN).

Heart-Rate Trends During Optokinetic Stimulation

Visual analysis of the HR time series data during optokinetic stimulation revealed that discrete HR periods or stages as defined by HR ranges, could be
identified in 25 of the 33 cases. Two types of discrete HR stages were found. In
the first type, no overlap between the consecutive stages was present. The "range-
change" in the second type was quite striking, but there appeared to be considerable overlap in the two consecutive ranges. Since the period lengths were identified
by visual observation, this raises methodological questions. Unfortunately, no adequate statistical method was available to discriminate between these time series.

The distinctive character of the stages was supported by *t*-tests, with the groups
characterized as follows: the HTLD subjects' dominant reaction was a type 1
phase-series. Their records consisted of alternating stages of low and high HRs,
with no overlap between them. Moreover, the series always started with a low
stage. Type 2 stages were found in the other groups with considerable overlap
between successive stages. As shown in Table 1, this lack of periodicity was found
for nearly half of the HTHD subjects.

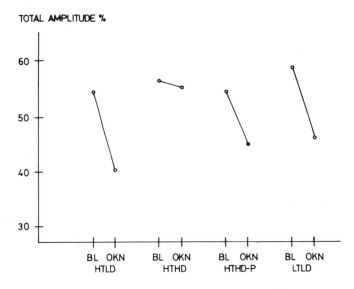

Figure 3 Average total spectral density of the 0.125-0.42 frequency region (resipatory sinus arrhythmia) by groups and situations as a percentage of total spectral amplitudes.

The findings from the 0-5 degree polynomial regressions indicated a general positive linear regression trend. HR tended to increase over time, except for the HTHD subjects, whose HR did not change systematically during the experiment. The results of the statistical analyses are detailed below:

1. Goodness of fit tests yielded nonsignificant Fs for the zero degree polynomials in 5 of the 8 analyses of HTHD data. Mean F values were lowest in this group, as compared to the other groups, for the zero degree polynomial. All but two of these Fs were significant for the HTHD group, and all but one for the HTHD- and LTLD groups.
2. The first degree polynomial was significant for 20 of the 33 subjects; these t-values were positive in 18 out of the 20 cases and were highest for the LTLD

Table 1 Distribution of four different kinds of HR changes

		Periods		No periods
		Type 2 with overlap		
Groups	Type 1 without overlap	Increasing	Decreasing	
HTLD	9	—	—	4
HTHD	1	2	2	3
HTHD-P	1	4	2	—
LTLD	2	2	—	1

group. For the HTHD group, the *t*-values were negative for 5 of the 8 subjects, but only one of these *t*s was significant. The higher degree polynomials did not yield consistent results for any of the experimental groups.

DISCUSSION

In the present study, optokinetic stimulation affected heart rate in the following way: In the majority of subjects, HR increased above BL during stimulation, while HR variability decreased. However, the means and variances for the parachutists differed on these measures from those of the HTLD and HTHD groups, primarily at baseline, rather than during the experimental phase. The spectral analysis revealed that the RSA tended to decrease during optokinetic stimulation, except for the HTHD group, for whom RSA increased.

The most prominent feature in the HR data plotted over time was that discrete periods of HR values, with some overlap in the ranges, were distinguishable over two consecutive periods for most groups. However, periods *without* overlap were characteristic of the HTLD subjects, and the HTHD group was distinguished by the absence of discrete periods in about half of the cases. The sample as a whole showed a tendency for heart rate to increase during optokinetic stimulation, with the exception of the HTHD group for whom the typical reaction was "no reaction," that is, zero degree regression being the best fit.

The biochemical findings indicated that the experimental procedure affected the HTLD group but had little effect on HTHD group. The heightened DBH values of the HTLD subjects at the end of the experiment were interpreted as evidence of a considerable stress reaction. Although the lower NA levels of these subjects appeared to contradict the DBH findings, this contradiction can be explained when the much shorter half-life of blood NA, as compared to serum DBH, is taken into consideration (Rush & Geffen, 1972). We may speculate that, in the case of the HTLD subjects, an initial stress reaction was followed by fast recovery, or perhaps even a rebound in parasympathetic or cholinergic functions. The rapid succession of heightened and lowered activation might manifest itself in the alternating stages of higher and lower HR of the HTLD, which were found in the histograms. A highly reactive nervous system may be characteristic of this group.

Neary and Zuckerman (1976) found high reactivity in high TAS subjects, as manifested in the electrodermal orienting reflex. The high TAS subjects, as compared to other groups, responded with a more intense EDR to the first presentation of the stimuli. However, no difference in habituation rates were found. Thrill and adventure seekers, or "vestibular sensation seekers" as we prefer to call them (Kulcsár, 1983; Kulcsár et al., 1984), seem to need variable environmental stimulation to make their regulatory mechanisms work effectively. If variable stimulation is presented, a biochemical equilibrium can be achieved.

The data for the high disinhibitor students, as compared to the HTLD groups, presented quite a different picture. No biochemical changes occurred in this group, and no special trends or stages of HR plotted against time could be found, although the HR increased during optokinetic stimulation. On the basis of these findings, it would appear that no stressful overload was experienced by the HTLD group.

What then caused their overall HR acceleration in the experimental situation? As noted earlier, accelerated HR might be expected for reward seekers when the stimulation has a reward character (Fowles, 1982). If so, this type of HR acceleration should have different biochemical concomitants than when HR increases are due to stress.

Optokinetic stimulation may be experienced as rewarding because of its effects on central vertibular mechanisms (Waespe & Henn, 1977), which may be similar to the effects of swinging or other low level vestibular stimulation. The effects of optokinetic stimulation on central vestibular mechanisms show considerable variation, depending on the kind of optokinetic nystagmus elicited (Dichgans & Brandt, 1978). The results of a previous study, demonstrating increased involvement of vestibular functions in HTHD subjects (Kulcsár et al., 1984), makes this interpretation of our data more tenable. The enhanced RSA of the subjects in the HTHD group in the OKN situation also seems consistent with this interpretation. Since RSA is vagally mediated, an increased vagal influence may be assumed for the HTHD subjects during OKN stimulation, which further supports the conclusion that these subjects did not experience a stress reaction. Rather than engaging in either passive or active coping, they seemed to enjoy the situation, which may have affected them like psychedelic drug.[†]

It should be noted that the HTHD parachutists differed considerably from the HTHD students, falling midway between the HTLD and HTHD student groups. Since biochemical measures were not obtained during the experiment, this interpretation is based solely on the HR data. While the increased HR found during baseline in the HTHD-P group seems puzzling, the increased variance in this group's IBIs in the OKN situation, resembled the heightened RSA of the HTHD students in the experimental situation. Since voluntary attention to the environment has been found to be associated with a decrease in HR variability (Porges, 1976), increased variability may reflect a lack of attention to stimuli by some members of the HTHD-P group. In the HTHD group, heightened RSA was interpreted somewhat differently, but the strategy of the HTHD subjects, as discussed above, also precludes voluntary attention replacing it by a vestibular reflex mechanism.

With regard to the HR data of the HTHD-P subjects, their intermediate position between the HTLD and HTHD groups seems to result from the fact that these Ss had periods with considerable overlap, whereas the HTHD Ss had no HR periods, and the HTLD Ss had periods without any overlap. Since HR periods are believed to be connected to resetting the baroreceptor feedback control, this function seems to be most evident in the HTLD group, expressed less often by HTHD-P Ss, and apparently absent in HTHD Ss. The intermediate position of HTHD parachutists may also indicate that HTHD characteristics can be lessened by risk-taking physical activity. For HTHD Ss who are vulnerable to psychiatric problems, extreme forms of physical activity, including vestibular stimulation, might be recommended.

In the introduction to this chapter, it was postulated that low sensation-seeking might be associated with two opposite forms of baroreceptor dysfunctions. LTLD

[†]A more parsimonous interpretation of the HR data of HTHD Ss is that their HR increased in the OKN situation because OKN involves some somatomotor activity. Obrist (1981) points out the possibility that even eye movement may represent somatomotor activity, since his experimental results show that eye movements and HR are in positive correlation.

subjects were thought to be inclined to both "passive coping" (low HR) and "rejection" of the environment (high HR). Although the limited number of subjects in LTLD group does not make it possible to draw firm conclusions, it should be noted that the LTLD group showed the most mixed picture across all of the measures that were analyzed.

CONCLUSIONS

The relevance of cardiovascular psychophysiology for sensation-seeking research was examined in this chapter and the findings of recent studies bearing on this topic were reported. Since both high and low sensitivity of the baroreceptor center appears to be associated with stimulus avoidance, optimal baroreceptor function would seem to be a prerequisite for stimulus-seeking behavior. This appears to especially important for TAS because seeking vestibular stimulation, which is the major characteristic of this dimension, requires a high degree of integrated cardiovascular regulation.

There is a special HR correlate of reward seeking that seems to be associated with the sensation-seeking Disinhibition factor. This involves incentive motivation, presumed to be related to the hypothalamic reward centers. This type of reward seeking induces increased HR without an associated biochemical stress reaction, a physiological pattern that should characterize high Dis individuals. In contrast, passive coping strategies correlate with low HR and stimulus avoidance, while other forms of avoidance (e.g., defense reactions) are characterized by high HR. Therefore, no characteristic cardiovascular reactions can be expected in low sensation seekers.

HR changes in thrill and adventure seekers (HTLD), and in two groups of high TAS/high DIS subjects (students and parachutists), were investigated during optokinetic stimulation, which was preceded and followed by intensive vestibular stimulation. In the HTLD subjects, HR increased, and HR variability and RSA decreased, during the optokinetic stimulation, reflecting voluntary attention and effort. The biochemical changes in this group—an increase in DBH followed by a decrease in NA—was thought to reflect an initial stress reaction followed by a rebound. The alternation of high and low HR stages during the experiment, without any overlap of the ranges, was interpreted as due to multiple sequential resetting of central baroreceptor mechanisms. This process, together with the biochemical data, was interpreted as the manifestation of a highly reactive CNS in HTLD subjects.

The increase in HR found for the HTHD students during the experiment, was accompanied by more, rather than less, RSA; but no biochemical stress reactions and no periodicity of HR were found for this group. The increased vagal tone and absence of stress reactions in the HTHD students lends support to the hypothesis that the HR increase in this group was due to the reward value of the optokinetic stimulation, that is, mild vestibular sensation, which was experienced as rewarding.

In summary, cardiovascular functions, or more precisely, variations in heart rate, appear to distinguish subjects with different scores on Zuckerman's Sensation Seeking Scale, especially, if real-life physical activity is taken into consideration.

We believe that our conception of the contribution of cardiovascular functions to sensory integration is supported by recent research findings.

REFERENCES

Adair, J. R., & Manning, J. W. (1975). Hypothalamic modulation of baroreceptor afferent unit activity. *American Journal of Physiology, 229,* 1357–1363.

Angyán, L. (1978). Cardiovascular effects of septal, thalamic, hypothalamic and midbrain self-stimulation. *Physiology and Behavior, 20,* 217–226.

Chess, G. F., Tam, R. M. K., & Calaresu, R. F. (1975). Influence of cardiac neural inputs on rhythmic variations of heart period in the cat. *American Journal of Physiology, 228,* 775–780.

Cox, D. N. (1977). *Psychophysiological correlates of sensation seeking and socialization during reduced stimulation.* Unpublished doctoral dissertation, University of British Columbia, 1977.

Dichgans, J., & Brandt, W. (1978). Visual-vestibular interaction: Effects on self-motion perception and postural control. In R. Held, H. W. Leibowitz, & H. L. Teuber (Eds.), *Perception* (pp. 755–804). Berlin: Springer.

Doba, N., & Reis, D. J. (1974). Role of the cerebellum and the vestibular apparatus in regulation of orthostatic reflexes in the cat. *Circulation Research, 34,* 9–18.

Dworkin, B. R., Filewich, R. J., Miller, N. E., Craigmyle, N., & Pickering, T. G. (1979). Baroreceptor activity reduces reactivity to noxious stimulation: Implications for hypertension. *Science, 205,* 1299–1301.

Elödi, P. (1981). *Biokèmia.* Budapest: Akademiai Kiadó.

Feij, J. A., Orlebeke, J. F., Gazendam, A., & van Zuilen, R. (1981). Sensation seeking: Measurement and psychophysiological correlates. In J. Strelau, F. Farley, & T. Gale (Eds.), *Biological foundations of personality and behavior.* New York: Hemisphere.

Fowles, D. C. (1982). Heart rate as an index of anxiety: Failure of hypotheses. In J. T. Cacioppo & R. E. Petty (Eds.), *Perspectives in cardiovascular psychophysiology* (pp. 93–126). New York: Guilford Press.

Fowles, D. C., Fisher, A. E., & Tranel, D. T. (1982). The heart beats to reward: The effect of monetary incentive on heart rate. *Psychophysiology, 19,* 506–512.

Hahn, W. W. (1973). Attention and heart rate: A critical appraisal of the hypothesis of Lacey and Lacey. *Psychological Bulletin, 79,* 59–70.

Honrubia, W. L., Downey, D. P., Mitchell, B. A., & Ward, P. H. (1968). Experimental studies on optokinetic nystagmus: II. Normal humans. *Actaoto-laryngologica, 65,* 441–448.

Hugelin, A., & Bonvallet, M. (1957). Tonus cortical et controle de la facilitation mortice d'origine reticulaire. *Journal of Physiology (Paris), 49,* 1171–1200.

Julius, S. (1981). The psychophsiology of borderline hypertension. In H. Weiner, M. A. Hofer, & A. J. Stunkard (Eds.), *Brain, behavior and bodily disease* (pp. 293–303). New York: Raven Press.

Katona, P. G., & Jih, F. (1975). Respiratory sinus arrhythmia: Noninvasive measure of parasympathetic cardiac control. *Journal of Applied Physiology, 39,* 801–805.

Kulcsar, Z. (1983). Sensation seeking: Its biological correlates and its relation to psychiatric vulnerability. *Pszichologia, 3,* 69–85.

Kulcsàr, Z., Kutor, L., & Aratò, M. (1984). Sensation seeking, its biochemical correlates and its relation to vestibulo-ocular functions. In H. Bonarius, G. van Heck, & N. Smid (Eds.), *Personality psychology in Europe* (pp. 327–346). Hess: Swets & Zeitlinger.

Lacey, J. I. (1967). Somatic response patterning and stress: Some revisions of activation theory. In M. H. Appley & R. Trumbull (Eds.), *Psychological stress: Issues and research* (pp.14–37). New York: Appleton-Century-Crofts.

Lacey, J. I., Kagan, J., Lacey, B. C., & Moss, H. A. (1963). The visceral level: Situational determinants and behavioral correlates of autonomic response patterns. In P. H. Knapp (Ed.), *Expression of the emotions in man..* New York: International University Press.

Lacey, B. C., & Lacey, J. I. (1977). Change in the heart period: A function of sensorimotor event timing withing the cardiac cycle. *Physiological Psychology, 5,* 383–393.

Lacey, B. C., & Lacey, J. I. (1978). Two-way communication between the heart and the brain: Significance of time within the cardiac cycle.*American Pyschologist, 33,* 99–113.

Malmo, R. B. (1961). Slowing of heart rate after septal self-stimulation in rats. *Science, 133,* 1128–1130.

Miura, M., & Reis, D. J. (1969). Cerebellum: Pressor response elicited from the fastigial nucleus and its efferent pathway in brainstem. *Brain Research, 13*, 595–599.

Neary, R. S., & Zuckerman, M. (1976). Sensation seeking, trait and state anxiety, and the electrodermal orienting reflexes. *Psychophysiology, 12*, 205–211.

Obrist, P. A. (1981). *Cardiovascular psychophysiology: A perspective.* New York: Plenum Press.

Pickering, T. G. & Sleight, B. (1977). Baroreceptors and hypertension. In W. de Jong, A. P. Provost, & P. Shapiro (Eds.), *Hypertension and brain mechanisms.* Amsterdam: Elsevier.

Porges, S. W. (1976). Peripheral and neurochemical parallels of psychopathology: A psychophysiological model relating autonomic imbalance to hyperactivity, psychopathy and autism. In H. W. Reese (Ed.), *Advances in child development and behavior* (Vol.11, pp. 35–65). New York: Academic Press.

Porges, W. S., McCabe, P. M., & Yongue, B. G. (1982). Respiratory heart rate fluctuations: Psychophysiological implications for pathophysiology and behavior. In J. T. Cacioppo & R. E. Petty (Eds.), *Perspectives in cardiovascular psychophysiology* (pp. 223–264). New York: Guilford Press.

Pribram, K. H. & McGuinnes, D. (1975). Arousal, activation and effort in the control of attention. *Psychological Review, 82*, 116–149.

Reis, D. J. (1981). Experimental central neurogenic hypertension from brainstem dysfunction: Evidence for a central neural imbalance hypothesis of hypertension. In H. Weiner, M. A. Hofer, & A. J. Stunkard (Eds.), *Brain, behavior and bodily disease,* New York: Raven Press.

Ridgeway, D., & Hare, R. D. (1981). Sensation seeking and psychophysiological responses to auditory stimulation. *Psychophysiology, 18*, 613–618.

Rush, R. A. & Geffen, L. B. (1972). Radioimmunoassay and clearance of circulating dopamine-beta-hydroxylase. *Circulation Research, 31*, 444–452.

Sandman, C. A., Walker, B. B., & Berka, C. (1982). Influence of afferent cardiovascular feedback on behavior and the cortical evoked potential. In J. T. Cacioppo & R. E. Petty (Eds.), *Perspectives in cardiovascular psychophysiology.* New York: Guilford Press.

Sayers, B. McA. (1980). Pattern analysis of the heart rate signal. In L. Martin & P. H. Venables (Eds.), *Techniques in psychophysiology.* New York: Wiley.

Sayers, B. McA. (1973). Analysis of heart rate variability. *Ergonomics, 16*, 17–32.

Svensson, T. H., & Thoren, P. (1979). Brain noradrenergic neurons in the locus coeruleus: Inhibition by blood volume load through vagal afferents.*Brain Research, 172*, 174–178.

Tranel, D. T., Fisher, A. E., & Fowles, D. C. (1982). Magnitude of incentive effects on heart rate. *Psychophysiology, 19*, 514–519.

Waespe, W., & Henn, V. (1977). Neuronal activity in the vestibular nuclei of the alert monkey during vestibular and optokinetic stimulation. *Experimental Brain Research, 27*, 523–538.

Walker, B., & Sandman, C. A. (1982). Visual evoked potentials change as heart rate and carotid pressure change. *Psychophysiology, 19*, 520–527.

Zuckerman, M. (1979). *Sensation seeking: Beyond the optimal level of arousal.* Hillsdale, NJ: Erlbaum.

Zuckerman, M., Buchsbaum, M. S., & Murphy, D. L. (1980), Sensation seeking and its biological correlates. *Psychological Bulletin, 88*, 187–214.

16

Light Stimulation as a Stressor Affecting Self-Stimulation of the Brain in the Albino Rat

Sniezyna Watras-Gans, Krzysztof Owczarek, and Jan Matysiak
University of Warsaw

The goal of the research reported in this paper was to test hypotheses about the neurophysiological mechanisms that underlie optimal arousal and the need for stimulation and the central mechanisms that regulate this need. Our investigations have focused mainly on specific brain self-stimulation directly following controlled changes in sensory stimulation, overstimulation and partial sensory deprivation. The present study is part of a larger research program in which animals were systematically overstimulated by means of pulsating light or understimulated via sensory deprivation. In this research, sensory overstimulation and understimulation were both viewed as aversive or stressful because of the influence exerted on spontaneous activity. The experimental results were evaluated in terms of the hypothetical mechanisms that regulate optimal arousal.

Matysiak (1980) has reviewed the results of numerous studies that support the hypothesis of Kish (1966) and Schultz (1965) regarding nonspecific motivation, that is, motives not connected with the gratification of natural appetitive drives that induce living organisms to actively seek sensory stimulation. Exposure to visual, auditory, and kinesthetic stimuli seems to provide positive reinforcement for many animals when this stimulation falls within defined intensity bands. However, sensory stimulation above or below these bands appears to be aversive and stressful because it results in overstimulation or deprivation, with associated behavioral disturbances (Schultz, 1965).

Not only do conventional sensory stimuli seem to have reinforcing qualities, but self-stimulation of the brain with electrical impulses produced by the instrumental responses of an animal appear to have similar effects. The degree of sensory reinforcement, as measured by the intensity of self-exposition to electrical stimulation, may fluctuate as a function of the novelty and complexity of the eliciting stimulus. However, these collative stimulus factors seem to have only transient effects (Matysiak, 1980).

In discussing variables that influence electrical self-stimulation of the brain, Matysiak (1980) cites the sensory reinforcement studies of Kish and Baron. These investigators found that preexposure to pulsating light completely inhibited self-exposition, whereas preexposure to continuous light only partially inhibited it. In both cases, however, the animal's responses returned to normal after a period of time. In departing from the assumption of a stimulatory drive with properties similar to primary drives, these authors attributed their findings to the effects of stimulation saturation.

Homeostatic theories assume that departures from an optimal level of stimulation influence cortical arousal by means of the reticular system, and that level or arousal motivates the organism to undertake activity to increase or reduce the intensity of incoming stimulation to a more optimal level (Matysiak, 1980; Schultz, 1965). Berlyne (1973) also theorized that the reinforcing properties of sensory stimulation depend on cortical arousal, but he assumed that a moderate increase in arousal was rewarding, whereas too great an increase was aversive. He also posited a facilitative interaction among the brain structures that regulate the level of activation and the structures that cause stimuli to acquire positive or negative reinforcing properties.

There is experimental evidence to support the hypothesis that self-stimulation of a reward system in the brain may have something in common with the stimulation that motivates the exploratory behavior of an organism. For example, Phillips and Valle (1973) found that rats that actively explored an open field situation had a higher mean frequency of self-stimulation of the hypothalamus lateralis than less active rats. In our laboratory, we found a significant positive correlation between the self-stimulation threshold, that is, the minimal intensity of current necessary to maintain self-stimulation, and the need for light stimulation. The finding that rats with higher self-stimulation thresholds showed more light exposure was interpreted as indicative of individual differences in the sensitivity of the central nervous system to activity directed at obtaining stimulation.

The experiment described below investigates the neurophysiological basis of the need for stimulation to verify an hypothesis formulated within the conceptual framework of optimal arousal and optimal stimulation theory. This hypothesis is based on the general assumption that behavioral activity aimed at supplying the organism with sensory stimulation is related to brain self-stimulation activity (Hinde, 1970). According to this hypothesis, the amount of brain self-stimulation should be smaller after satiation with light than after light deprivation. Self-stimulatory reactions were selected for study because they were regarded as drive behaviors (Sadowski, 1974); it was also assumed that motivation and reinforcement in self-stimulation were nonspecific and independent of natural appetitive drives (Valenstain, 1976).

METHOD

Subjects

The experimental animals were 12 three-month-old Wistar rats, weighing 280-320 grams. Each rat brain was implanted with bipolar wolfram electrodes. The coordinates of the location of the electrodes were: anterior-posterior (AP), 2.6 mm from integral line; lateral (L), 0.2 mm from the midline; ventral (V), 8.5 mm from the surface of the skull (cf., Pellgerino, Pellgrino & Cushman, 1967).

Apparatus

The stimulus was a 0.5 second series of rectangular two-phase electrical impulses (frequency 100 Hz; duration of single impulse 0.4 ms). Current intensity was regulated within a 50 to 650 microampere band. Self-stimulation was measured in a chamber consisting of an 80 × 30 × 20 cm cage with a wooden cover and sides 0.5 cm thick. In the chamber, there were two wooden bars (6 × 1.5 cm), which were placed at opposite ends of the cage and connected with a stimulator. Press meters and chronometers registered the duration of pressure on the bars. The cerebral electrical impulse was activated by alternate pressing of one bar, then the other bar. After a stimulus was exposed by pressing one of the bars, further pressing of this bar had no effect; the other bar had to be pressed in order for the next stimulus to be exposed. The experimenter could also switch on the stimulator by means of a special key.

In this study of the effects of pulsating light on self-stimulation, we used a chamber similar to the one described above, except that it was only half as long (40 cm) and without bars. Electrical bulbs for exposing the light flashes (intensity 3.8–4.0 Lx) were located in the ceiling of the outer cover of the chamber. Light of greater intensity was avoided in order to counteract any disorganization of behavior due to excessive stimulation. The duration of a single flash was 1 second; the interval between flashes was 7 seconds.

Previous parametric studies in our laboratory have shown that when rats were self-exposed to light stimuli, the mean number of presses per diem on a bar exposing a light of the same intensity was 170. In this experiment, there was a 30 minute pretest in which rats obtained 257 flashes. Thus, the procedure employed in this experiment can be classified as overstimulation.

The same chamber was used for the overstimulation and light deprivation conditions. The parameters of the pulsating light in the overstimulation condition were determined by a controlling signal which was tape-recorded. The wooden casing kept the chamber dark in the light deprivation condition. The electric bulbs were, of course, switched off in this condition.

Procedure

The rats were tested individually. After six days of post-operation convalescence the rats were taught the self-stimulation response. Trials took place every second day. When the animals had learned to alternately press the bars and stable response rates were obtained, self-stimulation thresholds were determined in the following manner. The intensity of the electric current under which the stable reaction had been obtained was diminished by 20 microamperes every five minutes. The value at which the reaction completely disappeared defined the threshold.

In the following session passive brain stimulation (priming) was used, beginning at a previously determined subthreshold current intensity. If the animal did not react, the intensity was increased by 20 microamperes every five minutes. The priming was stopped when the rat spontaneously began to self-stimulate. The perithreshold value of the electrical stimulus was defined as the smallest intensity of current at which self-stimulation continued for 15 minutes.

After individual self-stimulation thresholds had been established, on every sec-

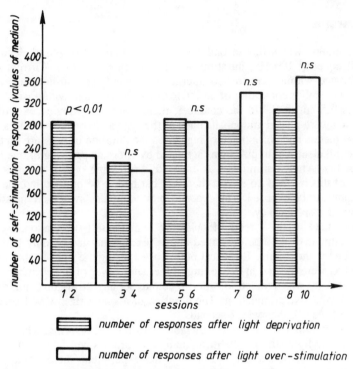

Figure 1 Median self-simulation rates for rats in a single session preceded by either light deprivation or over-stimulation.

ond day, an hour before self-stimulation, each animal was exposed to pulsating light or darkness by means of the apparatus described above. Each of these pretest conditions was used alternately, that is, after self-stimulation sessions that were preceded by the exposition of darkness, the rats went through a pretest trial with a pulsating light, and vice versa. Each rat was exposed to five pairs of self-stimulation sessions preceded by both pretests. In the first pretest, either pulsating light or darkness was presented randomly to each rat.

When the tests were completed the animals were put to sleep. Their brains were then examined to verify histologically the exact electrode locations.

RESULTS

In Fig. 1, each column graphically represents the median of self-stimulation rates of all the rats used in a single session. The shaded columns indicate sessions preceded by exposure to darkness; the blank columns represent sessions preceded by exposure to pulsating light. Analysis of data revealed a significant decrease in the frequency of self-stimulation following the pulsating light, as compared to self-stimulation following darkness ($p < .01$). However, significant differences were obtained only in the first 2 sessions; no differences were found for sessions 3-10. In successive sessions there was a tendency first to decrease the frequency of self-stimulation response (sessions 3 and 4) and then to increase the frequency of these reactions, as can be seen in Fig. 1. This increase was more apparent in trials which followed exposition of the pulsating light.

The first two columns in Fig. 1 refer to results obtained by animals after the first introduction of both pretests (session 1 and 2), the second group refers to sessions 3 and 4, and so on. Such grouping of results allows for the control of slight effects due to lesions around electrodes, which can appear when animals undergo prolonged self-stimulation. Significance of differences was measured using Wilcoxon's method (Siegel, 1956) applied to the results of successive sessions, such as 1 and 2, 3 and 4, 5 and 6.

Figure 2 shows the location of the electrodes. Sections of rat brains have been cut approximately perpendicular to the ventral surface of the brain; the atlas of Konig and Klippel (1963) has been used to verify the location of the electrodes. In 8 rats, traces of the electrodes were found in the midbrain tegmentum, dorsolateral from the interpeduncular nucleus in the proximity of the lemniscus medialis. In the remaining 4 rats, the traces of the electrodes were located between the lemniscus medialis and fasciculus retroflexus; in one rat, the electrode trace was in the middle of fasciculus retroflexus, and in the proximity of pedunculus corporis mamillaris in another.

DISCUSSION

The results indicated that the intensity of self-stimulation was lower after pulsating light exposure than after darkness, thus confirming the hypothesis. Thus, both partial light deprivation and overstimulation have a quite considerable influence on self-stimulation responses. The difference between the first two sessions was statistically significant. Failure to find differences in the other sessions was probably due to lesions which may have resulted from prolonged brain stimulation. This explanation is supported by the fact that, as early as the fourth session, animals were eliminated because of dramatic changes in their self-stimulation patterns.

The results of the present study corroborate those of Kish and Baron (1962), who found that pulsating light completely inhibited self-exposition of light. Kish and Baron interpreted their findings as resulting from the satiation of the sensory drive.

In the present study, the self-stimulation response after exposure to pulsating light was reduced or enhanced by prior manipulation of the light conditions, either by deprivation or overstimulation. Only partial inhibition was found in the self-stimulation response, perhaps due to the difference in the type stimulation. But we may also speculate that the reward consequences of self-stimulation can compensate for the aversive effects of over-stimulation, so that animals may have a tendency to self-stimulate despite drive reduction.

These results suggest that not only self-exposure, but also brain self-stimulation, is a factor in maintaining the optimal level of activation. Overstimulation by light causes a decrease in the rate of self-stimulation, while deprivation of light increases the self-stimulation rate. This could be interpreted as the additive effect of light and electrical stimuli and the attempt of the organism to avoid the aversive effect of over- and understimulation.

In the interpretation of our findings, it should by noted that both overstimulation and understimulation cause stress. Stressogenic factors involved in changes in sensory stimulation can also influence the motivational and reinforcement processes in self-stimulation, which can alter established reaction patterns. It should also be mentioned that histological verification of the location of these electrodes in the present study indicated that they were *not* implanted in brain areas associated with specific primary drives.

CONCLUSIONS

The findings of the present study verified the hypothesis that intracranial self-stimulation (ICSS) and sensory stimulation-seeking activity both contribute to

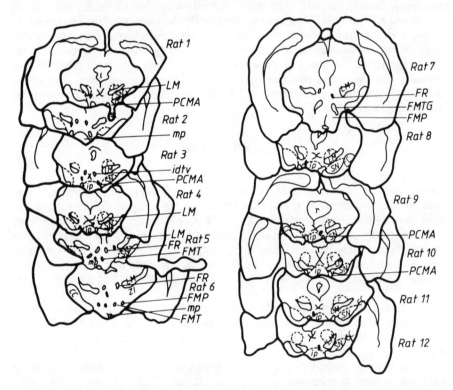

Schematic drawings made from stained frontal sections of rat brains demonstrating the deepest penetration of the electrodes

Explanation of the abbreviations:
CC – crus cerebri
FMP – fasciculus medialis prosencephali
FMTG – fasciculus mamillothalamicus
FR – fasciculus retroflexus
LM – lemniscus medialis
PCMA – pedunculus corporis mamilaris
SN – substantia nigra

idtv – nucleus interstitialis magnocellularis comissurae posterioris
ip – interpeduncularis nucleus
mp – posterior mamillary nucleus
r – nucleus ruber

Figure 2 Schematic drawings of rat brains cut approximately perpendicular to the ventral surface of the brain to show the location of electrodes.

maintaining an optimal level of activation. ICSS activity was measured in 12 male albino rats under two experimental conditions: After a 30-minute period of darkness, and following a 30-minute exposure to a blinking light. The hypothesis that the ICSS intensity would be lower after overexposure than following a period of light deprivation was partly supported. It was concluded that (a) light stimulation affects processes that determine level of activation; and (b) changes in light stimulation function as a stressor by altering the pattern of the brain self-stimulation response.

In self-stimulation, motivation or drive level may have something in common with a sensory drive, since both can be reduced or enhanced by prior manipulation of sensory conditions. The electrical stimulus in self-stimulation, as well as conventional sensory stimule, may influence the level of activation of an organism. Stress, resulting from sensory overstimulation and understimulation may have an additional effect on motivational and reinforcement processes in self-stimulation.

REFERENCES

Berlyne, D. E. (1973). The vicissitudes of aplopathematic and thelematoscopic pneumotology (or the hydrography of hedonism). In D. E. Berlyne & K. B. Madsen (Eds.), *Pleasure, reward, preference. Their nature, determinants and role in behavior.* New York: Academic Press.

Hinde, R. A. (1970). *Animal behavior. A synthesis of ethology and comparative psychology.* New York: McGraw-Hill.

Kish, G. B. (1966). Studies of sensory reinforcement. In W. K. Honig (Ed.), *Operant behavior: Areas of research and application,* New York: Appleton-Century-Crofts.

Kish, G. B., & Baron A. (1962). Satiation of sensory reinforcement. *Journal of Comparative and Physiological Psychology, 55,* 1007–1010.

Konig, J. F., & Klippel, R. A. (1963). *The rat brain: stereotaxic atlas of the forebrain and lower parts of the brain stem.* Baltimore: Williams and Wilkins.

Lipp, H. P. (1979). Differential hypothalamic self-stimulation behavior in Roman high-avoidance and low-avoidance rats. *Brain Research, 4,* 553–559.

Matysiak, J. (1980). *Roznice indywidualne w zackowaniu zwierzat w swietle koncepcji zapotrzebowania na stymulacje.* (Individual differences in animal behavior in light of the theory of need for stimulation). Wroclaw-Warszawa: Ossolineum.

Pellegrino, L. J., Pellegrino, A. S. & Cushman, A. J. (1979), *A stereotaxic atlas of the rat.* New York: Plenum Press.

Phillips, A., & Valle, F. (1973). Differences in reward value of brain stimulation in exploratory and non-exploratory rats. *Canadian Journal of Psychology, 27,* 4–11.

Sadowski, B. (1974). *Fizjologiczne mechanizmy zackowania* (Physiological mechanisms of behavior). Warszawa: PWN.

Schultz, D. P. (1965). *Sensory restriction: Effects on behavior.* New York: Academic Press.

Siegel, S. S. (1956). *Nonparametric stastistic for the behavioral sciences.* New York and London: Academic Press.

Valenstain, E. S. (1976). The interpretation of behavior evoked by brain stimulation. In A. Wauqier & E. T. Rolls (Eds.), *Brain stimulation reward.* Amsterdam: North-Holland.

IV

COPING WITH
STRESS AND ANXIETY

17

Anxiety, Worry, Prospective Orientation, and Prevention

Wolfgang Schönpflug
Freie Universität Berlin

INTRODUCTION

It is proposed that worries be analyzed analogous to stories, and techniques of story representation from cognitive psychology should be adopted for this purpose. Three formal features are distinguished which determine the structure of worry stories: Time perspective, branching, and concreteness. Psychological reasons are discussed why worried individuals should exhibit a tendency to elaborate their stories, to search for more information, and to engage in preventive actions. However, empirical evidence is presented for a strong focus of highly anxious individuals on their primary task and self-related problems. This focus seems not to be a favorable condition for cognitive involvement as necessary for elaboration, orientation, and preventive activity. It is, therefore, concluded that highly anxious individuals suffer from a conflict between the need to involve in prospection and prevention of negative events and the reluctance to invest effort and resources in future prospection and prevention. Possibly, this conflict is specific for emotionally anxious individuals as assessed by standard measures of anxiety. The empirical data presented stem from three experimental studies on behavior in achievement situations and from field research on hospitalized patients waiting for surgery.

WORRIES: ELABORATED
OR CONDENSED STORIES?

Worries are cognitions which relate individuals with external objects and environmental events, with internal physical or subjective states, and with physical and psychic functioning. Hamilton (1983) explains in detail that human memory stores a variety of worrying attributes like "does hurt" or "is painful" which are associated with referential concepts like "knife" or "fire" to which these attributes apply. Personality theorists involved in the study of anxiety have succeeded in demonstrating reliable individual differences in intensity of worries and in number of referents to worrying attributes (Hamilton, 1983; Wicklund, 1975; Wine, 1971). It has also been argued that worries call for conscious attention without or even against explicit intentions, interfere with ongoing information processing and are likely to deteriorate performance (Carver & Scheier, 1981; Müller & Pilzecker, 1900; Sarason, 1975).

Obviously, self-report questionnaires assessing the inclination to worry yield valuable information for ranking and classifying individuals. However, they do not indicate the semantic content and the logical structure of the worries experienced. Retrospective self-reports and association studies reveal immediate referents (e.g., in the statement "I worried about my illness"), but do not reveal the causal and procedural network which elucidates the links between immediate referents and worrying attributes. A detailed analysis of the structure of worry cognitions, however, is needed, in order to correlate them to general cognitive characteristics of individuals, to assess the mental load they constitute, and to determine their impact on behavior.

Indeed, worry cognitions can be rather simply structured. The simplest form to be conceived of can be reconstructed as a single proposition relating a predicate and an argument. Any worry attribute like *dangerous, hurt, painful* can serve as a predicate and be associated with an appropriate referent as an argument. Thus, propositions like *dangerous (lion)* or *hurt (knife)* originate. Such propositions may be processed very fast, and seem to be highly functional in eliciting elementary emotions like fear and hate, and primitive reactions like aggression and avoidance.

However, simple propositions are declaratory rather than explanatory. More inferences are needed to understand them. In order to understand *hurt (knife)*, at least three more propositions have to be kept in mind: (1) *cut (knife, finger)*; (2) *ache (finger)*; (3) *if (1), then (2)*.

Depending on topic, time, and location, still more sophisticated propositional structures can be conceived. They not only represent more extended process chains, but also more complex ecological settings. The further they can be elaborated the more degrees of freedom are granted for individual characteristics to operate. Unlike simple propositions they appear to form a basis for more differentiated feelings and activities.

Propositional models have gained high popularity in cognitive psychology during the last decade, mainly as tools for analyzing discourse (van Dijk & Kintsch, 1983). Alternative options are provided by graphic network models as the one described by Schank (1975), in which physical and personal states, events, goals, and styles are represented as nodes, and reasons, consequences, and initiations are represented as arcs connecting the nodes. Reference is made here to propositional models and network models because they have proven their value in the analysis of stories, and it will be contended that worries be analyzed analogous to stories.

Stories represent action-event sequences. They do not only represent sequences which have happened in the past. They also represent sequences which may happen in the future. Individuals have anticipations of the future, and they use the anticipations as bases for their personal involvement, active intervention and emotional reactions. This is at least the creed of cognitive behavior theory or action theory (cf. Frese & Sabini, 1985). Following this presupposition, worries appear as stories of future proceedings featuring unpleasant interludes and disastrous plots.

Worrying stories can, indeed, be very brief (e.g., "A truck will hit me," "I'm going to flunk my exam"). Their conciseness may veridically reflect the objective brevity of the action-event sequence as is often observed in real life (e.g., unforeseeable sudden accidents) and in the psychological laboratory (especially in stimulation studies, announcing or employing painful or annoying stimuli, conditioned or unconditioned). But short stories can also be interpreted as condensed versions of a more elaborated full story representing an extended and detailed sequence of actions and events. Individuals have high cognitive skills to make long stories short and short stories long. They apply macro-operators in order to filter out the gist or minimal content of a story, and they use elaboration procedures to express additional characters, motives and complications (cf. Kintsch & van Dijk, 1978; van Dijk, 1980). Whether anticipations of adverse action-event sequences are more elaborated or more condensed in states of anxiety is the central topic of this paper.

Features of Elaborated Worry Stories

In this section worries will be represented as networks. The elaboration of such networks will be discussed, and three features for estimating the degree of elaboration will be introduced: time perspective, branching, and concreteness. The term *time perspective* was introduced to psychology by Kurt Lewin (1948) and refers to the length of a series of coherent actions and events. If a person makes the statement: "I may become sick, and I have to go to the hospital" he or she may just be thinking of two consecutive states, *illness* → *hospital treatment*. This illustrates a short time perspective which can be extended, for example to:

$$illness \rightarrow \begin{array}{c} hospital \\ treatment \end{array} \rightarrow \begin{array}{c} failure \\ surgery \end{array} \rightarrow \begin{array}{c} stop \\ career \end{array} \rightarrow \begin{array}{c} loss \\ income \end{array} \rightarrow \begin{array}{c} loss \\ friends \end{array}$$

Sequential links of this sort have gained much emphasis in theories of achievement motivation. They define instrumentalities of action outcome as described by Nuttin (1953) and Vroom (1964), and form contingent paths as described by Raynor (1974).

The second feature of elaborated stories is branching. Branching refers to the parallel structure of events. If a patient states: "I am afraid my surgeon will not catch much sleep tonight and will be in bad shape tomorrow during my operation," this statement expresses a narrow view of the conditions of the surgeon's performance and the dangers of the operation. It can be represented by a linear chain: *sleep* → *surgeon* → *operation*. There are other factors which can be regarded as relevant for the surgeon's performance: a recent car accident or trouble with his family. Other actors who contribute to success and failure of the operation can be considered as well: the anestheist and the nurse. Each of these events and actors can be included in the story, thereby splitting the above version into different branches:

$$\begin{array}{ccccc} sleep & & & anesthesist & \\ family & \longrightarrow & surgeon & \longrightarrow & operation \\ accident & & & nurse & \end{array}$$

Psychologically, branching is relevant for the issue of causal attribution. Individuals attribute events and states to internal or external causes; this is also true for states and events lying in the future (cf. Meyer & Plöger, 1979). Branching indicates the number of causes individuals take into account, thus distinguishing monocausal and multiply determined sequences.

The third feature is concreteness. Concreteness refers to the specification of nodes according to sensory and motor criteria. The statement: "I shall be operated on my kidneys" is less specific and concrete then the statement: "My kidneys will be removed, and new kidneys will be transplanted from a donor." The former statement can be represented as a one-event node: → *kidney/operation* →.

An increase in concreteness occurs by replacing a node or a group of nodes by a more extended network. Thus, the latter statement in this paragraph can be represented by a net of at least three event-nodes:

ego: removal of kidneys
donor: removal of kidneys   →   *ego: implantation of donor's kidneys*

Through concreteness, anticipations of future events and actions gain some of the probative force and self-explanatory power of perceptions. They can serve as internal task models (Hacker, 1982) for which action plans can be developed.

What is the relation between the adverse content of worries and their degree of elaboration? If it is true that some people show an increased sensitivity for threatening signals (Epstein, 1972) it can be also postulated that these people will exhibit a stronger tendency to elaborate the frightening content of their worry stories. A long time perspective may aggrevate the seriousness of an unpleasant event by reference to its persistence, or of a pleasant event by reference to its deplorable aftereffects. Branching may exhibit the multiplicity of adverse proceedings, and concreteness may exemplify the severity of the situation. However, this may only be true for individuals operating in a sensitizing mode. With other individuals elaboration also gives a chance for entering mitigating thoughts: On better times following a period of immediate distress or on favorable consequences of unfavorable immediate events (with extended time perspective), on supportive and preventive factors balancing the threatening ones (with branching) and on the appeasement associated with realistic insight (going along with concreteness).

ORIENTATION AND PREVENTION
IN STATES OF ANXIETY

Orientation and prevention are intimately related to worries. Whereas orientation leads to the construction and verification of worries, predicting imminent dangers, preventive acts are designed and executed in order to modify the course of threatening events as anticipated without preventive intervention. Self-concern cognitions may, indeed, be stored in memory and invade the human mind as invariant structures and irrespective of the actual setting. But many worries are, in contrast, adjusted to varying life experiences, and are subject to change themselves. Thus, persons will actively search for information and draw conclusions to the worries they have. It can be assumed, that as with other stories (cf. Graesser et al., 1981), the cognitive structure of worry stories as built up at the present moment will guide the search for new information (e.g., the questions to be asked next). As far as adverse conditions have been identified in the anticipated sequences, preventive activities can be started which remove risks and barriers and provide new competence and support for mastering the risks (like learning of new skills or affiliation with benevolent partners). If preventive acts are effective, new information will permit new predictions regarding the course of events, thus leading to an alteration of the former worry story.

The concept of worry as used in this chapter is strictly limited to cognitions of imminent risks and dangers, as outlined above. It does not make reference to dynamic, emotional states. The emotional and autonomic involvement provoked by worry cognitions will be designated as anxiety. It makes good sense to suppose that highly anxious individuals will show much concern for their worries and will try hard to prevent imminent dangers. In consequence, highly anxious persons should show a sense for elaboration; they should ask more questions about further consequences (higher time perspective), should be more aware of additional reasons and agents (branching), and they should insist on details (concreteness). Since highly anxious individuals should also be more concerned about impending threats, they should engage in more preventive activities improving their prospects. With a higher variety of conditions and agents represented in their worry stories (due to augmented branching and time perspective) they also find more approaches to prevention; this should result in an increase of activities which Tomaszewski (1967) calls auxiliary.

Intense information search and active engagement have unfavorable side-effects: they increase the probability of false alarms and useless acts. Therefore, the more highly anxious persons elaborate their worries, the more they run the risk of including unrealistic or performance-irrelevant pieces of information as well as the risk of reacting to such information. However, in more complex and obscure situations, the validity of and the need for information are hard to evaluate; timidity, distrust, and insistence on more information may appear compulsive at times, on other occasions highly functional. The same appears to be true for the extent of prevention.

The literature supports this reasoning. Test anxiety is correlated with concern for self-evaluation (Spielberger, 1972). Highly anxious individuals suffer from more worries and other self-related cognitions not relevant for the task at hand, as frequently found in the tradition of Morris and Liebert (1970). Krohne & Schaffner (1980) have recently reviewed studies which demonstrate that anxious individuals take more time to prepare for scholastic tests.

However, orientation and preventive activity have their price: They consume time, effort, and external resources. Both activities can fail. Orientation, if failing, may produce inadequate anticipations and will inhibit rather than facilitate prevention. Preventive acts, if failing, may even create realistic conditions which are counterproductive. For these reasons, attempts at orientation and prevention may be risky. Depending on the situation, task relevant abilities, and motivation, persons may or may not be willing to take the risks. If they do not, they do not profit from the advantages of orientation and prevention, but they also avoid the disadvantages associated with orienting and preventing attempts. If they do, their engagement may pay off, but it may also prove to be inefficient. This way, a general model of behavior economy (Schulz & Schönpflug, 1982; Schönpflug, 1983) can be applied to the special case of orienting and preventing behavior. If anxiety goes along with high task involvement, anxious persons face two possibilities: sometimes their involvement will pay off, sometimes not, depending on situational difficulties and personal skills. Thus, anxious individuals may at times appear as achievers, at other times as nonachievers. From high achieving nonanxious subjects the anxious achievers should differ by exerting more effort, as has already been pointed out by Eysenck (1979).

Following these arguments, one may think of an anxious individual as a person who carefully elaborates the story of forthcoming events and vigorously reacts to disturbing details of this story. However, there is also counterevidence. Cognitive elaboration and skilled performance require differentiated information management, and it is well documented that in states of anxiety processing of complex information, working memory, and range of attention are impaired (for a more detailed analysis, see Eysenck, 1983). If this is true, the state of anxiety cannot be assumed to be a favorable condition for cognitive elaboration and diversified action. If this is true, anxious individuals will prefer to make long stories short, collapse branches and not look for details. They will neglect orientation and also omit preventive acts.

RECENT EMPIRICAL EVIDENCE

Viewed from the perspective of behavior economics, the old problem of facilitating and inhibitory anxiety can be analyzed in a more sophisticated manner. But the fact remains that the effects of anxiety are ambiguous, and cannot easily be predicted. Certainly, the explicit definition of functional and subjective factors which determine the effects of anxiety contributes to progress in theorizing. But as these factors are not easy to control and to assess, progress in empirical clarification has been slow. A good example for the difficulties encountered in experimental studies is presented by Mündelein & Schönpflug (1983). The subjects in their experiment were given the opportunity to prevent interruptions of a work procedure (system break-down during computer work). Consistent individual differences were observed which were correlated with reactivity scores (Strelau, 1972; Vorwerg, 1975). However, there were no correlations to trait and state anxiety scores (Laux, Glanzman, Schaffner, & Spielberger, 1981; Spielberger, Gorsuch, & Lushene, 1970), possibly because high involvement in the primary task due to anxiety also inhibited performance in the secondary task of prospective orientation and prevention (requests for state of the system and priority declarations). Observations of work procedures seem to constitute a better basis for discrimination of high and low achieving anxious subjects; apparently, a group of anxious individuals could be identified, who show no performance decrement as compared to nonanxious persons but a higher task involvement as indicated by number of checks and corrections, by time consumed, and by subjective ratings of effort (Schulz & Schönpflug, 1988; Wieland, 1985).

Possibly, the decision whether to elaborate or to show a narrow concern is experienced as a dilemma by anxious individuals themselves. Evidence for such a dilemma can be found in an earlier experiment simulating clerical work in the laboratory (Schulz & Schönpflug, 1982). The subjects in this experiment had to solve mental tasks like those which occur in public and business administrations. For instance, one task was to reply to a complaint addressed to a business firm: a customer complains that an order was not delivered to him. There may be many reasons for such a complaint. Possibly, there was a confusion of address labels in the packing department. Perhaps the order form was not filled out correctly by the customer, or there was some other reason. The subjects could assess the case, because they had access to additional information. For instance, they could inquire whether the missing package has been returned by another customer, which would point to a mistake in address or delivery. The search for relevant information from which valid conclusions could be drawn required careful study of the initial task.

The text of the task was shown on a screen. Additional information could be obtained by pressing defined keys. The subjects were free to study the task as shown on the screen as long as they wished. When they pressed the key for the first piece of additional information, the text with the task disappeared and the additional information appeared instead. The initial inspection time was taken as a rough index for orientation and preparation. If subjects are free to determine the time of task exposition before they start to call for more information, and if anxious subjects show a stronger inclination towards orientation and preparation, longer initial exposition times can be predicted for highly anxious persons. This prediction is correct, if nonevaluative feedback is given. Nonevaluative feedback means: subjects worked at their own pace; after their solutions, a "right" or "wrong" signal appeared which had no further consequences. The result is different if subjects are rated and paid according to the time needed. Under this condition, time required is communicated, and feedback includes information about premium payment (time-evaluative feedback). Under this condition, the initial inspection time for the task drops considerably, and high anxious subjects try to save more study time than low anxious ones (see Fig. 1).

Obviously, the two experimental treatments induced two different anticipatory structures. One was:

study ⟶ *search* ⟶ *conclusion* ⟶ *feedback*
task   *information*

In the other one a further consequence *premium* is added, and this consequence is enforced by a modification *speed,* which according to Graesser, Robertson, and Anderson (1981) can be classified as a style-node. This yields the following structure:

study ⟶ *search* ⟶ *conclusion* ⟶ *feedback* ⟶ *premium*
task   *information*

↓   ↓   ↓   ↑
———————————————————————— *speed* ————————————————————————

If concern for premium payment activates the style-node *speed* as a reason, a competition between fast and careful responding is initiated. The further interpretation is: high anxious individuals have a bias toward evaluative consequences, and therefore their concern for speed is activated at the expense of careful preparation and orientation. The first conclusion, then, may be: anxiety basically goes along with a sense for elaboration, but if speed is evaluated, anxious subjects show concern for high speed rather than for time-consuming elaboration.

A special condition associated with time evaluation was that total time was limited, and therefore preparation and execution were mutually exclusive. This need not be the case. The time schedule may be organized in such a way that preparation and execution cannot compete with each other. Examples are in sports, where each contest is preceded by a time of training, when no formal competition

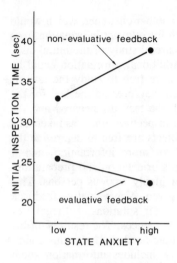

Figure 1 Initial inspection time for studying tasks: average scores for subjects varying in state anxiety and type of feedback (see Schönpflug & Schulz, 1979, p. 173).

is scheduled and no records are acknowledged. Foreperiods should give the chance for relaxation and reflection. But there are quite a few individuals who hate such foreperiods. They report they cannot concentrate on preparations, they feel blocked by worry, they feel excited and declare they cannot wait. Otto (1981, 1982) has studied this situation. He invited juveniles to participate in competitive races with miniature cars. The races followed a standardized schedule, but the subjects were not aware of this. There were two races for each subject, and before each race there was a waiting period which was attributed to technical and organizational reasons. Detailed recordings of overt behavior, telemetric heart rate measures and subjective responses were collected.

The subjects were able to engage in various activities during the waiting periods. An opportunity was given for orientation about both the forthcoming race and their own person. For instance, the person could ask for advice, could inspect the race course, could handle the cars. A person could also read magazines or have a drink—one of the few experiments where beverages were served. Among the most important variables were subjective estimates, how well they could cope with the demands of the waiting period on the one hand, and of the execution period with the race on the other. The first result: subjective estimates of the capacity/demand ratio for the executive situation varied considerably. The second result: coping capacity for the waiting situation was statistically independent from coping capacity for the executive situation. The third result: trait anxiety was moderately related to "waiting ability" (.30) and state anxiety (.41); the anxiety scores were not significantly correlated with racing ability.

In the experiment, heart rate was registered by means of a telemetric device. The scores exhibited considerable variation. The subjects who expressed that it is hard for them to wait have heart rates that were almost ten beats per minute higher than in the patient subjects. This is a difference which equals the average difference between high and low anxious subjects which has been found in other studies (Schönpflug & Mündelein, 1983). The subjects who rate their capacity for racing higher than the demands in the contest also have higher pulse rates during the waiting period (see Fig. 2). Objective arousal can be interpreted here as a sign of engagement or disengagement in the racing contest. Heart rate remains at the same level during the race in three groups. There is an upward shift of heart rate for the group which cannot wait, but engages in the competition (see Fig. 3). Although this group consistently has the highest heart rate, it reports only a moderate degree of arousal. Three groups give estimates which are in line with physiological recordings; the mean score of the competitive group which cannot wait is lower than would have been predicted from pulse rate (see Fig. 4). State anxiety scores follow the same pattern.

The discrepant group is of special interest. One might suspect that this group disregards or suppresses its anxiety (cf. Asendorpf & Scherer, 1983). An alternative explanation is possible which is not necessarily in conflict with the former one: impatient subjects suffer from a deficit in self-regulatory skills. This deficit is particularly important in waiting situations, where there are not external demands calling for immediate attention. The internal sensations of arousal constitute the main demands for regulation. If sufficient skills are lacking, impatient anxious subjects prefer to focus on the forthcoming task and disregard their own emotional state. Attempts to test this assumption have been made by detailed behavior analysis, but the data from direct behavior observation were not easy to interpret. Just one example will demonstrate the attempted approach. One class of activities which were recorded was related to the control of state of personal arousal. During the waiting period this class was represented by such items as "takes a cool drink, when feeling hot." During the contest "internal regulation" was scored, when subjects took a deep breath, or sighed "oh God" to get some relief from tension. During the contest, patient, nonanxious subjects scored highest, whereas impatient subjects with objectively high, though subjectively moderate arousal had the lowest scores (see Fig. 5).

In the light of these data, highly anxious achievers can be paraphrased as impatient individuals with high executive skills. They cannot cope with their internal arousal sufficiently, but they still manage to cope with the external demands. A look at their achievement scores, especially at their time to complete the race and the number of accidents, indicates that competent impatient subjects are not far below competent patient ones. Incompetent impatient subjects are even faster than the incompetent patient ones. It is hard to tell, how highly aroused, self-neglecting

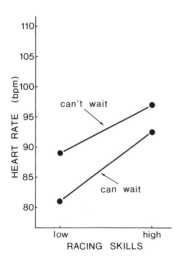

Figure 2 Maximal heart rate during a waiting period: average scores for subjects varying in racing skills and in the ability to wait (see Otto, 1981, p. 134).

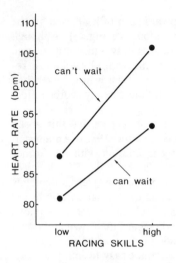

Figure 3 Maximal heart rate during a racing contest: average scores for subjects varying in racing skills and in the ability to wait (see Otto, 1981, p. 135).

achievers manage to maintain a high level of performance. They definitely do not compensate their shortcomings by increased orientation and preparation. This view is supported by five details from our behavior records for the waiting period. Impatient, highly anxious subjects have a longer time period of retreat and immobility; they show slightly more involvement in what we call substitutive activities or actions that are nonfunctional in the situation—like reading comics and magazines; they show less concern for the time after race; the time they devote to the inspection of the course takes about a quarter of the waiting period—the same portion as in the patient group; and they ask less for advice or available support. As Otto (1982) argues, these subjects anxiously expect the testing situation to come, but they are not in a state to elaborate their anticipations and to use the waiting period to improve their chances. Their emotionality seems to be an adverse condition for the cognitive operations performed during effective orientation and preparation.

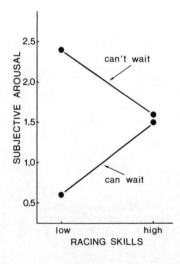

Figure 4 Subjective arousal during the experimental sessions: average scores for subjects varying in racing skills and in the ability to wait (see Otto, 1981, p. 133).

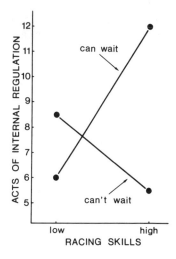

Figure 5 Acts of internal regulation during the waiting period: average scores for subjects varying in racing skills and in the ability to wait (see Otto, 1981, p. 139).

As a more direct test of story structure in states of anxiety, a study on hospitalized patients waiting for surgery was designed (Dutke, Frenzel, Raeithel, & Schönpflug, 1985). Interviews were done with patients whose treatment was scheduled several days in advance (as opposed to emergency cases). The investigators had a first interview on the preoperative day, a day which patients used for familiarization with the hospital, making personal arrangements and obtaining information on the operation and on narcosis. The investigators also escorted the patients on their way to the operation room and returned for another interview two days after the operation. Intuitive expectations were guided by the stereotype of the anxious and suspicious ruminating patient who asks many questions, makes sure that he is well attended to, and tries actively to arrange his environment according to his wishes (e.g., by distributing little presents to the nurses, supplying himself with beverages and magazines). Measures of anxiety (Laux et al., 1981) and emotionality (Ulrich & Ulrich de Muynck, 1979) were taken; questions regarding personal hopes and fears were asked, which also took time perspective and evaluation into consideration. Further questions referred to activity dimensions, execution of modifying acts, orienting behavior and passive endurance of others' actions (frequency, efficiency, objects, and agents).

The data are not as conclusive as was hoped at the beginning. Anxiety scores were not particularly high on the average, and most patients expressed optimism in regard to success of the surgery and later recuperation. There was a low correlation between anxiety scores and concern for possible negative consequences of the surgery, and no correlation with appraisal of positive consequences. Orienting and modifying behavior was not reported to be pronounced. There was definitely no increase in orientation for anxious individuals. It is rather the group with low anxiety who exhibits a tendency—though insignificant—towards increased orientation; low anxious persons also express more satisfaction about the information obtained from the doctors and nurses. What attenuates anxiety in many patients is obviously a voluntary transfer of control to the hospital staff. Doctors, nurses, medical equipment, and the hospital organization in general are included into the story of future events as competent and trustworthy agents. By inclusion of potent and benevolent agents the stories become rather short, as critical events and complications are excluded. Thus, neither a considerable portion of patients with high or with low anxiety could be detected which showed increased orientation and concern for cognitive elaboration of worries.

CONCLUSIONS

Apparently, the anxiety concept as used in this chapter and as assessed by the standardized instruments focuses on emotional and autonomic arousal; arousal may be high because of a lack of self-regulative skills. Arousal and lack of self-regulation emerge whenever anxious individuals encounter a threatening situation without the possibility of transferring control to other persons of competence and benevolence. As a strong emotional state, anxiety seems not to be favorable for sophisticated cognitive elaborations and detailed preparation and prevention. The stories which people have in mind during such a state are rather short and vague and do not close with a happy end. This type of an arousing but debilitating anxiety state should be contrasted with a constructive style of worrying. Constructive worrying should form a variant of vivid, rich and creative thinking. The search for inventive worriers should be continued. The inventive worrier should operate like a good detective or a safety expert, who is aware of a great variety of risks and also takes low probability events into account. He or she elaborates skillful scenarios for future developments, and is able to carefully design the steps to be taken in order to be prepared for impending dangers and demands. His or her behavior is not economical in routine situations; but prudence is highly valuable in sudden emergency situations. The inventive worrier may be cool or excited; but even if emotional, he or she will not lose self-control. The stories he or she will have to tell about the future will be extended, branched and detailed, and they will contain many negative features, although the inventive worrier will do his or her best to abolish risks and threats.

REFERENCES

Asendorpf, J. B. & Scherer, K. R. (1983). The discrepant repressor: Differentiation between low anxiety, high anxiety, and repression of anxiety by autonomic-facial-verbal patterns of behavior. *Journal of Personality and Social Psychology, 45*, 1334–1346.

Carver, C. S. & Scheier, M. F. (1981). *Attention and self-regulation.* New York: Springer.

van Dijk, T. (1980). *Macrostructures.* Hillsdale, NJ: Erlbaum.

van Dijk, T. A. & Kintsch, W. (1983). *Strategies of discourse comprehension.* New York: Academic Press.

Dutke, S., Frenzel, A. M., Raeithel, A. & Schönpflug, W. (1985). The self-regulative activity of medical patients as a co-determinant of their emotional states. In R. Schwarzer (Ed.), *The self in anxiety, stress and depression.* Amsterdam: North-Holland.

Epstein, S. (1972). The nature of anxiety with emphasis upon its relationship to expectancy. In C. D. Spielberger (Ed.), *Anxiety: Current trends in theory and research* (Vol. 2). New York: Academic Press.

Eysenck, M. W. (1979). Anxiety, learning, and memory: A reconceptualisation. *Journal of Research in Personality, 13*, 363–385.

Eysenck, M. (1983). Anxiety and individual differences. In G. R. J. Hockey (Ed.), *Stress and fatigue in human performance.* London: Wiley.

Frese, M. & Sabini, J. (Eds.). (1985). *The concept of action in psychology.* Hillsdale, NJ: Erlbaum.

Graesser, A. C., Robertson, S. P. & Anderson, P. A. (1981). Incorporating inferences in narrative representations: A study of how and why. *Cognitive Psychology, 13*, 1–26.

Hacker, W. (1982). Action control in the task-dependent structure of action-controlling mental representations. In W. Hacker, W. Volpert & M. V. Cranach (Eds.), *Cognitive and motivational aspects of action*. Amsterdam: North-Holland.

Hamilton, V. (1983). *The cognitive structures and processes of human motivation and personality*. Chichester: Wiley.

Kintsch, W. & van Dijk, T. (1978). Toward a model of text comprehension and production. *Psychological Review, 85*, 363–394.

Krohne, H. W. & Schaffner, P. (1980). *Anxiety, coping strategies, and test performance*. Osnabrück: Fachbereich 3 der Universität Osnabrück.

Laux, L., Glanzmann, P., Schaffner, P. & Spielberger C. D. (1981). *Das State-Trait-Angstinventar. Theoretische Grundlagen und Handanweisung.* Weinheim: Beltz.

Lewin, K. (1948). Time perspective and morale. In G. Weiss Lewin (Ed.), *Resolving social conflicts*. New York: Harper.

Meyer, W. U. & Plöger, F.-O. (1979). Scheinbar paradoxe Wirkungen von Lob und Tadel auf die wahrgenommene eigene Begabung. In H. Filipp (Ed.), *Selbstkonzept-Forschung: Probleme, Befunde und Perspektiven*. Stuttgart: Klett-Cotta.

Morris, L. W. & Liebert, R. M. (1970). Relationship of cognitive and emotional components of test anxiety to physiological arousal and academic performance. *Journal of Consulting and Clinical Psychology, 35*, 332–337.

Müller, G. E. & Pilzecker, A. (1900). *Experimentelle Beiträge zur Lehre vom Gedächtnis*. Leipzig: Barth.

Mündelein, H. & Schönpflug, W. (1983). Regulation und Fehlregulation im Verhalten. VIII. Uber primäree (unmittelbar ziegerichtete) und sekundäre (auxiliare und präventive) Anteile von Tätigkeiten. *Psychologische Beitränge, 25*, 71–84.

Nuttin, J. (1953). *Tâche, réussite et échec. Théorie de la conduite humain*. Louvain: Publications Universitaires.

Otto, J. (1981). *Regulationsmuster in Warte-und Vollzugssituationen*. München: Minerva.

Otto, J. (1982). Regulation und Fehlregulation im Verhalten. V. Anforderung und Kapazität beim Warten und beim Ausführen von Tätigkeiten. *Psychologische Beiträge, 24*, 478–497.

Raynor, J. O. (1974). Future orientation in the study of achievement motivation. In J. W. Atkinson & J. O. Raynor (Eds.), *Motivation and achievement*. Washington, DC: Winston.

Sarason, I. G. (1975). Anxiety and self-preoccupation. In I. G. Sarason & C. D. Spielberger (Eds.), *Stress and Anxiety* (Vol. 2). Washington, DC: Hemisphere.

Schank, R. C. (1975). The structure of episodes in memory. In D. G. Bobrow & A. Collins (Eds.), *Representation and understanding*. New York: Academic Press.

Schönpflug, W. (1983). Coping efficiency and situational demands. In G. R. J. Hockey (Ed.), *Stress and fatigue in human performance*. London: Wiley.

Schönpflug, W. & Mündelein, H. (1983). Operation-correlated heart-rate responses. *Psychological Research, 45*, 177–186.

Schönpflug, W. & Schulz, P. (1979). *Lärmwirkungen bei Tätigkeiten mit Komplexer Informationsverarbeitung*. Berlin: Umweltbundesamt.

Schulz, P. & Schönpflug, W. (1988). Anxiety as motivating and stressing factor. In C. D. Spielberger, I. G. Sarason, & P. D. Defares (Eds.), *Stress and Anxiety* (Vol. 11). New York: Hemisphere.

Spielberger, C. D. (1972). Anxiety as an emotional state. In C. D. Spielberger (Ed.), *Anxiety: Current trends in theory and research* (Vol. 1). New York: Academic Press.

Spielberger, C. D., Gorsuch, R. L. & Lushene, R. E. (1970). *Manual for the State-Trait Anxiety Inventory.* Palo Alto, CA: Consulting Psychologists Press.

Strelau, J. (1972). A diagnosis of temperament by non-experimental techniques. *Polish Psychological Bulletin, 3*, 97–105.

Tomaszeweski, T. (1967). Aktywność czlowieka. In M. Maruszewski, J. Reykowski & T. Tomaszewski (Eds.), *Psychologia jako nauka o czlowieku*. Warszawa: Książka i Wiedza.

Ulrich, R. & Ulrich de Muynck, R. (1979). *Das Situationsbewertungssystem SB-EMI-S*, Teil III, Testmanual. München: Pfeiffer.

Vorwerg, M. (1975). *Einstellungspsychologie*. Berlin: Deutscher Verlag der Wissenschaften.

Vroom, V. H. (1964). *Work and motivation*. New York: Wiley.

Wicklund, R. A. (1975). Objective self-awareness. In L. Berkovitz (Ed.), *Advances in Experimental Social Psychology* (Vol. 9). New York: Academic Press.

Wieland, R. (1985). Temporal patterns of anxiety: Towards a process analysis of anxiety and performance. In R. Schwarzer (Eds.), *The self in anxiety, stress and depression*. Hillsdale, NJ: Erlbaum.

Wine, J. (1971). Test anxiety and direction of attention. *Psychological Bulletin, 76*, 92–104.

18

Planning as a Method
of Stress Prevention:
Will It Pay Off?

Wolfgang Battman
Freie Universität Berlin

High and complex task demands, time pressure and additional environmental hazards have been quite unequivocally named as task related conditions responsible for the promotion of stress (cf. Cooper & Payne, 1977). The relation between task demands or work load and the individual's capacity (Kahneman, 1973) constitutes the core of most current stress theories (McGrath, 1976; Schönpflug, 1983). According to these models, stress is likely to occur if task demands tax or exceed the individual's capacity (Lazarus & Launier, 1978). Therefore, stress prevention must focus on the improvement of the demand-capacity-ratio by lowering the demands and/or enhancing the individual's capacity.

Control is a necessary prerequisite of preventing stress by improving the demand-capacity-ratio (Miller, 1979; Thompson, 1981). This condition is certainly met by capacity: as a joint function of ability and effort, capacity is under immediate control in its effort component (Kahneman, 1973; Schönpflug, 1983) and ability may be enhanced on a long term basis due to learning by experience and insight. Although the possibilities of resource management are quite obvious, it is only rarely taken into account that the load induced by task demands can be controlled also. Unlike life events, demands connected to a task are not isolated in their emergence but form a structured entity which can be formally described as a problem space (Newell & Simon, 1972). This interrelatedness of demands makes situations of high demand predictable. In consequence, the predictable situations of potential overload can be avoided: most tasks are characterized by 'degrees of freedom' (Hacker, 1978) enabling the individual to choose a way of solution corresponding to his or her abilities. The given predictability and controllability of demands does not imply, however, that all individuals will exert effective control. Whereas control in the psychological laboratory often is reduced to pushing knobs (Glass & Singer, 1972) or jumping over barriers (Seligman, 1975), exerting effec-

The study was supported by a grant of the Ministry of Interior to Dr. W. Schönpflug and is completely documented in Schönpflug & Battmann (1982). I am grateful to Dr. Schönpflug for his comments on an earlier version of this paper.

tive control in everyday life and at work is a complex process requiring extensive task specific knowledge and sophisticated strategies (Greeno, 1977; Bainbridge, 1978). Insufficient task specific knowledge and ineffective strategies are common causes of failure. They are a strong danger for the actor because of their subtlety: deficiencies in knowledge and strategy are not apparent until the efforts to solve a task fail, but are difficult to correct in a crisis requiring fast and accurate information processing. In addition, individuals differ in ability depending on their acquired skills as well as their capability of information processing. Reduced capacity due to low ability adds to the danger of failing the danger of premature exhaustion.

Therefore, strategies and knowledge should be acquired before a crisis in order to enable the individual to take advantage of the possibility of controlling task demands and to optimize capacity allocation. A familiar method of doing this is planning. The superiority of well planned action has been proved for everyday problems like errand walking (Hays-Roth, 1979, 1980), and cooking (Byrne, 1977) as well as for working life problems like electronic parts assembly (Skell, 1972) and railway operation (Hacker & Richter, 1981).

A plan can be defined as an ordered set of control statements to support the efficiency of action and the preparation of alternative actions for the case of failure (Sacerdotti, 1974; Schank & Abelson, 1977). During the planning process, future demands are identified and potential situations of overload can be avoided by the generation of preventive strategies (Hays-Roth & Hays-Roth, 1979; Hays-Roth, 1980). The execution of a good plan should reinforce the effectivity of action in several ways: (a) Higher capacity, that is, increased task-specific knowledge improves the individual's competence to cope with the task (Bainbridge, 1978); (b) Lower demands; as a result of the planning process, demands can be structured and capacity allocated to them in an way optimizing the person-environment-fit (French, Rogers, & Cobb, 1976); and (c) Saved resources; capacity normally wasted by suboptimal actions will be saved.

Doing well while executing a good plan also has, of course, emotional and motivational consequences (Miller, Galanater, & Primbram, 1960). Because interruptions which characterize failure and trigger stress (Mandler & Watson, 1966, Mandler, 1979) are improbable and are taken care of by already generated alternative strategies, the availability of the plan will be of special help for the individuals of a lower ability who can now expect and experience a "warm glow of success."

A good plan is an ideal method of stress prevention, but there are emotional and economical reasons why the good plan is only seldomly found. Planning improves capacity by optimizing the utilization and assembling of skills already available. Since new skills are not acquired, the individuals with low ability will realize that planning is a process of problem solving by problem generation (Getzels, 1979). The generation of efficient strategies requires the planning individuals to focus their attention on those areas of the problem space (Newell & Simon, 1972) which are most difficult to cope with. This may lead to unpleasant discoveries: the individuals may have to recognize that the course of action will be endangered despite accurate planning either due to external variable circumstances or because skills essential for success are lacking. If planners generate problems which they are unable to solve, justified worries will accompany and may even abort further planning.

From an economical point of view, planning can be characterized as an investment: considerable time and effort has to be spent in a process of complex information processing. This information processing can be more demanding than a solution by strategies generated on an ad hoc basis and may be illusionary, because a major part of the processed information will consist of hypotheses which may be disproved by reality during the execution of the plan. Therefore the investment planning can be regarded as profitable only if two conditions are met: (1) the generated plan is good and (2) the efforts invested into planning and plan execution are lower than those which would be required for a solution by ad hoc generated strategies.

These emotional and economical aspects highlight the uncertain payoff of planning. Provided a good plan is generated, it will certainly pay off on complex tasks which would have been unsolvable without planning. On the other hand, high task complexity makes planning difficult, particularly for individuals with low ability who may be unable to work out efficient strategies. In fact, for these individuals, planning may generate the worries it is intended to remove.

Most studies on planning have made use of relatively simple tasks and focus on the potential benefits of planning. Being interested mainly in the cognitive processes underlying planning, authors tend to neglect the possible negative effects of planning, including the adverse emotional states. The study reported in this article was conducted to test the hypothesis that the benefits of planning with regard to stress prevention and load reduction are limited and negative effects have to be expected if the ability of the individual is low. Low ability constrains the possible success of planning and plan execution will suffer if resources are heavily exploited already during plan construction. Furthermore, subjects may become worried if they cannot generate effective coping strategies or their deficient plans fail during execution. To analyze this pay-off function of planning, a realistic and moderately complex task environment was designed.

METHOD

The Simulated Task Environment

An adequate method of studying long-term cognitive activities like planning and their effects on the course of action taken by the individual seems to be a computer simulation of a complex task environment, which can be controlled directly by the subject. Guided by the "travelling salesman problem" (Dantzig, Fulkerson, & Johnson, 1954; Little, Murty, Sweeny, & Karol, 1963), we constructed a computer-simulated task environment in which the subjects were asked to take over the role of the supervisor of a chain of department stores scattered across a city. During the course of one day the subjects had to visit 10 stores where decisions about marketing strategies, accounting problems and so forth had to be made. At three of the stores, appointments with the storekeeper had been arranged in advance and the subjects had to keep them within a 10 minute time limit.

All the necessary information was displayed on a terminal. To acquire the necessary skills to handle the problem (i.e. to request information and enter decisions with the keyboard), all subjects worked through a training problem for 15 to 20 minutes.

At the beginning, the subjects received a "situational description" (Fig. 1)

```
    9.00          14.30

You are now at shop no. 1 .

Please decide which shop you want
to visit next.

Keep in mind the following dates:      Information 3

1. You have a date at shop no. 10
   at 9.45 am.                          FIXING NEW DATES

2. You have a date at shop no. 8
   at 11.00 am.                         You can fix new dates now. Please
                                        keep in mind that only the arrival
3. You have a date at shop no. 7        times can be changed.
   at 1.00 pm.
                                        Please enter the number of the
You can change this date  !             shop (07, 08 or 10):
                                        Please enter your new arrival
If you are not sure where to go         time (e.g. 12.45 or 13.15):
now request further information
or the map.                             When you are finished press
                                        'V' to continue.
Pushing key 'UT' you can get the
directory of available information.
When you have decided where to go
please enter the number of the shop.
```

Figure 1 Presentation of information on the screen: the situational description (left) and menu for changing dates (right).

specifying the current location, the prearranged appointments, and the current "system time."

By pressing appropriate keys, further information could be requested and was displayed on the right side of the screen. The information available on request consisted of (a) a town map, where the current position and the distances to all shops could be explored (Fig. 2); (b) a list of shops visited in which all shops already visited were noted; (c) feedback information about the average working time in the shops and the driving time between them; and (d) a possibility to change the appointments. By request of special information and entering the appropriate data subjects could inform shopkeepers if they wanted to change any one of the appointments (Fig. 1).

The subjects began their working day from a starting location (shop 1) at 9:00 a.m. system time. After collecting some information, they had to decide on their route and time schedule. Upon entering the number of the shop chosen on the keyboard, the town map was displayed with the starting and target shops blinking. Exposure time varied proportionally to the driving time between both places. Driving time was added to system time on a "clock-time" basis. Upon arriving at the destination, two administrative tasks (e.g. accounting problems, wage calculations, and marketing decisions) were offered to the subjects. After solving these tasks, subjects could again collect information and select the next shop to be visited. During these processes, the system time proceeded in real time. When all ten shops had been inspected, the trial ended with the selection of shop 12.

Keeping the appointments or arranging new ones was, of course, very important. Being late made a second visit necessary and being early meant waiting or coming back a second time. While it was possible for the subject to avoid changes and try to keep the prearranged appointments, it required a complicated and uneconomical schedule with long driving time. In addition, the requests for a change had to be made at least 25 minutes in advance to prevent short-term changes of appointments. Thus, arranging and keeping an appointment required an exact calculation of time and continuous schedule control.

The subjects had to work in this task environment for a total of three identical trials which lasted about 1.5 hours real time or 5 to 8 hours system time each.

All actions taken and information gathered by the subject were recorded on-line permitting a complete reconstruction of the stream of behavior. These performance data were complemented by a continuous on-line recording of several psychophysiological parameters (heart period, fingerpulse, electrodermal activity). Protocols of performance and psychophysiological state were matched after the session in order to obtain indicators of action dependent shifts in activation (cf. Schönpflug & Battmann, 1982).

Design and Subjects

A local labor agency offered the participation in the study as a one-day job to unemployed persons. All 72 subjects (32 female, 40 male) were volunteers and paid on an hourly basis. A 2 × 2 design with the factors planning and competence was constructed.

Half of the subjects were assigned to an experimental group, referred to as a "planning group" in the remainder of this article. This group received a short instructional text at the beginning of the first trial, which could be requested again as special "planning information" throughout the entire experiment. In this text,

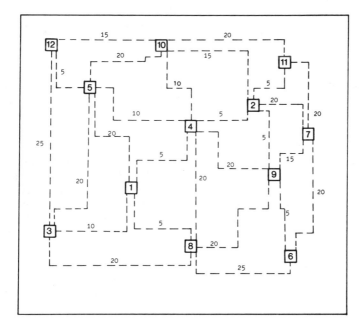

Figure 2 Presentation of information on the screen: the town map.

the subjects were asked to try to (a) plan extensively; (b) think about setting intermediate goals; and (c) enter their schedule at the beginning of each trial beside the town map.

The schedule entered by the subjects at the beginning of each trial was always displayed beside the town map when requested, but subjects were not committed to follow it.

The other half of the subjects (control group) were also free to plan but received neither an explicit instruction to do so nor the possibility to enter a plan beside the town map.

To permit an investigation of possible effects due to differences in competence, two groups—high- and low-intelligent subjects—were distinguished on the basis of their test scores on a well standardized intelligence test (Amthauer, 1971). The average standard score in this sample was 104 points with a standard deviation of 7.1 points. According to their standard scores, equal numbers of high- and low-intelligent subjects were assigned to the planning and control condition. Each cell of the design contains 18 subjects.

RESULTS

Performance

Control in this environment meant to keep appointments and, because the preassigned appointments did not allow an optimal schedule, it meant changing appointments. The quality of the plan and the competence of the individual is therefore indicated by the number of appointments kept. Figure 3 shows that planning instructions helped all subjects to cope efficiently with this barrier. The subjects given a planning instruction kept an average of 2.1 appointments, whereas control subjects kept 1.4 appointments; $(F(1/60) = 10.55, p = .001)$. Intelligence had no significant effect with regard to appointment keeping; $(F(1/60) = 2.26, p = .13)$. In addition, intelligence did not interact with planning; $(F(2/60) = 1.47, p = .24)$.

Because being late made a second visit to the shop necessary, punctuality should result in a shorter driving time and working day. The shortest possible driving time of 135 minutes establishes an optimal path between the starting shop (No. 1) and the terminal shop (No. 12). The deviation from this optimal path is shown as a second indicator of performance (Fig. 4). Corresponding to the number of kept appointments, subjects with planning instruction spent on average 59.5 minutes on driving from the starting to the terminal shop. This time is significantly lower than that of the control subjects (99.7 minutes); $(F(1/60) = 14.98, p = .001)$. As can be seen from Fig. 4, the subjects of the planning group, especially high-intelligent ones, are close to the optimal path. Furthermore, a significant effect of intelligence was found; $(F(1/60) = 4.92, p = .03)$, but planning and intelligence did not interact; $(F(2/60) = .40, p = .54)$. However, a comparison of both figures reveals a difference in the relation between the two parameters within the planning group: low-intelligent subjects of the planning group are as punctual as their high-intelligent counterparts. This correspondence is not reflected in the driving time: despite equivalent punctuality, low-intelligent subjects have a longer driving time in the second and third trial.

In addition to these two parameters, there are others indicating the superiority

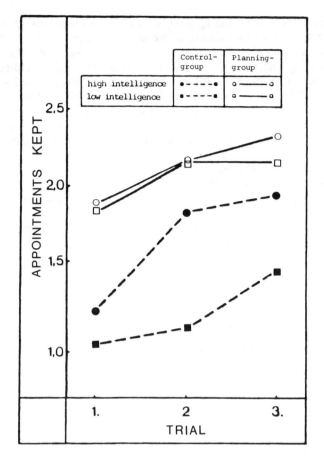

Figure 3 Number of appointments kept, differentiated for the factors planning and intelligence.

of well planned actions: (a) the optimal path was recognized and chosen by 19
(52%) of the subjects with planning instruction already in the first trial and by 22
(61%) in the last trial whereas in the control group, the maximum number of
subjects choosing this path never exceeded 7 (19%) (in the second trial); (b) the
number of repeated visits and suboptimal ways between shops is significantly
lower in the planning group than in the control group ($F(1/60)$ = 5.21, p = .03;
$F(1/60)$ = 14.99, p = .001).

Effort

As predicted, planning induced competence by urging the subjects to analyze,
anticipate, and derive preventive measures (Figs. 5 & 6). The effort invested into
the execution of the plan is indicated by the intensified information processing as
follows:

1. The subjects of the planning group requested the town map more often and for a longer time than the subjects of the control group in the first two trials. Figure 5 shows the number of requests of the town map over trials. The interaction between planning and the repeated measures factor (i.e. trials) indicates that a lower or equal involvement is reached for the planning group in the last trial only ($F(1/120) = 3.66$, $p = .03$). This result is supported by the time spent by the subjects on orientation and planning using the town map (orientation time). Planning subjects have a mean orientation time of 710 seconds per trial, while the subjects of the control group request the town map only for an average of 334 seconds ($F(1/60) = 76.20$, $p = .001$). The temporal distribution of orientation times corresponds with the requests of the town map as shown in Fig. 5. Again, planning and the repeated measures factor interact significantly ($F(1/120) = 14.00$, $p = .01$). No significant main effects of or interactions with intelligence were found for these parameters.

2. The attempts to control the situation are indicated by the number of appointments changed. Figure 6 shows that the punctuality of the planning group is based

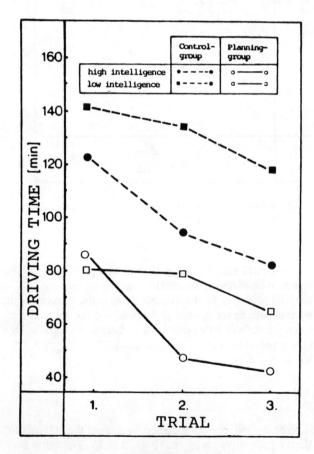

Figure 4 Deviation from the optimal path, differentiated for the factors planning and intelligence.

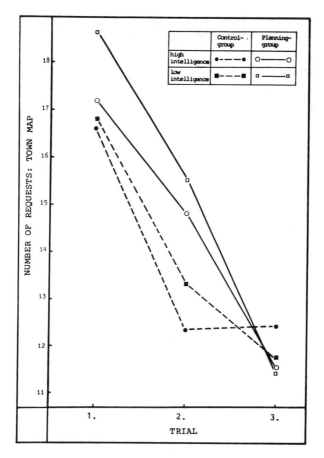

Figure 5 Number of requests of the town map, differentiated for
the factors planning and intelligence.

on the extensive use of the possibility to change appointments; ($F(1/60)$ = 12.78,
p = .001). Mainly due to the marked differences within the control group, a
significant effect of intelligence has to be noted also ($F(1/60)$ = 5.97, p = .02).

3. The intensive orientation and appointment keeping activity of the planning
group is guided by a careful evaluation of available feedback information. The
feedback information about the average time spent on the administrative tasks, a
vital factor with regard to keeping the appointments, was requested by the planning group more than twice as often compared to the control group ($F(1/60)$ =
4.12, p = .05).

Although these data primarily indicate the effort expended during plan execution, it must be noted that the generation of the plan in the planning group was a
long and intensive process: contrary to the control group, the subjects in the
planning group spent considerable time at the starting shop. With an average orien-

tation time of 180 seconds these subjects invest about three times as much time on orientation as controls before they actually start.

Heart Period

The high performance of the planning group is based on intensive information processing at the beginning. Heart period can be regarded as a psychophysiological indicator of the effort expenditure related to these processes and was therefore recorded during the entire experiment. To test whether planning constituted a higher load than other processes (e.g., working on the administrative tasks), we subtracted the mean heart period recorded during planning processes from the mean heart period for one trial. These intraindividual difference scores (cf. Gunn, Wolf, Block, & Person, 1972) are shown in Fig. 7. Two results are of special interest: (a) during the first trial, the subjects of the planning group are more activated than the subjects of the control group; and (b) planning and intelligence

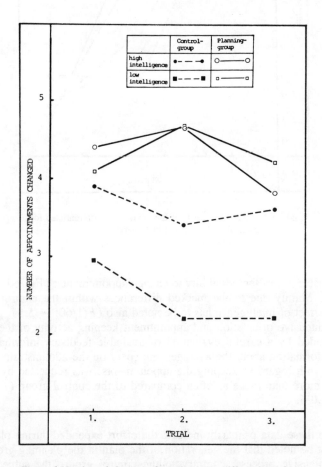

Figure 6 Number of changes of appointments, differentiated for
the factors planning and intelligence.

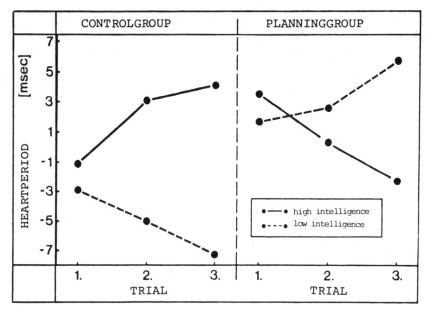

Figure 7 Intraindividual difference of heart period means while planning over trials, differentiated for the factors planning and intelligence.

interact significantly over the trials ($F(2/112) = 3.99, p = .04$). In the planning group, the activation decreases over time for high and increases for low-intelligent subjects, whereas in the control group the activation increases for high and decreases for low-intelligent subjects.

This result has an equivalent in the subjective experience of restitution and relaxation expressed by the subjects (Fig. 8). While there are nearly no differences in the control group, planning facilitated the relaxation of high-intelligent subjects. In contrast, low-intelligent subjects of the planning group seem unable to relax. The interaction between planning and intelligence is significant ($F(1/60) = 6.49$, $p = .02$).

Subjective Experience

The appointments on the time schedule constituted barriers in the task environment. Besides being a threat to the intended sequence of visits, they induced time pressure. Because planning subjects showed competence in making convenient appointments and keeping them, it was reasoned that time pressure should be reduced in this group. After the experiment, the subjects were asked if they experienced time pressure during work. As can be seen from the answers (Fig. 9), within the planning group time pressure is low only for high-intelligent subjects. Low-intelligent subjects of the planning group experienced enhanced time pressure. This interaction is significant ($F(1/68) = 4.59, p = .05$). Further analysis revealed that this time pressure, accompanied by feelings of strain of nervousness, was mainly caused by the threat of failing to keep the appointments: disordinal interactions similar to Fig. 9 were found on a more specific items like "Did you feel nervous because you had to keep the appointments" ($F(1/68) = 6.06$, $p = .02$). Furthermore, parallel findings indicating strain for low-intelligent subjects of the planning group were obtained for several additional rating scales constructed to measure feelings of tension, excitement, and uneasiness.

Obviously, increased competence as expressed in performance is not generally accompanied by enhanced confidence. In the planning group, appointments are competently changed and kept but do not lose their threatening character for low-intelligent subjects. Changes in anxiety can be regarded as an integrative indicator of positive or aversive emotional experience during the experiment (Spielberger, 1972). State anxiety was measured using the German version of the State-Trait-Anxiety-Inventory (Laux et al., 1981) directly before and after the experimental session. The postexperimental scores averaged 43 points for low-intelligent subjects in the planning group and 44 points in the control group while the corresponding means for high-intelligent subjects were 39 (planning) and 40 (control) points, respectively. This effect of intelligence is significant ($F(1/60) = 6.03$, $p = .02$). As there were no differences between low- and high-intelligent subjects at the beginning of the experiment, the postexperimental differences can be attributed to the task induced strain. This is supported by an examination of change scores in state anxiety calculated by subtracting the scores obtained before the

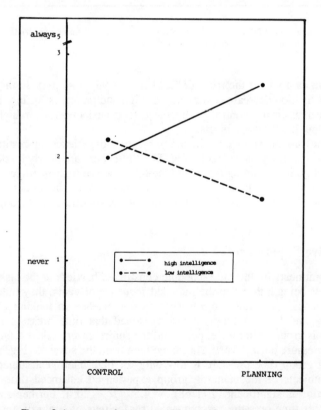

Figure 8 Answers to the statement "I was able to relax during the breaks," differentiated for the factors planning and intelligence.

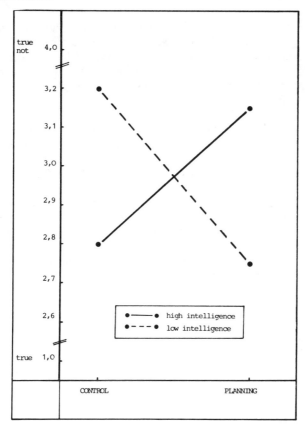

Figure 9 Answers to the statement "I experienced time pressure during work," differentiated for the factors planning and intelligence.

session from the score obtained after the session (Fig. 10). The result confirms that in low-intelligent subjects anxiety generally increased over trials; ($F(1/60)$ = 3.84, p = .053). The interaction between planning and intelligence is not significant. But there is, considering the performance, an important difference between the groups of low-intelligent subjects: for the subjects of the control group, enhanced anxiety is accompanied by a deficient performance, whereas anxiety in the planning group rises despite efficient control and high performance.

DISCUSSION

The complexity of the task environment is expressed in the performance and subjective data of the control group: with no help provided the performance of low-intelligent subjects did not increase over the trials. Their inability to keep appointments and lack of progress leads to a demotivation and emotional withdrawal from the task. Demotivation is expressed by decreasing activation (Fig. 7) and increased anxiety (Fig. 10) while the low scores on questions regarding task specific stressors like time pressure and threat (Fig. 9) indicate that these subjects tried to withdraw from demands. The performance of the high-intelligent subjects of the control group increased slowly and steadily but did not reach the level of planning subjects. This improvement was accompanied by intensified effort expenditure (Fig. 7) and a realistic assessment of the task specific demands. The increasing performance of these subjects shows that coping was possible but difficult without explicit help.

Planning was a notable help for all subjects: already in the first trial, even low-intelligent subjects attained a level of performance which high-intelligent subjects of the control group were unable to reach even after three trials and despite a steady progress (Fig. 4). This result confirms the benefits of planning with regard to performance reported in several studies (e.g. Hacker & Richter, 1981; Hacker, Plath, Richter, & Zimmer, 1978; Hays-Roth, 1980; Skell, 1972).

As expected, planning required considerable effort in this task environment. It must be noted that the effort related to planning is not restricted to the generation of the plan. Despite the fact that 50% of the subjects of the planning group discovered the optimal path before actually beginning the first trial, planning subjects processed relevant information more often and longer during the first two trials (Figs. 5 & 6). This result supports earlier findings (Skell, 1972) that a generated

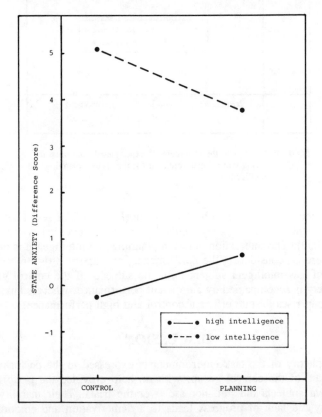

Figure 10 The change in state anxiety reflected in difference
scores between pre- and postexperimental state anxiety,
differentiated for the factors planning and intelligence.

plan is not merely executed, but verified until it proves sufficient and realistic. The load induced by planning is therefore a joint function of the efforts of plan generation and verification.

Considering only the performance data, it can be concluded that planning indeed had a stress-reducing effect: all planners were able to prevent interruptions (Fig. 3) and reduce the work load by minimizing driving time (Fig. 4). In the planning group, however, a marked difference between performance and subjective experience of the subjects, depending on their intelligence, needs further discussion. Only for high-intelligent subjects did planning prove to be beneficial in every respect: expending higher effort in the beginning (Fig. 7), effective strategies were generated. Using these strategies performance increased (Fig. 4), while the psychophysiological effort (Fig. 7) decreased. The warm glow of success is reflected in the subjective experience of the subjects: they report to relax well during the breaks (Fig. 8) and score low on items regarding the experience of time pressure or feelings of threat (Fig. 9).

Performance and subjective data do not, however, correspond for the low-intelligent subjects of the planning group. Despite their increasing ability to keep appointments (Fig. 3), performance decreased over the trials (Fig. 4), while psychophysiological effort increased (Fig. 7). Subjective data reveal that work was accompanied by intensified feelings of threat, time pressure (Fig. 9), and anxiety (Fig. 10).

For low-intelligent persons, planning not only solved, but also generated problems. To make use of the advantages connected with planned action, considerable effort has to be spent on the planning process itself. Increasing activation, feelings of time pressure, and threat indicate that a major portion of their resources was absorbed by the intensive planning process and during the concurrent plant verification in the first trial. As a result of this planning process, they learned the vital role of making appropriate appointments for a working day free of interruptions and committed themselves to further orientation and updating. But having already invested a major portion of their resources in the plan, this commitment became a heavy burden and subjects worked in constant fear of complete exhaustion.

CONCLUSIONS

Summarizing the results, planning cannot unhesitatingly be recommended as a method of stress prevention. The individual is required to bridge a considerable time lag until the investment planning will pay off. Efficiency increases only on a long-term basis but effort has to be spent immediately for the generation of the plan and its verification. This payoff function endangers persons with scarce resources: they will participate fully in the costs but only partially in the profits. While the observer may easily misinterpret their high performance as effective coping, actors judge their success on the background of the psychological costs paid for it. This balance is not necessarily positive and may find its expression in augmented anxiety and feelings of self-doubt.

In general, stress-triggering situations of overload can be avoided if individuals take advantage of the possibilities of controlling task demands by planning. But planning is an investment with an uncertain payoff: depending on the ability of the individual, it may cause emotional strain and generating a plan can be more demanding than a solution by ad hoc strategies.

REFERENCES

Amthauer, R. (1971). *Der Intelligenz-Struktur-Test 70.* Göttingen: Hogrefe.

Bainbridge, L. (1978). Forgotten alternatives in skill and work-load. *Ergonomics, 21,* 169–185.

Byrne, R. (1977). Planning meals: Problem solving on a real data base. *Cognition, 5,* 287–332.

Cooper, C. L. & Payne, R. (Eds.). (1977). *Stress at work.* New York: Wiley.

Dantzig, G. B., Fulkerson, D. R. & Johnson, S. (1954). Solution of a large-scale travelling-salesman-problem. *Operations Research, 2,* 156–187.

French, J. R. P., Rogers, W. & Cobb, S. (1976). A model of person-environment fit. In G. V. Coelho, A. H. Hamburg & J. E. Adams (Eds.), *Coping and adaptation.* New York: Basic Books.

Getzels, J. W. (1979). Problem finding: A theoretical note. *Cognitive Science, 3,* 167–172.

Glass, D. C. & Singer, J. E. (1972). *Urban stress: Experiments on noise and social stressors.* New York: Academic Press.

Greeno, J. G. (1977). The process of understanding in problem solving. In N. J. Castellan, D. B. Pisoni & G. R. Potts (Eds.), *Cognitive theory* (Vol. 2). Hillsdale, NJ: Erlbaum.

Gunn, C. G., Wolf, S., Block, R. T. & Person, J. R. Psychophysiology of the cardiovascular system. In N. S. Greenfield & R. A. Sternback (Eds.), *Handbook of psychophysiology.* New York: Holt, Rinehart & Winston.

Hacker, W. (1978). *Allgemeine Ingenieur- und Arbeitspsychologie.* Berlin: Deutscher Verlag der Wissenschaften.

Hacker, W. & Richter, P. (1981). *Spezielle Ingenieur- und Arbeitspsychologie* (Vol. 2). Berlin: Deutscher Verlag der Wissenschaften.

Hacker, W., Plath, H. E., Richter, P. & Zimmer, K. (1978). Internal representation of task structure and mental load of work: Approaches and methods of assessment. *Ergonomics, 21,* 187–194.

Hays-Roth, B. (1980). *Human planning processes.* Santa Monica, CA: Rand Corporation Report R-2670-ONR.

Hays-Roth, B. & Hays-Roth, F. (1979). A cognitive model of planning. *Cognitive Science, 3,* 275–310.

Kahneman, D. (1973). *Attention and effort.* Englewood Cliffs, NJ: Prentice-Hall.

Laux, L., Glanzmann, P., Schaffner, P. & Spielberger, C. D. (1981) *Das State-Trait-Inventar.* Weinheim: Beltz.

Lazarus, R. S. & Launier, R. (1978). Stress-related transactions between person and environment. In L. A. Pervin & M. Lewis (Eds.), *Perspectives in interactional psychology.* New York: Plenum.

Little, J. D. C., Murty, K. G., Sweeny, D. W. & Karol, C. (1963). An algorithm for the travelling-salesman-problem. *Operations Research, 11,* 972–989.

Mandler, G. A. (1979). Thought processes, consciousness and stress. In V. Hamilton & D. M. Warburton (Eds.), *Human stress and cognition.* New York: Wiley.

Mandler, G. A. & Watson, B. (1966). Anxiety and the interruption of behavior. In C. D. Spielberger (Ed.), *Anxiety and behavior.* New York: Academic Press.

McGrath, J. E. (1976). Stress and behavior in organisations. In M. D. Dunnette (Ed.), *Handbook of industrial and organisational psychology.* Chicago: Rand McNally.

Miller, G. A., Galanter, E. & Pribram, K. H. (1960). *Plans and the structure of behavior.* New York: Holt, Rinehart & Winston.

Miller, S. M. (1979). Controllability and human stress: Method, evidence and theory. *Behavior Research and Therapy, 17,* 287–304.

Newell, A. & Simon, H. A. (1972). *Human problem solving.* Englewood Cliffs, NJ: Prentice-Hall.

Sacerdotti, E. D. (1974). Planning in a hierarchy of abstraction spaces. *Artificial Intelligence, 5,*115–135.

Schank, R. A. & Abelson, H. J. (1977). *Scripts, plans, goals and understanding.* Hillsdale, NJ: Erlbaum.

Schönpflug, W. (1983). Coping efficiency and situational demands. In G. J. R. Hockey (Ed.), *Stresss and fatigue in human performance.* New York: Wiley.

Schönpflug, W. & Battmann, W. (1982). *Psychologische Effekte bei Langzeiteinwirkung von Verkehrslärm.* Berlin: Umweltbundesamt Bericht 82-10501304.

Seligman, M. E. P. (1975). *Helplessness.* San Francisco, CA: Freeman.

Skell, W. (Ed.). (1972). *Psychologische Analysen von Denkleistungen in der Produktion.* Berlin: Deutscher Verlag der Wissenschaften.

Spielberger, C. D. (1972). Anxiety as an emotional state. In C. D. Spielberger (Ed.), *Anxiety: Current trends in theory and research.* Washington, DC: Hemisphere.

Thompson, S. C. (1981). Will it hurt less if I can control it? A complex answer to a simple question. *Psychological Bulletin, 90,* 89–101.

Smith, A. B. ... ...
... ...
Thompson, ...
... ...

19

Information Processing
Strategies for Anxiety Reduction
and Changes of Activation Level
by Systematic Desensitization

U. Neumann
Frei Universität Berlin

J. Schellenberg
Humboldt Universität Berlin

INTRODUCTION

Systematic desensitization (SD) represents a highly effective psychotherapeutic method for the treatment of different neurotic disturbances, especially pathological anxiety. The various possibilities for the therapeutical use of SD, the simple, highly effective and economic applicability led in the last 25 years to an immense number of experimental and empirical investigations. Summarizing the results of these more than 2000 publications, it can be demonstrated that neither indicative disturbance-characteristics (kind, duration, severity), personality-characteristics (introversion/extraversion), nor objective components of the SD-method (relaxation, hierarchy, client-therapist-relation) represent definite determinants of therapy success. Up to now it has to be assessed that SD must be considered as a therapeutical efficient complex of variables but without any possibility of differentiation. Now as before the real process of anxiety- (symptom-) reduction due to SD and also causal conditions of therapy success are not clarified. Until now postulated components of SD efficacy have been characterized as global, heterogeneous, theoretical one-sided and empirical insufficient secured (Wolpe, 1958; Lader and Mathews, 1968; Birbaumer, 1973). SD therapy results in significant changes of emotional experiences and behavior. In order to guarantee a future of optimal and highly effective use of SD methods and to overcome the usual intuitive-pragmatical formation of SD, an analysis of causal conditions of symptom reduction during therapy process is needed.

Following this aim and in the view of existing results about the role of objective SD-components for therapy success and of new results of Cognitive Behavior

---

For the features f_6-personal-situational determined and f_9-emotional-ambivalent no category frequency could be observed. The reasons are discussed by Neumann and Schellenberg (1983).

Therapy (Beck, 1981; Ellis, 1977; Goldfried, 1978; Mahoney, 1977; Meichenbaum, 1979), the investigation of subjective changes provoked by SD (as an in sensu therapy) seems to be necessary. That is why the imagination of the problem (mostly anxiety eliciting) situations during the therapy, the associated internal representation, and information processing have to be analyzed. Consequently, the construct imagery represents the main point of our approach.

Typical for the few existing approaches concerning the analysis of imagery is the use of criterions like clarity, concreteness, controllability, and completeness of details. These criteria and their relation to the therapy success were analyzed by a pre- and postmeasurement with questionnaires. Such a procedure will be called "status-related measurement of imagery" (e.g. Rimm and Botrell, 1969; Davis, McLemore, and London 1970; McLemore, 1972). Using this procedure, significant correlations are more an exception than a rule. Only about 11% of published correlations reached the significance level (r between .30 and .40, see detailed Neumann and Schellenberg, 1983).

Besides the insufficient quality of the results this approach has to be criticized under the aspect of methodology. Using the status-related measurement of imagery it is not possible to registrate the stepwise changes of symptoms during the therapeutical process. Furthermore, published studies only measured formal, in this context, irrelevant, psychological criteria and their relation to therapy success. Cognitive, motivational and emotional components of human behavioral organization were not considered. This reduction of important psychological contents led to therapeutically irrelevant conception of imagery in SD.

Newer results of the Cognitive Behavior Therapy have shown the primary importance of the cognitive aspect for therapy success (Goldfried, 1978; Meichenbaum, 1979). Following this conception an obtained reduction of anxiety has to be regarded exclusively as the result of changed cognitive coping reactions. But the coping reactions were a priori and intentionally manipulated by the investigator. The changes were measured by status relation with questionnaires again. On the one hand it seems to be plausible that during therapy explicit induced changes of cognitive coping reactions will be reflected in the observed results. However, this kind of reasoning represents a dangerous tautology. In this way it is impossible to get any information about the pretended causal importance of the cognitive aspect for therapy success. On the other hand further psychologically important variables of human behavior were not explored and assertions about the therapeutical process are impossible.

In order to investigate the real (causal) importance of the cognitive aspect for therapy success the analysis of the natural development of coping reactions is needed. Thus the present approach has to carry out the analysis of imagery without any a priori inductions and manipulations of coping reactions during SD therapy. But further aspects of human behavior organization have to be considered (discussed later in this text).

In order to explore causal mechanism of therapy success by SD it must be concluded that instead of a status-related analysis of imagery ability and/or the single cognitive aspect, a combined status- and process-related analysis of imagery activity by a theory-founded approach is needed.

According to this, imagination activity in SD should be defined as conscious internal representation of situational and personal aspects of a mostly anxiety-eliciting situation (Lang, 1977). Imagination activity contains an anticipatory aim-

Table 1 Content analytic system of categories with 10 single features (f) for the analysis of the construct imagery activity

Cognitive aspect	Differential-motivational aspect	Emotional aspect
	Function	
Description and assessment	Explaining and reasoning	Intentional-valuation
	In anticipatory behavior organization	
f_1-Description of objective circumstances of the anxiety situation (location, time)	f_5-Personal-determination	f_8-Emotional-positive
f_2-Situational-specific reflections and concrete acting instructions	f_6-Personal-situational-determination	f_9-Emotional-ambivalent
f_3-Situational overlapping reflections and general acting instructions	f_7-Situational-determination	f_{10}-Emotional-negative
f_4-Imaginal (mental) defense and avoidance		

function and acting-function following the unity of cognitive, motivational, and emotional aspects. The cognitive aspect includes the analysis and processing of objective features of a problem situation and derived assessments, conclusions, and interpretations. That is why the cognitive aspect represents the descriptive-assessment-function in the anticipatory behavior organization. The motivational aspect includes the direct personal position to past and future behavior (cause, responsibility, possibility of taking influence, control). Those subjective arguments (explanations of responsibility, determination of causes) are serving for adjustment and aim-determination of behavior and have consequently to be considered primarily as motivation features. So the motivational aspect represents a more explaining-reasoning-function in this form of anticipatory behavior organization. Furthermore the emotional aspect as intentional-evaluation component of imagination activity has to be differentiated.

The three aspects—cognitive, motivational, and emotional—were operationalized in single features by the description of the possible therapeutical relevant meanings of the given definitions. For example, it seems to be reasonable to distinguish situational-specific reflections and general, situational overlapping reflections (cognitive aspect) or positive feelings and negative feelings during the confrontation with anxiety eliciting situations. The obtained 10 single features are illustrated in Table 1 in form of content-analytic system of categories for measurement of process-related imagination activity.

Furthermore, three questionnaires for the status-related analysis of imagination activity were worked out.

The causal analysis of SD therapy success conditions will be incomplete if there will not be an answer to the question of organismic costs (activation level) associated with information processing. Existing investigations (e.g. Lader and Mathews, 1968; Birbaumer, 1973; Lang, 1977) have to be criticized in the following points: (a) there were no simultaneous measurements of psychological and physiological data during therapy process, thus the interaction between the internal representation of a problem situation and changes of activation level represents an open question. The exclusive use (b) of control-group designs give no answer whether different therapy success of experimental groups is associated with different therapy-related changes of activation level in the case of equal treatment conditions. A comparison of extreme groups (treated successful and unsuccessful clients) is necessary. Both changes (c) of activation level overlapping the therapy duration in time and activation changes during general disturbance-irrelevant tasks were not analyzed. Until now a combined status- and process-related analysis of activation before, during, and after SD therapy was missing.

With the present approach it is intended to clarify the following questions: (1) What about the importance of features and aspects of imagination activity for therapy success? (2) Is the therapy success (anxiety reduction) associated with symptom-related decreases of activation level and with decreases of activation level during general tasks (general decrease of activation level)? (3) What about the interactions between the representation of anxiety situations and the physiological level of activation? (4) Does there exist an optimal psychophysiological feature complex determining therapy success? (5) Is the status-related measurement with questionnaires a suitable method to explain therapy success?

METHOD

Subjects

During a 3 year investigation period 35 socially anxious clients were treated with SD. The sample consisted of 14 male and 21 female subjects with finished university education. The mean age of the clients was 31.5 ± 10.4 years. All clients were treated over a period of 12 weeks.

Procedure of Systematic Desensitization

The traditional form of SD (see Wolpe, 1958) was used for therapy. Accordingly 10 anxiety-eliciting situations (anxiety items) of the clients were explored by using a standardized behavior analysis. After that these individual anxiety items were prepared for therapy strictly according to Lang's (1977) principle of the balance between stimulus- and reaction-propositions. The reaction-propositions contained only descriptions of subjective symptoms but no cognitive coping reactions or positive self-instructions (Goldfried, 1978; Meichenbaum, 1979). The anxiety items consisted of an equal number of words ($\bar{x} = 160.4$; standard deviation $s = 6.8$) and were arranged in a so-called anxiety hierarachy with 10 ranks.

During the SD therapy the client is asked to imagine the anxiety items and to react with relaxation. A presentation of an anxiety item consisted of a period of description by the therapist (1.5 minutes), a following period of imagination (1.0 minute) and after that a relaxation period (3.0 minutes). The clients should not interrupt their imagination if they feel subjective trouble during the description period or imagination period. The transition from one anxiety item (rank x) to the next (rank $x + 1$) was executed if the client did not signal anxiety or other unpleasant emotions during the imagination. In this way the clients were confronted step by step (rank by rank) with the anxiety items.

Effectivity of Therapy

An extensive psychodiagnostic test-battery consisting of 8 standardized questionnaires was used for measuring anxiety scores, vegetative symptoms and characteristics of personality. The questionnaires represent internationally well known methods which were adapted to GDR circumstances (e. g. Eysenck, 1965; Fahrenberg, 1970; Geer, 1965; see Helm, Kasielke, and Mehl, 1977; Spreen, 1961).

In order to be able to extract SD-specific internal information processes it is necessary to make a comparison with extreme groups (successful groups vs. unsuccessful groups, i.e., groups with or without therapeutically reduced social anxiety). For this purpose a 4-point measurement design with a pretreatment waiting group was used. That means before starting therapy a first diagnostic measurement (pre 1), a waiting period of 6 weeks (in order to control spontaneous changes of symptoms), and a second measurement (pre 2) had to be carried out. After therapy two measurements and a second waiting period of 4 months were followed (post 1, waiting period, post 2). Using this design no special control groups or waiting groups were needed. Furthermore individual psychodiagnostic feature patterns of the clients (pre 2, post 1) were analyzed by hierarchical cluster analyses, a principal component analysis and analyses of variance. The internal and external validity of the resultant classification of clients into therapy success groups were additionally tested in a behavior test (pre, post) and by means of a catamnestic exploration (post 2) four months after therapy. The behavior test represented a real stress situation and consisted of a free report to an unknown audience with a duration of 5 minutes. All clients heard the theme of the report only immediately before starting. The following indicators of the report were analyzed: (a) total number of spoken words, (b) duration of silence, (c) errors (repetitions, omissions, mistakes in speaking, grammatical errors), and (d) error index (mean number of spoken words without mistakes).

Status-Related Analysis of Imagery Activity

The status-related analysis of the aspects of imagery activity was carried out by using 3 special questionnaires constructed analogous to the 10 features of the process-related analysis of imagery activity. Negative cognitive schemes (Beck, 1981; Ellis, 1977), personal versus situational determination of own behavior (motivational aspect), and emotional valuations of anxiety situations (semantic polarity) were measured with a 7-point rating in the beginning, at the end of SD therapy, and after treatment of item 5 (rank 5) of the hierarchy.

Process-Related Analysis of Imagery Activity

For this purpose the client's descriptions of imagination of the anxiety items (ranks of hierarchy) 1, 3, 5, 6, 8, and 10 were classified sentence by sentence by trained independent judges. For this retrospective classification the above presented content-analytic system of categories with 10 features was used (see Table 1). There was a conformity among judges of $r = .89$.

Peripheral conditions (initial values, ability of verbalization, effects of forgetting, effects of training) which could influence the results were controlled exactly by using a retrospective procedure. A 14-day training period of visualizing was carried out in order to assimilate initial values (baselines). Before starting therapy effects of forgetting and the client's ability of verbalization were tested by asking the clients to imagine not disturbance-related items (e.g. "to lie in the sun and dream" or "how I put a thing into a cupboard"). The analysis of the imagination descriptions given by the clients included in this case the number of recalled parts of the item content. Effects of training which may occur because of a repeated realization of imagination tasks during therapy were controlled by testing if there was an increase of classified assertions in the feature-category system (f_2-f_{10}, see Table 1) independent of therapy success. Without any details it can be maintained that the mentioned peripheral conditions were of no influence on the following results. Consequently, the descriptions of imaginations could be considered as a valid copy of the functional coherence between imagined events (in mind) and recalled events (see Neumann and Schellenberg, 1983).

Process-Related Analysis of Activation Level

Specific-tonic and specific-phasic changes of activation level shall be distinguished in the context of imagined anxiety situations during therapy process. Physiological parameters of heart rate (HR, beat-to-beat-intervals), respiration rate (RR) and electromyographic activity (musculus brachio-radialis of the dominant arm, EMA) were registered across therapy.

Status-Related Analysis of Activation Level

These therapy-overlapping changes of psychophysiological activation (called general-tonic activation level) were analyzed by using pre- and postcomparisons (4 month interval) in the following manner. First, the heart frequency during the stress situations was registered (symptom-related in vivo). Second, the parameters HR, RR and EMA were registered during the client's imagination of anxiety situations (items) before and after therapy (symptom-related in sensu). Third, the three physiological parameters were registered during imagination of two neutral and two pleasing situations and cognitive tasks (general task-related in sensu).

Also in the context of changes of activation level, important peripheral conditions had to be controlled. It concerns all above physiological initial values (baselines), the reliability of physiological parameters, the analysis of activation changes due only to relaxation, nonspecific habituation effects of the parameters, variability of HR evoked by respiration and the test of the physiological data set according to Wilder's (1931; see Birbaumer, 1973) law of initial value. It can be concluded that these tested peripheral conditions did not influence the following physiological results.

RESULTS

Effectivity of Therapy

Both a hierarchical cluster analysis (ward- and single-linkage-method) and a principal component analysis of the individual psychodiagnostic feature patterns resulted in a classification of clients in three different therapy success-groups. (see Fig. 1). The distinction of the three extracted groups is a significant one (ANOVA, $F(2,36) = 89.96$; $p < .05$). Group 1 represents unsuccessful clients without changes of anxiety scores (group unsuccessful, NS, with 8 clients). Group 2 contains clients with positive changes of anxiety scores (group successful, SU, with 15 clients). Clients with high positive changes of test scores form the third group (group highly successful, HS, with 12 clients).

The catamnestic exploration verified the classification also under the aspect of time. In group NS no changes of c-values were obtained. In contrast to this a decrease of anxiety and of vegetative symptoms in the groups SU and HS could be demonstrated by a decrease of c-values on an average of 1.48 and 3.31 respectively.

The indicators of the clients' report during the stress situations showed generally significant positive changes in the three client-groups (pre- and postcomparisons, Wilcoxon, $p < .05$). This concerns an increase of the total number of spoken words and a decrease of the duration of silence. The amount of obtained changes varied depending on therapy success (number of words: HS pre 312, post 547, NS pre 253, post 357; duration of silence: HS pre 132.7 seconds, post 26.7

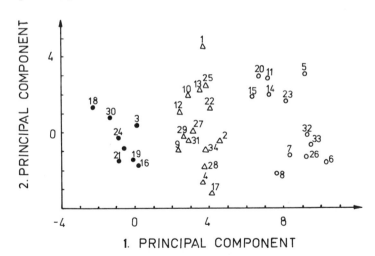

- • Not successful client-group (NS)
- Δ Successful client-group (SU)
- o High successful client-group (HS)

Figure 1 Projection of 35 clients on the first and second principal component using individual psychodiagnostic feature patterns and the marking of therapy success-cluster (Ward- and single-linkage-method).

Table 2 The results of the status-related analysis of the construct imagery activity*

Questionnaire	Cognitive		Differential-motivational		Emotional
	Measurement of negative cognitive schemes		Measurement of personal attribution of causes		Semantic polarity
Compared interval	Pre-rank 5	Rank 5-post	Pre-rank 5	Rank 5-post	Pre-post
High successful group	s^a	ns^b	ns	s	s
Successful group	s	ns	s	ns	s
Not successful group	ns	s	s	s	s

*p = .05 (Wilcoxon and Wilcox).
[a]s = Significant change.
[b]ns = Not significant change.

seconds, NS pre 156.5 seconds, post 90.3 seconds). In spite of a small increase of the number of words and a small decrease of silence duration in group NS (compared with the groups HS and SU) clients of that group made more errors (pre 27.5, post 48.5). Thereby an increase of the number of faulty spoken words (error index) could be observed. In the groups HS and SU there was no change in the amount of errors and additionally there was a clear higher number of spoken words. The consequence was a significantly positive change of error index.

Status-Related Analysis of Imagery Activity

Table 2 gives an overview of significant changes of questionnaire results within the therapy success-groups. It could be pointed out (H-test) that there were no significant differences between the groups before starting therapy (pre 2). The results show a reduction of negative cognitive schemes, an increase of personal determination of own behavior, and a new positive emotional valuation of anxiety situations not depending on success of therapy (critical differences, Wilcoxon and Wilcox). Consequently, a significant distinction of the three groups seems to be impossible with questionnaire methods.

Process-Related Analysis of Imagery Activity

Figure 2 illustrates the importance of the 10 features of the content-analytic system of categories for the therapy success strongly marked in a quantitative manner. Except for feature 1 (description of objective circumstances of a situation) all features allow a significant distinction between the three client-groups. Comparing the groups the features exhibit either an increasing category-frequency (f_3, f_4, f_7, f_{10}) from group HS, SU to NS or a decreasing category-frequency (f_2, f_5, f_8). According to this, in a discriminant analysis two different combinations of

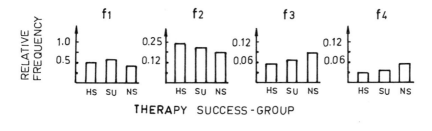

THERAPY SUCCESS-GROUP

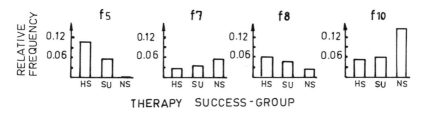

THERAPY SUCCESS-GROUP

HS - High successful client-group
SU - Successful client-group
NS - Not successful client-group

Figure 2 Relative frequency of the process-related features of imagery activity measured over the whole therapeutical process.

features could be extracted especially relative to their different value for the discrimination of the therapy success-groups (T^2 statistic, see Table 3). The two combinations of features represent the basic conditions of therapy success by SD and have to be interpreted as fundamentally different information-processing strategies for anxiety reduction. Only in this way can the clear discrimination between the process-related features and the therapy success-groups be explained. Furthermore, this conclusion has to be tested under the aspect of development of the strategies during therapy process (see Fig. 3). The variance-analytic verification of the learning process within the groups in the first and second part of therapy is

Table 3 Discriminant-analytic T^2-values of process-related features of imagery activity

Aspects	Feature configuration 1			Feature configuration 2
		T^2	T^2	
Cognitive	f_2-Situational-specific reflections and concrete acting instruction	7.08	1.89	f_3-Situational-overlapping reflections and general acting instructions
Differential-motivational	f_5-Personal-determination	4.56	2.05	f_7-Situational-determination
Emotional	f_8-Emotional-positive	3.82	.044	f_{10}-Emotional-negative

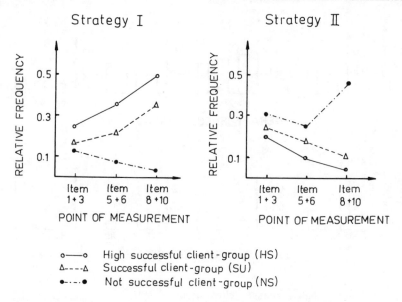

Figure 3 Development of strategies within the therapy success-groups during therapy process.

documented in Table 4. Summarizing these results it can be demonstrated that the therapy success-groups principally differ not only with regard to the quantity of the strategies 1 and 2 but also with regard to the development of the strategies in the groups during therapy process.

Process-Related Analysis of Activation Level

The specific-tonic changes of HR, RR, and EMA during therapy process for the first, middle and last presentation of anxiety situations are illustrated in Fig. 4.

Table 4 Variance-analytic verification of the development of the strategies 1 and 2*

	Strategy 1			Strategy 2		
	High successful group	Successful group	Not successful group	High successful group	Successful group	Not successful group
	$F_{(2,22)}$ $= 18.89$	$F_{(2,28)}$ $= 16.67$	$F_{(2,14)}$ $= 2.23$	$F_{(2,22)}$ $= 14.20$	$F_{(2,28)}$ $= 23.33$	$F_{(2,14)}$ $= 11.00$
First half of therapy	$s\uparrow$[a]	No change	No change	$s\downarrow$[b]	No change	No change
Second half of therapy	$s\uparrow$	$s\uparrow$	No change	No change	$s\downarrow$	$s\uparrow$

*$p < .05$.
[a]$s\uparrow$ Significant increase; [b] $s\downarrow$ Significant decrease.

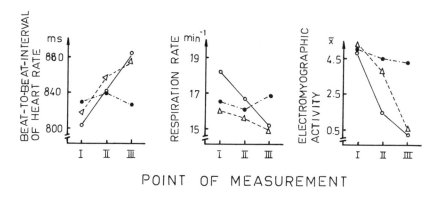

POINT OF MEASUREMENT

o—o   High successful client-group (HS)
△--△ Successful client-group (SU)
•--• Not successful client-group (NS)

I, II, III — First, second, last presentation of the description period
averaged over all anxiety items

Figure 4 Specific-tonic changes of activation level during therapy process (description period of anxiety items).

The variance-analytic verification of the obtained changes resulted in a significant reduction of activation level in the description period of anxiety situations, both for the groups HS and SU but not for the group NS [group HS; HR − $F(2,22)$ = 40.78, $p < .05$; RR − $F(2,22)$ = 21.53, $p < .05$; EMA − $F(2,22)$ = 42.99, $p < .05$; group SU: HR − $F(2,28)$ = 20.54, $p < .05$; RR − $(2,28)$ = 9.12, $p < .05$; EMA − $F(2,28)$ = 21.91, $p < .05$]. Equal results could be obtained in the imagination period; significant reductions of activation level for the groups HS and SU (an increase of beat-to-beat intervals in HR, a decrease of RR and a reduction of EMA) but no significant physiological changes in any registrated parameter for group NS.

For all groups there were no significant specific-phasic changes of activation level in the description period nor in the imagination period. That means that no specific-phasic reaction patterns typical for the strategies could be found. Furthermore it was impossible to point out a progressively decreasing trend of activation level over therapy (stepwise from one anxiety item to the next). The results of the physiological parameters in both periods show that the reductions of activation level are constant and stable. This occurs in each anxiety item in the same manner from the first to the last item of hierarchy despite increasing subjective difficulty from item to item.

Status-Related Analysis of Activation Level

Physiological general-tonic changes in the stress situations (symptom-related in vivo) are illustrated in Fig. 5. First of all there were no significant differences of the mean values of heart frequency between the groups at the beginning of SD-

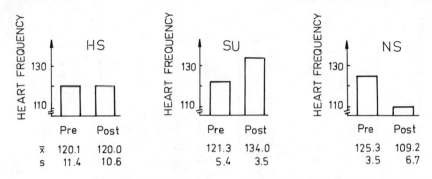

POINT OF MEASUREMENT — BEFORE (PRE) AND AFTER (POST)
THERAPY

HS - High successful client-group
SU - Successful client-group
NS - Not successful client-group

Figure 5 General-tonic changes of activation level (heart frequency) during the stress situations.

therapy (pre 2, H-test). Additionally, no significances between the variances of the prestress situation and the poststress situation of the client groups could be observed (*t*-test).

The main results of the stress situations were very surprising. It could be observed (pre- and postcomparisons) that there was a significant increase of heart frequency in group SU (t (14) = 7.82, p < .05), a significant decrease of heart frequency in group NS (t (7) = 4.82, p < .05), and no significant changes of heart frequency in group HS. Subjective anxiety reduction can also be connected with a tonic increase of heart frequency in a real stress situation (see group SU).

The pre- and postcomparisons (analyses of variance) of the results of symptom-related tasks in sensu showed significant decreases of activation level of the groups HS and SU—illustrated in increasing beat-to-beat-intervals of HR, decreasing RR and EMA. There were no significant changes of the physiological parameters in the group NS. The results correspond with the changes of activation level obtained during therapy process.

General-tonic changes of activation level in symptom-irrelevant tasks in sensu (neutral and pleasing situations, cognitive task) could not be observed for the groups HS and SU nor for the group NS. The results of HR given an exemplary demonstration: HS pre, 860.27 milliseconds, post 872.93 milliseconds; SU pre, 852.25 milliseconds, post, 865.91 milliseconds; NS pre, 831.46 milliseconds, post, 851.03 milliseconds.

DISCUSSION

The comparison of extreme groups which is necessary for analyzing the subjective basic conditions of therapy success by treatment with SD led to clear and corresponding results. Cluster analysis, catamnestic explorations and observed changes of clients' behavior in stress situations are indicators for a high internal and external validity of the discrimination of three therapy success-groups (client-groups).

In contrast to this it must be established that the attempt of discriminating the therapy success-groups by means of a status-related analysis of imagery activity with questionnaires did not bring interpretable results. For example, independent from therapy success there was both a significant reduction of negative cognitive schemes (operationalization of feature f_2) and a new positive emotional valuation of anxiety situations in the semantic polarity. With regard to theoretical positions of Cognitive Behavior Therapy (Beck, 1981; Ellis, 1977) our results encourage the following statement: the usual a priori induction or manipulation of cognitive aspects (coping reactions) and the following exclusive status-related measurement of changes have to be considered as not sufficient for analyzing information processing occurring during therapy. There are some doubts whether a status-related measurement of effects can clarify the underlying psychotherapeutical process. The often postulated isomorphy-relation between psychotherapeutical effect and psychotherapeutical process has to be tested with regard to its validity.

This argumentation is moreover supported by the results of the process-related analysis of imagery activity. Two different feature configurations could be extracted which are contrary with respect to the content. The configurations are representing in principle different information-processing strategies developed during therapy. Both strategies guarantee a permanent discrimination of the three therapy success-groups in the course of therapy. Consequently, the strategies have to be explained as causal conditions of therapy success by SD. Thereby strategy 1 is definitely pointed out as the primary causal condition for anxiety reduction. Strategy 1 is characterized by the interaction of concrete reflections and self-instructions (f_2 of the cognitive aspect) with a personal determination of own behavior (f_5 of the motivational aspect). This interaction results in an emotionally positive value of anxiety situations. Strategy 2, characterized by global reflections and self-instructions (f_3), by mental avoidance (f_4), by situational determination of own behavior (f_7) and by emotionally negative value (f_{10}) possesses another importance for anxiety reduction: this information processing strategy is hindering the process of anxiety reduction (see group NS, especially the second half of therapy).

Both strategies are changing distinctly during the therapy in all groups. The direction of changing is a criterion of therapy success or no therapy success. Clear differences between the three therapy success-groups could already be observed after the first half of therapy time. In group HS the increase of learning for anxiety reduction associated with strategy 1 is significant both in the first and in the second half of therapy (see Table 4). Additionally, there is a significant reduction of strategy 2. Therefore the learning progress of group HS represented on the basis of the strategies can be regarded as constantly under both the quantitative aspect and under the aspect of time. The learning course in group SU is more unstable. Significant changes of strategies were first obtainable during the second half of therapy. In group NS, contradictorily, no learning course could be observed (increase of strategy 2 in the second half of therapy).

These differences of the development of the two strategies in the three client-groups have to be interpreted in that way, how stable for utilization and how tight the strategies are integrated in the individual behavior repertoire. That is why it is necessary to speak of a different degree of interiorization of the strategies. Especially in comparing the groups HS and SU, a quite different degree of interiorization of the strategies can be observed. This explanation is also confirmed by the fact that the anxiety reduction associated with the strategies is in correspondence both with the indicators of the clients' report during the stress situation and with the group-classification.

According to this, all changes of activation level have to be interpreted. The therapy success determined by the strategies ($r = .87$) is associated with clear decreases of activation level (increase of HR, decrease of RR and EMA) during the imaginations of anxiety items in the therapy process (see Fig. 4). Contrary to this, in case of no subjective anxiety reduction (group NS) there were no significant changes of activation level. It can be stated that the extent of reduction of physiological activation level varied depending on the level of interiorization of the information processing strategies for anxiety reduction. There is clear evidence that changes of activation level have causally been evoked by the information processing strategies, especially by strategy 1 (see group NS vs. groups HS and SU). This statement must be precise, because the quantity of the observed reductions of activation level depends on the degree of interiorization of the strategies (see group HS vs. SU). The more interiorized the strategies, the higher the associated reduction of activation (the correlation coefficient between therapy success and process-related physiological changes reaches $r = .68$).

Corresponding to this the unexpected changes of heart frequency in the stress situations (general-tonic activation level in vivo) should be explained. The significant increase of heart frequency in group SU (see Fig. 5) can only be interpreted as an organismic adequate mobilization reaction to cope with the situation. The smaller degree of interiorization of strategy 1 and the competition with strategy 2 which has to be suppressed led to an increase of organismic effort. In group HS the automatic handling of strategy 1 and the failing competition with strategy 2 resulted in no significant physiological changes in the stress situations. The unexpected decrease of activation level in group NS can be regarded as a therapeutically acquired organismic defense reaction because of no development of anxiety-reducing strategies.

The further results in the context of general-tonic activation level (symptom-related and general task-related in sensu) were in accordance with the given interpretations. A decrease of physiological parameters in symptom-related tasks could be demonstrated only for the groups HS and SU but not for the group NS. Physiological changes during general tasks could not be observed for the two successful client-groups nor for the group NS. Stating this it must be doubted that in a physiological view neurotic anxiety can be defined as a general chronic overactivation (see Lader, 1980). Our results are favoring the definition of neurotic anxiety as a specific, situationally limited state of physiological overirritation. Both the failure of changes of activation in general tasks (in sensu) and the reduction of activation in symptom-related tasks on the level of activation observed during general tasks support this definition. Furthermore the results of the stress situations pointed out the validity of a positive relationship between anxiety reduction and the increase of organismic effort in human behavior organization. Consequently, anxiety and overactivation as well as anxiety reduction and reduction of activation do not exhibit the traditional one-to-one relationship.

Summarizing the results, the present approach represents a possibility for giving a theory-founded and empirically tested explanation of SD therapy success. The clients' internal information processing in anxiety situations and associated changes of activation level could be demonstrated as causal conditions of therapy success provoked by SD. Some results of discriminate analyses give an illustration of this fact. Using the optimal psychophysiological feature configuration a reordering of clients into the therapy success-clusters (groups) succeeded in about 90% of the cases. These results give a good explanation of the high multiple correlation between therapy success, strategy 1 and HR changes during therapy process of $r = .89$.

CONCLUSIONS

According to practical therapeutical work with SD, conclusions could be derived in the following direction: not the variation of objective frame conditions (hierarchy, relaxation) of SD will guarantee a further optimizing of the therapy method but only the explicit handling of extracted basic conditions of therapy success.

In the future further investigations have to explore the causal conditions evoking the development of extracted strategies. In this context new information could be expected by the investigation of real-life situations.

REFERENCES

Beck, A. T. (1981). *Kognitive Therapie der Depression*. München, Wien and Baltimore: Urban & Schwarzenberg.

Birbaumer, N. (1973). Uberlegungen zu einer psychophysiologischen Therorie der Desensibilisierung. In J. C. Brengelmann and W. Tunner (Eds.): *Behaviour Therapy-Verhaltenstherapie, praktische und theoretische Aspekte*. München and Wien: Urban & Schwarzenberg, pp. 136–164.

Davis, D., McLemore, C. W. & London, P. (1970). The role of visual imagery in desensitization. *Behaviour Research and Therapy, 1,* 11–14.

Ellis, A. (1977). Rational-Emotive Therapy: Research data that support the clinical hypothesis of RET and other modes of cognitive behaviour therapy. *Journal of Consulting Psychology, 1,* 2–42.

Eysenck, H. J. (1965). *Manual of the Eysenck Personality Inventory*. London: University Press.

Fahrenberg, J. (1970). *Das Freibnurger Persönlichkeitsinventar (FPI)-Hand-anweisung*. Göttingen: Hogrefe.

Geer, J. H. (1965). The development of a scale to measure fear. *Behaviour Research and Therapy, 3,* 45–53.

Goldfried, M. R. (1978). Reduction of test anxiety through cognitive restructuring. *Journal of Consulting and Clinical Psychology, 1,* 32–39.

Helm, J., Kasielke, E. & Mehl, J. (1977). *Neurosendiagnostik*. Berlin: Deutscher Verlag der Wissenschaften.

Lader, M. H. (1980). Körperliche Reaktionen auf Lebensveränderungen-ihre Beziehungen zu psychischen und psychosomatischen Störungen. In Katschnig, H. (Ed.): *Sozialer Stress und psychische Erkrankung*. München: Urban & Schwarzenberg, pp. 260–305.

Lader, M. H. & Mathews, R. M. (1968). A physiological model of phobic anxiety and desensitization. *Behaviour Research and Therapy, 6,* 411–421.

Lang, P. J. (1977). Imagery in therapy: An information processing analysis of fear. *Behaviour Therapy, 8,* 862–886.

Mahoney, M. J. (1977). Cognitive therapy and research. A question of questions. *Cognitive Therapy Research, 1,* 5–16.

McLemore, C. W. (1972). Imagery in desensitization. *Behaviour Research and Therapy, 1,* 51–57.

Meichenbaum, D. H. (1979). *Kognitive Verhaltensmodifikation*, München, Wien and Baltimore: Urban & Schwarzenberg.

Neumann, U. & Schellenberg, J. (1983). *Zur Analyse des Rekonstruktes Vorstellungstätigkeit in der SD unter kognitivem, motivationalem und emotionalem Aspekt. Eine psychophysiologische Untersuchung mit Relevanz für das a-priori-Konzept der KVT*. Unpublished Dissertation, Humboldt University Berlin.

Rimm, D. C. & Botrell, J. (1969). Four measures of visual imagination. *Behaviour Research and Therapy, 1,* 63–70.

Spreen, O. (1961) Konstruktion einer Skala zur Messung der manifesten Angst in experimentellen Untersuchungen. *Psychologische Forschungen, 26,* 205–223.

Wilder, J. (1931). Das "Ausgangswert-Gesetz", ein unbeachtetes biologisches Gesetz und seine Bedeutung für Forschung und Praxis. *Zeitschrift für Neurologie, 137,* 317–338.

Wolpe, J. (1958). *Psychotherapy by reciprocal inhibition,* Stanford, CA: Stanford University Press.

V

STRESS, EMOTIONS, AND HEALTH

20

Personality and Stress as Conjunct Factors in the Genesis of Lung Cancer

H. J. Eysenck
University of London

INTRODUCTION

The notion of psychosomatic disease, that is, that mental factors can give rise to physical manifestations of disease, has had a great deal of attention in recent years. It has also aroused a good deal of opposition and even ridicule, perhaps because it has been linked by many people with psychoanalytic speculations, projective tests and other methods and theories having little scientific basis. From the point of view of the Cartesian duality of body-mind, of course, psychosomatic disease presents both a paradox and an insoluble problem, but this is not the way behaviorists look at the problem of the body-mind relation in any case. As T. H. Huxley once pointed out: "No psychosis without the neurosis," that is, no mental event without an underlying physical event. On this basis, the "psychic" part of psychosomatics would be regarded as also based on *somatic* events, probably in the central and autonomic nervous systems, and hence the oxymoron "Psycho-somatic" would become a simple tautology: "Somato-somatic", which would present no philosophical or other difficulties (Eysenck, 1980a,b,c).

The so-called psychosomatic diseases have usually been disorders of a relatively minor kind, such as headaches, ulcers, asthma, and allergies; the idea that personality factors might be connected with more serious diseases like cancer, although occasionally put forward, has not been widely accepted or researched. Yet there appears to be some reasonably convincing evidence linking lung cancer, and possibly other cancers, with personality, and it will be the purpose of this chapter to look at this evidence, and try to suggest some causal connections which, although speculative, are certainly testable, and which, if along the right lines, may prove of both theoretical and practical importance. Lung cancer is usually linked with extraneous environmental factors, such as cigarette smoking, and it is often asserted that if people could be prevented from smoking, then something like 300,000 lives in the USA, (or 50,000 in the U.K.) could be saved. The argument involved usually relies on epidemiological evidence, and is methodologically and statistically suspect (Burch, 1976; Eysenck, 1980d; Oeser, 1979). It is not suggested, of course, that such agents as ultraviolet and ionizing radiation, chemical carcinogens and autogenic viruses are not concerned with the development of malignant tumors, but when we look at any specific agent, such as cigarette smoke, the evidence makes it clear that these agents are neither *necessary* nor *sufficient* causes. Out of 10 heavy smokers, only 1 will die of lung cancer; hence, smoking clearly is not a sufficient cause. Out of 10 people who die of lung cancer, one will be a nonsmoker; hence, smoking is clearly not a necessary cause. The situation is a very complex one, and simplistic solutions may do more harm than good in arriving at the truth. Certainly, none of the orthodox views about lung cancer would have predicted the observed personality relationships, and none could even begin to explain them.

In 1836, W. H. Walshe published a book in which he claimed that there seemed to be general agreement on the proposition that "women of high colour and sanguine temperament were more subject to mammary cancer than those of different constitutions". This suggestion, that there might be a relationship between cancer and personality, was taken up by several authors in recent years, but much of the work suffered from poor methodology and poor statistics; in particular, the tests used, usually of a projective kind, were unreliable and of unknown and very suspect validity. Nevertheless, they suggested to some research workers that cancer-prone persons were characterized by emotional reserve, and possibly by the suppression of emotional reactions; some references to this early work are given by Eysenck (1980d). Walshe's reference to the sanguine temperament suggests a relationship between cancer and extraversion; the temperament labeled *sanguine* by the ancient Greeks corresponds in many ways to the modern notion of extraversion (Eysenck, 1970). The first study to explicitly look at these relationships was reported by Kissen and Eysenck (1962). The patients tested were 116 male lung cancer patients, and 123 noncancer controls, both groups being patients at surgical and medical chest units, tested before diagnosis. Patients and controls were subdivided into age groups before a comparison of scores was made. Patients were also subdivided into those with or without psychosomatic disorders. As regards extraversion, there were no differences between cancer and control patients without psychosomatic disorders but, in comparing the groups with psychosomatic disorders, it was found that the cancer group was considerably more extraverted than the control group. This high extraversion score was found in all age groups, but most strikingly in the middle one (55 to 64 years). For the patients without psychosomatic disorders, a similar trend was found for the two younger age groups, but this was reversed in the oldest of the three control groups; as this group was also the smallest, containing only 10 cases, this may be a statistical freak, leaving open the possibility that in another sample a similar trend might be found to that in the younger groups.

As regards neuroticism, the control group had much higher N scores than the cancer group, regardless of psychosomatic involvement. It was also found that the two psychosomatic groups (cancer and control), had somewhat higher neuroticism scales than did the nonpsychosomatic groups. The results were highly significant, and suggested that the hypothesis linking cancer with lack of emotional expression was in the right direction.

Kissen (1964a,b) took up the investigation of the relationship between lung cancer and that of neuroticism; he again found that lung cancer patients had very significantly lower N scores than did the other patients. Kissen published a rather interesting paper (1964b) in which he tabulated lung cancer mortality rates per

100,000 men aged 25 and over by levels of neuroticism scores. He found that people with very low scores had a mortality rate of 296, those with intermediate scores a mortality rate of 108, and those of very high scores a mortality rate of only 56! The results obtained by him are again statistically significant, and suggest amazingly great differences between people having high and low scores respectively, on the neuroticism scale of the MPI. Very low scorers on N have about a six-fold possibility of developing lung cancer as compared with very high scorers. Most of these differences are almost entirely independent of cigarette smoking; if anything, high N scores smoke more than low N scores.

Kissen has published several other papers (e.g. 1963a,b; 1968) reporting general reviews of methodological problems, and an extension of the work so far discussed, using different methods of personality assessment. The general findings trend to support the original relationship between lung cancer patients, but this tend was rather weak.

Berndt, Günther, and Rothe (1980) have reported large-scale investigations, following up the work of Kissen and Eysenck, an undertaking at the Central Institute for Cancer Study of the Academy of Sciences of the DDR. Using Eysenck's EPI questionnaire, Berndt and his colleagues compared a control group of patients with patients who, after completion of the questionnaires, were found to suffer from breast cancer or bronchial carcinoma. He used a female control group of 953 patients, which was compared with a breast cancer group of 231. The male control group numbered 195, and the male bronchial carcinoma group 123. The female bronchial carcinoma group was very small, numbering only 20, which makes it almost impossible for this group to give significant differences from the controls.

In all three comparisons, the cancer patients had neuroticism scores *lower* than the controls, with the differences reaching a $p > .01$ level for the breast cancer group, and the male bronchial carcinoma group; for the female bronchial carcinoma group, the difference was significant on a one tail test, permissible because the study was testing a specific hypothesis. We may conclude that the Berndt investigation gives results essentially identical with those of the Kissen and Eysenck study.

Hagnell (1962) reported on the results of an epidemiological survey of the 2,550 inhabitants of two adjacent rural parishes in the south of Sweden. The survey was started in 1947 and included an interview during which a personality assessment was made on each subject. Ten years later, the procedure was repeated and the subsequent history of each subject examined. During this follow-up, it was observed that a significantly high proportion of women who had developed cancer had been originally extroverted in ratings. Hagnell was not concerned with lung cancer as such, but used amalgams of all cancers.

His finding was further strengthened by a study published by Coppen and Metcalfe (1963). Working in a general hospital, they used patients in two gynecological wards and two surgical wards, and outpatients attending the surgical clinic. Questionnaires were first filled in by the patients and at the end of the investigation the questionnaires were collected and scored and the diagnosis of each patient obtained. Forty-seven patients had malignant tumours; thirty-two had cancer of the breast, four had cancer of the uterus, eleven had cancer in other parts of the body. Two control groups were used, and care was taken that these should fall into the same age group as those with cancer. The cancer group had significantly higher extraversion scores than both control groups but here there was no difference in the neuroticism scores. It is possible that neuroticism is particularly highly related to lung cancer, and not to other types of cancer; there is not available a really large scale study comparing personality profiles of cancer patients where the malignant growths are in different parts of the body.

Greer and Morris (1975) also employed breast cancer cases in their investigations; they used consecutive series of 160 women in hospital for breast tumor biopsy, using a detailed structured interview and various tests, including the MMPI. The published results are based on statistical comparisons between 69 patients found at operation to have breast cancer, and a control group of the remaining 91 patients with benign breast disease. The principal finding was a significant association between the diagnosis of breast cancer and a behavior pattern, persisting throughout adult life, of abnormal release of emotions. "This abnormality was, in most cases, extreme depression of other feelings; extreme expression of emotions, though much less common, also occurred in a higher proportion of cancer patients than in the controls."

Another application, this time concerning lung cancer patients alone, was reported by Abse, Wilkins, Castle, Buston, Demars, Brown, and Kirschner (1974). In their study, 59 male patients were interviewed, 31 of them were later diagnosed as having lung cancer and 28 as having relevance to the hypothesis in question. Age was considered an important variable, and so patients and controls were subsequently divided into old and young. Scores were derived from the interview process. A highly significant differentiation was obtained, particularly for younger groups. Differentiation between lung cancer and control patients became *more* pronounced when comparisons were restricted to those patients who smoked more than one pack of cigarettes a day. The major differentiation showed that the (young) cancer patients showed a marked restriction in their interpersonal relationships, and reported less adequate or frequent sexual relationships. They appeared to have more problems in the handling of dependency needs. All of these differences were much less marked in older patients who were relatively difficult to distinguish from their age-matched controls.

In a recent study, Blohmke, Engelhardt, and Skelzer (1984) evaluated questionnaires of over 800 male patients with bronchial carcinoma. At the time of the examination, the patients questioned were not aware of the malignant nature of their illness. Healthy controls, and patients with various malignant lung diseases were used as comparison groups, and for the study reported, only results from smokers were investigated, making up 419 lung carcinoma cases, 419 healthy controls, and 162 nonmalignant lung cancer patients. Age and social status were controlled. The main finding of the study was that "carcinoma patients are less nervous, and show a higher degree of social conformity than persons of the two control groups". Blohmke and co-workers further concluded that "a low degree of external control is a further characteristic trait of smoking carcinoma patients". This agrees with the common finding that measures of internal versus external control usually show a correlation between external control and neuroticism so that the greater internal control of cancer patients would be expected.

These are, of course, all retrospective studies. A prospective study has been published in Yugoslavia by Grossarth-Maticek, Kanasir, Schmidt, and Vetter (1982), in which a sample of people in a small town were given personality inventories, their smoking history noted, and a follow-up study carried out to determine the cause of death for those who died. The questionnaire largely measured rational and nonemotive attitudes to life, and low scores (i.e., unstable emotional reactions) were found to be *inversely* related to death from lung cancer, and even more strongly and *negatively* related to death from all cancers. In fact, the statistical significance of these relations was very much stronger than the relation of smoking to death from cancer in general, or lung cancer in particular. A number of other, less direct, studies are mentioned by Eysenck (1980d), such as those by Ure (1969), Pettingale, Greer, and Tee, (1977), Achterberg, Simonton, and Matthews-Simonton, (1976), Krasnoff (1959), Evans, Stein, and Marmorston (1965), and Stavraky (1968). There seems to be little doubt, then, that there are relationships between cancer and personality, particularly with neuroticism (negative) and extraversion (positive), although it would be important to be sure of the relative specificity of these relationships, that is, whether there is a general cancer personality, or whether different types of cancer have different relationships with personality.

There appears to be a relationship between cancer and the third major dimension of personality, namely psychoticism. Bahnson & Bahnson (1964a) have suggested in the title of their paper that we may consider "cancer as an alternative to psychosis", although in Bahnson & Bahnson (1964b) they also found some support for the theory that denial and repression of primitive impulses and disturbing emotions is far more frequent in patients with malignant neoplasms. Eysenck (1980d) has reviewed the evidence linking psychosis, and in particular schizophrenia, with an absence of lung cancer, and indeed all cancers. Altogether it has been shown that the percentage of mental patients who died from cancer was considerably lower than that of the general population; 15% of deaths were caused by malignant neoplasms in the general population compared with 4.9% among the mentally ill. Other randomly selected causes of death such as cardiovascular disease and diabetes, showed no appreciable differences. In England and Wales, about 20% of deaths are caused by neoplasms compared with 6.9% of deaths in mentally ill patients. For Scotland, the figures are 17% and 5% respectively.

Schizophrenic patients seem to be more resistant to neoplasms than are patients suffering from other forms of mental illness. Of 2,145 state hospital deaths over 15 years, 60 were neoplastic and only 6 of these were among schizophrenics. The Kashenka hospital in Moscow reports the incidence of deaths from malignant neoplasm in schizophrenics to be only 0.1 to 0.2% from a yearly population of 2,500. Levi and Waxman (1975) had other supportive evidence. Eysenck (1980d) reviewed some of the theories regarding the apparent protection which schizophrenia and psychosis generally confers on patients as far as cancer is concerned; here we need only conclude that such a relationship exists and that it should be a task of primary importance to discover to what extent this relationship can be replicated in people scoring high and low respectively on the Eysenck psychoticism scale. Such a study has not, to our knowledge, been done so far, but a fair prediction may be made that high p scorers should be found less frequently among lung cancer patients than among controls.

One last study may be mentioned in connection with the relationship between the lung cancer and personality, because it contrasts the influence of smoking and personality, and it extends the relationship from a within-nation to a between-nation comparison. The study in question was carried out by Rae and McCall (1973), and relates extraversion and neuroticism on the one hand, and smoking on the other, to lung cancer. The authors attempted to demonstrate that an association between cancer and personality holds internationally. National extraversion and anxiety levels in 8 advanced countries, and statistics of the number of cigarettes smoked per annum in these countries were compared with mortality rates per 1000 of the population due to lung cancer (male and female separately) and cancer of the cervix (females only).

Rank-order correlations were then calculated between national personality levels and cancer mortality rates. There was a highly significant correlation between extraversion and male lung cancer (0.66) and between extraversion and female lung cancer (0.72). Corresponding correlations for cigarette consumption and lung cancer, for males and females combined, were quite insignificant (0.07). For cancer of the cervix the correlation with extraversion was again significant (0.64), whereas for cigarette consumption it was insignificant (0.45). Correlations between anxiety and lung cancer were negative and significant in both sexes (-0.52 and -0.71). This is an exceptionally interesting paper which deserves to be followed up on a much larger scale, showing that the findings of Kissen and Eysenck of the relationship between personality and lung cancer obtain also on an international scale.

Many of the writers in this field have followed Kissen in hypothesizing that it is *repression* or *suppression* of emotion which is the causal link in the relationship between neuroticism and lung cancer. On this point the writer ventured to disagree with Kissen, suggesting that low N scores may mean nothing but the absence of emotion; the simple score tells us nothing about the possible repression or suppression of emotion. This point is still unresolved, although there now exist methods of settling it. Weinberger, Schwartz, and Davidson, (1979) and Gudjonsson (1981) have shown that "sensitizers" and "repressers" of emotional reactions differ with respect to their L and N scores, with sensitizers having high N and low L scores, and repressers having low N and high L scores. This should make it possible to subject the argument between Kissen and Eysenck to an empirical investigation and solution.

It is difficult at first sight to find a rationale for explaining the observed relationships between cancer, on the one hand, and extraversion, absence of neuroticism and absence of psychoticism, on the other. Indeed, some of these relationships appear paradoxical. As we shall see, there is some evidence linking stress with cancer (Bammer and Newberry, 1981), and it would seem that neuroticism producing life-long feelings of anxiety and depression, and psychosis, producing severely disabling symptoms, would both produce very strong stresses indeed, so that one might have expected the correlations between cancer and neuroticism and psychoticism, to be positive, rather than negative. As regards extraversion, there is no obvious relationship one way or the other, and the usual interpretation of extraversion as being related to low arousal level in the cortex does not at first sight seem to provide an adequate explanation for the relationship with cancer. It may be useful to look at the literature relating stress to cancer in more detail, before trying to resolve these problems.

Sklar and Anisman (1981) have summarized the evidence, showing that there is a relationship between stress and cancer. Thus DeChambre (1981) has shown that several aspects of social conditions are capable of affecting cancer development in mice. It has been shown, for instance, that spontaneous mammary cancer and leukemia can be enhanced by isolation of animals. Pulmonary tumors induced by benzole-(a)-pyrene are similarly affected. The development of transplanted ascitistumors is promoted by changes from grouped housing to isolation. Other findings indicated renal involvement and psychosocial effects in ascititumors. The work summarized by DeChambre indicates immunological involvement; if an immunological attack on tumor cells is weakened by psychosocial stress, less cell lysis will occur. Riley (1981) has come to similar conclusions in his studies of psycho-neuro-immunological factors in neoplasmia. He concludes his survey by saying that "Some of the biological consequences of emotional or anxiety stress result in adverse influences upon identifiable elements of the mouse immune system". By utilizing an appropriate tumor-host model having an immunological equipoise that permits the detection of modest changes in the immunocompetence of the host, he demonstrated a tangible increased risk of the stress subjects with respect to either incipient or overt malignancies.

Jensen (1981) summarizes results from three research programs on the effects of stress in response to viruses. Experiments with mice showed that avoidance learning and confinement produced cumulative stress effects which increased their susceptibility to viral infections. Stressful conditions increased tumor incidence in response to polyoma virus, and stress conditions which influence virus susceptibility also impaired skin homograft rejection, bacterial phage clearance, inflammatory response and interferon production.

Bammer (1981) has reviewed evidence to show that stress can increase metastasis in animals, and there is also some evidence that this is true for humans. This can happen either by the physical action of the stressor or by stress-induced impairment of functions. Sklar and Anisman (1979, 1981), conclude from the review of the evidence that although many animal tumor systems had been shown to be responsive to stress, the animal studies have used such a variety of procedures that drawing general conclusions is difficult. They suggested much of the diversity in animal stress-cancer findings can be explained by differences between studies in the stressors and background environmental conditions employed.

In relation to the development of cancer in humans, retrospective studies have shown that life stress events frequently precede the appearance of forms of neoplasia, for example, Bahnson & Bahnson (1964), Greene (1966), Horne and Pickard (1979), and Jacobs and Charles (1980). Greene and Swisher (1969) succeeded in eliminating genetic factors by looking at leukemia in monozygotic twins discordant for the illness, and found that psychological stress was an important feature in the origins of this disease. Reviews by Bloom, Asher, and White (1978) give a good survey of literature.

One of the stressors most frequently studied has been loss of spouse and here again there are a number of studies (Bloom, Asher, and White, 1978; Greene, 1966; LeShan, 1966; Lombard & Potter, 1950; Murphy, 1952; Peller, 1952; Ernster, Sacks, Selvin, and Petrakis, 1979) showing that cancer appeared in higher than expected frequency among such individuals.

Eysenck (1983) has suggested the possibility that we might be dealing with an "inoculation" effect in relation to the determination of cancer by stress. There is good evidence that we must carefully distinguish between chronic and acute stress, and a failure to do so has led to the many divergent findings reported in the literature. Sklar and Anisman (1981) state that "Enhancement of tumor development has usually been reported in studies using acute, uncontrollable physical stress, chronic social stress or stimulating housing conditions. Chronic uncontrollable physical stress has tended to be associated with tumor inhibition. There is considerable correspondence between brain neuro-chemical responses to stress and cancer development under stress. Stress increases the synthesis and utilisation of compounds such as norepinephrine; if the synthesis does not keep pace with utilisation, brain depletion is observed. Brain neuro-chemical activity and cancer development have been shown to respond similarly to the difference between acute and chronic stress, to the availability of coping responses and, in some cases, to social conditions". They also found that there is evidence for changes in immune functioning under stress which causes response to neurochemical hormonal and tumor development effects. The neurosystems affected by stress are involved in hormone increase and immune reactions. Eysenck (1983) gives many examples of the inoculation effects of chronic stress in both the medical and psychological literature, and has elaborated this hypothesis in a later paper (Eysenck, 1984). He refers to the work of Newberry, Frankie, Beatty, Maloney and Gilchrist (1972), Newberry, Gildown, Wogan, and Reese (1976), Pradhan and Ray (1974), and Ray and Pradhan (1974) as indicating some evidence for the inhibitory effects of stress on tumor reduction. Other studies dealing with the inhibitory effects of shock on tumor growth are those of Jamasbi and Nettsheim (1977), Peters (1975), Peters and Kelly (1977), Marsh, Miller, and Lamson (1959), and Newberry, Frankie, Beatty, Maloney, and Gilchrist (1972). Other writers have used different stressors with similar results, for example, Gershben, Benuck, and Shurrager (1974), Molomut, Lazere, and Smith (1963), Pradhan and Ray (1974), Newberry, Gildown, Wogan, and Keese, (1976), and others; a good summary of all this work is given by Sklar and Anisman (1981).

As these last authors point out, "in addition to the inhibitory effects of chronic stress on tumour cell proliferation, (Newberry, 1978) it seems that adaptation to the effects of the stress occurs with repeated exposure." They give an example from their own work to show that a single session of inescapable shock, administered 24 hours after transplantation, enhances the growth of P15 mastocytoma; however, in mice that have been previously exposed to shock for either four or nine days preceding cell transplantation, the effects of subsequent acute stress were eliminated. "These data appear to indicate that adaptation to stress occurs at some level in the physiological process that governs stress-induced tumorigenic changes". As regards metastasis, it seems that acute stress may exacerbate metastasis, but under conditions of chronic shock administration, the formation and growth of metastasis is inhibited (Zimel, Zimel, Petrescu, Ghinea, and Tasca, 1977), very much in the way that chronic stress inhibits the induction and growth of primary tumors.

The observed relationships between chronic and acute stress on the one hand, and the development of neoplasms on the other, must raise the question of how emotional, psychosocial or anxiety-stimulated stress influences the growth of neoplasia. It is well known that such stress induced plasma concentration of adrenal corticoids and other hormones through well-known neuroendocrine pathways (Riley, 1981). It is well known that these corticoid concentrations injure elements of the immunological apparatus, and this may leave the subject vulnerable to the action of latent oncogenic viruses, newly transformed cancer cells, or other incipient pathological processes that are normally held in check by intact immunological apparatus. Riley (1981) describes studies supporting the view that increased concentrations of adrenal corticoids have adverse effects on the thymus and thymus-dependent T-cells, that is, elements which constitute the major defense system against various neoplastic processes and other pathologies. These studies also show that anxiety-stress can be quantitatively induced, and the consequences measured by specific biohcemical and cellular effects, always provided that proper base lines of these conditions are obtained in the experimental animals by the use of low-stress protective housing and handling techniques.

Sklar and Anisman (1981) summarized their very extensive review by reporting that there appears to be a remarkable parallel between the stress effects on neurochemical, hormonal, and immunological functioning. "Acute stress results in depletion of catacholamines and increases of ACh, increases synthesis and secretion of hormones, and immunal suppression. Adaptation in these biological mechanisms is observed in chronic stress, such that normal levels of functioning opposite to those induced by acute stress are apparent." They go on to consider biochemical and other causes of these effects, but it would take us too far to enter into discussion of these. Let us merely note that there is some evidence that acute stress reduces tumor *growth,* chronic stress tumor *reduction.* This effect is what we intend by the term "inoculation" effects; it is as if the previous experience of stress inoculates the animal against subsequent stress, making it less effective, or even reversing the biological changes produced.

It is suggested that along these lines we may find an explanation of the apparently paradoxical negative relationship between cancer on the one hand and neuroticism and psychosis/psychoticism on the other. How about the positive relationship between stress and extraversion? Eysenck (1984) has suggested that this may be accounted for by the remarkable fact that recent studies have shown that the immune reaction can be conditioned along Pavlovian lines (Ader, 1981; Ader & Cohen, 1975; Cohen, Ader, Green, and Bovbjerg, 1979; Rogers, Reich, Strong, & Carpenter, 1976; Wayner, Flannery, & Singer, 1978). These remarkable studies, and the more recent ones of Bovbjerg, Ader, and Cohen, (1982) have demonstrated the possibility of suppressing the immune reactions through Pavlovian conditioning, but they also seem to indicate that the immune reaction could be equally well strengthened through Pavlovian conditions—indeed, in everyday life, immune suppression is much less likely to occur than immunal enhancement possibly through chronic stress reactions, as pointed out above. If this were to be so, then clearly introverts, who form conditioned responses more quickly and more strongly than extroverts, (Eysenck, 1967), will benefit from this, and be more likely to acquire the strengthened immune reaction than would extroverts. Thus the reason for the greater susceptibility of extroverts to neoplasia may be their failure to acquire a conditioned immune reaction as regularly as do introverts; this would account for the observed correlation between cancer and extraversion.

It should be noted that the postulated effects of conditioning might also affect the negative correlation between neuroticism and lung cancer. Under certain specified conditions, strong emotions also facilitate the conditioning process, and hence anxiety and neuroticism can be found positively correlated with conditioning, (Spence & Spence, 1966). Thus, strong emotions may mediate better conditioning of immune reactions in high N scorers. The intense levels of emotion necessary to produce these effects are most likely to be found under conditions of environmental stress.

Though much in this paper is highly speculative, some of the postulated relationships, such as those between personality and cancer, are supported by relatively large collections of empirical data. These data seem to cry out for a theory to integrate them into the larger body of literature concerned with the genesis of carcinomas. However speculative, the relationships suggested here do have a basis in fact, such as the differentiation between acute and chronic stress, the contradictory effects of stress on the origin and growth of cancers, and the conditionability of the immune reaction. Whether these relationships will, in the long run, turn out to be as suggested here is, of course, another matter; only further research will be able to settle this issue.

REFERENCES

Abse, D. W., Wilkins, M. M., Castle, R., Buston, W. D., Demars, J., Brown, R. S., & Kirschner, L. G. (1974). Personality and behavioral characteristics of lung cancer pateints, *Journal of Psychosomatic Research, 18,* 101–113.

Achterberg, J., Simonton, O. C., & Matthews-Simonton, S. (1976) *Stress, psychological factors and cancer.* Fort Worth, TX: New Medicine Press.

Ader, R. (Ed.) (1976). *Psychoneuroimmunology.* New York: Academic Press.

Ader, R., & Cohen, N. (1975). Behaviorally conditioned immuno-suppression. *Psychosomatic Medicine, 37,* 333–340.

Bahnson, C. B. & Bahnson, M. B. (1964a). Cancer as an alterative to psychoses. In D. M. Kissen & I. I. Le Shan (Eds.), *Psychosomatic aspects of neoplastic disease.* Philadelphia: Lippincott.

Bahnson, C. B. & Bahnson, M. B. (1964b). Denial and repression of primitive impulses and of disturbing emotion in patients with malignant neoplasms. In D. M. Kissen & I. I. Le Shan (Eds.), *Psychosomatic aspects of neoplastic disease.* Philadelphia: Lippincott.

Bammer, K., (1981). Stress, spread and cancer. In K. Bammer & B. H. Newberry (Eds.), *Stress and cancer* (pp. 137–163).

Bammer, K., & Newberry, B. H. (1981). *Stress and Cancer.* Toronto: C. J. Hogrefe.

Berndt, H., Günther, H., & Rothe, G. Person: (1980). Ocjleotsstruktur nach Eysenck bei Kranken mit Brustdrüsen und Brochialkrebs und Diagnosever-zö durch den Patienten. *Archiv für Geschwulstforschung, 50,* 359–368.

Blohmke, M., Engelhardt, B., & Skelzer, O. (1984). Psychosocial factors and smoking risk factors in lung carinoma. *Journal of Psychosomatic Research, 28,* 221–229.

Bloom, B. L., Asher, J. J., & White, S. W. (1978) Marital disruption as a stressor. A review and analysis. *Psychological Bulletin, 85,* 867–894.

Bovbjerg, D., Ader, R., & Cohen, N. (1982). Behaviorally conditioned suppression of a graft-versus-host response. *Proceedings of the National Academy of Science, 79,* 583–585.

Burch, P. R. T. *The biology of cancer. A new approach.* Lancaster: MTP Press.

Cohen, N., Ader, R., Green, N., & Bovbjerg, D. (1979). Conditioned suppression of a thymus-independent antibody response. *Psychosomatic Medicine, 41,* 487–491.

Coppen, A., & Metcalfe, M. (1963). Cancer and extraversion. *British Medical Journal, 6 July,* 16–19.

DeChambre, R. P. (1981) Psychosocial stress and cancer in mice. In K. Bammer & B. H. Newberry (Eds.), *Stress and Cancer.* (pp. 43–58) Toronto: C. J. Hogrefe.

Ernster, V. L., Sacks, S. T., Selvin, S., & Petrakis, N. L. (1979). Cancer incidence by marital states: U. S. Third National Cancer Survey. *Journal of the National Cancer Institute, 63,* 567–585.

Evans, R. B., Stein, E., & Mormorston, J. (1965). Psychological-hormonal relationships in men with cancer. *Psychological Reports, 17,* 7–15.

Eysenck, H. J. (1967) *The biological basis of personality.* Springfield: C. C. Thomas.

Eysenck, H. J. (1970) *The structure of human personality.* London: Metheun.

Eysenck, H. J. (1980a). Man as a biosocial animal: Comments on the sociobiology debate. *Political Psychology 2,* 43–51.

Eysenck, H. J. (1980b). The bio-social model of man and the unification of psychology. In A. J. Chapman & D. M. Jones, (Eds.), *Models of Man.* Leicester: The British Psychological Society.

Eysenck, H. J. (1980c). The bio-social nature of man. *Journal of Social and Biological Structures, 3,* 125–134.

Eysenck, H. J. (1980d). *The causes and effects of smoking.* London: Maurice Temple Smith.

Eysenck, H. J. (1983). Stress, disease and personality: The inoculation effect. In C. L. Cooper (Ed.), *Stress Research,* (pp. 121–146). New York: Wiley.

Eysenck, H. J. (1984). Personality, stress and lung cancer. In S. Rachman (Ed.), *Contributions to medical psychology* (Vol. 3). London: Pergamon Press.

Gershben, L. L., Benuck, I., & Shurrager, P. S. (1974) Influence of stress on lesion growth and on survival of animals bearing parental and intracerebral leukemia L1210 and Walker tumors. *Oncology, 30,* 429–435.

Greene, W. A. (1966). The psychosocial setting of the development of leukemia and lymphoma. *Annals of the New York Academy of Science, 125,* 794–801.

Greene, W. A., & Swisher, S. N. (1969). Psychological and somatic variables associated with the development and course of monozygotic twins discordant for leukemia. *Annals of the New York Academy of Science, 164,* 394–408.

Greer, S., & Morris, T. (1975). Psychological attributes of women who develop breast cancer: A controlled study. *Journal of Psychosomatic Research, 19,* 147–153.

Grossarth-Maticek, R., Kanasir, O. T., Schmidt, P., & Vetter, H. (1982). Psychosomatic factors in the process of cancerogenesis. *Psychotherapy and Psychosomatics, 38,* 284–302.

Gudjonsson, G. H. (1981). Self-reported emotional disturbance and its relation to electrodermal reactivity, defensiveness and trait anxiety. *Personality and Individual Differences, 2,* 47–52.

Hagnell, O. (1962). Cancer in a Swedish village: A followup study. *Svenska Laki-Tidu, 58,* 492–498.

Horne, R. L., & Picard, R. S. (1979) Psychosocial risk factors for lung cancer. *Psychosomatic Medicine, 41,* 503–514.

Jacobs, T. H., & Charles, E. (1980) Life events and the occurrence of cancer in children. *Psychosomatic Medicine, 42,* 11–24.

Jamasbi, R. J., & Nettsheim, P. (1977). Non-immunological enhancement of tumour transplantability in x-irradiated host animals. *British Journal of Cancer, 36,* 723–729.

Jensen, M. M. (1981). Emotional stress and susceptibility to infectious diseases. In K. Bammer & B. H. Newberry (eds.), *Stress and cancer.* (pp. 59–70). Toronto: C. J. Hogrefe.

Kissen, D. M. (1963a). Personality characteristics in males conducive to lung cancer. *British Journal of Medical Psychology, 36,* 27–36.

Kissen, D. M. (1963b). Aspects of personality of men with lung cancer. *Acta Psychotherapeutica, 11,* 200–210.

Kissen, D. M. (1964a). Relationship between lung cancer, cigarette smoking, inhalation and personality. *British Journal of Medical Psychology, 37,* 203–216.

Kissen, D. M. (1964b). Lung cancer, inhalation and personality. In D. M. Kissen & C. L. Le Shan (Eds.), *Aspects of neoplastic disease.* London: Pitman.

Kissen, D. M. (1968). Some methodological problems in clinical psychosomatic research with special refeence to chest disease. *Psychosomatic Medicine, 30,* 324–335.

Kissen, D. M., & Eysenck, H. J. (1962). Personality in male lung cancer patients. *Journal of Psychosomatic Research, 6,* 123–137.

Krasnoff, A. (1959). Psychological variables in human cancer: A cross-validation study. *Psychosomatic Medicine, 21,* 291–296.

LeShan, L. L. (1966). An emotional life history pattern associated with neoplastic disease. *Annals of the New York Academy of Sciences. 125,* 780–793.

Levi, R. N., & Waxman, S. (1975). Schizophrenia, epilepsy, cancer, methionine, and folate metabolism. Pathogenesis of schizophrenia. *The Lancet, 5 July,* 11–13.

Lombard, H. L., & Potter, E. A. (1950). Epidemiological aspects of cancer of the cervix: Hereditary and environmental factors. *Cancer, 3,* 960–968.

Marsh, J. T., Miller, B. E., & Loamson, G. B. (1959). Effects of repeated brief stress on growth of Ehrlich carcinoma in the mouse. *Journal of the National Cancer Institute, 22,* 961–977.

Molomut, N., Lazere, F., & Smith, L. W. (1963). Effect of audiogenic stress in mice. *Cancer Research, 23,* 1087–1101.

Murphy, D. P. (1952). *Heredity in uterine cancer.* Cambridge, MA: Harvard University Press.

Newberry, B. H. (1978) Restraint-induced inhibition of 7,12-dimethylbenz(a)anthracene induced mammary tumors: Relation to stages of tumor development. *Journal of the National Cancer Institute, 61,* 725–729.

Newberry, B. H., Frankie, G., Beatty, P. A., Maloney, B. D., & Gilchrist, J. C., (1972). Mammary tumours. *Psychosomatic Medicine, 34,* 295–303.

Newberry, B. H., Gildown, J., Wogan, J., & Reese, R. L. (1976). Inhibition of Huggins tumours by force restraint. *Psychosomatic-Medicine, 38,* 155–162.

Oeser, vonH. (1979) *Krebs: Schicksal oder Verschulden?* Stuttgart: Georg Thieme Verlag.

Peller, S. (1952). *Cancer in men.* New York: International University Press.

Peters, L. J. (1975). Enhancement of syngeneic murine tumour transplan-tation by whole body irradation-a non-immunological phenomenon. *British Journal of Cancer, 31,* 293–300.

Peters, L. J. & Kelly, H. (1972). The influence of stress and stress hormones on the transplantability of a non-immunogenic syngeneic murine tumor. *Cancer, 39,* 1482–1488.

Pettingale, K. W., Greer, S., & Tee, D. H. (1977) Serum, IGA and emotional expressions in breast cancer patients. *Journal of Psychosomatic Research, 21,* 395–399.

Pradhan, S. N., & Ray, P. (1974) Effects of stress on growth of transplanted and 7,12-dimethylbenz(a)anthracene-induced tumours and their modification by psychotropic drugs. *Journal of the National Cancer Institute, 53,* 1241–1245.

Rae, G., & McCall, J. (1973). Some international comparisons of cancer mortality rates and personality: A brief note. *The Journal of Psychology, 85,* 87–88.

Ray, P., & Pradhan, S. N. (1974). Growth of transplanted and induced tumours in rats under a schedule of punished behaviour. *Journal of the National Cancer Institute, 52,* 575–577.

Riley, V. (1981). Psychoneuroendocrine influences of immuno-competence and neoplasia. *Science, 212,* 1100–1109.

Rogers, M. P., Reich, T. B., Strong, T. B., & Carpenter, C. B., Behaviorally conditioned immunosuppression: Replication of a recent study. Psychosomatic Medicine, 38, 447–452.

Sklar, L. S., & Anisman, H. (1979). Stress and coping factors influence tumour growth. *Science, 205,* 513–515.

Sklar, L. S., & Anisman, H. (1981). Stress and cancer. *Psychological Bulletin, 89,* 369–406.

Spence, J. T., & Spence, K. W. (1966). The motivational components of manifest anxiety: Drive and drive stimuli. In C. D. Spielberger (Ed.), *Anxiety and behaviour.* London: Academic Press.

Stavraky, K. M. (1968). Psychological factors in the outcome of human cancer. *Journal of Psychosomatic Research, 12,* 251–260.

Ure, D. M. (1969). Negative association between allergy and cancer. *Scottish Medical Journal, 14,* 51–64.

Walshe, W. H. (1836). *Nature and treatment of Cancer.* London: Macmillan.

Wayner, E. A., Flannery, G. R., & Singer, G. (1978). Effects of taste aversion conditioning on the primary antibody response to sheep red blood cells and Brucella abortus in the albino rat. *Physiology and Behavior, 21,* 995–1006.

Weinberger, R. A., Schwartz, G. E., & Davidson, R. J. (1979), Low-anxious, high-anxious, and repressive coping styles: Psychometric patterns and behavioural and physiological responses to stress. *Journal of Abnormal Psychology, 88,* 369–380.

Zimel, H., Zimel, A., Petrescu, R., Ghinea, E., & Tasca, C. (1977). Influence of stress and of endocrine imbalance on the experimental metastasis. *Neoplasma, 24,* 151–159.

21

Risky Health Behavior: Negative Subjective Competence of Cigarette Smokers

K. L. P. De Soomer and P. B. Defares
University of Wageningen

INTRODUCTION

In their review of research on behavioral risk modification, Leventhal and Cleary (1980) emphasize the need for new approaches for modifying chronic risk behaviors, such as smoking. Leventhal and Cleary assign particular importance to "the complex psychological and physiological processes underlying smoking and the tremendous individual differences in these processes" (p. 375). The authors state:

> New approaches are needed to deal with *the emotional structures* involved in the mainte-
> nance of smoking. The development and addition of these innovations to the already considera-
> ble armamentarium could result in a fairly dramatic increase in the practical success of anti-
> smoking efforts and a substantial increase in the sophistication of our theoretical models for
> educational intervention in other risk-inducing life-style behaviors. (p. 397)

We agree with Leventhal and Cleary that it is important to study how smokers think and feel about their smoking behavior, and how they view themselves vis-à-vis their smoking habit. The fact that many people try to quit, and fail to do so, suggests considerable ambivalence on the part of smokers. They want to quit, seeing the negative side of their habit, but they are unable to do so. An essential question is, "Why is it so hard to quit smoking?" One reason for this difficulty is that there is a positive side to the habit: People enjoy smoking. They feel that they benefit from it, in addition to being harmed by it. At the anecdotal level, smokers can see negative as well as positive sides to their smoking behavior. Other relevant factors in this regard are smokers' beliefs with respect to the different areas of health, social life and sense of self-esteem or competence. The beliefs of smokers

The authors highly appreciate the participation of W. R. Bowerman in preparing the pilot study and interpreting the results (De Soomer et al., 1983, unpublished manuscript). A grant from the Nether-lands Organization for the Advancement of Pure Research (ZWO) allowed him two monthly visits to our Department in Wageningen.

and the cognitions they maintain about themselves and the effects of smoking or quitting smoking on various aspects of their lives seem most relevant. The causal attributions smokers make concerning themselves are crucial determinants for the maintenance of risky behavior. Therefore, in addition to knowing the effects that people attribute to smoking per se, it is important to determine the degree to which people attribute the effects of smoking to themselves. Thus, smoking may be often linked to self-evaluations, guilt, and feelings of competence or helplessness.

It is also important to evaluate the extent to which smokers feel that their own smoking behavior, and their responsibility for it, has implications for positive and negative self-evaluations. Smokers may feel, for example, that their smoking habit bolsters their self-confidence or impairs it, or that nonsmoking might undermine feelings of competence. To the extent a person feels responsible for smoking and to which this habit has an effect on self-evaluation, a "second-order" self-evaluation concerning smoking might arise.

Bowerman's theory of subjective competence (Bowerman, 1978, 1981; see also De Soomer, Defares, 1984) provides a framework for investigating the issues at hand. We will briefly describe the theory and then indicate how aspects of it were used to gain insight into the positive and negative self-referent belief structures of smokers concerning their smoking behavior.

SUBJECTIVE COMPETENCE THEORY

Beliefs in subjective competence theory are called self-referent causal attributions and are structured as follows:

1. Action attributions acknowledge the occurrence or nonoccurrence of some behavior as being due to, or originating with, the self as an actor.
2. Effect attributions link the occurrence or nonoccurrence of some affectively neutral event to some action (which may be seen as occurring, or as not occurring, in any particular instance).
3. Affect attributions link the occurrence of a positive or negative affect to the occurrence of some effect.

While each of these beliefs or attributions is neutral in itself, as far as its implications for self-esteem are concerned, combinations of these beliefs can have potent implications for self-evaluation. For example, a person may believe that he or she is wholly responsible for the fact that he or she smokes (action attribution), that smoking leads to lung disease (effect attribution) *and* that lung disease is painful (affect attribution). This combination of beliefs, each of which is neutral in regard to self-evaluation, will jointly result in a negative self-evaluation, such as "I am freely doing something that will hurt me".

Figure 1 shows a series of three causal attributions: The actor (smoker) attributes smoking to himself ("I am smoking cigarettes"); the actor believes that smoking cigarettes is causally linked to lung disease; and the actor also believes that lung disease is painful. It should be noted that the second and third attributions are general beliefs, linked only to the self by their combination with the first belief. While each belief is innocuous in itself, as far as self-evaluation is concerned, the

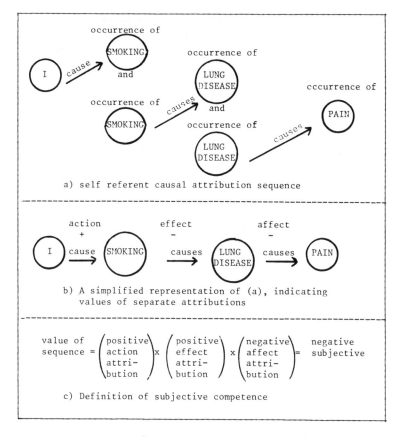

Figure 1 A *negative* subjective competence structure for a cigarette smoker.

three in combination are clearly negative in terms of implications for sensible action ("Why I am smoking? It is foolish").

Figure 1 illustrates how the three qualitatively different attributions may be linked together into an attribution sequence expressing positive or negative subjective competence beliefs. The positive or negative valence of subjective competence belief is defined as the product of the values of the three attributions elements: action, effect, and affect.

Positive action attribution, positive effect, negative affect, results in a negative outcome, $(+) \times (+) \times (-) = -$, and amounts to a negative subjective competence attribution "I am smoking cigarettes, which causes painful lung disease." In a formal model, the eight possible structures of subjective competence can be represented as in Table 1.

As stated earlier, the effect attribution connects the occurrence of an effect with the preceding action or nonaction. It is evident that the particular nature of the effect would then bear stronger relevance for the subject, if more personal involvement is implicated.

What aspects of the life-space of the smoker, to borrow a phrase from Lewin,

Table 1 Formal model of eight possible structures of subjective competence

Action	Effect	Affect	Subjective competence structure
	Positive		
committing the act (+)	effects (+)	positive (+)	+ + + = +
committing the act (+)	prevents (−)	negative (−)	+ − − = +
noncommitting (−)	effects (+)	negative (−)	− + − = +
noncommitting (−)	prevents (−)	positive (+)	− − + = +
	Negative		
committing the act (+)	effects (+)	negative (−)	+ + − = −
committing the act (+)	prevents (−)	positive (+)	+ − + = −
noncommitting (−)	effects (+)	positive (+)	− + + = −
noncommitting (−)	prevents (−)	negative (−)	− − − = −

might be relevant within this context? Since it is widely believed that smoking is harmful for one's physical well-being, aspects of health implications may be of great relevance in this context.

Another important area pertains to self-esteem, which is directly linked to subjective competence. Smoking may either enhance self-esteem as is sometimes suggested in tobacco advertising, or smoking may degrade self-esteem, as is the case when on is unable to quit smoking and feels ashamed about failing. A third set of items, covering yet another area, relates to social contacts. Positive and negative implications also pertain to smoking behavior in this respect. Smoking may create a cozy atmosphere, but smoking may also come fervently under attack by non-smokers, with the implication that smoking may endanger social acceptance and respect.

For each of the three value dimensions (health, self-esteem, and social contacts), eight items were constructed reflecting the eight structures of subjective competence as presented in Table 1. The complete list of subjective competence items comprises 24 items, 12 expressing beliefs of positive competence, and 12 of negative competence.

According to the subjective competence theory, competence refers to the capacity of the subject to transact with the environment in such a manner that this results in maintenance, growth or bloom (positive competence) or the very opposite, negative competence. A general assumption of the theory is that individuals are motivated to protect themselves from self-degradation; they attempt such self-protection by enhancing their perceived positive subjective competence (PSC) and by reducing their perceived negative subjective competence (NSC).

Ultimately, however, we are not so much interested in the sum scores of positive and negative beliefs separately, but rather in the integrated end score, in which the degree of overall negativity is represented.

This final overall score should not be computed, however, by means of simple subtraction of negatives from positives, as was originally suggested by Bowerman.

Instead, a more adequate procedure amounts to the following. The 12 scores of positive beliefs are summed as $\Sigma P = \Sigma(\text{items } 1\text{--}12)/12$. The same holds for the 12 scores of negative beliefs, $\Sigma N = \Sigma(\text{items } 13\text{--}24)/12$. The maximal subscore ΣP can theoretically be $60/12 = 5$, and the minimum score $12/12 = 1$. Simple subtraction of $\Sigma P - \Sigma N$ would inevitably lead to contaminated outcomes in cases of equal sum scores, as can be simply demonstrated in the following examples. The end scores (5-5), (3-3), and (1-1) all would amount to zero. The extreme scores 5 and 1 on the negative beliefs (ΣN), however, evidently have different implications.

The overall score for negativity, therefore, should be computed in such a manner that the proportionality is taken into account in a weighted end score, which is the case in the following formula: $\text{NSC} = (\Sigma N) \times [5 - (\Sigma P - \Sigma N)]$. The most favorable outcome (maximal ΣP and minimal ΣN) according to this formula would be $(1) \times [5 - (5 - 1)] = 1$. And the most unfavorable outcome (minimal ΣP and maximal ΣN) would be $(5) \times [5 - (1 - 5)] = 45$. In the examples of equal scores on ΣP and ΣN, the outcomes are, in the $(5 - 5)$ case in the $(5) \times [5 - (5 - 5)] = 25$; in the $(3 - 3)$ case, $(3) \times \{5 - (3 - 3)] = 15$ $(1 - 1)$ case $(1) \times [5 - (1 - 1)] = 5$.

According to this procedure, the $(5 - 5)$ case evidently is more unfavorable for the subject than the $(1 - 1)$ case, because of the relatively stronger impact of the negative beliefs, which according to the theory threatens the subject's self-esteem. In our formula the score of overall negativity is more unfavorable in the $(5 - 5)$ case (score 25) than in the $(1 - 1)$ case (score 5). The overall score of NSC reflects the degree to which subjects attribute unfavorable behavior to themselves. The higher the score on NSC, the more the subjects feel responsible for the negatively evaluated behavior.

SUBJECTIVE COMPETENCE AND COGNITIVE DEFENSIVENESS

NSC, indicating people's responsibility for their own negative behavior, implies a threat to self-esteem. According to Heider's balance theory (Heider, 1958) individuals are motivated to protect themselves from self-degradation. In terms of the subjective competence theory, they try to enhance their perceived PSC and to reduce their perceived NSC. Obviously, then, when a person's self-esteem is at stake, the person will be inclined to resort to defensive maneuvers. Perceived NSC, therefore, will arouse defensiveness, leading to defensive maneuvers, which also take place in situations of cognitive dissonance in decisional conflicts; this implicates defensive avoidance, manifesting itself as procrastination, shifting responsibility, or bolstering (Janis, 1977).

According to subjective competence theory, cognitive defensiveness can be assessed in two different ways. First, the model involves 4 positive and 4 negative beliefs, allowing the subject in case of strong negative beliefs to stress or exaggerate the corresponding opposed positive beliefs. Second, the theory specifies a more detailed and more differentiated manner to assess cognitive defensiveness. In order to clarify this point, one should more closely inspect the structure of the attribution sequence. The sequence involves a coherent series of separate attribution elements. Seven elements are distinguished, as presented in Fig. 2.

Bowerman suggests that cognitive defensive maneuvers can be engendered,

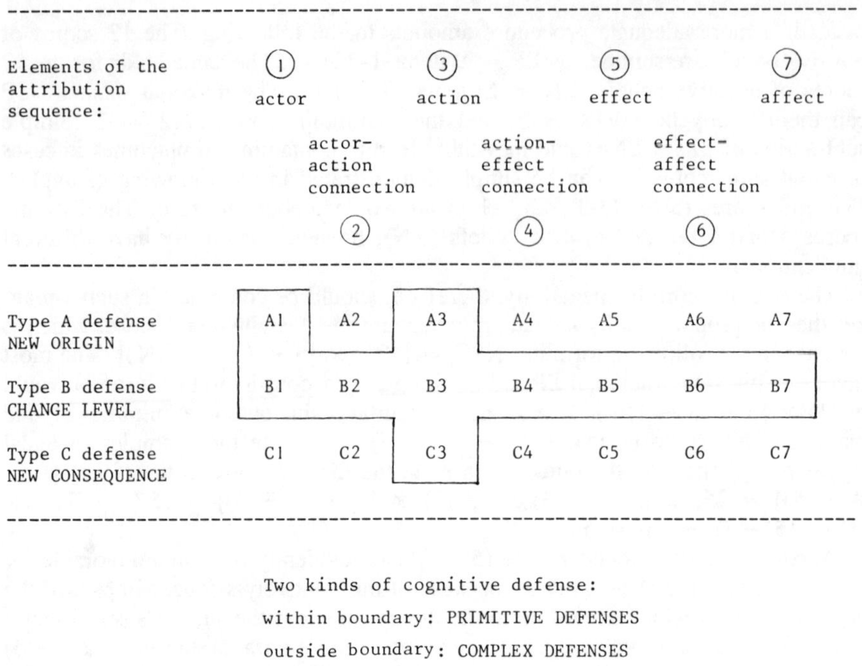

Elements of the attribution sequence:	① actor		③ action		⑤ effect		⑦ affect
		actor-action connection		action-effect connection		effect-affect connection	
		②		④		⑥	
Type A defense NEW ORIGIN	A1	A2	A3	A4	A5	A6	A7
Type B defense CHANGE LEVEL	B1	B2	B3	B4	B5	B6	B7
Type C defense NEW CONSEQUENCE	C1	C2	C3	C4	C5	C6	C7

Two kinds of cognitive defense:

within boundary: PRIMITIVE DEFENSES

outside boundary: COMPLEX DEFENSES

Figure 2 21 ways of cognitive defense in a subjective competence attribution sequence.

with the implication that the impact of NSC is weakened. The impact of each element of the attribution sequence can either be denied or weakened, and this may take place according to three basic maneuvers, labeled as new origin, change level, and new consequence.

First, an element Y in the attribution sequence attributed to element X is attributed to another element Xa, by which the exclusiveness of element X in causing element Y is undermined. Such defenses are called "new origin". An example would be: "Besides cigarette smoking there are many other factors that can cause health complaints." Second, an element X can simply be denied. This kind of defensive maneuver, called "change level," resembles "stopping thinking" in the dissonance model of Hardyck and Kardush (1968). An example would be: "I don't want to see medical information about health complaints caused by smoking." Finally, an element X in a subjective competence belief is supposed to cause element Y. By stating that element X also causes the (nonthreatening) element Ya, the negative impact of element X is weakened. These defenses are called "new consequence." An example would be: "When I should experience health complaints, an adventitious benefit would be that I could better reflect the sense of my life."

According to the theory, because there are 7 elements constituting the attribution sequence and forms of defensive maneuvers, 21 defenses can potentially take place. Bowerman suggests that the 21 defenses could be subdivided into primitive and complex defenses, the primitive defenses resembling the stopping thinking maneuver (see Fig. 2).

RESEARCH DESIGN

NSC indicates the degree to which individuals feel responsible for negative outcomes of their own actions. This feeling of responsibility implies that the subject is confronted with his own malfunctioning, which ultimately leads to a decrease of self-esteem. How strong is the influence of the assumed need for the enhancement of self-esteem in terms of behavioral change? A pertinent question in this context regards the influence of the condemnation of one's own behavior, in case NCS prevails. Would NSC be strong enough to engender behavioral changes? In order to investigate the impact of NSC upon facilitating behavioral change, a further specification of relevant variables seems essential. According to this model, NSC is considered as a predictor of behavioral changes. However, this in no way excludes the importance of the antecedent factors of NSC itself. What personality characteristics may play a role in inducing a lower or higher level of NSC of smokers? What kind of social and situational variables are to be specified in this context? While the subjective competence theory is an attributional theory, it seems highly probable that attribution style also might have an explanatory power. Finally, as NSC deals explicitly with matters of good and evil, right and wrong, it will most probably be determined by normative beliefs. In view of the previously mentioned considerations, NSC is conceived as an intermediate moderating variable. In the research design, presented in Fig. 3, NSC is explained by personality variables, attribution style, normative variables, and social and situational variables. Consequently, NSC moderates psychological conditions that facilitate or block behavioral changes. Let us briefly inspect each cluster of variables.

ANTECEDENT CONDITIONS

Personality Variables

It is frequently and fervently argued that cigarette smoking is detrimental to health. Taking into consideration that good health is to be conceived as a positive value, the belief that smoking threatens health might cause anxiety. Trait anxiety seems most relevant in this context. High anxiety subjects will most probably be more strongly influenced than low anxiety subjects by the threat due to the negative health implications of smoking. Consequently, high anxiety subjects will perceive more NSC. In order to assess anxiety levels, the Dutch version of the State Trait Anxiety Inventory (STAI) (van der Ploeg, Defares, Spielberger, 1979) was administered in this study.

Another relevant personality variable concerns trait self-esteem. Individuals with low self-esteem are supposedly less equipped to cope with threat. The negative implications for self-esteem will be stronger for low self-esteem subjects than for high ones. Therefore, low self-esteem subjects will experience more NSC. A trait version of Janis' Scale for the measurement of self-esteem was used for this purpose (Janis, 1982).

Furthermore, a Social Anxiety Scale was included, indicating the degree to which individuals feel uneasy and tense in social settings. High social anxiety subjects suffer from a heightened sense of vulnerability, due to their sensitivity in dealing with other people, and will experience more NSC. The Dutch Scale for

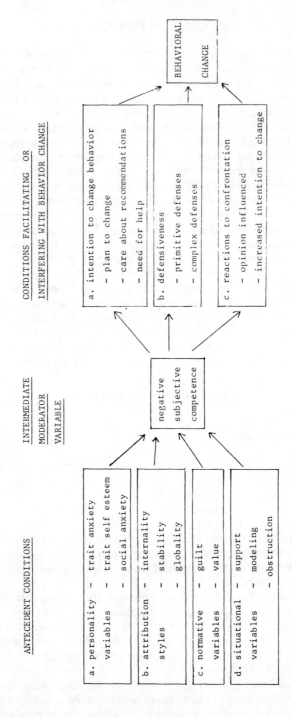

Figure 3 research model for the study of negative subjective competence.

Social Anxiety (Willems, Tuender-de Haan, and Defares, 1973) was administered for this purpose.

Attribution Style

While subjective competence is an attributional concept, it is assumed that differences in attribution style might influence subjective competence. And because NSC explicitly deals with the attribution of unfavorable behavior, it is also to be expected that the dynamics of learned helplessness may bear some relevance. The learned helplessness phenomenon refers to expectations based upon a noncontingency model. People learn that the outcome is independent of their own responses. As Miller and Seligman (1982) pointed out, learned helplessness will be strongly influenced by stability, globality, and internality concerning the attribution of failure. It is to be expected that individuals who generally demonstrate more stability, globality, and internality in the attribution of failure outcomes will experience a higher degree of NSC.

Normative Beliefs

An important cluster of variables refers to normative beliefs. Individuals with a highly positive attitude towards smoking are supposed to stress or overemphasize the positive implications of smoking (the 12 PSC items), and to ward off the negative implications (the 12 NSC items). Therefore, a positive attitude toward smoking will lower the overall score of negativity, reflected in the NSC score. Attitude toward smoking was measured with a 5-item Osgood attitude scale, representing the value-dimension (Krech, Crutchfield, & Ballachey, 1962).

In view of the moral implications of health-risk behavior, the concept of guilt may also be relevant to a negative evaluation of smoking. In studying NSC, guilt, indeed, seems to be a very critical variable. NSC indicates the degree of responsibility a person may feel with regard to his or her defective behavior and unfavorable outcomes, which is attributed to the self as an actor. To the extent that this explanation does not take the concept of guilt into account, the explanation would be morally neutral because the degree of NSC will be conceived as due to factors which are beyond the personal responsibility (e.g. personality variables, social and situational factors, or even the influence of culture and socializing agents). Whenever a person's responsibility is at stake, however, a moral explanation is involved. Guilt should be considered a variable in its own right, which cannot be reduced to the previously mentioned factors. The absence of empirical research and test construction concerning guilt is a notable neglect in psychology.

Recently the authors of this article developed the Netherlands Guilt Scale (NSGS), a scale for measuring guilt. As the scale is in press, we will briefly give an impression of its construction. In a preliminary phase, 30 subjects were interviewed on their beliefs and feelings concerning situations that may arouse guilt feelings. On the basis of the data, 112 statements were formulated, indicating diverse aspects of guilt. In a later phase, these statements were presented to 180 subjects, using a five-point scale format. The data were condensed by way of factor analysis. On the basis of the amount of explained variance, two significant factors emerged and finally 14 items with the highest loadings were selected.

The first factor, comprising 8 items, reflects a negative assessment of one's own functioning concerning both physical and psychological aspects. The items indicate that feeling guilty is associated with feelings pertaining to worrying about self, feeling uneasy, or feeling uncertain. The second factor, comprising 6 items, reflects the feeling of being rejected with reference to a negative evaluation of one's own behavior. The items of this factor indicate that feeling guilty is associated with statements such as "I cannot prove myself," self-blame, and accusation by others. Factor 1 evidently refers to distress in a more general sense. In contrast, Factor 2 more specifically reflects the guilt element.

These 14 items were explicitly linked to smoking behavior in order to diagnose the extent to which subjects experience guilt concerning smoking. An example of this procedure amounts to the following. The general statement, "feeling guilty makes me feel uncertain," was rephrased as "smoking makes me feel uncertain". It seems likely that in this manner guilt feelings concerning smoking can be adequately assessed. In the context of the research design it is important to note that the variables of the previous clusters deal with personality per se without reference to smoking, while the normative variables (value and guilt) explicitly deal with smoking.

Situational Variables

Several situational factors may operate in inducing positive or negative feelings, associated with smoking or with the decision to quit smoking. With reference to the work of Bandura, it seems most likely in this context that modeling effects may play a prominent role. Modeling is defined as "the tendency for a person to reproduce the action, attitudes, and emotional responses by a real-life or symbolic model" (Bandura, 1971). It seems obvious that when significant others smoke, there will be less chance that a modeling effect will engender NSC. If the subject's own partner, friends and relatives are smokers, a modeling effect might potentially lower NSC.

Another important situational factor pertains to social support. It is generally accepted that emotional support reduces perceived threat, the strongest emotional support being assigned to one's own partner (Cobb, 1976). When smokers believe that their own partners would be highly appreciative if they quit smoking, then it seems most likely that the smoking habit will be associated with the partner's disapproval. Consequently, quitting smoking is associated with the partner's approval. The negative implications, and consequently NSC concerning smoking, will be enhanced. In contrast, when smokers believe that their environment thwarts intentions or endeavors to quit smoking, then they might perceive the social environment as counteracting their strivings. In that case there will be no social support for quitting. The negative implications of smoking will not be stressed by the social environment and eventually NSC might decrease.

Clearly, the previously mentioned situational variables are in no way exhaustive. However, they may be conceived as important social and situational influences which may affect the degree of NSC. Summarizing the antecedent conditions of the research design, NSC, reflecting the degree to which subjects feel themselves responsible for negative outcomes, is explained by personality variables, attribution style, normative variables, and situational factors.

EFFECTS

In as much as NSC is conceived as a central mediator variable, the degree of this variable may predict conditions either facilitating behavioral change or interfering with change (see Fig. 3, right column).

1. More strongly experienced NSC will increase the perceived negativity of smoking, and consequently will promote the intention to change one's behavior. In our study, the intention to change smoking behavior was assessed with items referring to the seriousness of intentions to quit smoking, the degree to which subjects are willing to accept recommendations to stop smoking, and the perceived need for support.

2. Research on attitude and attitude change has firmly established, however, that mere intention is not a valid prediction of behavioral change. In the Fishbein model (Ajzen & Fishbein, 1980), 3 important factors which may influence behavioral intentions are mentioned; namely, attitudes, normative beliefs, and motivation. The Fishbein model does not explicitly refer to cognitive defensiveness as a separate variable interfering with the materialization of intended behavior. The importance of cognitive defensiveness is stressed by subjective competence theory, and assessment of specific defensive maneuvers is an essential element of the theory. As was previously mentioned, two different types of cognitive defenses were specified, that is, primitive defenses and complex defenses. According to the theory, primitive defenses are to be expected in the case of lower NSC, and complex defenses are to be expected in the case of stronger NSC.

3. After completion of the subjective competence scale, subjects were deliberately confronted with the negative health implications of smoking. This was done by introductory texts, suggesting the expert knowledge of distinguished authorities. This procedure was meant to create a vivid confrontation and also to assess whether the confrontation would have varying impact, depending on the specific level of NSC. In the closing sections of the questionnaires, the subjects were asked to indicate whether the "participation in this research" had influenced their opinion about smoking, and whether their intention to quit smoking was strengthened because of this participation.

The research reported here was based on a single test session. In principle, it would be of great relevance to gather information concerning the relationship between different levels of NSC and actual decisions to quit smoking. Obviously, the intention to stop smoking is not a satisfactory predictor of genuine behavioral change. Too many smokers want to stop, promise to stop, or even execute such plans for a while, but become devoted smokers again. Furthermore, even when an addicted smoker indicates that he seriously cares about recommendations to stop smoking, the actual behavioral change often falls short of initial intentions. This does not, however, imply that explicit behavioral intentions are unimportant for altering a tenacious habit.

Pilot Study

Prior to the main project, a pilot study was carried out with 85 cigarette smokers: 61 male and 24 female students of the Agricultural University of Wageningen, all indicating they smoked at least 15 cigarettes daily. The subjects completed the scales on subjective competence, cognitive defensiveness, and trait self-esteem. The pilot study was mainly intended to test whether the items used were adequate and unequivocal. We will skip the data of the pilot study. The outcomes did warrant the inclusion of these variables in a more extensive study, which would allow for empirical testing of the model presented.

Subjects in the Main Project

In the main project, in which all the variables, presented in Fig. 3, were included, subjects were recruited by means of an advertising campaign in local newspapers in Wageningen (31,000 inhabitants), Ede (85,000 inhabitants) and Arnhem (139,000 inhabitants). In the announcement, cigarette smokers were invited to participate in a study on beliefs and feelings concerning smoking. The daily minimum was fixed on 15 cigarettes a day, irrespective of sex. Age of subjects was between 18 and 50. A one-hour questionnaire was completed in the presence of the investigators. As a compensation for travel costs and for their effort, subjects received ten Dutch Guilders, which is equivalent to the price of two packets of cigarettes and a regular bus ticket. Two hundred seventy subjects participated and completed the questionnaire: 175 male and 95 female, mean age 25.8 years ± 8.1 years (s.d.). During the sessions subjects were allowed to smoke, and interestingly 510 cigarettes were counted after the session, which approximates an average of two cigarettes per subject. All subjects accepted the money except one subject, who asked us to donate the money to the Dutch Asthma Fund.

RESULTS

Before presenting the results concerning the research design tested in this study, we should first mention that no significant differences in NSC were found between men ($N = 185$) and women ($N = 95$) (two-tailed t-test for independent samples). Neither was there a significant correlation between age and NSC. We may conclude that neither sex nor age determine the degree of negativity in terms of subjective competence.

In order to test the model, presented in Fig. 3, we proceeded as follows. NSC was conceived as a central mediating variable. By means of multiple regression analysis, the potential predictive value of the antecedent variables was assessed, and by means of one-way analysis of variance, the probability of consequential events was assessed.

The potential predictive value of each separate cluster of antecedent variables was assessed by means of multiple regression analysis, with NSC as the dependent variable. Basically this procedure may be conceived as an empirical testing of the model so as to assess the construct validity of the theoretical assumptions. In a subsequent overall analysis, all antecedent variables were entered into the regression analysis. This overall analysis indicates which variables possess the strongest explanatory power, and are of special relevance in terms of empirical validity (see Kerlinger, 1973).

When the three *personality variables* are entered into the regression analysis, the amount of explained variance NSC is rather modest; yet the outcome is defi-

Table 2 Multiple regression of negative subjective competence by personality variables

Entered independent variables		
Trait anxiety	Trait self-esteem	Social anxiety
$F = 4.604$	$F = 0.085$	$F = 2.940$

$R = 0.24$; $R^2 = 0.06$; $F = 5.57$; $Df = 3,251$; $p = .01$.

nitely significant, and interestingly the strongest explanatory power is clearly represented by trait anxiety (see Table 2). This indicates that trait anxiety accounts for a significant portion of the variance of NSC.

When variables of the *attribution cluster* are entered into the regression analysis, the amount of explained variance of NSC is of the same magnitude as in the former analysis (see Table 3). In this cluster the strongest explanatory power is represented by stability: NSC is most strongly explained by stable attributions of failure outcomes.

Restricting the regression analysis to the *normative variables,* an impressive amount of the variance is explained by guilt, whereas attitude-value is also clearly significant (see Table 4).

Finally, when the *situational variables* are entered into the regression analysis, the amount of explained variance is less pronounced than in the case of normative variables, yet stronger than in the case of personality variables and attribution variables (see Table 5). In this cluster the strongest explanatory power is represented by the belief that one's partner will appreciate quitting smoking. This belief evidently enhances NSC. Another significant variable in this cluster refers to actual smoking behavior of the partner, indicating that negative health risk behavior of the partner may act as a precondition for reduction of NSC.

In a subsequent overall analysis, all mentioned variables were entered conjointly into the regression analysis. As Table 6 shows, three significant predictor variables are maintained, namely guilt, attitude-value, and the perceived approval of the partner. On the basis of this overall analysis, we may conclude that the degree of NSC of smokers concerning smoking can be predicted by guilt concern-

Table 3 Multiple regression of negative subjective competence by attribution style

Entered independent variables		
Stability	Globality	Internality
$F = 7.133$	$F = 1.120$	$F = 0.003$

$R = 0.26$; $R^2 = 0.07$; $F = 6.48$; $Df = 3,261$; $p < .01$.

Table 4 Multiple regression of negative subjective competence
by normative variables

Entered independent variables	
Guilt	Value
F = 95.723	F = 18.143

R = 0.62; R^2 = 0.38; F = 80.56; Df = 2,262; p < .01.

Table 5 Multiple regression of negative subjective competence by situational
variables

Entered independent variables in the regression			
Modeling (friends)	Modeling (partner)	Partner's disapproval	Thwarting environment
F = 2.554	F = 4.681	F = 41.328	F = 0.399

R = 0.38. R^2 = 0.14; F = 11.00; Df = 4,260; p < .01.

Table 6 Multiple regression of negative subjective competence
by all antecedents conjointly.

Independent variables entered in regression	
Personality variables:	
trait anxiety	F = 0.056
trait self-esteem	F = 0.295
social anxiety	F = 0.427
Attribution variables:	
stability	F = 0.302
globality	F = 0.001
internality	F = 1.055
Normative variables:	
guilt	F = 55.969
value	F = 12.261
Situational variables:	
modeling (friends)	F = 0.723
modeling (partner)	F = 1.919
partner's approval	F = 8.474
thwarting	F = 0.195
environment	

R = 0.64. R^2 = 0.41. F = 14.71. Df = 12,252. p < .01.

ing smoking, negative evaluation of smoking, and the belief that one's partner will appreciate quitting smoking.

According to subjective competence theory, beliefs of NSC indicate that individuals attribute the responsibility for the negative outcomes to themselves as the *actors* or origin of the attribution sequence. The results of the regression analysis corroborate that normative beliefs are the strongest predictor of NSC. From the point of view of conceptual theorizing, we may conclude that NSC is a normative construct, to a large extent explained by normative variables, such as guilt, attitude-value, and partner's disapproval.

In a subsequent section of the model, presented in Fig. 3, it is suggested that NSC, conceived as a central moderator variable, determines the probability of consequential events: the intention to change the smoking habit, cognitive defensiveness, and vulnerability when confronted with negative health implications. The potential influence of NSC was analyzed with one-way analysis of variance. The subjects were subdivided into three groups: low, medium and high NSC. Two different criteria for subdivision were utilized. First, extremely low NSC was defined by a cut-off point of 1 standard deviation (s.d.) below the mean ($N = 43$); extremely high NSC was defined by 1 s.d. above the mean ($N = 44$); the remaining 183 subjects comprised the group of medium NSC according to this procedure. The second criterion was a straightforward subdivision into three groups of equal size, encompassing low scores on NSC ($N = 90$), medium scores ($N = 89$), and high scores ($N = 91$) (see Table 7).

In view of the large number of subjects, the latter procedure might in principle outbalance contaminations due to idiosyncratic extreme scores on both ends of the continuum. The results indicate that practically no differences in explained vari-

Table 7 One-way analysis of variance of dependent variables by levels of negative subjective competence

		Criterion: standard deviation			Criterion: groups of equal size	
		mean =	N =		mean =	N =
	Low NSC	7.6591	43	Low NSC	9.1451	90
	Medium NSC	12.9246	183	Medium NSC	12.7446	89
	High NSC	19.7806	44	High NSC	17.6654	91
Cluster	Dependent variables	F =	p =		F =	p =
1. Intention to	-stronger intention	22.57	.0000		25.64	.0000
	-care about recommendations	16.93	.0000		24.62	.0000
	-need help	0.44	n.s.		0.16	n.s.
2. Defensiveness	-complex defenses	6.49	.0018		10.62	.0000
	-primitive defenses	6.85	.0013		5.66	.0039
3. Reactions to confrontation to stop	-opinion influenced	5.43	.0049		15.11	.0000
	-increased intention	14.63	.0000		21.62	.0000

Mean low, medium and high scores on negative subjective competence (NSC) grand mean: NSC = 13.2033; s.d. = 3.9583.

ance of the dependent variables emerged. For the sake of brevity, we restrict our presentation to data based on the latter procedure. We will deal with each separate variable.

Three variables represent the cluster indicating the intention to quit smoking. The differences between levels of NSC are graphically presentcd in Fig. 4.

High NSC subjects demonstrate a stronger intention than low NSC subjects to quit smoking.

High NSC subjects also seem to be more inclined to care about recommendations to quit smoking, than low NSC subjects. With regard to the perceived need for help to quit smoking, no significant differences were found. We may conclude that high NSC concerning smoking is a favorable precondition for quitting smoking.

The second cluster of dependent variables, potentially predicted by different levels of NSC, contains two cognitive defensive modes. On the basis of subjective competence theory, 21 different defenses were formulated. A factor analysis of the data resulted in two clear factors. Factor 1, explaining 27% of the variance, contains 3 items with factor loadings > .40. These items belong to the so-called complex type, namely (according to the legends in Fig. 2) the defenses C4, C5, and C6. Factor 2, explaining 16.3% of the variance, contains 4 items with factor loadings > .40. These items belong to the so-called primitive type, namely the defenses presented in Fig. 2 as B1, B5, B7 and A1.

The graphs in Fig. 5 indicate that high NSC subjects seem to have more complex defenses (i.e. higher factor scores on factor 1) than low NSC subjects. In contrast, high HSC subjects have fewer primitive defenses (i.e., lower factor scores on factor 2) than low NSC subjects. These findings corroborate a basic assumption of subjective competence theory. These data converge with the findings from the "intention cluster," namely that high NSC is a more favorable precondition for quitting smoking.

In the third cluster of dependent variables, two variables refer to the impact of the confrontation with threatening health consequences of smoking.

The graphs of Fig. 6 show that the opinion concerning smoking of high NSC subjects is more influenced by the threatening confrontation. Moreover, intentions of high NSC subjects to quit smoking were increased to a stronger extent. The importance of high NSC as a favorable precondition to quit smoking is once again corroborated by the findings concerning reactions to a threatening confrontation.

DISCUSSION

High NSC clearly contributes to a much higher extent than low NSC to the intention to stop smoking. High NSC also implicates a more complex and differentiated defense system compared with the more primitive defenses of low NSC, and high NSC subjects seem more willing to face warnings concerning health risk consequences. Good intentions, less primitive defenses, and readiness to accept external pressure, are only to a moderate degree indicators of genuine behavioral change. Having these intentions and readiness, however, is undoubtedly a better precondition than their absence in this respect.

The degree of NSC was explained by personality variables, attribution style, normative variables, and situational factors. Notwithstanding the relevance of other factors, it was clearly demonstrated that the normative variables exert the

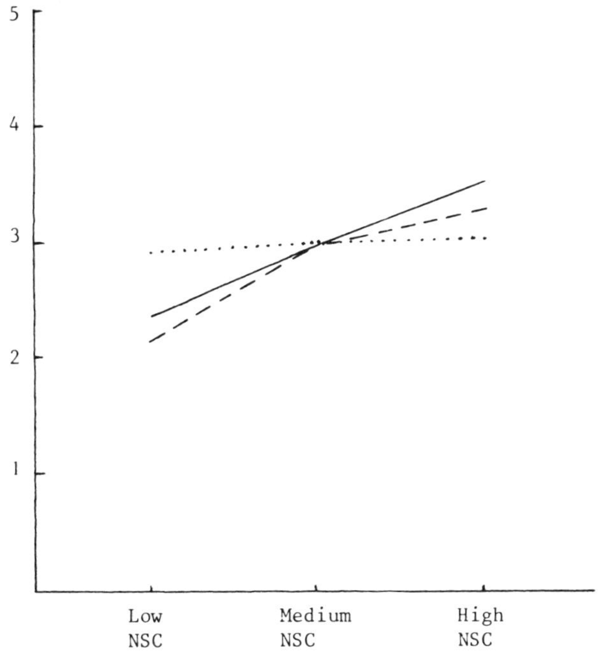

Legenda:	———————	- - - - - - - -	···········
Dependent Variable:	ACTUAL INTENTION TO STOP	CARE ABOUT RECOMMENDATIONS	NEED HELP TO STOP
Oneway. F-ratio:	F = 25.64. p = .0000	F = 24.02. p = .0000	F = 0.16. n.s.

Mean score on dependent variable:

NSC 1 (N = 90):	2.33	2.15	2.93
NSC 2 (N = 91):	3.02	3.01	3.01
NSC 3 (N = 89):	3.56	3.30	3.06

Differences of the NSC-levels:	T =	p =	T =	p =	T =	p =
NSC1 - NSC3:	-7.437	.000	-6.978	.000	-0.36	n.s.
NSC1 - NSC2:	-3.877	.000	-4.965	.000	-0.21	n.s.
NSC2 - NSC3:	-3.088	.002	-1.595	n.s.	-0.53	n.s.

Figure 4 One-way analysis of variance: differences in variables indicating the strength of the intention to stop smoking, for three levels of negative subjective competence (NSC).

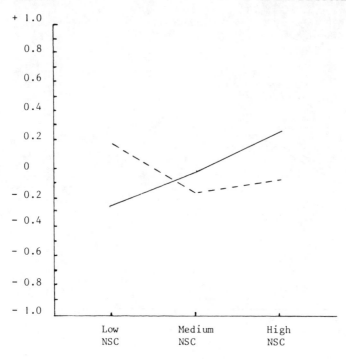

Legenda: _____   --------------

Dependent Variable: FACTORSCORES   FACTORSCORES
                                  COMPLEX DEFENSES   PRIMITIVE DEFENSES

Oneway. F-ratio: F = 10.69. p = .0000   F = 24.02. p = .0000

Mean score on dependent variable:
                NSC 1 (N = 90):   -0.26   0.21
                NSC 2 (N = 91):   -0.02   -0.16
                NSC 3 (N = 89):   0.28   -0.06

Differences of the NSC-levels: T =   p =   T =   p =
                NSC1 - NSC3:   -4.555   .000   2.251   .026
                NSC1 - NSC2:   -2.143   .033   3.372   .001
                NSC2 - NSC3:   -2.460   .015   -0.862   n.s.

Figure 5 One-way analysis of variance: differences in factor scores indicating complex and primitive defenses, for three levels of negative subjective competence (NSC).

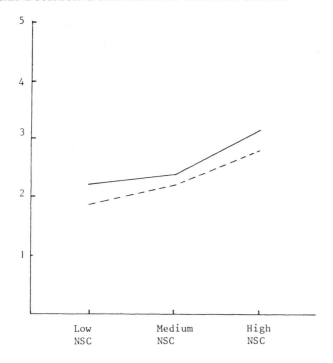

Legenda:

Dependent Variable:	OPINION INFLUENCED		INTENTION INCREASED	
Oneway. F-ratio:	F = 15.11. p = .0000		F = 21.62. p = .0000	
Mean score on dependent variable:				
NSC 1 (N = 90):	2.21		1.86	
NSC 2 (N = 91):	2.44		2.20	
NSC 3 (N = 89):	3.15		2.80	
Differences of the NSC-levels:	T =	p =	T =	p =
NSC1 - NSC3:	-5.214	.000	-6.773	.000
NSC1 - NSC2:	-1.261	n.s.	-2.397	.018
NSC2 - NSC3:	-4.040	.000	-3.941	.000

Figure 6 One-way analysis of variance: differences in degree of influence due to confrontation of health for three levels of Negative Subjective Competence (NSC).

most powerful influence. Anti-smoking campaigns, however, most frequently use anxiety-inducing procedures, stressing the horrible and painful health risk consequences of smoking. The psychodramatic therapy for heavy smokers proposed by Janis (1982), is an example of extreme anxiety provocation in group settings. According to our findings, the most effective tactic to evoke behavioral change would be in our view the induction of guilt feelings, guilt feelings being the most powerful explanation of NSC, and higher NSC being a better precondition for behavioral change. Guilt feelings clearly represent an unpleasant emotional experience, but this does not exclude the potential effectiveness of these feelings for bringing about changes in order to terminate undesirable behaviors. In the history of psychology, the potential positive impact of guilt feelings has been neglected. Positive effects are obviously not to be expected in the case of neurotic and unjustified guilt feelings. However, the rejection of the function of unjustified guilt may have obscured the functionality of justified guilt.

The results from the reported study support the plea for a positive function of guilt feelings, as launched by O. Mowrer (1960), and endorsed by D. Campbell (1975) and by D. Phillips (1982). Further research on this topic is recommended in order to investigate whether guilt feelings can be utilized in the context of therapeutic and preventive maneuvers, especially in the field of addiction, pertaining to smoking, eating disorders, alcoholism, and drug abuse, or even more generally in different areas of unwanted behaviors, such as vandalism and antisocial behavior.

REFERENCES

Ajzen, T., & Fishbein, M. (1980). *Understanding attitudes and predicting behavior.* Englewood Cliffs, NJ: Prentice Hall.

Bandura, A. (1969). *Principles of behavior modification.* New York: Holt, Rinehart, and Winston.

Bowerman, W. R. (1978). Subjective competence: The structure, process, and function of self-reference causal attribution. *Journal for the Theory of Social Behavior, 8,* 45–75.

Bowerman, W. R. (1981). Applications of a social psychological theory of motivation to the language of defensiveness and self-justification. In M. M. T. Henderson (Ed.), Mid-America Linguistics Conference paper. Lawrence, KS: University of Knasas Linguistics Department.

Campbell, D. T. (1975). On the conflicts between biological and social evolution and between psychology and moral tradition. *American Psychologist, 30,* 1103–1126.

Cobb, S. (1976). Social support as a moderator of life stress. *Psychosomatic Medicine, 38,* 300–314.

De Soomer, K. L. P., Bowerman, W. R., & Defares, P. B. (1983). Subjective competence of smokers concerning smoking. Unpublished manuscript, Wageningen.

De Soomer, K. L. P., Defares, P. B. (1984). Riskant rookgedrag: Subjectieve competentie, zelfwaardering en gezondheid. Gedrag. *Tijdschrift voor psychologie, 12,* 82–100.

Hardyck, J. A., & Kardush, M. (1968). A modest modish model for Dissonance Reduction. In R. P. Abelson (Eds.), *Theories of cognitive consistency: A sourcebook.* Chicago: Rand McNally.

Heider, F. (1958). *The psychology of interpersonal relations.* New York: Wiley.

Janis, I. L., & Mann, L. (1977). *Decision making: A psychological analysis of conflict and commitment.* New York: Free Press.

Janis, I. L. (Ed.) (1982). *Counseling on personal decisions: Theory and research on short-term helping relationships.* New Haven: Yale University Press.

Kerlinger, F. N. (1973). *Foundations of behavioral research* (2nd ed.). A Holt International Edition. London: Holt, Rinehart & Winston.

Krech, D., Cruchfield, R. S., & Ballachey, E. L. (1962). *Individual in society: A textbook of social psychology.* New York: McGraw-Hill.

Leventhal, H., & Cleary, P. D. (1980). The smoking problem: A review of the research and theory in behavioural risk modification. *Psychological Bulletin, 88,* 370–405.

Miller, S., & Seligman, M. E. R. (1982). The reformulated Model of Helplessness and Depression. In R. W. Neufeld (Ed.), *Psychological stress and psychopathology.* New York: McGraw-Hill.

Mowrer, O. H. (1960). *Learning theory and the symbolic processes.* New York: Wiley.

Phillips, D. L. (1982). De lof van de schuld: Moraliteit en schuld in de moderne tijd. *De Gids, 145,* 145–162.

van der Ploeg, H. M., Defares, P. B., & Spielberger, C. D. (1979). *Zelfbeoordelings vragenlijst.* Lisse: Swets & Zeitlinger.

Willems, L. F. M., Tuender-de Haan, H. A., & Defares, P. B. (1973). Een schaal om sociale angst te meten. *Nederlands Tijdschrift voor de Psychologie, 28,* 415–422.

22

Interactions of Stressful Life Changes, Cognitive Factors, and Depression in Myocardial Infarction Patients: A Life-Span Development Study

Paul R. J. Falger
State University of Limburg School of Medicine

In current behavioral medicine research it is recognized that several psychologic and social determinants may interact in the etiology of coronary heart disease (CHD).

A specific behavioral disposition—the Type A coronary-prone behavior pattern—constitutes an independent psychosocial risk indicator in the pathogenesis of myocardial infarction (MI) (Brand, 1978). The adult coronary-prone person is characterized by a habitual manner of acting in an alert, hasty, overly responsive and aggressive manner, by a chronic sense of time urgency, by an utterly competitive involvement in work, or, in short, by an exaggerated need for personal recognition through achievement (Friedman & Rosenman, 1971). This psychosocial risk indicator for CHD holds true for employed, middle-aged men and women in the United States (Waldron et al., 1977; Chesney & Rosenman, 1980; Hayes & Feinleib, 1982), and, with similar degrees of association, in employed, middle-aged men in Western and Eastern Europe (Appels, Jenkins, & Rosenman, 1982; Kornitzer, Kittel, De Backer, & Dramaix, 1981; Zyzanski, Wrzesniewski, & Jenkins, 1979).

An unprecedented exposure to stressful life changes (LC) in the last years prior to MI also may be a particularly important psychosocial risk indicator (Rahe & Romo, 1974; Siegrist, Dittman, Rittner, & Weber, 1980; Theorell, 1980; Byrne & Whyte, 1980; Thiel, Parker, & Bruce, 1973). MI cases may assess such LC in a peculiar cognitive manner, that is, they perceive these changes as causing much more emotional upset or distress in their lives than (healthy) referents do (Byrne, 1980; Siegrist, Dittman, Rittner, & Weber, 1982), or as requiring more psychologic and social adjustment (Byrne, 1983; Lundberg & Theorell, 1976; Lundberg, Theorell, & Lind, 1975).

Another aspect of adult social life, one's occupational status, is also considered

Part of the research that is reported in this chapter was supported by Grant 31.010h/1981 from the Dutch Heart Foundation (Nederlandse Hart Stichting).

a psychosocial risk indicator for CHD (Jenkins, 1971, 1976). A few decades ago only the highest occupational strata in Western society were afflicted with CHD, but nowadays this picture is almost completely reversed. That is, it is the un-skilled, poorly educated industrial laborer that is suffering most from MI, with the least chance of survival (Marmot, 1982).

The picture with respect to psychosocial determinants in the development of premature MI is not all drab, however. In several studies it was demonstrated that social support, when embedded in a network of meaningful social relations, may serve as a most powerful moderator of life stress. This relationship holds in partic-ular with regard to the incidence of CHD and MI (Berkman, 1982; Cobb, 1976).

These studies have provided discerning insights into the complex intertwinings of behavioral, psychosocial and cultural determinants in the pathogenesis of MI. Yet they have almost completely neglected an equally intriguing question, namely, how those factors may have come about to play such a decisive role in the lives of MI-patients. Stated differently, what specific developmental trajectories did those patients follow during their life course that ultimately destined them to suffer from premature MI, or even sudden cardiac death? To what extent have MI cases been able to exert control over their own lives? That is, could they have encountered LC of particular idiosyncratic relevance that inexorably changed their lives? In what peculiar manner might the Type A coronary-prone behavior pattern have inter-acted with the occurrence and subsequent coping with LC in different developmen-tal domains? Would a rather universal ontogenetic pattern lead to premature MI in adulthood? Or, on the contrary, would specific cohort effects that account for unique historical-environmental constellations provide better explanatory power (Falger, 1983b)? And, to address finally a crucial issue that was not brought up yet, to what extent do heart patients suffer from manifestations of vital exhaustion and depression in the last months before MI *as a final common pathway* toward breakdown in psychosocial adaptation, as is suggested to some extent by the litera-ture on psychic factors in sudden cardiac death? (Greene, Goldstein, & Moss, 1972; Kuller, Cooper, & Perper, 1972; Alonzo, Simon, & Feinleib, 1975; Kuller, 1978; Rissanen, Romo, & Siltanen, 1978).

THE SOUTH–LIMBURG LIFE HISTORY
AND MYOCARDIAL INFARCTION STUDY

Some of these developmental issues mentioned above, were addressed in the South-Limburg Life History and Myocardial Infarction Study.

First, in this case-referent investigation our interest is directed foremost to the question whether the life course of MI-cases is characterized by an appreciable exposure to LC in different developmental domains, and whether there may be any clearly discernable cohort effects in this respect. Second, the particular cognitive manner in which MI-cases may assess those LC, that is, whether in the perception of the cases under study each reported event has contributed in any positive sense to his psychological and social development, or on the contrary, has proven detri-mental, is of importance, as is the extent of social support that is associated with each LC. Third, there is interest in the cohort-specific prevalence of the Type A behavior pattern in relation to coping with LC. Fourth, previous findings of ours could be replicated in this study, that is, that manifestations of vital exhaustion and depression may destine a future case's emotional constitution in the last months prior to MI (Appels, 1980; Falger, 1983a; Falger & Appels, 1982).

METHOD

The exposure to 51 LC in three developmental domains, (a) childhood, youth and adolescence, (b) work and career, and (c) family and social life, and, in addition, the psychological perceptions, coping strategies, and social support associated with each reported event, are all assessed by means of a *structured interview scheme*. This interview scheme was constructed after extensive interviews with some 35 MI-cases, and on the basis of the results from a pilot study on 136 healthy, middle-aged men (Falger & Appels, 1982).

At the end of the interview session, each participant is categorized as either Type A (coronary-prone), or Type B, according to the original Structured Interview assessment (Rosenman, 1978).

Further, all participants complete the Maastricht Questionnaire (MQ) that was developed earlier to measure prodromal symptoms of vital exhaustion and depression (Appels, 1980). The MQ has been used in a number of retrospective and prospective studies on MI-cases and several referent groups. The MQ pertains to the last half year prior to MI, or interviewing. (For a review of these studies, cf. Falger, 1983a).

An average interview session will last some 2.5 hours.

Subjects

In this case-referent study, three groups of subjects are involved, i.e., MI-cases, healthy neighborhood referents, and hospital referents.

1. An MI case is defined as a male person, between 35–70 yrs. of age, hospitalized with *first* MI that is clinically documented by ECG and serum enzymes max classifications. All patients come from the two largest hospitals in the South-Limburg Region, and are visited personally by us in the hospital within a few days after admission. Participating cases complete the MQ in the hospital and are interviewed at home some one/two month(s) after their release. After completion of an interview, a healthy neighborhood referent is sought.

2. A healthy neighborhood referent is defined as a male person, between 35–70 yrs. of age, without documented MI (self-report), living in the immediate vicinity of an MI-case from our study. All neighborhood referents are selected by means of a complete list from the telephone directory, containing all persons on the street where the MI-case is living. Then, those referents are asked, by means of a standard letter, in a random order, and one at the time, to participate in this study if they comply with our definition. The neighborhood referent then also is interviewed at home.

In this manner, the developmental trajectories in MI-cases can be compared with an equal number of healthy neighborhood referents, controlled for socioeconomic status (Miettinen, 1982).

3. A hospital referent is defined as a male person, between 35–70 yrs. of age, without documented MI (hospital record), hospitalized with a presumably non-stress related ailment (e.g., hemorrhoids, prostate hypertrophy, inguinal hernia,

cataract, etc.). All those referents come from the same hospitals as the MI-cases. All hospital referents are asked, by means of the same standard letter that applies to healthy neighborhood referents, to participate in this study if they comply with our definition. All hospital referents are interviewed at home, about one/two month(s) after their release.

Including this second referent group allows for further clarification of the crucial question whether the life-span developmental patterns in MI-cases are identifiable by a singular structure with respect to exposure to particular LC during the life course, regarding idiosyncratic coping strategies, or with respect to social support associated with each LC (Miettinen, 1982).

Design

The design of this study is such that all MI-cases and both referent groups are assigned equally to seven cohorts of five years each, spanning the age range from 35–70. There are 15 MI-cases, 15 healthy neighborhood referents, and 30 hospital referents of 35–39 years of age, 40–44 years of age, and so on, adding up to 105 MI-cases, 105 neighborhood, and 210 hospital referents.

In this manner, specific cohort influences in the developmental patterns of MI-cases and referents could be identified (Baltes, Cornelius, & Nesselroade, 1978). Also, in employing this particular design that by implication covers the largest part of the human life trajectory, some of the inherent restrictions of a cross-sectional approach could be alleviated (Schaie, 1973).

RESULTS

The South-Limburg Life History and Myocardial Infarction Study was begun in December 1980;* at the time of writing it was not yet completed.[†] Therefore, the results that are presented here still bear a preliminary character.

Given the limited size of this paper, we will confine the range of available data to the evidence pertaining to prodromal symptoms of vital exhaustion and depression prior to MI. Then we will proceed to an examination of the occurrence of LC. and of the particular manner in which MI-cases perceive these events as they occurred in their life courses.

The Prodrome of Vital Exhaustion and Depression

In all case-referent studies in which the MQ on vital exhaustion and depression was employed, it was demonstrated that middle-aged MI-cases in general suffer from appreciable prodromal symptoms of vital exhaustion and depression prior to premature MI (Appels, 1983; Falger, 1983a). In the present study, the mean MQ scores of all MI-cases ($N = 121$) and neighborhood referents ($N = 108$) that

---

*All data were compiled, and all statistics were programmed and computed (SPSS) by Jan van Houtem and Jos Bekkers, assistants to this research project.

[†]Early in the course of this investigation it became apparent that older heart patients would be much easier sampled than younger ones, for the obvious reason of vast differences in cardiovascular morbidity rates. Since we wanted to comply with the design in order to be able to study cohort effects, *more* than 15 MI-cases were allowed to be included within each cohort (with a *maximum* of 25), and subsequently a like number of same-aged neighborhood referents.

could be included so far, are 90.2 and 68.9, respectively (t (229) = 6.74, $p <$ .001, one-sided). These results on the MQ should be read as indicating: The higher the score on the MQ, the more clear-cut is the prodrome of vital exhaustion and depression. The minimum score on the MQ is 50, the maximum score 150. When calculated separately for each cohort of MI-cases and neighborhood referents according to the design, the same degree of significant differences in MQ-results is obtained (not shown here).

In summary, it could be said that a majority of MI-cases report a specific constellation of emotions, that is termed the prodrome of vital exhaustion and depression, in the months prior to their first coronary event. This prodrome may indicate a final breakdown in resources to cope with the psychological and social burden occuring in their lives (Appels, 1980, 1983; Falger, 1983a).

In the remainder of this paper, we will examine whether this general breakdown in psychosocial adaptation before premature MI could possibly have emerged from particular developmental patterns.

Stressful Life Changes and Appraisal in the Life Course

The results in this section are presented in a different manner than in the previous one. Here the data pertain to three *combined* cohorts: 35–49, 50–59, and 60–69 years of age. A detailed analysis of differences in all cohorts would be beyond the limited length of this paper. Also, the total number of referents is larger than in the earlier analysis. This is obtained through combining the healthy neighborhood referents with the hospital referents that have been interviewed so far (N = 74), after analyzing possible differences with respect to the occurrence of LC in both referent groups. Significant differences, (i.e., chi-squares) emerged only with respect to 5 out of 51 LC.

Further, the results are presented either in the form of chi-squares, corrected for 2 × 2 contingency tables, or as significant odds ratios. The odds ratio (i.e., relative risk) is an epidemiological measure, indicating the degree of association of a specific parameter with the illness in cases under scrutiny, as compared with referents (Miettinen, 1982). An odds ratio of 1.0 implies that there is no difference in degree of association. All corresponding chi-squares, corrected for 2 × 2 contingency tables, are significant at the .05 level, or less, one-sided (not shown here).

Exposure to Stressful Life Changes

In Table 1 are presented the odds ratios—associated with significant chi-squares—with regard to exposure to LC in the developmental domains of (a) infancy, youth, and adolescence, (b) work and career, and (c) family and social life, respectively. The first domain contains 12 events, the second one 16, and the last one 23.

In summary, the life courses of young MI-cases (*cohort 1*) are characterized by some potential disadvantages (sleeper effects) in developmental opportunities occurring in infancy, youth, or adolescence. The work and career domain does *not* seem to contain clearly definable developmental impairment in cases. In the family and social life domain, on the other hand, some distinctive LC can be identified. The most disruptive one, of course, might be divorce, occurring 4.6 times more

Table 1 Occurrence of stressful life changes in three cohorts of male myocardial infarction patients

	Odds ratios[a]		
Event	Age 35–49[b]	Age 50–59[c]	Age 60–69[d]
Infancy, youth, adolescence			
Prolonged living away from our home	2.82	n.s.	n.s.
Prolonged unemployment of family head	2.21	2.67	n.s.
Prolonged financial problems in family	2.66	2.02	n.s.
Prolonged serious conflicts in family	n.s.	2.21	n.s.
Subject having to work while still at school	n.s.	2.31	n.s.
Work & career			
Compelled to look for other job(s)	1.99	n.s.	n.s.
Prolonged period(s) of unemployment	n.s.	3.54	n.s.
Work place(s) closed down	2.28	n.s.	n.s.
Prolonged period(s) of overwork	2.28	n.s.	n.s.
Prolonged/serious conflicts with supervisor	n.s.	2.72	3.42
Prolonged/serious conflicts with subordinates	n.s.	2.76	3.42
Home & social life			
Divorce first spouse	4.59	4.18	n.s.
Death first spouse	n.s.	n.s.	3.33
Getting children	n.s.	2.52	n.s.
Prolonged/serious illness children	n.s.	3.45	n.s.
Death children	n.s.	2.60	n.s.
Prolonged/serious educational problems with children	2.45	13.50	n.s.
Prolonged/serious conflicts with children (in law) living on their own	4.41	15.39	5.88
Moving	3.79	n.s.	n.s.
Prolonged/serious marital conflicts	n.s.	3.85	2.31
Prolonged/serious illness of subject	n.s.	3.03	n.s.
Prolonged/serious illness of spouse	n.s.	n.s.	2.25
Prolonged/serious conflicts with family members	n.s.	3.72	n.s.
Prolonged/serious financial problems	2.21	3.80	n.s.
Effected considerable loan	n.s.	n.s.	2.11

[a]Associated chi-squares, $p > .05$, (one-sided);
[b]Cohort 1: MI-cases = 41; Referents = 87;
[c]Cohort 2: MI-cases = 41; Referents = 54;
[d]Cohort 3: MI-cases = 39; Referents = 41.

often in cases than in referents. In addition, problems related to bringing up one's children appear to be of a rather chronic character, since those problems appear to continue even when the children have left their parents' home, and are living on their own.

The events in *cohort 2* provide us with a rather detailed image of the particular developmental course that may be conducive of MI in middle adulthood.

In summary, it is observed again that potential developmental disadvantages (sleeper effects) when being young, that were found in younger MI-cases, also have occurred in the lives of middle-age cases. Further, the pattern of probably chronic problems with one's children is replicated here, with additional threat- or loss-related events, like serious illness or even death in children, to reinforce the disruptive scope of this image. The problematic character of married life in cases also appears to be obvious. With respect to working life it is apparent that unemployment and the closing down of the work place may constitute unequivocal developmental "breaks" in psychosocial development in the lives of cases. It should also be noted that a pattern of possibly chronic conflicts with others characterizes the working life of MI-cases.

The life course of the oldest MI-cases (*cohort* 1), in summary, is characterized first by the circumstance that there is no discernable difference between cases and referents with respect to LC in the formative years. Second, the two discriminating events in working life refer to possibly chronic conflicts with others, and are as such reminiscent of the same events occurring in the second cohort. As was already observed in the youngest and the middle-aged cohorts, once again the family and social life domain yields most differences between cases and referent, although considerably less so (in a quantitative sense) than in the middle cohort. In oldest MI-cases also, chronic conflicts with children (who have left home) are most outspoken. This is the only LC, then, from the interview that figures in all three cohorts.

In elderly cases and referents who were living single at the time of interviewing, the developmental "break" of "death of spouse" had occurred 3.3 times more often in the lives of MI-cases.

It should be noted here that all results in the present section of developmental structures as yet cannot provide insight into the temporal sequencing of those LC over the life course. Thus, it cannot be determined yet to what extent these disruptive events that pertain to family life may have formed specific *clusters* in the respective developmental structures. However, as we have traced as precisely as possible the year(s) in which all reported events have happened, in future analyses we will be able to do so.

Appraisal of Stressful Life Changes

Table 2 provides a different picture concerning the role of LC in the lives of MI-cases. Here are presented all significant differences with respect to the appraisal of the reported events in the three developmental domains. More specifically, these differences pertain to the fact that MI-cases have evaluated these events as predominantly of ambivalent character with respect to their psychosocial development, either shortly after the event occurred (S), or as regarded from the different perspective of the time of interviewing (L). These results on the ambivalence of appraisal are presented here regardless of the fact, whether the LC under study occur more frequently in the life course of MI-cases, or not.

For example, the event "prolonged period(s) of overwork" is the single one in *cohort 1* to occur more frequently in MI-cases, as well as to be evaluated as predominantly ambivalent directly after it occurred. (Referents typically would say instead: "I did not like it, but I could use the extra money at that time.") Yet, an event like "spouse having a job," although apparently not occurring more often in the lives of cases in *cohorts 1 and 2,* obviously holds an ambivalent and strong emotional grip over MI-cases. (Or, as one patient put it: "Our lives went a separate way. She became much more involved with the tragedies of the children in the

Table 2 Ambivalent appraisal of stressful changes in three cohorts of male myocardial infarction patients

	Chi squares		
Event	Age 35–49[a]	Age 50–59[b]	Age 60–69[c]
Infancy, youth, adolescence			
Moving (L)[d]	6.08*	n.s.	n.s.
Hospital admission(s) of subject (S)[e]	n.s.	4.80*	n.s.
Coping with school period of subject (L)	n.s.	5.74	4.92*
Work & career			
Coping with work beginning (S)	7.35**	n.s.	n.s.
Coping with work beginning (L)	n.s.	4.71*	n.s.
Prolonged period(s) of unemployment (L)	5.13*	n.s.	n.s.
Work place(s) closed down (S)	n.s.	n.s.	7.00**
Prolonged period(s) overwork (S)	5.86*	n.s.	n.s.
Searching after other job(s) of own accord (S)	n.s.	5.69*	7.18**
Searching after other job(s) of own accord (L)	n.s.	n.s.	6.39*
Compelled to look for other job(s) (S)	n.s.	n.s.	6.55*
Compelled to look for other job(s) (L)	n.s.	5.90*	n.s.
Increased responsibility at work (S)	n.s.	7.61**	8.93*
Irregular working hours/shift work (S)	n.s.	n.s.	5.43**
Home & social life			
Getting children (S)	n.s.	6.16*	5.23*
Getting children (L)	6.64**	12.66***	4.05*
Children leaving home (S)	n.s.	8.31**	5.64*
Children leaving home (L)	n.s.	21.63***	n.s.
Others moving in with subject and spouse (S)	n.s.	n.s.	6.53*
Others moving in with subject and spouse (L)	n.s.	n.s.	4.84*
Prolonged/serious illness of subject (L)	n.s.	5.96*	n.s.
Prolonged illness/death of family members (last 5 yrs.) (L)	n.s.	4.45*	n.s.
Prolonged illness/death of relatives/friends (last 5 yrs.) (S)	6.17*	n.s.	4.63*
Prolonged illness/death of relatives/friends (last 5 yrs.) (L)	6.17*	n.s.	4.92*
Spouse having job(s) (S)	13.74**	13.96***	n.s.
Moving (S)	n.s.	4.05*	n.s.
Effected considerable loan (S)	n.s.	n.s.	4.67*
Effected considerable loan (L)	n.s.	5.23*	n.s.

[a]Cohort 1: MI-cases = 41; Referents = 87;
[b]Cohort 2: MI-cases = 41; Referents = 54;
[c]Cohort 3: MI-cases = 39; Referents = 41;
[d](L) = Long-term perspective
[e](S) = Short-term perspective
*$p < .05$
**$p < .01$
***$p < .001$

nursery home where she was working, than with the problems of our own two adolescents.")

In summary, events that may signify possibly unexpected (nonnormative) developmental breaks in the youngest cohort, like (a) moving, (b) unemployment, or (c) death of a relative, or events that may indicate the beginning of a new developmental sequence, like beginning to work, or getting children, are predominantly evaluated as ambivalent in contributing to subsequent psychosocial development, or as not falling in their proper place, so to speak.

Combined with the observed, probably chronic nature of conflicts in family and social life (cf. Table 1), these findings suggest that a possibly self-evoked, chronic struggling with conflictual situations may form a quintessential aspect of the life of young MI-cases.

The latter suggestion is strongly reinforced by the findings on the ambivalent nature of specific LC in *cohort 2*. That is, events that constitute *novel* or (normative) aspects in youth, work, and family and social life, like coping with (the exigencies of) school life or with beginning to work, with increased responsibility at work, with getting children, and later, with children leaving home, among other events, are invariably met with ambivalent emotional feelings, sometimes both shortly after the event occurred, as well as in retrospect. In the Discussion we will argue that such findings could be interpreted as congruent with the notion that MI-cases perceive their personal environment as predominantly uncontrollable, in spite of their sometimes vigorous efforts. In other words, they habitually may experience a considerable discrepancy between their invested efforts in life and ensuing results.

The previous reasoning with respect to ambivalent emotions about novel events in the three developmental domains is further corroborated by the findings in *cohort 3*. The oldest MI-cases to a large extent report the same ambivalently experienced events as the middle-aged cohort does, such as coping with school, with work beginning, with increased responsibility at work, with getting children, and with children leaving home. In addition, ambivalent emotions with respect to (nonnormative) events like irregular working hours, and to work place being closed down, are found. Also, others moving in with subject while being married (most often this implied "A complete lack of freedom, since my old mother still wanted to control everything going on"), and illness and death of relatives and friend ("It's growing empty around me") constitute other such examples.

DISCUSSION

In summarizing the findings concerning the life course of MI-cases, two aspects appear to be important.

First, in all three cohorts MI-cases have been exposed to more LC (in the course of their entire lives) than same-aged referents. The differences in exposure to LC between cohorts are substantial, however. The largest discrepancy occurs in the second cohort, aged 50–59, where no less than 18 LC are reported more often by MI-cases than by referents, followed by the youngest cohort (10 LC), and the oldest (7 LC). Most of these LC are associated with (nonnormative) developmental "breaks," that is with events that may signify disruptions in the 'normal' developmental pattern within a particular cohort (Baltes et al., 1978). Only a single event, chronic conflicts with children who have left home, occurs in all cohorts. Eight

LC occur in two consecutive cohorts. The remaining 16 discriminating LC, however, occur in one particular cohort only.

These findings appear to argue in favor of a rather unique life course structure in different cohorts of MI-cases. However, some (predominantly nonnormative) events appear to be of such pivotal concern that they occur in two or all cohorts, thus probably regardless of the specific historical context that may be associated with the occurrence of the other discriminating LC. In other words, we do *not* find here some universal psychosocial pathway conducive of MI, as is found in most retrospective investigations of this type (Rahe & Romo, 1974; Theorell, 1980).

The second aspect appears to be of even more importance. We find that some LC to which cases have been exposed more frequently than referents are also the ones that are evaluated as predominantly ambivalent. This could have been expected from the results of earlier studies (Byrne, 1980, 1983; Lundberg et al., 1975.) Rather, it is observed that about *half of the nondiscriminating events are evaluated as predominantly ambivalent with respect to subsequent psychosocial development in MI-cases*. In this respect, again a single profound LC, getting children, figures in all three cohorts, and is evaluated as ambivalent both shortly after the event, as well as in retrospect. It should be noted here that normative LC like going to school, beginning to work, or in this instance, getting children, of course hardly can be expected to yield different prevalence rates between cases and referents. However, these events that generally mark the beginning of a new developmental sequence, that as such could yield significant differences in prevalence of subsequent LC, quite obviously appear to be perceived as rather emotionally different.

All ambivalently evaluated LC can be said to deal with either novel, but rather expected events in psychosocial development (e.g., coping with school, work beginning, getting children, children leaving home), or with rather unexpected changes that may induce profound adjustment with respect to subsequent psychosocial development (e.g., moving, unemployment, effecting a considerable loan, death of relatives or friends).

In this manner, these particular LC may constitute a considerable additional psychosocial burden in the lives of MI-cases, but rather differently so in different cohorts. As was observed before, such life courses may in most instances be associated with prodromal symptoms of vital exhaustion and depression in the months prior to infarction.

It appears appropriate here to mention some current progress in thinking about the etiologic relationship between LC and the subsequent development of depression. As was demonstrated in several studies on cognitive characteristics of LC and subsequent depression (Fairbank & Hough, 1979; Hammen & Mayol, 1982; Silver & Wortman, 1980), it is particularly LC that are perceived as relatively controllable, internally caused, intended, and likely to reoccur that appear to be most conducive to depression. This tendency is clearly apparent in the LC from the family and social life domain, that receives most emphasis in all cohorts of MI-cases. It could be argued, now, that MI-cases who lack emotional support in their daily familial environment (Berkman, 1982; Cobb, 1980), for which particular failure they feel to be held responsible themselves, cannot cope adequately any more with the additional stressful burden of working life, when LC associated with this domain do constitute a severe disruption in psychosocial development, as we observed in these coronary cases. This peculiar constellation of lack of emotional support, combined with overburdening by events that are perceived as controllable, but occur to be uncontrollable could lead, then, to prodromal symptoms of vital exaustion and depression, and finally to premature MI (or sudden cardiac death).

Another highly relevant line of reasoning, linking dysfunctional behavior with respect to coping with LC to the development of depression, is provided by the general concept of learned helplessness (Abramson, Seligman, & Teasdale, 1978), and by further specifications for adult Type A coronary-prone subjects as well (Glass & Carver, 1980).[‡] As was discussed elsewhere (Falger & Appels, 1982; Falger et al., 1984), the former concept states that depression is the outcome of specific learning processes in interpersonal development that are characterized by a considerable discrepancy between invested efforts and ensuing results. One of the core aspects of the Type A coronary-prone behavior pattern, that is, the dimension of situationally determined, perceived controllability may be particularly relevant in this respect (Krantz, Glass, & Snyder, 1974; Matthews, 1982).

From the series of laboratory experiments by Glass (1977), it can be concluded that a learned and probably lasting inability to respond properly to a personal environment that is perceived as predominantly uncontrollable may account for this peculiar feature. According to these experiments, a subject exhibiting the Type A coronary-prone behavior pattern will habitually be striving hard for control over his personal environment. Challenging exigencies from this environment, in particular when these incentives provide an opportunity for enhancing control, will initially be met with a hyperreactive response pattern that is anchored in physiological arousal. This habitual arousal could set highly complex regulatory systems in motion that may be conducive to cardiac malfunctioning (Buell & Eliot, 1983; Sterling & Eyer, 1981). However, when such efforts appear to fail, eventually, in spite of prolonged striving for control, a hyporeactive phase may emerge. In this peculiarly vulnerable state, that also can be described as such from a psychophysiological and neurohormonal regulatory point of view (Frankenhaeuser, 1983; Sterling & Eyer, 1981), a subject may no longer be capable of performing adequately. Hence, he or she may begin to develop manifestations of vital exhaustion and depression. It is conceivable, now, that the ambivalent evaluation with respect to novel LC, and to LC that may require profound adaptation, that occurred unequivocally in the life courses of the MI-cases under study, could considerably enhance the emergence of a cyclic sequence of hyperreactivity, in order to grasp control over novel situations induced by LC, and hyporeactivity, when efforts to control are failing, sometimes after extensive trying (cf. the chronic character of many reported events).

In his first review article on psychological and social precursors of CHD, that appeared in 1971 in the *New England Journal of Medicine,* C. David Jenkins, one of the outstanding pioneers in this field, wrote the following:

> *The best combinations of the standard (clinical) risk factors fail to identify most new cases of CHD. . . . A broad array of studies point with ever increasing certainty to the position that certain psychological, social, and behavioral conditions do put persons at higher risk of clinically manifest CHD. (Jenkins, 1971)*

[‡]Although no preliminary prevalence data on the Type A coronary-prone behavior pattern are included in this paper, this psychosocial risk indicator may constitute a substantial modifier with regard to the present data. Hence, its possible function in shaping the relationship between determinants and illness-outcome should be recognized here.

We do hope that the results from this investigation so far may have underscored the rightfulness of this position. At the same time we fully realize that the psychosocial life trajectories to premature MI in middle-aged men most probably may pass many more crossroads than we were able to sketch here tentatively.

REFERENCES

Abramson, L., Seligman, M. & Teasdale, J. (1978). Learned helplessness in humans: Critique and reformulation. *Journal of Abnormal Psychology, 87*, 49–74.

Alonzo, A., Simon, A. & Feinleib, M. (1975). Prodromata of myocardial infarction and sudden death. *Circulation, 52*, 1056–1062.

Appels, A. (1980). Psychological prodromata of myocardial infarction and sudden death. *Psychotherapy & Psychosomatics, 34*, 187–195.

Appels, A. (1983). The year before myocardial infarction. In T. Dembroski, T. Schmidt & G. Blümchen (Eds.), *Biobehavioral bases of coronary heart disease.* Basel: Karger.

Appels, A., Jenkins, D. & Rosenman, R. (1982). Coronary-prone behavior in the Netherlands: A cross-cultural validation study. *Journal of Behavioral Medicine, 5*, 83–90.

Baltes, P., Cornelius, S. & Nesselroade, J. (1978). Cohort effects in behavioral development: Theoretical and methodological perspectives. In T. Collins (Ed.), *Minnesota symposia on child psychology,* Vol. *11.* Hillsdale, NJ: Erlbaum.

Berkman, L. (1982). Social network analysis and coronary heart disease. *Advances in Cardiology, 29*, 37–49.

Brand, R. (1978). Coronary-prone behavior as an independent risk factor for coronary heart disease. In T. Dembroski, S. Weiss, J. Shields, S. Haynes, & M. Feinleib (Eds.), *Coronary-prone behavior.* New York: Springer International.

Buell, J. & Eliot, R. (1983). Behavior and the pathophysiology of coronary heart disease in humans. In T. Dembroski, T. Schmidt & G. Blümchen (Eds.), *Biobehavioral bases of coronary heart disease.* Basel: Karger.

Byrne. D. (1980). Attributed responsibility for life events in survivors of myocardial infarction. *Psychotherapy & Psychosomatics, 33*, 7–13.

Byrne, D. (1983). Personal determinants of life event stress and myocardial infarction. *Psychotherapy & Psychosomatics, 40*, 106–114.

Byrne, D., & White, H. (1980). Life events and myocardial infarction revisited: The role of measure of individual impact. *Psychosomatic Medicine, 42*, 1–10.

Chesney, M. & Rosenman, R. (1980). Type A behavior in the work setting. In C. Cooper & R. Paine (Eds.), *Current concerns in occupational stress.* New York: Wiley.

Cobb, S. (1980). Social support as a moderator of life stress. *Psychosomatic Medicine, 38*, 300–314.

Fairbank, D. & Hough, R. (1979). Life event classifications and the event-illness relationship. *Journal of Human Stress, 5*, (2), 41–47.

Falger, P. (1983a). Behavioral factors, life changes, and the development of vital exhaustion and depression in myocardial infarction patients. *International Journal of Behavioral Development, 6*, 405–425.

Falger, P. (1983b). Pathogenic life changes in middle adulthood and coronary heart disease: A life-span developmental perspective. *International Journal of Aging and Human Development, 16*, 7–27.

Falger, P., Appels, A. & Lulofs, R. (1984). Ontogenetic development and breakdown in adaptation: A review on psychosocial factors contributing to the development of myocardial infarction, and a description of a research programme. In J. Cullen & J. Siegrist (Eds.), *Breakdown in human adaptation to 'stress'. Towards a multidisciplinary approach* (Vol. 1). Den Haag: Martinus Nijhoff/ Commission of the European Communities.

Falger, P. & Appels, A. (1982). Psychological risk factors over the life course of myocardial infarction patients. *Advances in Cardiology, 29*, 132–139.

Frankenhaeuser, M. (1983). The sympathetic-adrenal and pituitary-adrenal response to challenge: Comparison between the sexes. In T. Dembroski, T. Schmidt & G. Blümchen (Eds.), *Biobehavioral bases of coronary heart disease.* Basel: Karger.

Friedman, M. & Rosenman, R. (1977). The key cause—Type A behavior pattern (1974). In C. Monat & R. Lazarus (Eds.), *Stress and coping.* New York: Columbia University Press.

Glass, D. (1977). *Behavior patterns, stress, and coronary disease.* Hillsdale, NJ: Erlbaum.

Glass, D. & Carver, C. (1980). Helplessness and the coronary-prone personality. In J. Garber & M. Seligman (Eds), *Human helplessness: Theory and applications.* New York: Academic Press.

Greene, W., Goldstein, S. & Moss, A. (1972). Psychosocial aspects of sudden death: A preliminary report. *Archives of Internal Medicine, 129,* 165-174.

Hammen, C. & Mayol, A. (1982). Depression and cognitive characteristics of stressful life-event types. *Journal of Abnormal Psychology, 91,* 165-174,

Haynes, S. & Feinleib, M. (1982). Type A behavior and the incidence of coronary heart disease in the Framingham Heart Study. *Advances in Cardiology, 29,* 85-95.

Jenkins, D. (1971). Psychologic and social precursors of coronary disease. *New England Journal of Medicine, 284,* 244-255; 307-317.

Jenkins, D. (1976) Recent evidence supporting psychologic and social risk factors for coronary disease. *New England Journal of Medicine, 294,* 987-994; 1033-1038.

Kornitzer, J., Kittel, F., De Backer, G., & Dramaix, M. (1981). The Belgian Heart Disease Prevention Project: Type A behavior pattern and the prevalence of coronary heart disease. *Psychosomatic Medicine, 43,* 133-145.

Krantz, D., Glass, D. & Snyder, M. (1974). Helplessness, stress level, and the coronary prone behavior pattern. *Journal of Experimental and Social Psychology, 10,* 284-300.

Kuller, L. (1978). Prodromata of sudden death and myocardial infarction. *Advances in Cardiology, 25,* 61-72.

Lundberg, U., & Theorell, T. (1976) Scaling of life changes: Differences between three diagnostic groups and between recently experienced and non-experienced events. *Journal of Human Stress, 2,* 7-17.

Lundberg, U. Theorell, T. & Lind, E. (1975). Life changes and myocardial infarction: Individual differences in life change scaling. *Journal of Psychosomatic Research, 19,* 27-32.

Marmot, M. (1982). Socio-economic and cultural factors in ischaemic heart disease. *Advances in Cardiology, 29,* 68-76.

Matthews, K. (1982). Psychological perspectives on the Type A behavior pattern. *Psychological Bullitin, 91,* 293-323.

Miettinen, O. (1982). *Principles of epidemiological research.* Unpublished manuscript, Harvard University, Department of Epidemiology and Biostatistics.

Rahe, R. & Romo, M. (1974). Recent life changes and the onset of myocardial infarction and coronary death in Helsinki. In. D. Gunderson & R. Rahe (Eds.), *Life stress and illness.* Springfield: Thomas.

Rissanen, V., Romo, M. & Siltanen, P. (1978). Premonitory symptoms and stress factors preceding sudden death from ischaemic heart disease. *Acta Medica Scandinavica, 204,* 389-396.

Rosenman, R. (1978). The interview method of assessment of the coronary-prone behavior pattern. In T. Dembroski, S. Weiss, J. Shields, S. Haynes, & M. Feinleib (Eds.), *Coronary-Prone behavior.* New York: Springer International.

Schaie, K. (1973). Methodological problems in descriptive developmental research on adulthood and aging. In J. Nesselroade & H. Reese (Eds.), *Life-span developmental psychology: Methodological issues.* New York: Academic Press.

Siegrist, J., Dittman, K., Rittner, K., & Weber, I. (1980). *Soziale Belastungen und Herzinfarkt.* Stuttgart: Enke.

Siegrist, J., Dittman, K., Rittner, K., & Weber, I. (1982). The social context of active distress in patients with early myocardial infarction. *Social Science & Medicine, 16,* 443-453.

Silver, R. & Wortman, C. (1980). Coping with undesirable life events. In J. Garber & M. Seligman (Eds.), *Human helplessness: Theory and applications.* New York: Academic Press.

Sterling, P. & Eyer, J. (1981). Biological basis of stress-related mortality. *Social Science & Medicine, 15E,* 3-42.

Theorell, T. (1980). Life events and manifestations of ischaemic heart disease: Epidemiological and psychophysiological aspects. *Psychotherapy & Psychosomatics, 34,* 135-148.

Thiel, H., Parker, D. & Bruce, T. (1973). Stress factors and the risk of myocardial infarction. *Journal of Psychosomatic Research, 17,* 43-57.

Waldron, I., Zyzanski, S., Shekelle, R., Jenkins, D., & Tannenbaum, S. (1977). The coronary-prone behavior pattern in employed men and women. *Journal of Human Stress, 3,* 2-18.

Zyzanski, S., Wrzesniewski, K., & Jenkins, D. (1979). Cross-cultural validation of the coronary-prone behavior pattern. *Social Science & Medicine, 13A,* 405-412.

Index

Acculturation, misunderstandings of, 97–98
Achievement-related stress, 82
Adaptation level (AL), 126
Affect, and learned helplessness, 81–96
Aggressiveness, 105
Ambiguity, 167
American Psychological Association, 30
Anger, Type A, 113–122
Anonymity Scale, 73
Anthropology, and theory of functionalism, 97
Anticipatory stress, 167–179
Anxiety:
    assimilation theory of, 3–13
    cognitive and conditioned, 12–13
    cognitive changes as function of, 207–210
    as dimension of determining stress, 159–161
    in high school students, 65–79
    implications of modern conditioning theory, 7–9
    introverted and neurotic tendencies of, 200
    measured by skin conductance response rate (SCR), 200, 202
    and performance, 199–217
    prevention, 245–257
    primary and secondary, 4–6
    problems in experimenting on mental task in, 215–216
    relevance of psychophysiological measurement, 200
    research direction in, 11–13
    social, 53–62
    (*see also* Stress)
Anxiety state (A-STATE), 199

Arousal, 235–241
Assimilation theory of anxiety, 3–13

Behavior:
    impact of loss of control on, 81
    individual differences in, 158
    smoking, 307–327
    of teacher in test anxiety, 73–77
Bortner scale, 113–115, 120

Caffeine, 216
Cancer:
    as alternative to psychosis, 299
    lung, 296, 300
Cattell's 16 Personality Factors, 194
Character structure, 155
Cigarette consumption, 300
Classroom climate and test anxiety, 72–77
Cognition, 3–13
    defensiveness and subjective competence, 311–312
    factors in myocardial infarction, 329–341
    in helplessness, 88–92
    in learned helplessness, 81–96
    in shy males, 53–62
Cognitive Behavior Therapy, 277–278
Competence expectancy, 69
Conditioning theory, 7–11
Control, 81–82, 259
Coping:
    individual differences in, 158
    with noise, 125
    in school environment, 66
    with stress and anxiety, 244–292